Richard Jacobs

Searching for Beauty
Letters from a Collector to a Studio Potter

To Vickie —

[signature]

kestrel
books

A copy of the British Library Cataloguing in Publication data is available from the British Library
ISBN 0-9548840-6-X

First published in the UK by Kestrel Books Ltd 2007

Kestrel Books Ltd
2 Cwrt Isaf
Tythegston
Bridgend

www.kestrel-books.co.uk

Designed by Adam Evans

Photographs by Toril Brancher
Photograph on page 14 by Mary Mar Keenan

Printed by HSW Print, Tonypandy, Wales, UK

Acknowledgements

I want to express my love and appreciation to my wife, Judy, who supported and helped me from the beginning of this effort. Judy has provided, throughout this venture, positive affirmation of this rather improbable late-life effort of mine. She proofed each letter after its completion and her comments were always insightful.

I need to offer a special expression of appreciation to Christa Assad, a wonderfully talented American potter, who not only graciously agreed to receive these letters but provided constant reassurance of their value to her and their potential value to other makers of craft and art.

I wish to express my gratitude to David Jones, an important British ceramic artist and writer of great intellectual breadth, who has been invaluable in helping these letters get published and has generously reaffirmed my work in so many ways. I must extend my gratitude to Mark Hewitt, a remarkable potter and insightful and articulate writer on pottery who has been most supportive and helpful. I wish to thank my publisher, Anthony Childs-Cutler of Kestrel Books, for his willingness to take a chance on an unknown writer from far away California and his patient advice during my introduction to the bewildering world of book publication.

I want to extend a more general and generic appreciation to all the potters represented in my collection and beyond that, to all working potters struggling to practice their craft with devotion and integrity and still meet the demands of daily subsistence. You have made my life richer by the gifts of your talents and efforts. These letters are my tribute and homage to you.

Lastly, I find special satisfaction in having these letters published in Britain. I have lived in and visited Britain many times during my life. I consider it my second home. I first visited Britain when young. Involved and agonized over Civil Rights and Anti-Vietnam war movements in America, I briefly went into self-exile in Britain. I have always been received with great kindness and hospitality during all my visits. I am gratified that the publication of this book will give me further opportunities to visit Britain again. I hope this book forms a modest reciprocation for the generosity I have always experienced there.

Richard Jacobs
Glendora, California

Foreword
by Christa Assad

For nearly five years now I have pored over a private collection of missives written by a gifted thinker. I have read, re-read, highlighted and lectured on the content of these letters – yet selfishly hoarded the majority of them for myself. Like any devoted collector, I reveled in the near-exclusivity of the relationship I had developed with this collection – a collection that only I possessed in full. As the years passed, and the stack of manila envelopes bearing my name and address grew, I began to realize that the magnitude and power of these words had long surpassed typical, personal correspondence. Brilliant and moving, these letters filled me with emotion, concern, and the realization that although written to me, they were meant for a much greater purpose and a wider audience.

When I first met Dr. Richard Jacobs in July of 2002, I was potting full-time in San Francisco. My studio was tucked away in back of a boutique gallery I co-owned with two other potters, and I had grown accustomed to the routine questions posed by tourists in search of souvenir trinkets, sourdough bread and the nearest public restroom. I had underestimated the effects that any walk-in visitor might have on my day's work, let alone my ethical beliefs, political stance, or my long-term goals as a craftsperson. Richard changed that. It was a chance meeting when he walked into my gallery while vacationing with his wife, Judy. Richard was eyeing one of my pots, a long-necked vase with delicate slip-trailing, and when he learned I was the maker he began an enthusiastic critique. I listened.

That initial conversation revealed a glimpse of who Richard Jacobs would become to me, yet I could never foresee the impact he would make on a larger scale, forging a path through the arena within which we craftspeople fight to defend our cause and our existence. We found common ground in our exami-nation of cultural relevance, championing the handmade object amidst the shift toward high-tech industry and virtual relationships. Though a generation apart, we were united by a respect for the history of craft and the role of maker as definitive characters in the story of our culture.

The *Letters* outline a series of ideas and concepts introduced by Richard for my consideration. Sourcing his many and varied interests – collecting, gardening, music, reading, politics, philosophy, theatre, global and environmental concerns – he draws parallels between daily activities and making pottery. Our worlds merge and join forces over a common cause: the preservation of our rich cultural history. Richard is a spokesperson for the craft world. His beliefs and ideals mimic mine, but leap off the page as eloquent, lively writing that vocalizes the things I could never express so clearly. He references a dazzling array of sources, other authors and historians. He asks many questions, yet does not profess to have all the answers. More importantly, he inspires curiosity, examination and action. His questions are not meant to discourage or dissuade me from my course, but to clarify my intent, my purpose and my goals as a potter.

Some of the letters arrive with unbelievable synchronicity to events in my life. A letter discussing the relevance and value of the artist's signature, for example, came just as I was contemplating a change from the traditional potter's chop (stamp) to a handwritten, or inscribed, full signature. In this way, I see how Richard's ideas would affect others and have particular meaning to a much larger readership. The letters, though written to me, are actually speaking to any maker, art appreciator, humanitarian, or curious onlooker. As the original focus of the letters, I see myself as Richard's model for his discussions: a concrete, living example in his exploration of culture. Our fortuitous meeting, my pottery and my lifestyle were the springboard for this project, but Richard has moved on to a much broader purpose. His motivation is genuine, as proven to me. His goal is clear: to share his passionate views on the preservation of culture, in the hope that we can continue to revere, rather than eliminate, all things handmade. I truly believe *Searching for Beauty* is a unique and powerful assemblage of essays that speaks to each and every one of us.

I leave you with one of my favorite passages. In a letter dated February 4, 2003, Richard writes:

"I mourn the devaluing of skill, the actual historic loss of the expertise of the human hand. This is further aggravated by the incorporation of this loss within the rhetoric of pride in progress. What is left for us is the patronizing appreciation of 'folk art' created by 'underdeveloped' people, relics of their primitive status that provides props for our interior decorators... The generations of skilled crafts people, except for a few recalcitrant potters, are largely gone, their knowledge and skill buried with them. My sons have not expressed any interest in planting roses in their gardens. They take too much time and trouble. Alas, my pruning genius will soon be lost. I am told that the modern rose is another example of human progress. It is true, there are more roses on the bush, but the wonderful fragrances are mostly missing now. Are we conscious of the trade-offs? Did we really improve them? In a democracy we should vote on this issue of rose fragrances. During my entire life, authorities of my culture and my world have told me that all those things that have changed in my world represented something called progress. I want that fragrance back!"

May we all recapture and cherish that sweet scent of forgotten times and peoples, when beauty and tradition were much easier to identify, and were simply ours to enjoy.

Christa Assad
Kansas City, Missouri, USA
July 4, 2007.

Introduction
by David Jones

"Shadows have more style, but I prefer people". William Stafford, American poet

Richard Jacobs is a collector of pots and a generator of insights. That he is also a human being should normally go unremarked but it is his humanity and particularly the depth of his self-deprecating humour that pervades every page of this insight into a life and its multiplicity of connections; connections to ideas, to objects, and most particularly to people. It is this latter quality that makes what is essentially a book of aesthetic reflections (traditionally a very dry subject) into a fascinating read, and, most importantly, in a completely accessible language. As 'a read' this book of essays is like an old, wise and often quite outlandish friend purifying a lifetime of experiences 'recollected in tranquillity', glass of whiskey in hand, beside the fire. When we first met, on a panel discussion I had organised at the NCECA conference in Louisville, I used a quote that now sums up to me Richard's attitude to the great works of man: "Like a frog at moonrise I am impressed but not reverent." (William Stafford).

So first then to the man: he is an alchemical distiller of the special essences that are embodied by simple containers. In this series of meditations he allows the vessels in his collection to overflow their function of containment and to make rare and strange connection to other worlds of ideas.

This book of essays is a putative series of letters to a fine potter – a real woman – with her hands in real clay. Yet Christa stands also as a symbol. She represents the muddied world of making, of aesthetic and functional decision and indecision, of risk taking, and problem solving. This soiled and sullied existence of the clay-bespattered maker is a far cry from the ethereal world of the collector. For the latter the minute particles of mud and dirt never really existed. Their amorphous, multi-potentialled existence is experienced only after a chemical change, when, as a liminal object, they are changed utterly. Those particles have penetrated the barrier of ceramic firing and are fused into a finished and final *form*. Here they begin their new life as counters in an aesthetic game of position and juxtaposition within a collection, and, notwithstanding an earth-quake on the San Andreas Fault, they are as nearly eternal as any human product; yet they stand for examples of the quotidian, and this is the essential nature of useful pots.

Richard's use of the pots is not that of the occupant of the kitchen. He has ripped them from that context and superimposed the new hermeneutic (inter-pretative) environment of the private gallery. Through that distancing they have adopted a new significance, which is no longer the importance of their ability to contain drink or food but of their juxtapositions – one to another.

He deals with the pieces, not in the manner of the art historian /archaeologist / surgeon, who dissects the victim until only parts remain. His methodology in this writing is like that of a director of epic theatre – a theatre that does not build to dramatic climaxes in a search for catharsis – but more a theatre of reflection that teaches lessons about the world. His writing is a search for beauty in the Brechtian *gestus* – the signature of the potter that sums up her, or his, unique contribution to creativity. Jacobs is searching here for a poetics of engagement that allows the mind to wander discursively and to paint in the detail in the manner of the vast canvasses of the nineteenth century Russian novel. The epis-tolary form he employs is reminiscent of Richardson's *Pamela*, and is ideally suited to his style which takes in the panoramas of contemporary life through the *conceit* of writing personal and private letters. His style is intimate and confid-ing, yet also wide-rangingly philosophical. Jacobs can be placed firmly in a crit-ical pragmatist tradition calling on John Dewey and William James as the sensible arbiters of taste and reason. Richard Jacobs is certainly not the Kantian ideal of the objective and dispassionate thinker. Indeed he must be one of the most opinion-laden human beings I know; but he questions every intellectual and philosophical position – particularly his own. In this book we shall meet not just the objects and their makers but also the thinker who through ownership estab-lishes his own existence amongst the world of things. And it is a very human presence – one wryly aware that the very experience that has provided such a rich perspective on human, and ceramic, existence has also exacted a toll on his body.

Walter Benjamin is one of the first philosophers to emphasize that collecting is first and foremost an all consuming passion of children, and Richard Jacobs betrays that still child-like amazement with objects and journeys and the flights of fancy conjured by language. Children do not collect because of the monetary value of the object, its place in a historical schema, nor yet because of an appar-ent understanding of use. Instead, like the rich who own all that they need for their subsistence, children can engage in the "transfiguration of objects". For them a "fetish value" is ascribed to the new object, (or idea or words). Richard adds an object to his collection and it makes new relationships with the other objects there. He has focussed almost exclusively on the utilitarian item which is revalorised by its new context within the collection. When he writes about it he makes connections to other ideas. Richard Jacobs riffs on the lives of objects in great looping arcs of association; like an improvising jazz musician he places an idea of the ceramic object at its centre and takes us (his readers) on a meta-physical journey. Here, in these thought-provoking essays that have ceramics at their core, he creates links to contemporary politics and as well as to aesthetics, mirroring the juxtaposition of the highly individualistic pots in the collection. It is a kind of hypertext created by a devotee of William Morris and Ruskin. The values are deeply with tradition and longevity as opposed to the ephemeral vicis-situdes of fashion – but the references anchor the reader to the contemporary world. We inhabit that same sphere, alongside his beloved pots, and through his writing he enables us to comprehend more of that mad(e) world.

"The world is what you see outside your window, plus what you think of."
  William Stafford

David Jones
Leamington Spa, England.
July 2007.

One

July 31, 2002

Dear Christa,

Thank you for the note, vita, and kind gift of the ceramic periodical that celebrates your beautiful pots. Your vita documents the dedication and commitment to your talent that will allow you to exist and flourish through your art and craft. I enjoyed our brief chat and wish to extend my remarks through this correspondence. Forgive me my inflated pretension - I depend upon the self-conscious appreciation of my own ultimate absurdity as an essential survival strategy - but I am still going to subsume further remarks under the rubric of "Letter To A Young Potter".

This is a dual tribute - to an earnest young person I briefly met and the beautiful benefit from that encounter - a pot on a shelf situated where I can now rotate my gaze from computer to shelf and back as I compose my thoughts and tap my fingers on the keys. You must share this tribute with Rainer Maria Rilke - a remarkable German poet of the last century whose ten letters to an aspiring young poet who sought his counsel is entitled "Letters To A Young Poet". This small book has become a classic - indeed you might very well be familiar with it.

First of all, I do not believe my extended duration on the earth provides any true seniority or greater wisdom. Indeed I have found that the simple accumulation of time and experience for most people merely reinforces through repetition the habit of prejudice and conformity. So I do not claim any advantage. I do now have the luxury of time for reflection. And the awareness of extended age that time is a finite gift of mortality that I confirm each morning with some gratitude.

As a former professor who was always an institutional heretic and troublemaker, I was always far more interested in intellectual engagement over conventional academic work. They are not the same thing. The sterile accumulation of inert information - the professor as the passive docent of the objective fact -

the transfer of this mountain of academic sludge to the institutional inmates through tactics that require feats of faithful memorization - this never suited my temperament or purpose.

My favorite passage from Rilke is in his fourth letter. He advises his young friend:

"You are so young; you stand before beginnings. I would like to beg of you, dear friend, as well as I can, to have patience with everything that remains unsolved in your heart. Try to love the questions themselves, like locked rooms and like books written in a foreign language. Do not now look for the answers. They cannot now be given to you because you could not live them. It is a question of experiencing everything. At present you need to live the question. Perhaps you will gradually, without even noticing it, find yourself experiencing the answer, some distant day. Perhaps you are indeed carrying within yourself the potential to visualize, to design, and to create for yourself an utterly satisfying, joyful, and pure lifestyle. Discipline yourself to attain it, but accept that which comes to you with deep trust, and as long as it comes from your own will, from your own inner need, accept it, and do not hate anything."

That young man was fortunate indeed to be the recipient of that advice. But all relationships are reciprocal, whatever the surface difference in age and situation. Without personal cynicism, the motivation for generosity always contains the self service of human need - even if in this case it could be the pleasureful excuse for self-rumination. As someone whose childhood was spent in splendid isolation - drawing and painting, with almost daily trips to the branch library at the end of my dead-end street - to experience the books that provided the furniture for the fantasies of my inner existence - in a family where mother and father, younger and older brothers - did not enter the door of my private domain. In my youth, I met my best friend, Eugene, in "Look Homeward Angel" and we confided in each other through the difficult years of adolescence. I would speculate in my dreams that I must be an orphan placed on their doorstep - how else could I be so different from the other members of my family? I marched to my own drumbeat before I could even start to compose the lyrics of my life.

I have always been a risk taker, and at this point perhaps you might think this communication somewhat eccentric. Even intrusive in seeking some exchange beyond the commercial transaction that is the only evidence of our previous relationship. In your note you indicate appreciation for supporting your career. However modest that support, I do acknowledge that it is a function from which I derive much satisfaction. I do think your pot was worthy of my purchase - and I am pleased that you directly benefited - but again self-interest played an important part. I do not mean some calculated financial investment for future gain - indeed I frankly do not care if your career eventually inflates the value of that vase. Nor do I celebrate the acquisition of a commodity that increases the inventory of my private possessions. Your pot contributes daily to the enrichment of my domestic life. I house it in order to meet it each day. The true aesthetics of art do not reside in highly refined and esoteric discussions of critics and academics. The engagement of an artifact with human sensibilities is a pedestrian and ordinary event - I wash the dishes, take out the trash, and engage my pottery. They are all necessary actions and behavior to maintain my life and sanity.

Nor do I hold with the modern arrogance of the artist that does not recognize or respect the eventual custodian of the artifact. Although you are indeed the artist, the creator of that vase, the placement of that vase in the context of my life has both changed my life and the vase. Your vase now has many new friends that have already influenced its appearance and meaning. The fundamental weakness of the gallery and museum is that it seeks - pretends - to isolate each artifact for individual scrutiny. Even an imposed thematic cohesion does not truly bind the artifacts. William Morris was right - only the integration of the object in intimate domestic surroundings provides the coherent collage that is a single reality. The juxtaposition of divergent objects provide a new, creative, and total composition. Your vase is just one actor. Just as any painter knows that each new brushstroke changes all formerly applied brushstrokes, the addition of your vase enhances and changes everything. But the fate of your vase is to endure assimilation - and Americans should know the price of assimilation, some more than others.

I am going to leave now. I wish you the very best. I hope that the gallery continues to flourish. I once had dreams of becoming an artist. The discontinuities of personal relationships; the detour to teaching; and the numerous noble but losing crusades to liberate my students, bring peace to the world, and save the environment were distractions that somehow consumed my lifespan. The irony and eventual triumph of life is not surrender - whatever the losses - but to endure the failures in order to secure the validity of personal integrity. Learning is a series of reasonable failures. Life is a series of reasonable risks.

Take care,

Richard

Two

August 6, 2002

Dear Christa,

Received your postcard announcing your exhibition at the gallery in Berkeley. I was grateful for your note regarding my previous letter. I appreciate your invitation to attend the opening reception on August 17th and would very much like to see your new work but I will not be able to make that date. Please keep me informed about your continuing exhibitions. Given your encouragement I will continue my correspondence with another message, my second "letter to a young potter".

You mentioned in your initial note appreciation for my support of your 'career'. I respect your determination to achieve excellence as a potter/artist. Indeed you have already achieved a level of technical proficiency that gives you options and choices in determining the character and aesthetic attributes of each piece. The recognition by your peers and others is documented in your vita and in workshops and exhibitions such as the coming Berkeley event. However, the shape and character of your pottery is not ultimately going to be determined by your expert technique but by the shape and character of you. Your central task is not devising cunning strategies for your career but to construct and create the personhood that can sponsor complex explorations and honest experimentations.

The observable integrity of the individual pot is a representation of the integrity of the person who created it. Ironically, this stumbling struggle to attain mastery only becomes convincing when it also demonstrates the fallibility of your human status. You are embedded and enshrined in the artifact - including the unconscious orientation of your time and place, the world view grafted on you at birth, the parochial elements of the neighborhood of your youth.

You cannot ever erase all evidence in the pot of the world that made you. You can only add self-conscious elements that form the truly creative aspects. This dual struggle requires great energy - to create yourself and those self advertising artifacts that celebrate that self - all at the same time. You must surely learn to love yourself - forgive yourself - and go on. In fact perhaps the greatest triumph will occur when you find yourself in the pot, when the pot represents a personal identity that you could never understand any other way. Perhaps each pot becomes a self revelation to yourself as you fuse person with pot.

The essential weakness of perfection is that it must meet absolute and universal standards at the cost of the particular. The 'international' architecture of the last century attempted to reach that goal and the standardized glass boxes attempted to shed all evidence of the local site and culture. The closer it came to that single perfection, the more sterile and empty they became. The achievement of perfection will not arrive when you successfully eradicate the last evidence of your own 'inadequate' identity in the pot - the achievement of mastery will emerge when your humanity permeates every aspect of that pot. The flaws of your fallibility could be the necessary scar tissue that forms the source of true wisdom. These flaws, visible in the pot, could be more distinctive and truer than the attempts to provide a seamless surface free from imperfections.

Scientists will tell you that it is the failed experiments that negate the offered hypothesis that represents valuable science. The nullification of failed experiments reduces the unknown and forms the pathway to greater knowledge. For science, as with art - you need to ask the right questions and not be impatient to receive premature answers. The comfort of closure also terminates any further exploration in the area of the answer. That is a very high price to pay for the supposed security of absolute truth. Growth is only possible when you have doubts. Confessed ignorance is the rich promise that sponsors the pilgrimage.

That brings us back to Rilke who pointed out in his advice to that young poet, it is the questions you must learn to live with and experience, the answers will come when you least expect them. I taught over 20 years in a polytechnic state university that was essentially a job training center. The forced recruiting of students into majors was really an attempt to restrict their study to a narrow and fragmented segment of curriculum that would conform to some future occupational or professional job slot. The most promising students were recruited as disciples of the discipline, slotted for the graduate work that forms the breeding and perpetuating domains of the academic guild.

I was an 'interdisciplinarian' and 'generalist' who refused to surrender my intellectual curiosity to become a valued 'specialist'. I was always surprised when my colleagues who had amassed vast inventories of warehoused data had such great trouble attaching value and meaning to that same data. They explained that the interpretive function of the making of meaning was the task of yet another group of academic specialists - the Philosophy Department. The reality was that they lacked the intellectual capacity to attach their specialized knowledge to the context of the whole web of human experience and knowledge.

For the intellectual, placement is not defined by the taxonomy but rather within the dynamic context of ad hoc variables that comprise human reality and experience. You cannot achieve this placement without attributing normative value and providing relative meaning. Nothing else will stand still while you are performing this intellectual feat of placement and meaning. You are moving in the world and everything around you is moving. The connections you make reflect their inherent interdependence. This is the principle of ecology, the most important paradigm of this century. This is the difference between academic knowledge and personal knowledge. You are of course placing yourself as you place the knowledge. In this case subjective bias is simply the ethical preference of expressed principle.

This discussion leads me to consider the words of Soetsu Yanagi - the Japanese philosopher and dear friend of Bernard Leach, the renowned English potter who revived the arts and crafts movement in England during the last century. In his remarkable book, "The Unknown Craftsman: A Japanese Insight into Beauty", Yanagi speaks in the English language through the paraphrasing of Leach, in his chapter entitled "Irregularity":

"Why should one reject the perfect in favour of the imperfect? The precise and perfect carries no overtones, admits of no freedom; the perfect is static and regulated, cold and hard. We in our own human imperfections are repelled by the perfect, since everything is apparent from the start and there is no suggestion of the infinite. Beauty must have some room, must be associated with freedom. Freedom, indeed is beauty. The love of the irregular is a sign of the basic quest for freedom".

In placing the vernacular 'folk craft' of the uneducated village potter as the highest realm of sublime art, Yanagi and Leach are challenging the dominant Western insistence that professionalism is the successful eradication of the exotic savagery of the untutored pot. Remember it was the Western Anthropologist who discovered the customs and pottery that resulted in the placement of the bones and pots of non-Western peoples in Natural Science Museums, not cemeteries or art museums. Just how civilized does a pot have to be in order to achieve the status of art?

Yanagi would not approve of the deliberate imperfections of modern Western art and craft - those satirical attacks on traditional art that form the basis for much of 'pop', 'funk' and 'contemporary art'. He was looking for:

" . . .a freedom without overtones of willful artistry, free of formulas. Speaking with respect for the traditional craftsmen - 'Such deformations as they contain were born, not made, unlike the kind of distortion that is current today. Their oddness was unplanned. Contemporary 'free form' is willful and unfree. In fact it can be said that the pursuit of freedom has led to prison gates - the prison of self'."

I do not think we Westerners can remove our self-conscious awareness that Yanagi deplores, "The difference is between things born and things made". We cannot sponsor a natural birth of art or ceramics in this society. We have tasted of the fruits of formal knowledge in a culture of mass produced commodities, where handmade craft no longer has cultural meaning or function. We will only substitute the handmade pot in the gallery for the obvious plastic container when the handmade object has some special distinction for some special people. Shopping at Wal Mart for Tupperware is a more normal and natural cultural event in our society than shopping at the Sebastian Ward Gallery. If the consumer really just wants some container to hold the leftovers from the Chinese-To-Go or that micro-waved T.V. dinner, the chances are they will go to Wal Mart, not to that Berkeley Gallery. I guess what I am saying, to you and Yanagi, is that we cannot recover the innocence, we cannot go back, we cannot go home again.

In this society, your handmade pot is always going to be a novelty, severed from the traditions of the crafts of the Native American, or those immigrant settlers and pioneers that made their own soap and furniture. We must create our own integrity and our own community, our own traditions, and seek company and friends from those in the past and present, from diverse cultures. What are the ingredients of a contemporary aesthetics that would make sense of your inefficient production methods and sentimental, even reactionary desire to make things by hand? Some potters are escaping this quandary by collapsing and smashing the functional pot and saying that their slabs of free form clay are now elevated to art since they have no function and cannot be used, only admired. The prices usually go up and the reputation is enhanced. Christa, tell me, why are you holding on to the obsolete and quaint pot when you could be making "ART"?

I am an environmentalist who prefers, in the heat of summer, air conditioned interiors to the natural atmosphere. Aside from that minor discrepancy, as a native southern Californian, I maneuver freeways with great skill, soak in my hot tub (turned off in the energy crisis), garden, listen to my extensive collection of classical CDs, watch videos with subtitles, and read. The only dislocations I must suffer are self-inflicted. Even if the risks are self-imposed, I must be active in the world. The most powerful leaders are those who have nothing to gain. That is, what they are doing is not for self-interest, but for principle. The most powerful artists, I suspect, are those who simply must live that life where art is the purpose of life and life is the purpose of art because there is no separation or distinction between their art and life.

I wish you the very best in your exhibition at Berkeley,

Richard

Three

August 17, 2002

Dear Christa,

In this 'third letter to a young potter' I welcome the continued opportunity to communicate my thoughts to you. I am seated at my desk, staring at the monitor as letters appear magically and form words on the screen. Words somehow form sentences, apparently inspired and connected to my busy fingers. I look at the results, willing to take responsibility, but still marveling at the corrupt ease of the act. Never before have so many avenues of media been available for commercial and personal expression. Yet the common currency of commercial culture and electronic 'chat-rooms' reveal the appalling poverty of thought and expression. Does the democracy and gross accessibility of self-projected messages diminish and trivialize the communication? Is this why the very essence and formality of 'fine art' as an experience seems so old-fashioned and obsolete in our culture? We read that the compositions of Beethoven and Brahms and others were engaged as the common events of ordinary society. Pottery was once actually used as instruments of domestic existence. The awful bifurcation of popular and classical culture has never been so complete. The brave and audacious step you and your colleagues have taken - to place a studio and gallery in the very bowels of commercial tourism and franchise outlets is indeed worthy of great respect. Your refusal to create production lines to assemble ceramic Golden Gate Bridges or miniatures of Alcatraz, while commendable, does reveal a lack of marketing savvy that surely must compound your continued challenge to exist.

I have just finished our telephone conversation. I needed assurance that these communiques were welcome. I think we have established mutually agreeable protocols for future exchanges. I find it wholesome and refreshing that individuals can connect and communicate, not by 'spamming' thousands of potential targets through technological aggression, by the uninvited invasion of private space, but by the personal creation of an authentic correspondence to a specific individual. My progressive instincts require the belief that significant issues of common concern provide the excuse for civic discourse, however distant the parties. While our life cycles barely overlap, and biographical details of the other remain a mystery, we can locate our common humanity through the central issues that form a context and shared territory for this exchange.

What is the fate of the pot? You make them and I collect them. What responsibilities does the potter and the collector have to the pot? I do not pour from them, few rarely hold flowers. Containers without content - objects without objectives. They sit in rows on shelves, splendid and quiet friends who make little demands of me and reward me each day by their very existence. No rare trophy pieces here for investment purposes, rather an eclectic and inclusive collection that documents my great affection for hand made craft. I partially justify my collection by offering custodial protection. They are safe. I dust them weekly and bravely await the next California earthquake, knowing that museum wax secures them to the shelf. I have an alarm system and punch in the numbers on the small keyboard on the hallway wall each time I leave the premises. I do not know what this says about our culture, or the low state of the criminal mind, but I suspect that thieves would sooner swipe silverware and computers. I take care anyway, assuming there might be one criminal with good taste in the vicinity.

And, by God, I do enjoy them. I invite neighborhood children and take them on tours of the cottage. Each pot has a story of acquisition, many in some far-off land. Each pot contains memories of associations with people and places that form the vita of my last twenty five years on earth. At some point, I don't remember when, they replaced the camera snapshots that used to record my adventures in the world. Some are antiques, and like a true Californian, I join their youthful reverence at anything over twenty five years old. I assert to my young charges that indeed some are even older than me, and despite their incredulous response, share their wonder at these objects which existed before our time and that might survive after our demise. Like the California Redwood tree, ceramics has historic durability that is not typical in our disposable consumer culture.

As for the young potter, is your pot a projection of the future I will not share and certainly be unable to understand? Will the pot take me with it and teach me new possibilities or make my orientation obsolete? If I cannot understand or absorb the new pot at my advanced age, should I reject the pot and resign myself to the comforts of a recognizable past? Do you want a bridge to the past or a break with the past in your pot? Some contemporary pots have a real 'attitude' that I do not always share. Relationships with my pots are at least as complicated as my relationships with people.

I hope that you are capable of being sentimental about your pots and care about them as much as I do. You must not casually abandon them. Do you put them all out for sale or perhaps tuck one or two away because you cannot bear to part with them? I assume that the creative process is not simply the repetitive motions of habit. I know you must make a living but I insist on the romance that you love what you are doing and it is out of devotion, not concern about the gas bill, that inspires your daily activity. I can arrange visiting privileges if you wish to see your pot again.

The potter must go on to the next pot - to further discoveries and possibilities. A sequence of pots might form a montage of serial images and experiences that lead to somewhere new for the potter. Collectors might want to stifle that dynamic process - to request a dependable product that is predicable. Many artists succumb to suffering in their success by repeating their first commercially successful pot over and over again in order to perpetuate and secure continued popularity. That first really popular pot can damn the potter to creating the logo pot associated with her name and reputation. It is hard for us to keep track of the potter if they change too much. Thus the pressures of conformity are much greater for the successful potter than the unknown one.

Each object has the ability to tell many stories. Pottery has narrative ability. The inherent story of the potter told through the pot; the story of the cultural arti-fact anchored in time and place; and the contextual story of the collector who appropriates strangers and domesticates them in new surroundings. Pottery has the potential to revise their stories by assuming meanings unintended by those who shaped their form. Pottery has stories to tell that change with time, long after the potter has finished and disappeared. I learn something about myself in the act of selecting and obtaining that one pot in preference to the other pots. I learn something about the potter and the choices made in the creative process. I am also aware that the pot has a longer life span than I do and will be recycled after I have vanished. The pot is the likely survivor, and the potter and collector must be envious of its extended lifetime beyond them.

I have moved your pot without your permission. The subtle hues were in shadow from the play of weak light from the window against the back wall. It is closer to me now, sitting at the desk a few feet from the shelf. It now enjoys a generous cascade of sunlight that illuminates the constrained discipline of its classic demeanor. It is fortunate that pottery is portable. Some pots must reside in several rooms before I arbitrarily decide their final destination. A few remain ambiguous occupants of particular space, not yet at home. Some pots keep moving, permanent orphans that do not seem to belong anywhere. Still I cannot bear to store any of them. All objects must be seen in order to exist. I cannot exile them to some dark obscurity.

I do truly marvel at the infinite invention of the human imagination as demonstrated in the variety of form and character of pottery. I cannot speculate on their ultimate fate - it could break my heart. One son likes to torture me by indicating he will call the Goodwill truck to pick them up after my demise. I threaten that they will be buried with me. Like some ancient Egyptian pharaoh, I will insist that wife and pots will share my immortal resting place. I cannot tolerate the thought that their next owner will neglect them.

I wish to return to an idea that I explored in the last letter. What is art and what is craft? Do those terms have any meaning? I mentioned Soetsu Yanagi, the Japanese philosopher, critic and founder of the Mingei movement. The concept of Mingei, which means literally 'popular art' defines the natural methods of production, a certain kind of beauty born out of 'unconscious creation' as explained by Brian Moeran in his book, 'Folk Art Potters of Japan'. Moeran quotes Yanagi:

"This movement of ours is most active in the field of crafts, but it is not simply a craft movement. Rather what we are really aiming at is a clearly spiritual movement. Thus the Mingei movement cannot be said to exist without its ethical and religious aspects... I am not suggesting that a craftsman has to be a moralist or religious preacher; each man can keep to his own profession. What I do say is that a craftsman is first and foremost a human being, and as a human being his life has to be founded on spirituality... The problem of beauty is not simply a problem of beauty; beauty cannot exist unless it contains elements of truth, goodness, and holiness. If we reflect on this, we will realize that it is impossible to come to terms with a folk art movement that is not spiritual. In this sense, the Mingei movement should try to be a cultural movement".

Can the modern educated potter, who has tasted of the mortal sin of self conscious knowledge, ever regain the necessary innocence to make that simple and honest pot of complete integrity? How can we expect or demand truth, goodness and holiness from you and your pots? It must be a struggle just to make the damn things and keep your head above water. Can you save the world through your pots? Should you even try? William Morris thought you could. The seductive pull of nostalgia for some preindustrial communal world greatly influenced Morris, who wanted to rediscover the golden age of the Middle Ages where art, craft and life were truly integrated in a seamless reality. There is such irony in this history - Morris, the socialist Utopian and child of the upper class, seeking the reactionary site of the feudal middle ages to regain a workers paradise of self-reliant communities. This in contrast to his own reality, where despite the rhetoric, only the wealthy could afford the hand made artifacts of his own shop.

Young potters like yourself can rightly claim all of the past potters as your heritage. You are simply joining a long historical parade that extends back to the dawn of human existence to those anonymous individuals whose shards of clay embedded in the sand define past civilizations. It really doesn't matter if you didn't personally know them, or could speak their language, or even agree with their ceramic intentions or results. Whatever historical or cultural discontinuities and divisions exist in the tortured tangle of the past, people today are still making pots. It might not be the world's oldest profession, but surely it qualifies as one of the world's oldest professions. Student or professional potter, regardless, human hands are still shaping clay. Fires burn or power is generated. Wheels turn or slabs are piled together. Educated or naive, functional or decorative, art or craft, indigenous or commercial commodity, the potter's work goes on. It is hoped - I hope - that this activity is as essential to human culture as any endemic aesthetic performance - be it on the stage, on canvas, or with a slab of marble.

I cannot calibrate my wonder and joy based on some contrived definition or standard that dictates to me the value of what I have just experienced. I embrace all pottery. I cannot collect just one style or period or potter. Their very diversity is a compliment to the diversity of the human imagination. The only bad pot is the dishonest pot. I have my favorites, but it is only my private passion that affects the choice. I have no exclusive standards or rigid demands to make of the pot. Carl Rogers insisted that we should have an 'unconditional personal regard' for people that accepted their sometimes difficult differences. I am not always successful in applying this to people, but quite good at applying this to pots.

It is time to leave again. In a family of teachers, the end of summer is the beginning of school. Whatever the needs of students for new clothes, notebooks and backpacks, teachers must gear up for the school year. My two sons have followed me into the classroom. My wife is teaching at the university where I once taught for over twenty years. While I am now on the sidelines, observing their annual rituals of preparation for the school year, I realize that fall is a return to an interior existence - of home and classroom. I do not know all the impli-cations of this for your gallery and studio. I hope the regular rhythms of your studio; the slapping and shaping of clay; distant buzz of the street; affirmative exchanges with those who discover and purchase your wares; conversation of friends engaged in mutual endeavor; collective hopes and dreams for the gallery realized, all fit within the four walls of your gallery and studio, all form a pattern of security and success for you. There must be a place in the world for what you do. I would not want to live in a world that did not encourage and celebrate the gifts that emerge from the potter's wheel.

Your friend,

PS Many thanks for the photo you sent recently.

"The potter must go on to the next pot – to further discoveries and possibilities."

Four

September 1, 2002

Dear Christa,

Warm greetings from a very hot place. I sit comfortably at my desk, safely barricaded behind the window, observing the intensity of the sun defeated by air-conditioning. No gardening today. Plants don't do well in this kind of weather. The flowers wilt and the plants do not have the energy to grow. No breeze from the bay for us. We wait for relief, dependent upon the uncertain predictions of television weather reports.

We live in a valley close to the foothills. The air quality has improved so much that the mountains that were formerly obscured for several months each summer are mostly clear and near. From the crest of a nearby hill, we can now actually see the placement of our home above the freeway and below the ridge line of mountain ranges. We live in a 'Mediterranean' climate that is rare in the world. I have compromised this habitat by the placement of dozens of sprinkler heads that allow a lush garden with plants that cannot claim indigenous status. In the abstract, as a matter of principle, I endorse the untouched natural environment as seen in the mountains above me. In practice, I have created a garden environment that could not exist without my constant intervention. I rationalize that this kind of honest confession at least partially excuses the violation.

What has been the importance of geography in pottery? Certainly the availability of clay extracted from the earth located many potteries in the past. Before the swift transportation of clay, I would imagine the qualities of the local clay influenced the quality and character of the local pot. There was often some distance and disparity between the rural areas where appropriate clay was discovered and the urban centers where it would be appreciated and purchased. I have never visited Zanesville, Ohio and do not want to be prejudiced, but I suspect that the origins of this site as a center of American art pottery had more to do with its natural rather than cultural resources. North Carolina is an interesting example where a long history of indigenous rural potters co-exist with imported eastern seaboard potters with their galleries in Asheville. Many of these newcomers have established studios in the countryside. How many old traditions and emerging styles co-exist in the same territory? I do not know but I would hope that all can learn from each other and new work reflects elements of multiple traditions and possibilities.

The topography of geography affects the character of culture. Physical isolation can better preserve a single tradition. San Francisco has a history as a port of entry for immigration. The spectacular beauty of the physical environment and the periodic landings of divergent peoples form a mosaic of traditions and ceramic examples of diverse cultures. Does the chronic attitude of some modern artists that traditions must be overthrown in order for new pottery to flourish allow the tribute of active ceramic traditions in their own work? The ultimate compliment, consciously realized or unconsciously present, is that in overthrowing the tradition, the reference point is still that tradition. All the energy expended in the rebellious effort is yet another tribute to the same source. Whatever the eventual fate of the theories of Freud or Marx, the revisionists must deny their validity and significance only by creating documents that attest to their towering importance. In creating the ceramic counterpoint, the counterpot is still commentary on the absent inspiration.

In the 19th and 20th centuries, many potters moved across oceans and lands, seeking more favorable sites and opportunities for their expanding skills and talent. A few of these itinerant potters were among the most talented. The peripatetic Frederick Rhead, a giant among American art potters, was born in England, developed his skills at Wardle Pottery, came to America in 1902 - first at Avon Pottery Works in Wheeling, West Virginia, then Weller Pottery in Zanesville, and later Roseville Pottery in the same city - moved on to Jervis Pottery in Oyster Bay, Long Island, traveled to University City, Missouri at University City Pottery, then joined the exodus to the promised land, golden California, where he worked in Fairfax at the Arequipa studio. After that it was on to Santa Barbara, where he founded his own studio, finally ending his career with the American Encaustic Tiling Company and Homer Laughlin Pottery Company back in Ohio. As David Rago summarizes in "American Art Pottery", "During the forty years that Rhead potted and decorated in this country, he significantly influenced or managed ten companies, including small studios, large factories, well-intentioned experiments, and even a sanatorium." Sounds a bit exhausting. But his pots were dynamically changing as he was moving, working and learning. Rhead provided both leadership and art as he moved across time and territory.

In reviewing your vita, I see that you share this traveling tendency with Rhead. I think you probably have the advantage of jet planes and mileage plus arrangements over him. Are all professional potters vagabonds and transients? I do not know your origins or place of birth or place of upbringing, the first citation on your vita reveals the Midwestern site of your Master of Fine Arts at Indiana University in Bloomington, Indiana. Prior to 2000, you studied in West Virginia, Post-Bac Study in Nova Scotia, Canada as a visiting Fulbright Scholar, BA at Pennsylvania State University, artist in residence in Snowmass Village, Colorado, study abroad at the University of Leeds, England, and now in San Francisco, California. I have skipped over other references on your vita and the sequence of travels is not quite in order, but it reveals an intrepid spirit that is willing to venture into foreign lands and distant parts in a quest to develop and hone your craft and teach and learn from others. Your pots travel and you travel, sometimes to different destinations. You might beat Rhead's record yet.

There is an international infrastructure of potters, galleries, art centers, institutions of higher learning, associations, agencies and individuals devoted to the promotion and support of ceramics. Young potters may go forth in the world and place themselves in perpetual jeopardy, creating visible extensions of their own personhood and supposed talent. I try to remember this when I approach a pot in a gallery. Even rejected, the pot survives, worthy of respect. I do not need to issue an indictment of the pot to justify my rejection or alternative choice.

The demanding expenditure of time and effort is an investment in the unknown speculations of possible success. Your work is judged and juried by the masters and experts of the craft. Publications cite the appearance of your pots and awards and grants can emanate from that recognition. So a career is possible and many today are pursuing that ambition. I do not know if there is real justice in all of this. Is innate talent the ultimate determinator of success, or like so many other human enterprises, does packaging, marketing, the right connections and pandering to popular taste determine success? Do you measure success by the quality of the pot on the shelf or the amount of money in the bank? Can you really have both?

Definitions and possibilities for excellence are inclusive of all life functions. I do not believe you save your excellence for just one task. Given our natural limitations, your excellence might be more obvious in some areas, but people who strive for excellence tend to give their best in all circumstances. Michael Polanyi, in his book, Personal Knowledge, states, "The freedom of the subjective person to do as he (she) pleases is overruled by the freedom of the responsible person to act as he (she) must." I believe excellence has something to do with this self-enforced commitment. This commitment is made after the rational realization that it is not necessary or required. When excellence achieves worldly success as the desired outcome, when success is the intended goal of the original effort, excellence is reduced to a mere methodology for self-bribery. The fruits of something called success, monetary or material, have no organic connection with this trait called excellence.

Can some enterprising potter emulate the success of Thomas Kincade? I notice that many painters are making excellent quality reproductions by laser and electronic methods which they sell as 'original' reproductions, numbered and signed. You can't really tell the difference, or so it is said. Who will be the art potter to pioneer the same approach? Five hundred original vases, all the same, only requiring the incised signature of the potter as the only hand made element in some new technological process. After all, American genius in the form of Ford created the capacity for the worker to own an automobile, and Levitt utilized the same formula to mass produce affordable housing tracts that contributed to the great expansion of the middle class after World War II. Why not bring that kind of democracy to ceramics? You could sell your pots through Wal-Mart. Doesn't the rarity of the single and unique handmade pot create a false market scarcity just to keep the prices high? The overpowering global domination of the American corporate system in all areas of our existence provides unchallenged opportunities for entrepreneurs and hustlers. No one with any brains majors in the Humanities or Liberal Arts anymore. The business majors far outnumber all the rest, and the School of Business rules in American higher education.

I follow the pots, sometimes the potter. I too love to travel and selectively sort through the ceramic antique remnants of foreign civilizations and the fresh creations of contemporary potters. We lived in England in 1984 on sabbatical, Judith looking at special education in elementary and secondary schools while I was a visiting faculty member at the University of Surrey at Guildford. We visit England often, have friends there, and always make our pilgrimage to The Craft Potters Association on Marshall Street in London. This association is the only national body in Great Britain representing studio potters. I stroll around the shop with my wife, then make a second, more serious tour. My wife and I confer on the possible selections. She controls the purse strings in the family, pays the household bills. We are truly partners in our travels and pottery acquisitions. In this kind of partnership, you need at least one sensible and reasonable person to moderate the spontaneous infatuation that the other seems to enjoy with almost every pot. Judy performs this function very well.

Knowing you spent time in England in 1989, I am sure you know of this wonderful shop in London. I am quite proud of the variety of fine pots we have amassed over the years from Great Britain. I regard England as a second home, comfortable and familiar, not at all foreign to me. On one lovely visit we purchased the directory of potters from the Craft Potters Association, which contains a map identifying studio locations. We rented a car and traveled all over Great Britain visiting potters in their studio or gallery. I remember one search in the Welsh countryside, maneuvering the car through narrow country lanes, looking around each bend for some sign of the studio, and the joy of discovery. Another trip we made the grand pilgrimage to all the Leach studios, wife, son, and grandson. What an amazing family tradition. Vivid memories of strolling the streets of St. Ives, the seaside village that was, and still is the home of so many artists. My small cottage is a depository of so many British artifacts. Pottery originated with a journey to a particular place, a site that forms still recognizable pictures in my mind. Each pot in my collection triggers these reveries of past journeys.

We must plan our future travels. I expect to see your future itineraries eventually recorded on your resumé in the form of awards, exhibitions and honors. I will continue my explorations of the world, secure that where there is human community and culture, there will most likely be pottery.

Your friend,

Richard

Five

September 12, 2002

Dear Christa,

The mountains above us are on fire. The fires of war are gathering in the nation. The smoke dims the sunlight. Talk of war fills the newspapers and media. Ashes leave a gray film on every surface. Generals and politicians prepare us for the calculated costs of planned violence. We are told that the flames were not sponsored by nature but more likely by some slight human mistake. Generals in uniforms and politicians in suits debate, in civilized discourse, plans to eliminate remote people and terminate foreign governments. The flames are advancing and if caught by a breath of wind could consume a home and a lifetime of family possessions in mere seconds. The winds of war launch weapons of such intelligence that they can successfully eradicate carefully chosen people and buildings without personal contact. Homes are built in areas that defy and defile nature and threaten the habitat and life of other species. Fire sponsored by war leaves terrible scars on the human landscape. The creative benefits of fire might only make sense to the potter who wisely restricts it to the kiln. Decisions will soon be made and things will happen, and the consequences will sear my conscience and burn holes in my heart. I am an old man who is surely living at the apex of human civilization.

I fear that all the potters and poets of the world cannot save me. The romance of my life consisted in the belief or illusion that art was the highest expression of a noble species and that war and bigotry were the dysfunctional symptoms of injustice and oppression. The inventory of wars, holocaust and atrocities during my lifetime could make me a fool. I look to my books and pots, seeking comfort and reassurance. In seeking guidance, I have just reviewed the written statements and manifestos that many potters and other artists offer to explain their motivation and intention in creating their pots and art.

Joseph Addotta, who creates wonderful bronze sculptures of animals, states that his work "… reflects a profound feeling for the living beauty of nature". I view his sleeping cat, so delicate and detailed, so heavy and so small. I share his reverence for "the living beauty of nature". I could cite a bibliography of work and a pantheon of giants whose moral vision, formed in artifact or text upon the page, would reinforce this commitment. But Joseph Addotta is not being quoted in the media today and I do not see the operational implemention of this profound feeling for nature in the public policy of those in power.

Perhaps I expect too much. If the pen is truly mightier than the sword, why does civilization triumph through mere survival after so much death and destruction? When will the preventive power of human testimony and nobility as magnified through art triumph prior to the deadly act? The performance of Beethoven's Ninth and the finale of 'Ode to Joy' after the Berlin Wall came down was memorable but why couldn't a prior performance have prevented the wall? I must be truly naive.

Ned Rorem, the American composer, in a recent L.A. Times book review, stated that, "Art is unrelated to morality: it does not make us better, or even change us; art makes us more into what we already are by reminding us of all the things we know." He compounds this somewhat pessimistic appraisal by remarking, "… that great artists aren't necessarily great human beings, while many saints are second-rate artists." In contrast, Bernard Leach believed in the 'ethical' pot. Born of honesty and simplicity, conceived in aesthetic innocence, and useful in daily function. I assume that if pots could be ethical, Leach would extend that ethical status to the potter and the potential user.

I carefully reviewed your statement, Christa, that accompanied your pot along with the vita. It is a fine and honest statement. You found certain virtues in the creation of your work. "Clarity, as well as harmony, is essential in the attachment of handles, the fit of lids, curve of spouts." Observing your pottery, I can certainly affirm that clarity and harmony. Your forms are solid, almost architectural, and knit together in single form and function. Indeed I can find such harmony in many of the objects that fill my house. I can find harmony in my own arrangement and placement of objects in each room, rectangular compositions in space that envelop you as you enter each room. If harmony can be achieved in art, with some discipline and practice, why is it so absent from the morning newspaper and the 6 o'clock news? Why does the artist so value harmony while it is so abused and neglected by others?

In your statement you place yourself within the contemporary tragedy of September 11. You state, "To try to stay focused in the midst of this devastating time of terrorism, I calm myself with the familiar motions of forming cups and bowls on the wheel." I too participated in the national penance of watching, time and time again, those planes smash into the towers. The repetition only increased the agony. The pain and hurt increased as the media researched the individual biographies of the victims and their families. I wept and grieved with the nation. All the victims were innocent. The vast majority of people who end up casualities of wars have always been innocent.

How must I revise myself to survive? If art cannot lead, then it can at least become a therapy for those of us who create and those who appreciate. If the realism of evil must exile the dreams of idealism, we must accelerate the manufacture of bombs and body bags and forget the silly notions that art can educate and ennoble humankind. War is transformative, not art. The great inventions of this technological age were inadvertent products of war. It is war that is good for the economy. It is war that unites us in common purpose. Art is for sissies and dilettantes. I want to protect myself by becoming cynical and tough. It would increase my popularity and sense of belonging. I could then listen to talk radio shows and identify my new-found masculinity with a patriotism that reduces life to an athletic contest in which we 'kick ass' thanks to our superior military capacity.

The concluding sentence in your statement reminds me that the elegance of pottery results from interaction with the earth. You state, "Crafting handmade, useful objects from 'mud' continually reminds me of just how basic, how elemental, life can be." Looking at human history, pottery is at least as elemental as war. As your insight fully states, we make art with mud. Art is not a frill or extracurrular activity, as often represented in public schools. It is essential and functional to the human spirit and useful to our daily lives. Pottery is not as hard or tough as a gun or tank. But weapons of war quickly become obsolete, and shards of pottery define ancient civilizations. I am grateful for the assurance derived from all possible evidence. I have a friend who just completed the construction of an adobe house. He is off the grid and completely self-sufficient in energy and water. Here in Southern California we still have old adobe houses, now museums and monuments, from pre Gold Rush days. Mud is an honorable material for durable houses and great pottery. It is fitting that the play of childhood, the squeezing of mud through the fingers of a child has graduated to the adult shaping of mud to create art. It is a single progression that only reinforces its primal origins and essential activity.

John Ruskin, the fountainhead of the Arts and Crafts movement, established the Guild of St. George in 1871. In this community, as Kaplan and Elizabeth Cumming explain in 'The Arts and Crafts Movement', "Guild members were obliged to live and work according to Ruskin's religious and moral principles and contribute to Guild funds; in return they received fair pay and enjoyed healthy work and shared in communally owned farms and industries." The authors then concede, "Attracting minimal immediate response, it did little to improve the general run of society but it provided a precedent for later craft guilds." How can you have an aesthetic of pottery without an ethic of life? How can you care about pottery without caring about 'the general run of society'?

Collis Glaspy, a contemporary potter from the American Southwest, provides a most positive and wholesome statement:

"Pottery speaks to me of the love between myself and all of creation... I describe myself as a healer as well as a potter and I channel healing energy into each pot I throw. This is my gift to the earth based clay. I feel it supplies the harmony between myself and my earth, this harmony essential to my spirit."

I am beginning to see connections between your statement and the statements of other potters. Both of you speak of harmony and pay tribute to the earth, source of the raw material of your art. Does Collis go too far in describing himself as a healer? Does the pot only heal the potter or can it heal others who come into contact with it? It is fairly obvious that the sheer physical exertion of throwing a pot might be therapeutic, most physical exercise is good for you. But can the visual engagement of the pot provide therapy? Are all potters in love with 'all of creation'? If I had the resources to do a clinical survey, would potters as a group be any less neurotic or aggressive than the rest of us? Remember, I am preparing to go to war and I must become a warrior citizen if I am to hear the daily body count without weeping. I will abandon my sentimentality about potters and pottery. Cut out the love and harmony bullshit and let's get ready for war.

A contemporary potter in Idylwild, California, Greg Kennedy, who has provided me with two beautiful pots, stated in his 'A Potter's Soliloquy', "To go out among the people of the earth. To put yourself at risk. To discover that there is really no reason for fear. To see your changing reflection reflected so differently in each facet of the varied mirrors of the many possible existences. To fall so fully in love with experience that you want to experience everything entirely. And then to be consumed in the realization that you are already a part of it all and that the all is already within." I am accumulating impressive and convincing testimony. Despite my earlier bravado, I will never be ready for war.

I look at the sweet face of my grandchildren, the youngest, Sydney, only a few weeks old and I cannot believe that war is a natural and normal activity for individuals or nations. We have reason to fear the fanatical terrorist. We know what they can do. But the glory of America is the hope it holds for all the peoples of the world. I went to New York a few weeks after the tragedy. The ruins of the World Trade Center were still smoldering and the smoke was visible in the sky. I saw American flags everywhere, huge sheets on tall buildings, small stars and stripes on lapels, waving flags on cars. Can we follow the advice of Greg Kennedy and remain "… among the people of the earth" and "… place yourself at risk" and "… fall so fully in love with experience that you want to experience everything entirely"? Greg might say I am taking his words out of context in light of September 11. But are all the words of potters I have quoted in this letter just for peacetime application? The world has been at peace only a few scattered years in the total history of world civilization. If you can only utter and apply words of peace and harmony in times of peace there might never be an appropriate or convenient time to do so.

I collect the pots and words of potters. Maybe I take them too seriously. Pots are inherently gentle creatures. They arrive only when you invite them and they do not disturb the peace. I do not know as many potters as I know pots. I would like to think potters are also gentle and would not disturb my peace. During the course of writing this letter the fires in the mountains above me are now contained. The sky is free of smoke. Our leaders are still talking of war. Seen from an historical perspective, the hopes and aspirations of Ruskin and Morris largely failed. In a few months I might have to face the reality of war that would make the words of my potter friends failed pledges of unrealistic affirmation.

Sometimes my letters might fail to entertain. Sometimes I cannot even find escape or peace amidst my pottery.

Take care - your friend,

Richard

Six

October 2, 2002

Dear Christa,

I can see the front garden from my desk, looking through the open blinds, past the leaded glass window and driveway to the small fountain. Perennial plants merge to form a density I first discovered and loved in English gardens. Years ago, I removed the original grass lawn with a sharp shovel, clod by clod. I refused to become an expert gardener, preferring the unintended delights and risks of uninformed experimentation. Plants surprised me by their enthusiastic size and unexpected generosity of clustered flowers. Small trees surprised me as they grew tall and spread shade over areas that demanded plants that felt comfortable in shadow. Specks and dots of lavender are sprinkled throughout the more prevalent greens. One plant, I think it is called 'Tiger's Tail', responds with spikes of orange that do not harmonize but provide an eclectic diversity that also suits my taste in pottery. I love to trim and shape the varied vegetation, assuming creative control over the natural chaos that emerges when I fail to tend the garden for more than a few days. A high hedge of pink roses surrounds the front and side, pressing against the split rail fence that is the boundary line of my corner house.

A private garden, a secret garden, except for the driveway that opens up the garden on one side. On the other side, a small Victorian gate of wrought iron, with an arbor of red roses overhead. Neighborhood children play in the garden and my grandchildren explore the paths of flagstones that meander through high walls of flourishing plants. A few butterflies dance and explore, hummingbirds hover over the flowers. I am sadly reminded of the far more plentiful butterflies of my father's garden so long ago. Where have all the butterflies gone? I sit on the bench in my front garden at different times of the day, listen to the splash of the fountain, gaze at the profusion of plants, grateful I have the abundance of time to experience and occupy the site.

Perhaps it is the slowing pace sponsored by the ageing process, or the absence of deadlines and a demanding schedule. The manual operations of living each day tend to become ceremonies in which my hands perform calculated and repeated maneuvers that bring inherent satisfaction. My hands 'work' in the garden - dirt under fingernails, occasional cuts from thorns. I make tea in the early afternoon, not as elaborate an experience as the Japanese, but requiring several steps that bring satisfaction in their sequential execution. My hands are not specialized, but as a generalist I do not make excessive demands. The hands of the potter are so crucial. When did you discover you had the hands of a potter? How did they let you know? Are you still conscious of their actions in shaping the pot?

Diane Ackerman, in "A Natural History of The Senses" explores the importance of hands:

"In these days of mass-produced objects, we treasure things that are 'hand-made'. . . Sometimes working hands seem to perform with a cunning sensitivity that defies explanation... A hand moves with a complex precision that's irreplaceable, feels with a delicate intuition that's indefinable..."

I cannot accept that the vicarious connection between the manipulation of the computer mouse and what happens on the screen, however elaborate the graphic result, can equal the direct involvement of the human hand in creating objects of art. The etched designs of the laser cannot duplicate the integrity of the hand carved and sculpted wood and clay. Will we eventually lose the full ability to use our hands, as we apparently did the prehensile toe, in the electronic triumph of mechanical superiority? Hands are the most direct instruments of our empowerment. We express and communicate our thoughts and emotions with hand gestures; we work with tools designed to fit the hand, and our hands create the intricate objects of aesthetic value. Our increasing dependence on the yellow pages reflects the inadequacy of the hand-held ordinary screwdriver to repair the tiny intricacies of electronic circuits. If robots can assemble better cars, how far away can be the surrender of the artist's hand? Some day potters might be the last group of human beings involved in the manual labor of the creative process. Some day someone will proudly display the truly innovative pot never touched by hands.

Hands allow us to make mistakes. Mistakes are the ultimate proof of our humanity. Perfection, according to Plato, allows only one template. We stretch and exercise our hands to transcend previous limits and boundaries. Just as old records in Olympic competition are shattered, the genius and endurance of the artist pushes the aesthetic and technical boundaries. We will never achieve the seamless perfection of the machine. Art contains our insecurities and physical

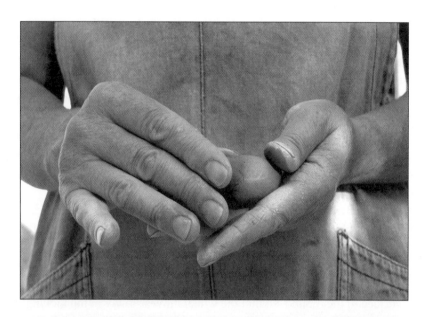

limits as well as our talent. Even what we celebrate in our art is there to bring some comfort and get us through the night. We must reach definitions of excellence that forgive and complement the labor of our hands.

I look at my hands, see the 'age spots' that decorate the back of them; stubby fingers that no longer possess the tensile strength to fulfill every command. Opening the stubborn bottle top might require assistance, pushing the shovel into the earth to make a hole for some new plant requires greater patience now, with an increased repetition of small efforts that eventually produces results. But my hands are still friendly to my wishes, and loyal in response. Strangers become friends when they 'shake hands'. The hands introduce the clay to the potter and the relationship is defined by that interaction. I do not think one could become a potter if one did not like the substance of clay, the feel of clay. I would imagine the better potters are best able to establish sensitive rapport with their hands. Hands are the scouts that report back useful information.

Kenneth R. Beittel, in 'Zen and the Art of Pottery' spends much of his book describing the movement of the potter's hands. In discussing centering the clay, Beittel states:

"... the potter rhythmically clasps the palms of both hands, fingers relaxed, on the surface of the mound, so that the wheel moves slowly in the kicking direction." Beittel describes the urgent role, and potential disaster, as the hands perform dynamic and delicate maneuvers at the potter's wheel:

"The hands slowly but steadily move up toward the top edge of the mound, so that a tall narrow cone shape is achieved. The back and inside surface edge of the palms are the pressure points that move and lift the mound. If the hands move too fast from bottom to top, a spiral will be created; too little pressure with the hands, and the cone will not be formed; too much pressure, and the clay will be tweaked off at the top."

He continues the discussion of shaping the clay:

"For shaping and thinning, the right hand should be relaxed, falling into a natural cupped and rounded form,... The fingertips of the right hand should lightly encircle the stem,... The left hand then finds the inside center, presses down slightly and sweeps out against the bowl-like shape of the restraining right hand."

He goes on in several segments to further describe the elaborate choreography of the two hands working together, identifying how finger and thumb have

essential roles to play in the creative process. For this lay person, the narrative implies that the myriad maneuvers necessary in split second precision does not allow the potter time to consciously direct the hands. They must know what to do beforehand. Practice over an extended period of time provides the unconscious patterns of learned behavior. Beittel terms this integration "hand and wheel in partnership".

I assume that each potter has her own 'moves'. As with classical pianists, even with the same composition, the physical experience at the piano is quite different and the interpretation is never exactly the same. In the audience, I can observe the posture and facial expression, the movement of the hands and fingers as they slide up and down and hammer and caress the keys. I do not know if there is a classical potter's hand, the ideal hand for the potter. Is a big hand more impressive? How about long fingers? What about the wear and tear on the hands? I imagine the wrists also are at risk. Do you have the equivalent of carpel tunnel syndrome? Do your hands dry out from the constant moisture? Could some enterprising entrepreneur make a fortune selling potters some special cream or lotion that would restore your hands to their natural condition? Show me a potter's hand, tell me if I should recognize some obvious trait that reveals the true potter. Is there any carry over to other activities? I would like to feel that potters could be as clumsy in other pursuits as the rest of us. Can you catch a ball? Paint a fence? I do not begrudge you your talent, but a democracy of mediocrity in at least some areas would make me more comfortable.

Hands are agents of purposeful activity. They are attached in obvious and visible ways. They can make obscene gestures and provide physical overtures to sensual contact, even love. I don't really believe that they reveal either the future or your character, although some people apparently make a living 'reading' them. What about the long haul and the ageing process for you? For baseball players, I recall that the knees are usually the first to go. What about the potter? Are the hands all that durable, given that they work so hard? Where do old potters go? I have so many questions, and unlike most teachers, they are honest questions because I do not know the answers. I remember Otto Heino sitting in front of his studio in Ojai on a bench with his dog nearby. Otto must be over eighty now. He still throws pots, still functions. His hands look as old as the rest of him. The multitude of pots on the shelves of his gallery tell you that his hands retain their contact with clay, and still form that clay into distinctive shapes. A long lifetime of bending over that wheel, engaging the clay with hands that contain all the wisdom of that lifetime.

Do potters compare hands the way they compare pots? How do you 'work out' to keep your hands in shape? I am aware that you would have to cease all activity as a potter to have the time to properly answer my questions. How do

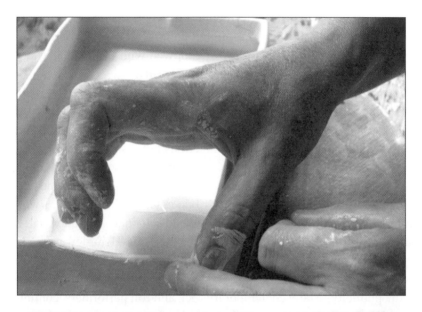

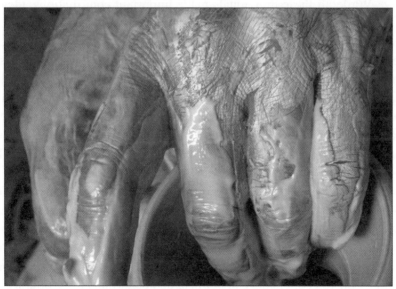

you remove your occupational mud at the end of the day? The coal miner has a real problem, the coal dust seeps under the fingernails and in the folds of wrinkled skin. How persistent is clay against soap and scrubbing? Are you proud to display your clay-soiled hands as a badge of your honorable profession? Would you increase your artistic reputation if you insured your hands with Lloyds of London for three or four million dollars? It is so pleasant to write as a lay person rather than as the professor endowed with complete mastery. My questions do not reveal incompetence, just curiosity.

If you could somehow achieve celebrity status, you could be the first potter to make the cover of People magazine if you play your cards right. I do not know if Paris dress designers could be persuaded to create a special wardrobe for potters. Like classical musicians, if serious potters such as yourself decide to remain outside the popular culture, your obscurity will limit the box office impact of your pottery. What a dilemma: grab fifteen minutes of fame or pursue artistic integrity and cultural invisibility? I do not know of any potters who have the contrived eccentricities that the media would celebrate. Salvador Dali caught the attention of the media with his bizarre mannerisms, Hemingway became the living stereotype of his own creation, Andy Warhol presided over a circus of friends in acts of tragic self destruction that gladly accepted notoriety as a source of media publicity. Many contemporary rock and roll performers continue that legacy. While all these individuals made important contributions, they also ended up being used as entertainers and clowns for the popular culture. Eighteenth and nineteenth century Romanticism permitted poets to be promiscuous if they promised to die at an early age. I remember a film I saw as an adolescent, so young that I did not know how really awful the film was, of the life of Chopin, spitting blood on the piano keys. I had aspirations to be a genius, a great painter, and to suffer in Technicolor. I thought there was a direct correlation between weak lungs, spitting blood and artistic greatness. I had serious pneumonia when I was an infant, almost died, and thought at the time I saw the movie that I was half-way home to fame and greatness.

Even the Booker prize judges, reported in the British newspaper 'Guardian Weekly', are recommending turning from 'pompous, portentous and pretentious fiction' to more popular fiction in awarding their annual prize for authors of fiction. According to the article, "they vowed to cast their net wider to more plebeian literary forms, and even into the lower depths of genre and 'popular fiction'." Can you both believe in political democracy and be a cultural elitist? To the average citizen, Kirk Douglas is still Van Gogh and his most important career move as an artist was to remove one ear and send it to a prostitute. Please, please, Christa, don't emulate Douglas/Van Gogh and lop off a finger in a misguided attempt to jump-start the next phrase of your career. Your many accomplishments, including the recent citations in "The Art of Contemporary American Pottery" by Hluch, attest to your emerging greatness, and besides, it could impede your performance at the wheel. Given the expectations of the culture, life could be both more exciting and dangerous if potters desire the role of artist rather than crafts person.

I am left-handed, the great curse of my life, the ultimate stigma from which I have never recovered and that determined my life destiny. I remember the elementary school teachers that tried to force me to change to the right hand in my penmanship exercises that revealed my complete lack of moral character with my misshapen left handed smudges of the alphabet. As I recall, lefties make lousy second base players and bad golfers, (maybe it was bowling). How about left-handed potters? What is their fate? Can you tell a left-handed pot from a right-handed pot? Beittel in his book tells you what to do with each hand at the wheel. If you were left-handed, could you exchange the role of hands and not upset Beittel and still make great pottery?

One should not underestimate the metaphorical impact of hands. Many non-profit agencies seeking peace and conflict resolution have logos of sets of over-lapping hands, often of difference hues and shades. In sharp contrast, that masculine metaphor for force, the closed fist, inspires the possibilities of aggres-sive, possibly lethal damage. As a grandfather, I know about the painted print of the child's hand in finger painting or pressed in clay at school. The profile of the child's hand is often the first lesson in drawing. The non-threatening hand gestures of the potter are firm and tender in their effectiveness, careful not to tear or dent the fabric of the clay. Do potters ever have to clench their fists?

Hands are vehicles of sacred mediation. The manipulation of hand-held beads in Middle Eastern countries and in the Roman Catholic and Orthodox traditions combines prayer and reflection. The unity of hands together in prayer is one of the hand gestures of the faithful. Bernard Leach and Kenneth Beittel would agree that the making of pottery comprises stylized rituals of sacred meaning. I do not know if the average professional potter, preoccupied with keeping to a production schedule, is attuned to this sacred potential. Here Beittel discusses the 'Great Tradition', originating in Japanese Zen beliefs, where there is:

"…a turning from the heart toward wholeness. Zen in the art of pottery is no more nor less than centering the body-mind by dwelling with a beginner's mind in the heart of the simplest act. It is a meditation in action in which the humblest bowl and the largest sphere arise from the same deep peace… "

The hands of the potter in this tradition perform the action that reflects the inner integration of person and nature. Pottery becomes the discipline through which unity and peace are achieved. Perhaps in the West we are asking too much to expect this experience. The walls between secular and sacred have been carefully built here. The attainment of 'Enlightenment' in our tradition was the triumph of reason over the sacred and their permanent separation.

There is a tradition in our school system, the five paragraph essay in which students are instructed to provide a neat and complete conclusion in the last paragraph. Teachers and academics have a lot of trouble with ambiguity. In my mind, ambiguity is one of the essential elements of intellectual complexity and subtlety. How absurd that our Hollywood movies require a happy ending and so do our school assignments. This letter, my sixth to you, will disappoint that tradition. My beloved garden, the price of fame, and the significance of hands, please tie them all together in a neat bundle if you can. I am not even going to try. The process of integration must be the imaginative enterprise of the reader, not this writer.

Take care. Your friend,

Richard

Seven

October 29, 2002

Dear Christa,

Our relationship had a most improbable beginning. A visit to San Francisco with my wife several months ago; hotel near Fisherman's Wharf, a walk through The Cannery, an old fruit cannery converted to shops; a chance discovery of a ceramics studio and gallery, Verdigris, scanning the shelves and identifying beautiful pots; a brief but stimulating conversation with the potter, someone named Christa Assad; the purchase of a pot and departure. Then the risk, sending you my first letter, announcing my bizarre intentions to initiate an ongoing correspondence with you based on the model of Rilke's "Letters to a Young Poet". What a range of possible disasters in perception. These scenarios could be unflattering to both of us. An old man with nothing to do, perhaps attracted in some abnormal way to this young woman potter, pioneering a novel way of stalking through postal correspondence; insipid commentary from a collector dilettante who confessed ignorance of the actual work of the potter; diversion and interruption of creative activity to placate this harmless senior citizen in a new kind of ceramic outreach - the potter as gerontology social worker.

On the other hand, to be fair and balanced, another scenario; mature intellectual discovers young potter; enriches her existence by a series of brilliant letters only to discover complete lack of intellectual curiosity, uncomprehending response that reveals shallow and superficial individual; further exposé of corrupt and conniving potter willing to sell her artistic soul to make big time success. I could go further with this proposed script but I must announce immediately that these perceptions have been effectively demolished by our last meeting. I am of course only speaking for myself in this regard but remain hopeful that you share this conclusion.

It has taken me two paragraphs just to say that I was so pleased by our meeting. Sometimes the art, noble and humanistic, woefully, does not represent the artist's character and temperament. Beethoven was cruel to his nephew, Cezanne was a most unpleasant man, and Gauguin deserted his wife and children and dallied with native women in the South Seas. I met your pots first, then shortly afterwards met you. Your pots, even at first glance, were strong, disciplined, and orginial. After our last meeting, it became apparent to me that they inherited these traits from you. This of course leads me to the theme of this letter and the inevitable questions. Do potters have the time, in their competitive efforts to stay afloat, for friendships beyond the instrumental contacts to facilitate their careers? Are potters inherently loners, more at home in solitary interaction with their wheels than in the social matrix of family and friends? Do their beautiful pots attract more friends than the potters who made them? Do potters just hang around with other potters and interbreed to perpetuate their insular guild? It is important that you answer all the questions posed in all of my letters. Of course, you have no obligation to inform me of the answers. To the degree the questions cause you unease or an excuse for introspection, the answers might be useful for self reflection and self-critique. Lying to others can in some circumstances be forgiven, lying to yourself should never be tolerated. If my commentary and questions are relevant, you only need to satisfy yourself in order to satisfy me.

I note here the observation that you have already partially answered my questions. Your trusting relationship with your partners in the studio enterprise was evident. You work together in rather tight quarters, depend on each other, and yet each creates quite distinct pottery. The pottery studio can be a collective enterprise, you and your friends have already proved that. Some potters seek grand goals in common purpose. Others might form temporary associations to pragmatically reduce expenses, willing to co-exist at the same site in order to survive individually. I don't know the human, material or aesthetic glue that holds your experiment at Verdigris together, but I did sense real respect and friendship. You are close friends and neighbors in that gallery/studio who truly help each other.

Your shared studio does not resemble the description of Garth Clark in "The Potter's Art" of the emergence of industrial pottery in England in the seventeenth century, "… the fruits of a complex industrial collaboration in which many pairs of hands have been involved, a collaboration which is known impersonally as the 'production line'." He further deplores the working conditions. "The early industrial potteries were exceedingly unhealthy working environments and the workers paid a lethal price for their participation." Exploited potters of the world, unite! You still probably share the long hours; twelve hours were the norm according to Clark. You are most vulnerable in this barbaric society that in some instances resembles the harsh conditions of long ago England. To be self-employed, without the 'fringe benefits' central to your security such as pension and health plans is really living dangerously. Although your self-exploitation is voluntary and made by conscious choice, how you exist signifies a society that does not seriously sponsor or support art or artists. The values and priorities of countries are evident in their public budgets and financial allocations. A society whose political discourse always provides the better argument for guns than art is a place where lust for power is more compelling than the celebration of culture.

The Arts and Crafts potters of the late nineteenth century were often gentlemen intellectuals who still practised the division of labor in which they designed and perhaps decorated the pots but often did not throw them. The thought preceded the pot. Ideological perspectives divided individuals and groups. Ceramic art pottery began to carry the signature, initials or mark of the maker. The human dimensions of friendship were often compromised or nullified by emerging disagreements. It is both a sign of human complexity and integrity that abstract principles can unite and then divide people. Hurt and disappointment can more often emerge from idealism than cynicism. Friendships of fact based on solid affection and respect can wither over differences of aesthetic abstraction. The studio potters of the twentieth century often worked in isolation to create unique pots that represented the personality of that individual. But common purpose often inspired utopian communities and joint efforts.

Dartington in Devon was such an experiment during the early twentieth century. Composed of reformers and intellectuals with common interests, production of crafts was central to their aspirations along with a progressive school that sought to integrate the wisdom of East and West. Founded by the wealthy Elmhursts, it still exists to this day. According to Tanya Harrod in "The Crafts in Britain in the 20th Century", discrepancies and contradictions abounded, with one investigative report stating, "... there was no real link between the ideals associated with a 'Dartington' philosophy and what he saw as a grim industrial manufacturing environment, albeit in a rural setting... Dartington was meant to be classless and unhierarchical. But in fact those who were deemed artists were accorded the greatest privileges by the Elmhursts - although, as in a princely court, these privileges could be suddenly withheld." There were numerous other brief experiments in utopian communities, brief unity among potters, manifestos issued with a flourish, breathless declarations of immutable aesthetic truth. Few lasted long. Aesthetic absolutists, convinced that they alone have the formula for truth, can be as fanatical and narrow-minded as those who claim they alone have heard the word of God.

I always preferred to launch my daily crusades with the pretense and inspiration of a superior ethical vision. Perhaps my efforts to reform institutional life in public education required the imposed drama of a noble struggle to get through the tedium of that repetitious life. Actually institutional racism and sexism were real and their impact devastating. I needed the greater context of moral purpose to fuel my modest efforts to alleviate the inherent humiliations of a mass professional treatment in the classroom that seemed to standardize and rank individual humans according to cultural origin and gender identity.

Friendships require reciprocal exchange and some attention. I have never had the energy or time to maintain too many friendships and really do them justice. One positive variable is the sheer endurance of the changing landscape of lives and personalities over an extended period. The real triumph of friendship is the trust and caring that provides sanctuary in joint company. Mutual interests and goals can be central. Shoji Hamada, in the foreword to "The Unknown Craftsman" describes the friendship of Soetsu Yanagi and Bernard Leach:

"Yanagi and Leach shared a similarity of approach during fifty years of close friendship, even when they were half a world apart. In fact they were never apart. Yanagi is gone, but the friendship has deepened. Leach has translated a selection of Yanagi's essays in a way that no one else could have done, and this in itself is a creative continuance of that friendship."

We know what happened to the friendship of Gauguin and Van Gogh. Friendship is a risk because rejection and repudiation of a friend comprises the severest form of critical commentary.

I am not oblivious to possible gender distinctions in discussing friendship. In the popular culture of my youth, women were not thought capable of friendship with other women. According to this logic, due to the need to compete for men, they were natural competitors in the sexual and marital arena. Embedded in western culture, the fraternal urges of men for other men's company was considered normal and natural, be it the exclusive gentlemen's club of the nineteenth century or the college fraternity of the twentieth. Sports promoted the team spirit of those athletics dominated by boys and men. I know that much has changed in our culture and I am not sure how the impact of that historical residue still haunts the efforts of women.

What about contemporary potters? Your pottery partners are women. Do men control the galleries, ceramics publications, university ceramics departments? To what degree are these issues safely buried in the past and to what degree do they still operate in your world? Sexism did not only restrict the temporal advancement of women, it also sought to define their very character and nature. In my youth, you would have been counseled into Home Economics classes to prepare you for domestic chores. I ended up in 'shop' classes where I made things with wood and metal. There was an invidious reverse side to this.

My memories of gender bias as a boy and young man involved in the arts was the vague unease of family and friends. For a boy caught drawing and painting, for a young man to aspire to be an artist was not only a retreat from the manly contests of the marketplace but a sign of 'effeminate' tendencies. We must further discuss these issues in a later letter.

Thank you again for your generous gift of the vase on my recent visit. To share your beautiful pottery with me was an act of friendship that I can only meagerly repay with the words on this page. I look forward to future contact and collaboration. Please don't get discouraged: the value of your work is evident to those who encounter it. Your national reputation is growing. Your resolute determination and commitment will carry the day.

Your friend,

Richard

Eight

November 10, 2002

Dear Christa,

Fall has sponsored the first rain of the season. I am not fond of weather. The very demonstration of weather is traumatic for Southern Californians. As a former teacher, I knew that the shattering impact of rain outside the classroom windows was a dangerous source of discipline problems. In the same sense that fish do not know water, Southern Californians do not know weather. It has rarely intruded in my life. We are encased in an unchanging cocoon that does not allow significant contrasts. The impact of seasons on my garden are blurred and faint. A few leaves falling, plants activated with flowers at different times but blooms in the garden all year around. Variation in heat requires minor adjustment to the interior thermostat that controls the air conditioning unit. The umbrella is stored in the closet, a largely unused and exotic accessory. The weather in Southern California rarely has the power to determine our behavior or plans. It gets very little attention. Our notoriety with others is based on earthquakes and smog, not hurricanes or tornadoes, not banks of snow or flooding rivers.

I used to have trouble appreciating some poetry, in particular the genre that so celebrated spring with the metaphors of human renewal. I am beginning to understand the literary references that compare the life cycle to the seasons. The cycle of seasons has become connected with the rhythms of my body. I am now approaching winter with increased apprehension, dread commemorated by another birthday in January, fears that the bronchitis that afflicted me last winter could return. I just did not know how cruel winter could be in other places, and as a result, remained unprepared and unrealistic about the vicissitudes of increased age in the winter of my own existence. Metaphors only become real when they are directly experienced.

The given variables of daily life at any one location are rarely challenged. What is considered necessary is defined by local conditions, and becomes the submerged presuppositions of tradition and habit that frame mentality and world view. To construct your own existential personhood requires an act of will and rigorous intellectual activity. Conformity as a human trait is rarely self-discovered, only those who refuse to conform are aware that it exists. A cultural renegade requires not only courage (that comes later) but first the supreme critical consciousness to surface the embedded notions that govern those around her, and then summon the courage to overthrow them in public. The creative and critical act is always subversive. The contemporary potter will never make it big. I know of no sitcom television program where the hero is a potter or, apart from the 1990 movie, 'Ghost', a film with potter as protagonist. I know of no toy or comic book where the potter has been portrayed as superhero or politicians who have bothered to frame a seductive message to entice potters to support them. I know of no potter who has been enlisted to model sexy underwear in magazine and TV adds. My interest in pottery only adds to my personal eccentricity that family and friends tolerate.

Does making pottery make cultural sense? How can we make the argument that handmade pottery is a human necessity? I can go to museums and view things that are not made anymore. Horse-drawn carriages, steam engines, and ice boxes are not made anymore. They became more valuable curiosities because they are now obsolete. What potter will achieve the ultimate fame by making the very last pot? The great popularity of the Antiques Roadshow on television, both here and in Britain, where old pots and vases, previously unappreciated and stored out of view, are hauled out of attics and closets, provided intense media attention, declared to be of surprising monetary value, and newly celebrated with honored placement on the mantelpiece. In American culture, anything, no matter how chipped or cracked, can assume great respect if some expert assigns it a considerable price tag. I have instructed my sons that if only they will keep all my pots intact for the next hundred years, the pots will qualify as antiques and their heirs will be rich. Surely contemporary potters trying to make a living must deeply resent those battered and ancient pots which inspire such awe and high prices. Looking at the unsold beauties on their own shelves, this resentment is understandable.

I find it a bit strange that in a society that dreads the ageing process, the antiques trade is flourishing. You will lose considerable value if you strip old furniture or erase the patina, but the plastic surgeon is completely unaffected. It is of some comfort for old people to have old things that have survived adversities long before their own birth. Unfortunately few of us will become antiques. Contemporary potters need to place all their new pots in a time capsule. Your grandchildren or heirs can take them to the Antiques Roadshow and express the required shock and delight when they are determined to be priceless. Your reputation will be assured, even if you are not around to enjoy the benefits. Better still, destroy most of your work before you expire so that your pots become precious and the market value increases. If you are really serious and sincere about your pottery you should be willing to wait a century or two to be recognized and validated.

If pottery remains an obscure cultural event, can it be claimed as a significant attempt to retrieve balance and simplicity with nature? Here I look back for guidance to Henry David Thoreau. His mission at Walden Pond still resonates with contemporary dissidents:

"I went to the woods because I wished to live deliberately, to front only the essential facts of life, and see if I could not learn what it had to teach, and not, when I came to die, discover that I had not lived. I did not wish to live what was not life, living is too dear; nor did I wish to practice resignation, unless it was quite necessary. I wanted to live deep and suck out all the marrow of life, to live so sturdily and Spartan-like as to put to rout all that was not life, to cut a broad swath and shave close, to drive life into a corner, and reduce it to its lowest terms, and, if it proved to be mean, why then to get the whole and genuine meanness of it, and publish its meanness to the world; or if it were sublime, to know it by experience, and be able to give a true account of it in my next excursion."

If potters seek historical roots in our culture to draw substance, I firmly believe that we have intellectual traditions that document the importance of handmade artifacts in seeking a life that reconciles human nature with the natural environment. Later on that same page in 'Walden', Thoreau exclaims, "Simplicity, simplicity, simplicity!" Can it be possible that pottery, indeed art, is an essential element in the simple life rather than merely a decorative adornment for the wealthy few?

Both the American and English intellectual traditions question the devastating development of technology that represented the industrial revolution. Here Thoreau and Emerson join Ruskin and Morris in deploring the impact of industrial technology on the lives of artisans, workers and the environment. In a wonderful new book, "Against the Machine: The Hidden Luddite Tradition in Literature, Art and Individual Lives", Nicols Fox explores the broad dimensions of this thinking:

"As a theme, resistance to technology appears in Romantic and Victorian literature, in transcendentalism, in the Arts and Crafts movement, the agrarian movement, the environmental movement. It is present today in the writers who cling to their typewriters, the fine cabinetmakers who cherish their old tools; the handweavers and basket-makers, and potters and needlework enthusiasts, who keep to their craft against all logic; the herbalists and organic growers who are convinced that what they do is important and brook no argument - all those who cling consciously in whatever manner or degree to the old ways."

What is the state of this issue among potters today? I can't remember if the wheels in your studio are plugged in or get their power from your feet. Does it make a difference? Is there some organic integrity with feet powered wheels or are they obsolete now? I do remember that you have electric kilns. I know it would be difficult to forage for kindling wood or cow dung along Fisherman's Wharf to feed the fire. Is your arrangement a compromise born of expediency or can you justify the use of power appliances in your craft? Does it matter in the kind of pottery you create? The wood turner uses a lathe and it is still considered a craft. Has some accepted authority determined and defined what represents a hand-crafted object? At some point, does the extensive use of electric appliances disqualify a craft product and turn it into a manufactured product?

Is it simply the inevitable conservatism of old age that motivates tentative and uncertain reservations about technology? Ruskin and Morris failed in attempts to find a utopian paradise based on medieval practices. The sound of the train invading the countryside appalled Thoreau. I hide in my secret garden, seeking to escape the hum of the nearby freeway. As in politics, where my vote usually guarantees the candidate's defeat, I must be careful not to be a sore loser in the cultural battles of my time.

I am not sure what to label myself without offending friends, becoming foolish, or revealing my lack of sophistication. How can one confess affinity with nineteenth century romanticism without suffering ridicule? In a chapter entitled 'Romantic Inclinations', Nicols Fox describes this impulse:

" 'Romantic' was a way of seeing, a certain cast of light that could transform anything. In this new illumination, the imagination could play with the unfamiliarity of familiar things, accentuating the strangeness of the half-visible. This sensation of newness, of possibility, of transformation defined the word. This was the mind at playful work, allowed to range and create and interact with the ever-changing nature of reality. The Romantics' priorities were with the exercise of imagination, with excess, with the mystical and, at times, the irrational. The natural world was a powerful and important place where God dwelt; human emotion, intuitions and yearnings were not simply valid, but vital, and could be trusted."

In my experience on the academic campus, the romantic impulses of the artist conflicted with the dominant mode of the objective and detached knowledge of science. The danger that this powerful methodology will objectify the arts into dependable taxonomies of regulated fact are great. The presence of the arts on an academic campus is simply unnatural. The conversion of the artist and intellectual into academicians was a form of institutional domestication that Emerson, Morris and Thoreau would never have tolerated.

I must declare my moderate stance regarding environmentalism simply because my lifestyle would document the hypocrisy of a purist position. I do adjust the thermostat to maintain creature comfort, keep my hot tub at a high temperature for instant use, fly jet planes whenever time and money permits, and rely on my CD player for the music that enriches my life. I could go on with this inventory but would prefer not to. On the other hand, we recently purchased a hybrid car that gets excellent mileage and emits very low pollution fumes. Lights are turned out when I vacate a room and I use a manual can opener. I am trying. I have a sentimental desire to preserve the natural environment though I rarely visit it. I enjoy the romance of the landscape through the art that was directly inspired by it. The exploitation and destruction of nature is a moral issue for me. It is as offensive as the exploitation and destruction of human beings.

My two sons have forfeited the eating of meat. They were not raised that way. One daughter-in-law has become a vegan. I am in danger of losing the moral leadership of my family. Aside from eating my fellow living creatures (they are butchered first), I indirectly support the terrible exploitation in the Amazon rain forest necessary to establish those huge cattle ranches. Thus the American hamburger is not innocent and it is very costly for the natural world. I can carry personal reform and reconstruction only so far. I do not hunt or fish. My hands are clean. What happens at the dinner table is completely divorced from the moment of slaughter. Technology magnifies the ability of the petty crimes of individual lifestyles to become collective environmental atrocities of global impact. The interdependence of ecological systems explains how damage to one aspect of that system can threaten the entire system. We do not see the results of our minor offenses at the scene where we commit them. The hole in the ozone layer or the destruction of the rain forest are the culmination of minor offenses that can be traced to acts committed each day by all of us. What does this have to do with pottery? Is making pots just a job? Can you have an aesthetic of pottery without an aesthetic of nature? I rarely answer my own questions in these letters but I will this time: the answer is no.

You must join me with mutual confessions of environmental compromise. Potters use the earth. Do you leave scars and holes in the ground? Can I locate some spoiled location where generations of potters have extracted clay? If the earth is not renewable for oil and gold, is it endlessly renewable for potter's clay? When will you run out of clay and have to resort to plastic? Much to my disillusionment, I have found out that lumbermen do not care about the preservation of trees and fishermen overkill and threaten to extinguish species of fish. They are there for sheer short term profit, not as stewards. Do potters revere the earth that they manipulate on the wheel? Do potters associate clay with reverence for the earth?

I need to at least seek coherence in my flawed performance. Perhaps my personal incompetence with any form of machinery aggravates my condition. It is possible that the 'clean' technology of the computer will bring about the promised land. I do not play games on the computer, do not chat with strangers, and wish for very little information about things that do not matter to me. I remember the story you told me about the visitor to your studio/gallery who tried to persuade you to abandon the handmade pot and make pottery by computer. He offered to help you set up the program. He was convinced that a standardized perfection and more efficient production would prove superior to your old-fashioned ways. You were properly offended.

Take good care of yourself. I promise not to judge you by the number of electrical outlets in your studio.

Your friend,

Richard

Nine

November 30, 2002

Dear Christa,

We are preparing to leave for Washington, DC. We will stay there for about a dozen days. Where people holiday and what they do when they get there is a very solid indicator of who they are and what they value. Vacations are very special events for most Americans. Commentary from foreign critics suggest that we are a work-obsessed people who have a harsh and cruel social contract that awards very little compensated time away from the workplace. Americans work as hard at having fun on vacations as they do at the work site. For many people commercial tourist packages now dominate vacation decisions. They find special deals on the internet, arrive at tourist sites that are fully prepared to raid their pocketbooks, and return home with enough T-shirts for all their relatives and friends. You know this better than I do, with your studio/gallery on Fisherman's Wharf in San Francisco.

For some needy souls, vacation is an escape from the drudgery of the workplace, requiring isolation on some seashore, away from all the normal events in their lives that make them so miserable. To merely sit on the sand and vegetate for two weeks represents the meager yearly span of temporary liberation. As lifelong academics, and now retired, Judy and I have some advantages. We had the space between semesters, summer, and extended periods around the holidays to travel and explore. As educators, we did not have the money to go for extravagant cruises and first class hotels. When the children were young and accompanied us, the logistics and itinerary were rather different than now. These factors were not considered a handicap, as the quaint bed and breakfast facilities in old English coaching inns, with the children often on folding beds next to us, was quite charming. Crooked thick walls and low ceilings with ancient beams that seemed to bow with the weight of the structure was the stuff of romance. My oldest son, not yet a teenager, memorized the complete succession of English royalty and became a convinced monarchist. We bought brochures, read them faithfully, and participated in the conducted tours of the estate houses of British aristocracy. We dragged the kids to every available museum and historical site. That was the beginning of our collecting I think, but instead of T-shirts we started to collect pottery.

I don't want to be defensive in trying to explain why we started to collect pottery. We could have bought a bigger house instead, or invested in Wall Street, or a faster car. We could have sent the money to some worthy cause, but no, we spent the money on pottery. Why do people collect? Perhaps childhood trauma or savage parental abuse; surely collecting must have its origins in some kind of pathology or psychological dysfunction. Overcompensation for the insecurities of life, rat packers who prefer their stuff in the circular shapes of vases, rather than old newspapers stacked to the ceiling or bottle tops or baseball cards or automobile hubcaps or Germans dolls of the nineteenth century. Everything is now a 'collectible', waiting to be assembled on shelves in the den or family room, proud collectors proclaiming the discovery and capture of items at obscure locations such lawn sales or some old barn. We have distinguished ancestors as collectors, royalty filled their palaces with pottery while the masses starved, robber barons in the Gilded Age had many pots in their mansions while exploited workers toiled in their factories, and colonizers and conquerors looted ancient lands and civilizations for their pottery. Today we too are proudly able to prize our pots in our little cottage in Glendora.

I do not need to justify my motivation. I know a need from a want. I want pottery because I have an obligation to support human imagination and creativity in a world where human destruction and tragedy often appears to be triumphant. I need pottery because I am daily enhanced and enriched by the presence of pottery within the domestic chambers of my family life. Surely history proves that art is an endemic activity shared by all groups. I can only offer my own testimony and experience that the celebration and appreciation of art is as natural and necessary as its creation. Collecting cannot be explained, since it is not a rational pursuit and depends on an unlikely duality - obsession with beauty and a lust for private ownership of beautiful things. Bankruptcy becomes a distant danger if this obsession cannot be controlled. Who can tell you when you have enough French Impressionist paintings or sufficient pots? When is enough really enough? The finite shelf or wall space in your home cannot be the measurement of your appetite. That would represent a cruel limitation. Mortality is the great unspoken curse of the collector. The inevitable approach of that mortality sharpens the race, a monopoly of some category of art must be achieved before you falter and weaken, this is the great contest that energizes memorable collectors. It is simply good sportsmanship to donate the collection when your demise becomes evident and unavoidable. I must be realistic. There are no collector's genes in succeeding generations of family members. I will pass on to them the pots, but cannot provide them the passion for collecting them.

I would claim an impulse, the aesthetic sensibility embedded in my youth as a young artist and art educator, supported by my enthusiastic spouse, with joint forays of discovery and acquisition in galleries, antique shops, museum shops, and the studios of potters. Collecting pottery has been a great organizing agent for planning vacations. If the location is new and previously unvisited, the research commences to identify the sites mentioned above. This never becomes a 'business' trip in some compulsive manner. The sites are usually urban, because our holiday must include concerts, gardens and the theater. We regularly subscribe to the Los Angeles Philharmonic Orchestra and to the subscription plays of two downtown theaters. We are members of Pasadena Heritage, a wonderful preservation group that seeks to save those marvelous California Craftsmen bungalows, and sponsors a yearly conference on the American Arts and Crafts movement, the Huntington Library and Gardens that has a magnificent William Morris collection, and the Los Angeles County Arboretum. I am listing these activities only to suggest that the best of all worlds is where your holiday is not an escape from reality because you must escape that reality in order to recover from it; but rather your holiday is a reinforcement and expansion of those life enriching activities that already form the very basis for your daily existence and happiness.

There is a chapter entitled 'Tribute to a Collector' in the book "Color and Fire - Defining Moments in Studio Ceramics 1950-2000" by Jo Lauria. The contents represent selections from the Smits Collection and Related Works at the Los Angeles County Museum of Art and was the inspiration for a touring exhibition I viewed at the museum a few years ago. The tribute is a touching statement by Gretchen Adkins, the daughter of the collector Gwen Lauries Smits.

As Adkins relates, her mother too had modest resources:

"She was sharing her purchases with Dad when he recognized the impassioned urgency in her voice. This was a woman with a conviction. 'Why not collect pots instead of paintings?' he said. 'We'll set aside $100.00 a month.' He was content to let her make the artistic decisions, since he had always been more of a patron of his wife than of the arts. It was one of the nicest presents my father ever gave my mother. From then on she eschewed paintings and started to openly admit she was a collector of ceramics."

This is a great story for two reasons. Gwen Smits was not motivated to purchase expensive trophy pieces to compliment her silver service and the decor of her interior designer. Nor was she was originally an expert whose mastery of knowledge led her to calculated acquisitions. She fell in love with pottery and everything else followed. As her daughter informs, she was an art enthusiast who supported art in her community and desired to grace her own home with objects of beauty. Adkins describes the struggle:

"Collecting is a demanding taskmaster, if given free rein. It drives the daily schedule. It dominates the thought. And it dictates how money is spent. Mother had a hard time keeping within the pot allowance. She started to devise ways for her budget-respectful soul to allow her ceramics-besotted heart to have its way."

If you are a 'ceramics-besotted' collector, you must not grieve over the pots you cannot afford, but embrace those pots that are both beautiful and affordable. I do not begrudge Gwen Smits but this pioneer collector of American pottery started before the competitive market in ceramics became active and the prices started to climb. The best of all worlds is when you see pottery of great merit by a potter unknown to you, and confirm that you can actually afford to buy it. I first encountered a potter by the name of Christa Assad that way. How do you know who are the 'promising' potters on their way up and - on the other hand - those pots you love and buy that will join you in perpetual anonymity? On one level I do not care - if I like the pot I will buy it if I can - but on another level - to buy the pot and then discover on the supplied resumé that this potter is a Full-bright scholar and winner of several ceramic distinctions and considerable recognition - becomes a confirmation of judgment that can't help but be pleasing. The ego of the collector becomes dependent upon the reputation of the potter to vindicate the decision of purchase. A potter is judged by her pots, a collector is judged by his judgment.

I have both pity and compassion for those people who only live for the weekend and two weeks of the year. My social conscience tells me that in some instances this is the result of involuntary circumstances, but the consumer acceptance of commercial popular culture tells me that most of this misery is self-inflicted. Robert Hutchins and Mortimer Adler formed the Great Books movement in the early twentieth century with the belief that all people had the capacity to understand and benefit from the great books that form the legacy of previous civilizations. Both elitists and realists might now reject that assumption for different reasons. The elitist might believe that only a special and privileged group could enjoy the subtlety and complexity of sublime culture. A problem is that this attitude often assumes that this special position of wealth and privilege is the result of some intrinsic endowment rather than the favorable circumstances of birth and station. The contrasting position of the lower classes would be the fault of their own defective nature.

The realist would offer schemes to provide bread and water supplemented with vocational job training, great literature and pottery could wait. The romantic might create a fantasy of expectation projected through a grand vision of an improbable future, would provide the books and pottery and suffer deeply the inevitable disappointments. William Morris's utopian classic, "News From Nowhere" is an example of the latter. In the 1934 Centenary Edition for the Nonesuch Press, G.D.H. Cole in the Introduction explores the nature of Morris's writing:

"He was letting himself dream of a society that would let him do without stint everything he thought worth doing, and would not upset his pleasure in what he did by the sense that others were lacking a like freedom. He wanted to be free to make beautiful things, not merely for a fortunate few who could afford to buy them, but for everyone who would get pleasure out of having and using them. Through most of his life, nothing hurt him so constantly as the knowledge that his pretty things were out of the reach of most who liked them - except in the sense that most people had not been given a chance of finding out whether they liked them or not. He believed in his bones that the appreciation of beauty was a vitally important part of the art of living, and that a people devoid of artistic appreciation was inevitably a dead people, destined to slavery and decay. He believed that it came naturally to men to have this sense of beauty in the everyday things of common use, and that a society in which they had it not was fundamentally 'unnatural' - a society out of which half the pleasure and happiness had been banished. He believed that the quality of beauty in common things, and in man's relation to them, affected the whole way of living, impoverishing any society that went without it, however men might pile up material riches. He believed that the ordinary things men made ought to be so made as to be 'a joy to the maker and to the user,' and that where most men spent their working days joylessly making ugly things, the death of civilization was at hand."

I read William Morris for inspiration, not for a blueprint to the promised land. Most of my heroes were assassinated in the 1960's. It can be dangerous in America to have dreams. It is always underestimated how dreams of human hope and universal liberation threaten those whose privileged position might be displaced if these dreams were realized. At best, when dreams are activated they become ideas and principles that can combine in a powerful and compelling reform movement. That has happened in the past. There is no such impulse today. The closest thing we have is the environmental movement but it is presently in political exile. A purposeful and powerful aesthetic should motivate creation. A society that regularly slays its dreamers is not conducive to those artists who create art in order to create a better society.

The holiday season has arrived. Turkey leftovers in the refrigerator are proof of a joyous family event. The garden must wait, it is raining today and my trip will soon take me away. I hope things are going well for you. I am complimented by your continuing attention to these letters. You must accept that these letters are really a petition to plead for your continued creation of beautiful pottery. I must accept and model the inherent optimism of Morris - there is much to be grateful for in our lives. Unlike Morris, I have achieved my utopian paradise. Except for just a few more pots.

Take care,

Richard

Ten

December 16, 2002

Dear Christa,

We are back from Washington, D.C., ready for the family gatherings and rituals of Christmas, adjusting to a series of rain storms after surviving snow and freezing conditions back east. Regional distinctions exist and do matter. They build different kinds of houses and wear different kinds of clothes than we do in Southern California. Things happen to the natural environment back there that is completely skipped in the changes of seasons here. We saw the naked skeletons of trees. I discovered that they are not really dead and there are as many varieties in the forms and twists of their trunks and limbs as in the former shapes and colors of their lost leaves. We visited every memorial devoted to past presidents and heroes of previous wars. Perhaps the evident limitation of space on the Washington Mall for further memorials will influence decisions about future wars. Despite the climate, and with the help of the fine subway system, we visited almost every museum and gallery, paying tribute to art collected from all realms of geography and culture.

When you visit a previously unknown land, it is important to look as carefully at the totality of the landscape as the fixed objects organized to receive your stare in the museums. The entire world becomes quaint in your voyage of discovery. The people encountered only exist during your visit, surely they cannot live in that weather beyond your own endurance. Because you must actively overcome the prejudices of your own time and place in encountering new experiences, it is valuable that you first observe the 'other', whatever that might be, in the innocent bias that allows incredulous astonishment. The heavy price of assimilation and acceptance is to reduce the exotic to the familiar. Few individuals, in my view, are able to consistently renew passionate encounters with familiar objects and landscapes. They are just too comfortable to make the effort. The dislocation of travel inspires fresh insights into your previous orientation.

If those naked trees can be aesthetically satisfying, then form can indeed triumph over decoration. This is an issue of endemic importance in ceramics. I look over my collection, I recall the multitude of ceramics encountered in my recent trip, and I see unreconciled divisions over this issue stretched over thousands of years in diverse cultures. What are the factors that motivate the contemporary potter to ignore decoration and seek purity in the naked outline of the form itself? What are the cultural traditions and personal temperaments that insist that added decoration either weakens or enhances the already established shape? Can the single glaze of one color and visual texture of that single color satisfy both potter and viewer? When do you stop and why do you stop there? I gaze at the inventive and intense decoration of French porcelain created for their royalty, and spontaneously wince in my modern posture at the rococo elaboration. The delicate bouquets of flowers and figures painted or formed on the bright surfaces, often encircled with flowing gilded patterns, are rich delights that are just too sweet for me.

What constitutes 'over-embellishment'? Were Ruskin and Morris right about the Victorians? Can the abstracted and disciplined form provide enough to satisfy the human spirit? If 'form follows function' then applied decoration can only be secondary and unnecessary. In our American culture, the Arts and Crafts movement followed the Protestant, Puritan dislike of elaboration. The form and shapes of the natural materials were deemed sufficient decoration. You do not find many framed paintings on the walls of the Gamble House in Pasadena. That aesthetic austerity has guided many contemporary potters. The rational formulas of 'design' are favored over the extravagant passions of expression.

There are many parallels with other arts. My own private preferences in my youth reveal my aesthetic disposition; the endless inventories in the long-winded hymns of Walt Whitman; the verbose and convoluted language of Thomas Wolfe and Eugene O'Neil; long strings of words, verbal narrations that became monologues of rambling thought; the shimmering images of Bonnard - with hot colors of nudes in the tub or fruit on the table that raise the fever of the canvas and glow with intensity; the extended and thunderous symphonies of Bruckner and Mahler that roll and groan with great anguish and turmoil. Further confession, I did purchase a few years ago, in a charming and dusty old pottery shop in Madrid, a 19th century vase complete with pasted flowers, yellow ceramic braid, elaborate handles and assorted bright colors. When does floral become florid? How many flowers does it take?

But I must quickly add, not to lose favor with you, Christa, that I celebrate and value those economical statements that get to the essence of things. I do believe that the getting of wisdom is a subtractive process, not an additive one. In my old age, I prefer the distilled rigor of chamber music over the spectacular contrasts of the philharmonic orchestra, the small incisive drawing over the huge mural, the simple traditional Japanese pot over the fancy baroque creation. But having said that, I must further weaken my argument by stating that I really enjoy them all, want to experience all media, all genres, all possible modes of expression, in all the arts. Does that make me inclusive and cosmopolitan or a man without taste or standards? In the same sense that I try to enter the world of a foreign culture to appreciate the artifact, I also attempt to honor the temperament and orientation that produced that particular artifact. If excellence is achieved within the logic and values of that orientation, I will join in the tribute by embracing the artifact. I do have limitations with a modern aesthetic that seeks to terminate standards and the rigors of craft as an unacceptable burden. Even here, I make a personal choice and claim no universal authority.

In the book "Techniques of the World's Great Masters of Pottery and Ceramics", a section written by Colin Sheaf entitled 'The Monochrome Tradition' explains this tradition:

"No nation of potters has taken the production of ceramic forms, decorated with a single-color glaze, to a more refined level than the Chinese. Western potters traditionally regard a vessel's biscuit or glazed surface as a canvas, an area to be decorated cosmetically. However, a few twentieth century studio potters have been directly influenced by the Orient. Chinese and Japanese connoisseurs have always seen virtue in the plain surface and have always taken pleasure in the texture and form of the vessel, and the hue of the integral glaze. It is an approach and a taste very remote from that of the Europeans... The plain shapes and natural ceramic forms focus attention, but unlike western equivalents they are integral to the vessel, not mere vehicles for the pattern."

It was this tradition that enchanted Bernard Leach and so influenced what he brought back to England. Leach was a painter before he was a potter and thought painting and drawing as important as pottery. He later modified this desire to illustrate the pot after living in Japan.

There have been counter revolutions of potters who reject this particular tradition, and move toward either a non-functional direction or a more expressive and pictorial one. I do believe it is possible to exercise an expressive vocabulary of visual symbols and patterns on clay without vandalizing or cheapening the object. There are Asian traditions that have employed this approach. In the same book mentioned above, in a section entitled, "The Influence of Japan and the Kakiemon Style", William Tilley describes this particular cultural vocabulary:

"For example, the 'flaming tortoise' is simply that Japanese symbol of longevity, the minogame, a freshwater tortoise of such a grand age that a long tail of pond-weed has grown on its shell. The 'banded hedge' is the brushwood fence commonly seen in Japan, and the quite impossible 'pairs of phoenixes' are the equally mythical Japanese ho-ho birds which do appear in pairs, usually to herald matters of auspicious portent. Other designs incorporate tigers with plum blossom or bamboo, quail with millet, various other birds such as doves and the long-tailed paradise fly-catcher, and flowers, especially fuyo, the Japanese hibiscus."

How do contemporary potters make up their minds about this challenge? To decorate or not to decorate is the question. I suppose it is not possible there will be any consensus or agreement from potters about this. Which potters could be singled out as employing iconic vocabularies that provide a symbolic shorthand of our age and time? Do you choose abstract patterns or do you tell a story? Is one better than the other? For the purist, doesn't the concealment of the clay itself with a glaze constitute a severe compromise? Can you transfer the continuum of perspectives in two dimensional painting regarding abstraction and realism to three dimensional pottery? With the same arguments on each side? When does the exactitude of literalism become sentimental in a visual vocabulary? Surely the attainment of a precise decoration requires its own high standards. Do you judge the quality of decoration simply by judging the difficulty of arriving at that decoration? Is the very definition of craft defined by the amount of work or difficulty in achieving the result? Can ease of execution, available to everyone, bring about great art or great pottery? I am so pleased with the speculative possibilities of these questions that I am not sure a single answer would satisfy me.

I look at your two pots on the shelf, standing side by side. You have used your 'gingerbread' glaze. There are variations in value and intensity. The shapes are vertical, with long necks. There are straight edges and curved forms. On one, slender threads of white, widely separated, send traces down the vase. On the other, these white traces form small pools, begin halfway down with the expanded body of the vessel, white threads that fade as they run to the bottom. Your pots are decorated but the decoration does not seem to be placed over the surface but embedded in the very form. It is not an afterthought, nor does it take attention away from the entirety of the vase. It does not distract but it does complete the subtle complexity of the piece. It is obvious you made conscious decisions regarding all this and you had the skill to execute it. I do not think a pot is made the same way you would make a cake. There the decoration and icing has little to do with the cake underneath. You do not know if the cake is chocolate or white until your bite includes the cake. If the pot is really right and you have made all the right decisions, the decoration completes the shape and character of the form. You do not have random choices in the icing.

The counter-argument for decoration has modern supporters. Brenda Pegrun, in her book, 'Painted Ceramics: Colour and Imagery on Clay' states:

"Most potters represented in this book, despite the technical complexities and extra time and labour involved, paint on pots because they find it exciting and challenging. Image-making and the instinct to embellish a plain surface by drawing or painting is innate and can be powerful. Pots in ancient times were painted with expressive imagery which appears to have served as a protective charm."

While exploring the creative possibilities of painting the surface of ceramics, she also includes the difficulties:

"Ceramic surfaces are usually curved, either convex or concave, posing problems of draughtsmanship not experienced by painters of flat surfaces. Picasso observed that drawing slipped away from him on the convex curve of a ceramic ball. On the concave curve of a dish, drawing comes towards you. Either way, the curve forces adaptation, the steeper the curve and the larger the image, the greater the distortion of imagery."

While most potters attempted to reconcile and integrate form and painting, Pegrun quotes that American maverick Peter Voulkos:

"I brush colour on to violate the form and it becomes a complete new thing which involves a painting concept on three-dimensional surface, a new idea. These things are exploding, jumping off. I wanted to pick up that energy... get more excitement going."

Some, like Voulkos, use painting to move pottery as craft to painted sculpture as art. I do not accept the premise that pottery needs painting, or decoration for that matter, to be called art. Of course most potters do not have to choose exclusive preferences. Even if one decides to emphasize form or to develop intricate forms of decoration, the wide spectrum of choices are always available. Only if the potter feels the need to issue some dogmatic manifesto that indicts those who work differently can a divergent approach become offensive. This has often been the case of 'schools of painters' who become movements of single purpose. I do not know if potters are as combative or argumentative about their approaches. My collection does not have a single viewpoint.

I accept the post-modern notion that our very language is embedded with the cultural presuppositions that form our world view. The very word 'decoration' inherently connotes an add-on, superficial scraps and dabs to make something pretty. Even Pegrun's use of the term, 'painted ceramics' indicates the same idea. Art cannot be completely organic. Art requires the artifice of the human hand. That interference in the composition of the original natural element - clay from the earth - has to compromise and complement whatever qualities that natural element contains. The Arts and Crafts movement, both in England and here, emphasizes the beauty of the natural wood and stone. I think that their architecture largely benefits from this view. I am less sure about the pottery. I have held in my hands - I could not afford to purchase it - a beautiful green Grube vase valued at $17,000 dollars. In the fantasies of my collector's desire, I would joyfully add that Grube green vase to my shelf but I would soon detest my collection if all my vases were smeared with that same damn green glaze. As an environmentalist, I accept that 'more is less' and 'small is beautiful' makes sense. I am not as sure I would apply this to all pottery.

After those comments, please Christa, don't try to please me by adding rosettes to your pottery. Somehow they won't fit. I truly appreciate your resolve. I will continue to be occasionally dazzled by the seductive lure of colors and elaborate decoration. But I will discipline my judgment as the potter must discipline their craft and ultimately I will choose substance over glitter. I find the placement and juxtaposition of highly decorated vases next to the sublime simplicity of another vase to enhance both. I fully accept the decision of the potter in this regard. As long as the vase in its finished condition represents the integrity of the potter and the craft, I can make my choices as a collector according to the aesthetic pleasures that each pot evokes. My preferences must never become so dogmatic and exclusive that I shut out vast domains of art and craft.

I hope the holidays provided you with happiness and joy. This 10th letter will soon be followed by the new year. I know that it will be a promising and productive one for you. May you flourish in the coming year and may your pottery be celebrated for the excellence it truly represents and deserves.

Your friend,

Richard

Eleven

January 10, 2003

Dear Christa,

I have just made a great discovery. Pottery does not move. There is no action. Some say that films are the great American art form (others would disagree and offer jazz or musical theater). Films move. The big box office favorites make a lot of movement, with car chases and the spectacular, loud and fast achievements of 'special effects'. What kind of competition can pottery offer? Maybe that's why I like pottery. I refuse to see a film that has special effects. That is almost as offensive to me as a happy ending. I don't see many American films. I want complex characterizations from fine actors, a good, literate script, and films that represent the contradictions and endemic predicaments of the human condition. The actors don't have to do a lot, I just want them to talk to each other about things that really matter. I don't even need a conclusion; in fact I love the way that some foreign films end, apparently in the middle of things, with people just going on in their attempts to stabilize their lives and cope with their fallibilities. I have heard the gasp of audiences who feel surprised and cheated when 'Finis' is flashed on the screen. I respond with feelings of assumed superiority that I am convinced originates in the more refined subtlety of my existential soul.

Aside from pottery, I also collect graphics, mostly antique but some contemporary prints. I have been collecting the etchings of Guadalupe Goas, visiting her gallery in Ensenada, B.C., Mexico. While I enjoy her rich etchings of landscapes with plant, ocean, and sky, I prefer the three etchings of hers on my walls that inventory objects placed in rows on the shelves or on the table. This genre in art is called the 'still life'. In an old college text from my days as an art major, Helen Gardner in 'Art Through The Ages', defines still life as "A painting representing inanimate objects such as flowers and household articles". Gardner describes the painter, Chardin who, "… made a specialty of simple interiors and still life, which he painted masterfully in his own mode, rivaling the Dutch masters of the previous century". This information further documents the pattern of my bias.

Etched objects in repose, frozen actors whose visual drama relies on their relationship with other objects; the significance of placement and detail; happily residing at fixed sites with quiet backgrounds. My pottery does the same thing. They are objects of meditation that do not threaten to disrupt my peace with unexpected behavior. I can be the only agent to disturb their settled composition. I am gentle in the occasional change of placement. I do not want them to get upset. I live near the freeway, I have enough movement around me without my pottery coming to life. They remain still - along with Guadalupe's objects on the shelves and tables she constructed in the etchings. Everything is 'still' in my house, even I move slowly through the rooms. As I age, I too am becoming a part of a larger still life, sitting, reading, and observing the surroundings of my domestic composition. Hand gestures, even turning the page, would galvanize attention if others were present. Small movements become more dramatic as action becomes more scarce. The deep green chile on Guadalupe's table, along with the very red apple, sitting on the white table, convey as much intensity as the vivid sunset over the ocean in another of her etchings. These scenes are as dramatic and satisfying as anything I could see outside through the windows. The subtle movement in my garden when motivated by an occasional breeze is all the action I need in my daily life.

Surely the 'still life' cannot be satisfying to contemporary tastes. The toys of my grandchildren move and talk, often with a greater vocabulary than the child playing with it. What used to be a 'wind-up' toy with spring is now powered by batteries, with a restless energy that extends far beyond the child's attention span. Even dolls now emulate their real life friends by organic activity that requires the changing of diapers. Children are no longer in charge of play activity, the toys speak with authority and organize the child's response. No wonder, as I observe my grandchildren, that they soon abandon these expensive toys and find true pleasure in the pots and pans in the kitchen. The older generation of youth have been raised on video games, hand-held or on the big screen, that act out murder and mayhem at the slightest maneuver and command. You target people and they explode, scores increase as enemies from outer space and other locations are decimated. Pottery just stands there on the shelf. How will it compete at the box office with the next generation of potential collectors? What would happen if you installed batteries and pots moved and talked? How about pots that automatically self-destructed? I believe that particular fad attracted much attention a few decades ago in the 'fine arts'.

One art movement that personified the dynamic force of technologically empowered movement was futurism. Many of the foremost artists of this Italian based movement in the early twentieth century embraced Mussolini and Italian fascism. Futurist manifestos celebrated with the fascists a joint love of power. The description of their values in 'Arts & Ideas' by William Fleming explains this attitude:

"Theirs was a vision of a state ruled by a mechanical superhuman mind, in which the people would be reduced to cogs in the gigantic wheel of a fully mechanized society. Above all, the futurists projected an art for a fast-moving, machine-propelled age. They admired the motion, force, speed, and strength of mechanical forms, and in their pictures they wanted more than anything else to include the dynamic sensation of motion."

Motion, force, speed and strength, all the virtues of the masculine persona. Every male film actor now needs his own personal trainer to get sufficiently beefed up to play action heroes in summer-season movies. I recently went to see a film and couldn't avoid the previews in which a series of coming films created a montage of noise, violence, and physical mayhem. The noise was not background music but the sounds of objects and human beings colliding. The speakers were turned up high and the sheer blast of sound reverberated through the restricted space. Special effects were magnificent as cars crashed through buildings and slammed into each other, great bonfires of flame engulfed everything, and people flew as they punched and kicked each other in mid-air. I heaved a sigh of relief when the five-minute ordeal was over. Galleries and museums are so quiet. They wouldn't dare put in speakers, would they, to boost attendance?

Pottery stands still. The motor is missing. It does not change. It does not even visibly age. It does not perform. It becomes an active appliance only when it is picked up by the human hand. We do not consider the very movements of that unplanned choreography, the reaching, the grasping, the filling and pouring with the pot - we do not consider that an integral part of the pottery. I do not pose with my pots and have pictures or videos made, attempting to enrich and integrate the meaning or significance of the pot. We do not really collaborate - the pot and the collector. My function, if there is any function - and the pot's function, if it has any function, are after or before the status of pot as art is experienced. I am separated from my pottery during the time it is art. I cannot remember seeing pictures in ceramics magazines or pottery books of people actually using the pots - the pots are represented at rest and alone.

In those ceramic book pictures they don't put flowers in the vases. Why? How important is the pot to the Japanese who practise the art of flower arranging? If the functional value of pottery is so important to some, why aren't the contents of the vase considered important and included in the aesthetic of the pottery? Would all pots be enhanced if they had something sticking out of them? Would a proud potter forbid such activity? Should the potter give instructions or determine what the collector should put in her pots? Why doesn't the potter have any ideas as to the preferred wallpaper or interior decor that would best complement the pot? Can a pot be so beautiful and important that the potter should insist that the interior surroundings be designed around that pot? Pots were once designed and used as chamber pots and placed under the bed for convenience. Could the chamber pot potentially qualify as art, or would it have to be designed for the more noble function of holding flowers? Any problems with that? Why don't museums and galleries have exhibitions around the theme of chamber pots instead of tea pots? Embarrassed by their unsavory past?

Many contemporary painters have abandoned painting, no longer brushing paint in some fixed configuration on a flat canvas, forever still and final after the last brushstroke. They have moved to video art. When I walk into museums today, I will often encounter multiple video screens, sometimes stacked high: images move across the screens, waving patterns and quick shifts of action. This is modern art for modern times. The images usually move faster than I want them to do. My eyes represent my feelings and grow impatient, not wanting to stare or blink in coordination with the dazzling shafts of dark and light movements on the screens. I grow nervous at all the visual activity. I cannot keep track of all the screens at once. After a few minutes, the repetition of images provide ripples of anticipated effect. I usually do not stay long.

Alexander Calder, who began his artistic career as an engineer, gives sculpture movement by using currents of wind to set his mobiles in motion. Siegfried Giedion, in 'Mechanization Takes Command', in his brief discussion of Calder, attributes the love of motion and machine to the very essence of American civilization.

"… a gearing of the American man with the machine, with mechanism, with the mobile. No other people is in such close touch with these abstract structures. Calder absorbed the modern means of expression, slowly amalgamating them with his own background until, by 1931, he had attained a sensitivity to states of equilibrium that he stressed in his 'mobiles'. He was carrying on the tradition of his artistic forerunners, now blended with the American consciousness… The solution of motion problems never loses its fascination over the American mind. This urge takes the form of an obsession - no matter how bluntly the inventor's reason may tell him to work on for the sole purpose of making money. In Alexander Calder's mobiles, this urge for the first time found its artistic reality."

Hirokazu Kosaka was a student of mine forty years ago in my junior high art class. Today he is an internationally renowned performance artist. He is also an archery master, Buddhist priest, flamenco guitarist, and Visual Arts Director of the Japanese American Cultural Community Center in Los Angeles. His performances integrate movement, music and the essence of Japanese culture and the experiences of the Japanese Americans in this country. Many of these vignettes are inspired by memories of Hirokazu's youth. These performances are not literal plays with a single story. The choreography of movement often relies on the abstraction of symbolic props and visual representation for this live art. In an interview for a newspaper review of his art, Hirokazu explains the use of archery in his performance:

"When the curtain opens, an arrow shoots," Kosaka says. "The image of a small, split-second of an arrow-path reminds me of the first generation. I think art needs to be the life, not separate from it, and that's what I'm trying to do," he declares. "It almost becomes religious."

At the end of the newspaper article, Hirokazu finishes the interview with a story:

"I remember my father taking me to a garden," he says. "His friend, who was a priest and lived in a 13th-Century temple, had asked us to come on August 15, at 8:30 in the evening, to see his garden, and we went. We sat on the veranda and for me nothing happened, but my father said, 'Yes' and walked away. And I really couldn't understand what it was. But after another 15 minutes I cracked - just laid back and laughed. Because on August 15, a full moon comes up on the far side of that garden and, at 8:30, if you looked very carefully at the rock formations - the tall protruding rocks on the gravel - you could see the shadow created by the moon write 'Spirit' in Chinese. That's the kind of sensitivity I'm trying to get."

I'm not reactionary. I respond to movement and I appreciate 'performance' as an aesthetic event. Nor is my resistance to the vulgar action and noise of our time simply a dysfunction of age. I need to look as carefully at my pottery as Hirokazu's father looked at that rock formation. Discipline in perception and performance are simple tasks that require great concentration and focus.

What is the necessary 'sensitivity' for the collector. Does your temperament determine the nature of the collection, or could the environment of the collection profoundly modify your temperament? When I am with my pottery, I am doing a 'piece' as my friend Kosaka would say. My performance demands that I move though rooms, hesitating, stopping, scooping up objects with my eyes, patterns and shapes that are positioned on individual vases yet often merge in combined patterns that do not need to be completely harmonized. Perhaps I should stage my work, this behavior of the collector. The stage, the space, the room is important. I brag to visitors that I know when any pot has been moved just one inch by others. I determine placement and I know the arrangement of objects as the very composition and theater of my daily life. As with the philosophical question of the tree falling in the forest, the pottery in my home does not exist until my presence brings it to life. The performance begins when I move into the space.

What about your performance? I remember your remarks about how making pots is hard physical work. Is there beauty in throwing the pot? Poetry in motion? Centering the clay centers the soul? Or just hard work after all? Is it exciting to watch? I think of the painter - daubing with a paint brush. I think I would be bored, literally watching the paint dry. No wonder Jackson Pollock became an overnight sensation with that Life magazine article. Throwing and dripping paint, standing and moving across and around the canvas. Now that is exciting. Can you tell how talented a potter is by the way she throws a pot? Men are stronger, aren't they? Can't they throw bigger pots? Does size matter in ceramic performances?

Craft has value because it exists in context. Art is valued because it can claim it doesn't need context. Art can define itself with the arrogance of individual genius. Craft is historically chained to some folk and region. Even when an individual signature is affixed to the object the artifact is still the representation of geography and custom. Some assert that the qualification for art is dependent on the successful eradication of parochial properties that could give away its origin. In western culture, something called 'design' has been used and defined in the last hundred years as the process through which modern materials and modern technology could achieve the goal of art through the elimination of local culture as visible reference. Modern designers often do not claim local citizenship in their work. Frank Gehry can place the same sheets of fantastic shapes on the exterior of his buildings in Bilbao or Los Angeles. He apparently doesn't think it matters. Great art and architecture thus could be universal icons in the aesthetic globalization of the world. I think that is a very heavy price to pay for world unity or the successful careers of super artists. I think many potters are infatuated with this idea because their vitas and biographies become a large part of the possible book or article that later celebrates them, along with a few shots of their pots of course. The potter as 'The Fountainhead' might make some potters and Ayn Rand happy, but I don't need it.

While the glamour of modern machines and technology might maintain their mystique, they are indeed consistently powerful, those artists who seek to emulate them as dynamos of great energy and art must inevitably disappoint their admirers. I for one do not need or want insider information about the human frailties and fallibilities of those whose art I admire and experience. I am just indicating that you should be careful what you wish for in this commercial, media driven culture. The stardom of the individual artist rests more upon the lurid disclosures of celebrity than the significance of the art. What an unfair price to pay. While the economy might indeed be dependent upon modern technology, I am still resistant for art or pottery to be defined or considered as dependent for their fame and fortune on the same sources. Are painters still doing still lives? I'm frankly happy that pots don't move or make noise.

You are now the official collector of my letters. To be the repository of my letters is a very great responsibility. Don't feel you need to frame and exhibit tthem. I just want you to know the importance of your new role as letter collector. You might want to expand someday and start collecting the letters of Lincoln or Nixon. Now I'm going get up from the desk and take a walk through the house and encounter my pottery. Lights! Camera! Action!

Your friend,

Richard

Twelve

February 4, 2003

Dear Christa,

Pruning roses is an act of faith, a slow deliberate process that allows me to demonstrate my veteran skill. It is an investment in eventual spring, that the small red swelling evident on the stem will someday burst into green growth. There are no witnesses to my brilliant display, no accolades or applause, still I please myself with my deft cuts of extraneous growth, exercising severe judgment about what will survive my intense gaze and pruning shears. I follow up with the pruning seal, then the squeeze of the plastic container that contains the dormant spray that seeks to protect the plant from dangerous insects. This precise ritual, spread over several weeks because of the profusion of rose brushes that fence my corner house, constitutes one of my major duties and joys as homeowner and gardener. Pruning is a perfect way to start each year. I just hope you derive as much satisfaction from throwing pots as I do from pruning rose brushes.

So expert at pruning that I can afford reveries, I meditate on foreign affairs and personal issues. I do not hurry, not wanting efficiency but preferring the feel of the faint warmth of the winter sun on my back. I am content to simply exist there. I have achieved mastery in at least one area in my lifetime. I worry about the fate of other rose bushes in my neighborhood, convinced that no other nearby occupant has my refined knowledge and subtle skills. The immediate rewards of mastery can inspire the arrogance of superiority. I must remind myself that there are many other areas of doubtful performance in my life. The acknowledgement salvages my humility.

I mourn the devaluing of skill, the actual historical loss of the expertise of the human hand. This is further aggravated by the incorporation of this loss within the rhetoric of pride in progress. What is left for us is the patronizing appreciation of 'folk art' created by 'underdeveloped' people, relics of their primitive status that provide props for our interior decorators. Even the middle class can obtain them at Cost Plus. The generations of skilled crafts people, except for a few recalcitrant potters, are largely gone, their knowledge and skill buried with them. My sons have not expressed any interest in planting roses in their gardens. They take too much time and trouble. Alas, my pruning genius will soon be lost. I am told that the modern rose is another example of human progress. It is true, there are more roses on the bush, but the wonderful fragrances are mostly missing now. Are we conscious of the tradeoffs? Did we really improve them? In a democracy we should vote on this issue of rose fragrances. During my entire life, authorities of my culture and my world have told me that all those things that have changed in my world represented something called progress. I want that fragrance back!

A purist becomes an extremist when articulating a singular point of view that denigrates all that falls outside the boundaries of that viewpoint as evil or wrong. I must moderate my message - to be labeled 'luddite' is rather like being a 'tree hugger'. Why do all the invidious labels that I resist describe the virtues I most value? My resistance can be contained with the further shame of being called 'politically correct'. I need to experiment at expanding the cultural vocabulary. My cultural adversaries seem to have the current advantage.

Apparently painting and sculpture can exist without a consensus of standards, indeed the modern era represents a series of successful overthrows of previous standards. Anything placed on a museum wall or floor qualifies as art from the very placement at that site as long as it is sponsored by an individual artist willing to be associated with that act. Does pottery really want to achieve that advanced stage of liberation? Do those who want to 'elevate' pottery from craft to art want the same liberation as the painter or sculptor? By definition, can a craft be a craft without agreed upon standards of performance and product? If art by modern definition requires the breaking of previous conventions, are standards of performance just habits or notions of time and place? How can the very integrity of the piece be so defined that the overthrow of the practice embodied with that integrity results in the loss of that integrity? Why does change and experimentation in art have to assume the pose of rejection and repudiation of former modes of expression? Technological changes have always assumed they were superior to the previous technologies that they replaced. Do changes in art need to share that same arrogance?

In the introduction to "Color and Fire - Defining Moments in Studio Ceramics, 1950-2000", Jo Lauria explains this historical progression as she...

"... surveys the major stylistic movements in the history of ceramics during the second half of the twentieth century - from pure functionalism, to functional references and the nonfunctional, to the ultimate privileging of ideas and content over material and craft."

Commentary regarding this movement often assumes the prose of progress, as if previous approaches were inferior steps in the revolutionary overthrow of hopelessly dated and obsolete stages. Jo Lauria, in the same book quoted above, credits Rose Slivka, editor of Craft Horizons, with a significant article in 1961 concerning 'The New Ceramic Presence', in which she celebrates both pottery and sculpture in terms of "release from the tyranny of traditional tools and materials".

The narrative regarding changes in artistic approaches often reads similar to the implicit triumphalism in historical narratives - the glory story of America's emerging power as world empire is mirrored by the victorious army of American artists who have wrested power away from Paris and now are undisputed conquerors of the art world. We Americans are used to seeing change - technological change, historical change, and artistic change, as the inevitable march of an incremental superiority.

Art changes as our automobiles change. Why don't American consumers understand that a yearly adjustment in bumper or body style does not represent an improvement in quality of the engine or design? Why is the past assumed to be the result of unthinking habit and custom while contemporary changes are the result of courageous genius? The art gallery parallels the automobile showroom, where trendy or sensational novelties deliberately render last year's model or artist obsolete, old, and passé. Art made for immediate sale in a gallery showroom is as cheap and superficial as a film made for summer audiences.

There is a difference between optimism, surely a wholesome element of American character, and the arrogance of power that cannot depend upon previous historical examples for proof of permanent endurance. The reality is that stable traditions in human societies are always most fragile and can be easily overthrown when penetrated by powerful forces. One McDonald's can destroy the integrity of a local architecture and cuisine in a foreign city where previous influences were the vernacular culture of that historical site. It is assumed that each innovative artistic impulse renders all previous artistic practices obsolete. This is really an American mythology - the rigid grip of previous cultural tyrannies on the tender impulses of the individual creative artist. On the contrary, human culture is as fragile as the natural environment. The nullification of culture equals the destruction of our rain forests. The termination of indigenous cultures is keeping up with the termination of animal species. When you denigrate previous cultural traditions, you are clear-cutting the growth of thousands of years of communal living and achievement. We do this without thinking or reflection. I am tired of reading 'art books', written by Europeans or Americans that provide an imperial analysis of the changes in art as a metaphor for the continued progress of humankind. According to this approach, the mythic Peter Voulkos successfully demolished the ceramic traditions of all previous civilizations. That assumption is implicit in the narratives of too many ceramic 'experts' I have been reading lately.

Referring to non-functional ceramic objects that can be called sculpture, Susan Peterson, in her recent book, "Contemporary Ceramics", declares that some of these objects "… find their way into art galleries and museums and may command large prices. The art market has developed sophistication." Peterson, a highly respected potter and ceramic authority, goes on in the next paragraph to state:

"The struggle now seems to be to find a difference, any difference, from what has gone before. Following the ceramic explosion of the 1950s, embellishment on the themes established by Voulkos, Price, Mason, Soldner and their circle has been expanded by the following generation up to the 1990s. No more breakthroughs are discernible, and it may not be possible to top what has been done in claywork in the second half of the twentieth century."

I am not sure what words like 'breakthrough' mean in terms of pottery. Does Jackson Pollock represent a breakthrough as contrasted with Rembrandt or Van Gogh? How do you 'top' previous generations of artists or aesthetic movements of distinction? Has the 'world art market' really developed sophistication when the implications of this statement are followed with a discussion that implicitly equates the merchandising strategies of the commercial art market with the profound integrity of previous approaches and traditional cultures?

A small group of potters, with the legendary Peter Voulkos as the chief figure, really did change things. Voulkos recently died and has received proper homage in current publications. Like Picasso, his early work is cited to prove that he could deconstruct traditional forms only after he had mastered them. I certainly respect his importance and talent. His reputation is not limited to clay. His historic dimensions resonate with a cultural need to establish the individual artist as a radical maverick whose persona needs to be as excessive and colorful as his art work. In the introduction to "Clay Today: Contemporary Ceramics and Their Work" Martha Drexler Lynn describes this group:

"Initiated by the predominantly male abstract expressionist potters, such as Peter Voulkos, Paul Soldner, and Jerry Rothman, the macho sculptor/potter image emerged in the 1950s from the Otis Art Institute in Los Angeles. Working around the clock, making prodigious numbers of nonfunctional, large-scale, process-oriented, sculptural pieces, Otis artists often punctuated their working sessions with impromptu parties, wrestling matches, and all sorts of horsing around. This new template for the ceramist's life-style incorporated a romantic sensibility that yearned for larger-than-life idols."

Voulkos is the dividing line, according to most conventional narratives in contemporary ceramics accounts. However revisionists might quibble in the future concerning Voulkos, the individualism of the culture reinforces the impact of the iconoclastic dismissal of the past and the romance of the solitary rebel. Legends emerge of this individual from living memory. Rick Newby and Chere Jiusto, give their account of the importance of the Archie Bray Foundation in Montana in giving a young Peter Voulkos his start, in the book, "A Ceramic Continuum: Fifty Years of the Archie Bray Influence". They describe his early rebellion:

"In 1957, with ruthless candor, Peter Voulkos clarified his revolutionary position regarding the relationship between art and craft when he served as juror for an exhibition of works by the designer-craftsmen of the Mississippi Basin."

Only three years after leaving Helena, Voulkos had become, according to the show's catalog:

"Leader and envy of every pedestrian potter . . . . Vigorous breaker of meaningless boundaries, scourge of the dull and too-often-repeated."

Newby and Jiusto go on to quote Voulkos in his juror's statement:

"Lack of stimulation leading to lack of conviction, idea and intensification seem to be the general rule of the... show... .not only this show but most craft shows... A few techniques at hand, seemingly passed off for art... people associated with craft work tend to confine themselves in a very tight little sphere refusing for some reason the contamination of any of the fields of creativity."

I do not have any cosmic or final judgment about the actual work of Voulkos. I do not think you have to abandon craft in order to embrace art. I do not accept the artificial division of the 'applied' or 'decorative arts' from the 'fine' arts. It reminds me of another contrived separation deeply embedded in the Western world view. In the eighteenth and nineteenth centuries the emerging Western academic discipline of anthropology placed the looted artifacts of non-Western cultures in Natural History museums, not Art museums, where you would find the art of the Western world. This custom continued well into the twentieth century. The racist presuppositions confirmed the observations that primitive natives did not have religious beliefs, they had superstitions; their way of life simply quaint and exotic customs; their art stacked and stored with the bones of their robbed tombs as remnants of uncivilized tribes on the back shelves of natural history museums.

You and every other working potter must confront him and explain either your devotion to or rejection of Peter Voulkos. He deliberately placed himself outside the tradition of functional pottery as craft, and worked clay as the substance of sculpture. That move encouraged later generations to further explorations in which creative integration of both traditions result in vestiges of containers that express further elaborations of individual imagination. Others have fully separated themselves from any remnant of the pot, and use clay as the raw material for form, in preference to stone, metal or wood and other materials.

I do not think that the quality of life or art has anything to do with the chronology of occurrence or appearance. I do not believe the immediate present is the inevitable zenith and summit of all previous existence and effort. Contemporary technologies can make cheaper or more plentiful commodities but not necessarily better quality. I make important discoveries when I walk in my garden. I cannot make those kinds of observations of my surroundings when I am driving my automobile on the freeway. Food from the garden does taste better than the frozen processed food placed in the microwave. Air and water, basic to human survival, are polluted by acquaintance with humans and their modern appliances. We need 'breakthroughs' that will return quality and care to both art and nature.

As a collector of pottery, I cannot follow the path of Voulkos. I do not know if my attitude is more the result of my modest financial resources or my aesthetic sensibilities. I value experimentation in all fields of human endeavor and the employment of critical intelligence and creative imagination. I value the preservation of the natural and historical, built environment. In the same spirit, I value the diverse achievement of previous and traditional cultures and wish to honor and preserve their achievements. As an old rebel and outsider in my own life as an educator and activist, I am not retreating from reform and change. It is not old age or modest means that ultimately determines my position. I can marvel at the audacity of Peter Voulkos and his originality. I do not need to nullify Bernard Leach to do so. No one has the last word. Voulkos has the advantage of later historical placement but it is a temporary advantage.

I have no affinity for numbers but a few are worth considering. This is the twelfth letter addressed to my potter friend in San Francisco. I had my sixty-ninth birthday last week. I graduated from high school over fifty years ago. I am the grandfather to three grandchildren. I review this impressive information so that both my sense of perspective and proportion can be enriched. I am still honing the craft of living. It is at least as demanding and complex as the craft of the potter's wheel. I do not need a breakthrough, I just need more time and insight to better understand how the resources of my past can further enhance the understanding of my present state. Just making it through the day with some grace and humor requires a lifetime of trying. Life has its own pruning process. I do not have the time or energy to waste, I must cut back to the essentials.

Take care, your friend,

Richard

Thirteen

February 23, 2003

Dear Christa,

Rain keeps me inside. It is a good excuse to narrow my behavior to interior routines. Reading is my chief domestic activity, in addition to cleaning toilets, dusting pots, and vacuuming the floors. Marital agreements confirm my duties. Judy teaches part-time at the university and supervises student teachers in the public schools. I maintain the house. Such is the drama of retired life, we had a crisis yesterday in the kitchen. I accused our cat, Chloe, of peeing on the back kitchen door, only to find later that the ice maker on the back of the refrigerator was leaking. Judy insisted I apologize to the cat. Given my mechanical dysfunction, I sought refuge and aid in the yellow pages. Later in the day a man knocked on the front door, spent one hour in the kitchen, and my crisis was resolved. I don't know if I can take that kind of excitement every day. You think you have problems.

I attempt to inflate my daily struggle to epic proportions, defying my exile to the obscurity of my present situation. It is difficult to develop metaphors for the decline of the western world or the threat of global warming from the dust on my dresser or the fine webs spun by tiny spiders in the corners of rooms. I remove them on discovery, encouraged by my efficiency. I remain significant in my own existence and try to avoid simply reliving the memories of the past. Given the symbols of status in this culture, I must have known that the surrender of my appointment book and the deletion of my resumé on the computer were vital steps in my current irrelevance. On the sidelines, I observe the frenetic activities of others and loyally pay attention to my own commentary. There are compensations; time is a limitless indulgence; my daily schedule emerges from immediate whim; I do not require the approval of friends or strangers to ratify my thoughts or actions.

The unregulated life is the romance of the artist. The iron cage of employment provides the security of obligated time and dependable income. In the past, most potters worked for potteries based on the industrial model. Marx made a compelling argument for the alienation resulting from the surrender of one's hired labor to impersonal tasks that do not bring the closure of individual accomplishment. Today, the potter is an independent entrepreneur. You can claim the product and the profit as your own. Your own situation is complicated by your duties to maintain regular hours at the studio. How do you balance the flexibility of individual freedom with the obligations of keeping commercial time? Perhaps the reality of such freedom is an illusion. I am sitting in my house and you are sitting at the potter's wheel in your studio; we will never know if entirely out of personal choice. We unconsciously enforce rigid restrictions on ourselves and often mourn the result. The very definition of maturity is the voluntary decision to do what otherwise might be imposed on you by others. We become our own parent. We are the final authority. We often attribute our situation to the powers of others because it is so difficult to overthrow ourselves. When I was a rebellious youth I thought that the price of maturity was surrender. Now I know that it really comprised a shift to an imposed self-supervision that could not promise a more benign regime.

Our biographies do not just happen. At what point do we assume responsibility and biography becomes autobiography? At what point do we claim authorship for our own lives? Do we dare defy our origins and create ourselves in the unpredictable patterns of our unique gifts? Can you fashion your life with the same creativity and verve as you fashion that unique pot that only you could create? Some great poets remained bank clerks or insurance salesmen. I am sure you can claim credit for the journey that brought you to San Francisco and your solid reputation as an important young potter. We all have stories to tell, naturally enhanced by self-love. Some of us just don't have the time or energy to record our glorious life adventures. For some, I suspect that they add the meaning later on, although we would all like to think that personal principle is the precursor of our behavior.

I started my professional life as a junior high art teacher in a Mexican-American community. Years later when I was teaching a course at the University of California Riverside, I came across a passage in the book that I had ordered as the class text, "Educating The Powerless" by Stanley Charnofsky. Charnofsky was a professor at a university close to the community where I was teaching that junior high class. He described the inherent racism of schools at that time and the administrators that domesticated teachers in that system:

" One secondary school principal refused to permit student teachers to teach in the art department of his school because '… there are no teachers in our art department I would care to have any young teacher be exposed to. Boys are uncontrolled in some of those classes, and the leadership is quite poor.' Yet, the students at that school (largely Mexican-American) were most appreciative of the specific teacher whose boys were 'uncontrolled'. He wore a beard and an open shirt. He was Anglo, but he spoke Spanish. He was educated, but he lived in the barrio where the children lived. He was sensitive, unstructured, nonconforming, and thoroughly loved. And no student teachers were allowed in his class."

The passage brought back vivid bittersweet memories, long buried. Charnofksy did not identify that nonconforming Anglo by name but I knew it was me. I called him, met with him, and he confirmed the fact. My struggle, so many years ago, to help Mexican-American youth to survive a racist institution that ignored and insulted their cultural identity was recorded on a published page. Years of being ostracized by my peers and punished by the principal for defending those students was vindicated decades later.

Promoting life-affirming principles deserves attention and recognition in art and life. This cannot be promised and surely can't be the motivating factor. It is completely different from the media-created celebrity of the synthetic heroes of our popular culture. An opportunist or careerist can never receive the citation that only commitment and character can bestow. I am convinced that significant art demands the same ingredients as all other courageous behavior.

I meet many people through their biographies. They become immortal in their capacity to inspire and mentor. The lessons are embedded in their lives and art. Some of my best friends are maintained on the shelves beneath my pottery, dependable and always available for guidance. Two important leaders of American culture, Louis H. Sullivan and Candace Wheeler, presented to me in two separate experiences and volumes, converge at the World's Columbian Exposition in 1893 at Chicago. They more recently converged in my life.

I first 'met' Candace Wheeler a few years ago at the New York Metropolitan Museum of Art. There was a major exhibition of her art. Prior to this event I was totally ignorant of her contribution. I was so impressed with the examples of her work on display. A book, "Candace Wheeler: The Art and Enterprise of American Design, 1875-1900" by Amelia Peck and Carol Irish, documents her life and catalogs her work for the exhibition. The inside flap of the book provides a concise description of Wheeler:

"Candace Wheeler (1827-1923) changed the course of textile and interior design in nineteenth-century America and was a driving force behind the professionalization of women in the design field. ... Wheeler founded the Society of Decorative Art in New York. The organization offered instruction in the applied

The young man

Non-conformist teacher

Educationalist, activist,
thinker

Collector, curator, author

arts to women and helped them sell their work, providing them some measure of economic independence. Wheeler was acquainted with leading figures in the New York art world and, as a textile specialist, went into partnership with Louis Comfort Tiffany in an interior design firm ... In 1883 Wheeler formed her own firm, Associated Artists, which produced both hand-wrought and machine-made textiles and was staffed entirely by women. Artistically, Wheeler had begun by taking as her model the accomplishments of advanced British designers such as William Morris and Walter Crane. In the course of her career she absorbed elements of Japanese design and developed a sophisticated American textile style in which the natural forms of native plants were interpreted as free-flowing designs ... she took up the challenge of producing fabrics that were not only beautiful but also affordable and practical for use in middle-class homes. To accomplish this she explored unusual weaving and printing techniques, and in some cases invented new ones."

Wheeler was appointed director of design for the Women's Building of the 1893 Exposition in Chicago. Her leadership at this Exposition included the Hall of Honor where murals celebrated the progress of women. The hall housed art by female artists from around the world. This must be viewed in the context of the late nineteenth century, where few women were permitted to assume active roles of public leadership in the arts and business. She lived a long life, active to the end. Just a few days ago I attended a seminar on her sponsored by the Gamble House in Pasadena. The references can only multiply as this significant person is discovered and rediscovered.

Louis Sullivan, in his "The Autobiography of an Idea" (what a great title for a book!) first published in 1924, father of the modern skyscraper, developed an architecture that married form to function, building to site, and structure to nature. He believed that the organic spirit of architectural design could organize society. Influenced by John Ruskin and his ideas of nature rather than history as the source of form and decoration, Sullivan was later the mentor of Frank Lloyd Wright. In the book "Art Nouveau - 1890-1914", edited by Paul Green-halgh, in a chapter entitled 'Louis Sullivan and the Spirit of Nature', Lauren S. Weingarden described Sullivan's contribution to the 1893 Chicago Colombian World's Fair Exposition:

"Sullivan's polychromed, wholly ornamented Transportation Building provided a unique alternative to the core of the World's Fair ... Sullivan's building was in a more informal setting. Sullivan combined 30 hues, dominated by red with varying tones of blue, yellow, and green, into the delicately interweaving patterns of his frescoed ornament. Viewed from a distance, the building emitted a radiant crimson effect. This optical illusion was reinforced by the Golden Doorway at the building's centre. Comprising a series of concentric half-circles within a monumental square frame … faced with gilded variation of Sullivan's low-relief ornament."

Both individuals were leaders because they had the capacity to see their art as advancing human civilization. Both practised the use of patterns derived from nature in their art. They lived in a very optimistic time in American history; with the emergence of new inventions such as elevators that made tall buildings possible, electricity, railroads that opened up the entire nation; growing national power that challenged old world power. Both lived to witness the heart-rending tragedy of World War I. Wheeler lost three grandchildren in that war. Both were visionaries, hopeful creators of new worlds. Even after the war and personal loss, Wheeler declared:

"I see ahead of us an era of righteousness and prosperity such as has never existed before, because for the first time in the world's history women will be working side by side with men, the mature home women bringing the schooling they have had as executives and economists to bear on the advance of real civilization. They will head all charitable societies and all work dealing with the fortunes of women and children. Always the producers of the race, they will become its conservers, bringing the woman's point of view to bear on every situation."

I was not introduced to Candace Wheeler in the education of my youth, not even as a university art student. She did not appear in the textbooks, was not heard on radio, was not the subject of a television show. She did not fit the stereotype of her time as a domestic woman who performed the hobby of textiles as feminine refinement; nor did she fit the modern stereotype of a bohemian maverick at war with the culture. She was both conventional and radical, all at the same time.

Louis Sullivan, in his "Autobiography of an Idea", expresses his vision with compelling power. I must consciously forgive his use of man as universal. He is an old friend of another time.

"Our dream shall be of a civilization founded upon ideas thrillingly sane, a civilization, a social fabric squarely resting on man's quality of virtue as a human being; created by man, the real, in the image of his fruitful powers of beneficence; created in the likeness of his aspirant emotions, in response to the power and glory of his true imagination, the power of his intelligence, his ability to inquire, to do, to make new situations befitting his needs. A civilization that shall reflect man sound to the core and kindly in the exercise of his will to choose aright. A civilization that shall be the living voice, the spring song, the saga of the power of his Ego to banish fear and fate, and in the courage of adventure and of mastership to shape his destiny."

How should we regard their art and visions now? We are in a different time, and have even more evidence to make us cynical and wary. Many of Sullivan's buildings have been demolished, and the tender fabric of Wheeler torn and faded. The buildings at the Chicago Exposition were pulled down after closing and much of the interiors were discarded or lost. It is hard for most to reach across the hundred years or more and embrace them. Yet they endure and their art survives.

Why do I waste your time in this letter? You are a potter. They were not potters. When I taught students at the university, I announced that I did not care about their eventual jobs, this was not a trade school but a university. I wanted them to become more complicated; to help them become more complicated was the task of the professors and the university. The preface to the pot is whatever the potter brings to the wheel. Everything, every life experience, thought, hope, understanding and vision guide the hands and form the clay. I cannot believe the pot can contain more subtlety and wisdom than the potter. The pot, even if forever empty, always contains the character and intelligence of the potter. The pot is your best character reference. They are the mighty instruments of your hopes and vision for all of us. They form the illustration of your biography.

I think that is when the crafts person becomes the artist. It has nothing to do with the media or technique. It has to do with intention and purpose. The artist takes responsibility for her art, and at the same time, takes responsibility for the world. Art is both implicit protest against the inadequacies of the present and concrete testimony of hope for the future. Art does not have the single purpose of isolated function, but the greater purpose of enhancing and ennobling those who encounter it. I believe a pot can do this. Do most potters believe this too?

I do hope that Candace, Louis and you become good friends. Don't worry, I won't shift my correspondence to them. I am not confident they would respond.

Take care - your friend,

Fourteen

March 10, 2003

Dear Christa,

Winter is still sponsoring the weather. Dark clouds hover over the foothills. The threat of rain and war combine to provide a daily anxiety. We are still early in the year and early into the new century. Much was said a few years ago about the glorious hopes and visions as we celebrated the new millennium. The old pathologies of previous centuries are being continued into this one. The world waits for war. It is easier for the young to wait out the present crisis and plan for hopeful possibilities beyond. I do not have the luxury of an extended future. We planned to leave this month for Europe. Our departure appears to coincide with the plans of Bush to initiate the invasion of Iraq. I do not think he will change his mind and we do not wish to change our plans. We will leave March 26th if the world is not shut down. I reject terrorism as a strategy of the oppressed and I reject military terrorism of the state as foreign policy. Both private and official violence leave citizens as victims. Not even smart bombs know how to avoid the innocent. The seeds of future violence are embedded in the outcome of previous violence. Wars can never bring peace, only the commitment to peace can bring peace. The consequences for human civilization are costly and dreadful for all participants, whatever the outcome of the initial bloodletting.

It might be instructive to view the art world of another millennial year just over one hundred years ago. The assessment that inevitably arises from the end and beginning of centuries offers opportunities for both despair and celebration. Is it "Twilight or Dawn?" as the question is posed by Robert Rosenblum in "1900: Art At The Crossroads". The cultural and intellectual context of that time was aptly summarized by Maryanne Stevens in the same book:

"Indeed, the closing decades of that century were shaped by a myriad of new and powerful, but often contradictory, forces: socialism rose beside right-wing reactionary extremism, nationalism and anti-semitism; the absolute authority of science was challenged by spiritualism and a return to religious faith; the understanding of man's existence was extended both by the psychological inquiries of Charcot and Freud and the sociological investigations of Durkheim; and cultural establishments experienced increasing assaults from a proliferation of potent avant-gardes."

I observe few permanent casualties of history here. Most of these conflicting forces, perhaps camouflaged in a more contemporary prose and setting, still compete in our new century. Victory seems to be consistently preferred over reconciliation in human history. Many invidious and toxic causes, defeated at one time or place, simply abandon the lost host and acquire a new sponsor elsewhere.

I once read with ironic amusement the harsh verdict that a writer issued about Winston Churchill, that he was essentially a man of the nineteenth century, whatever part he played in the politics and policies of the twentieth century. Birth and place anchor your world view, and you cannot escape or outlive your origins. Now I too, late in life, venture into another century, knowing that I am as obsolete in orientation as the typewriter I was forced to abandon not so long ago. You have the advantage, Christa, here. You will spend most of your life in this new century, witness the vast majority of it, and some day look back with your own amusement at the dated relics and fashions of this past century. I look back and see the historical evolution of ceramics. I too can date pottery by appearance. What will the contemporary pottery of this new century look like? Like the biographies of the deceased, beginning and ending calendar dates are often attached to descriptions of pottery, be it termed Arts and Crafts, Art Nouveau, Art Deco, etc. Is the traditional pot timeless? Are some ceramic variables immutable? Are your pots going to ever look dated? Is some ceramic expert going to say in 2075, "Oh, that is a Christa Assad pot, how quaint! Not bad for early 2000 San Francisco stuff." What label do you think the experts will call you and your work someday? Do you care?

Today there is apparently little agreement or solidarity regarding a singular or dominant style. Perhaps that is a good thing. Martha Drexler Lynn identifies the proliferation of current styles in "Clay Today: Contemporary Ceramists and Their Work":

"The contemporary ceramic vessel world includes many variations of clay work. The brown pot, expressive pot, message pot, postmodern pot, and pretty pot all thrive. Many artists combine these styles in idiosyncratic ways to communicate content. This pluralism reflects growth in the attitudes held by ceramicists and their audience and echoes the development of clay from craft into art."

According to this particular expert, you have endless choices with your pots. Your post-modern freedom allows you permission to do any thing you want to do. Why do your pots look the way they do? How can personal conviction about these things withstand the next wave of some new movement or idea that will pressure you to get with it, to get on the bandwagon. How can you resist the emulation of that slightly more famous potter who is currently the rage in galleries and ceramic periodicals?

I forgive youth. It is a significant sign of my humanity in old age. I forgive youth for being young. You will outlast me. For those in the past who have provided me personal and direct injury, their eventual and natural death is the only retaliation that can bring me justice. I am not capable of any other retribution. If religion has not convinced me of the romance of afterlife, then a rigorous objective analysis of the mortality of my existence must somehow be softened to allow relief. Art is a superior fiction, pottery a clay confection that provides at least temporary insulation and escape from the actuary tables of insurance companies and the reoccurring wars, natural disasters, and physical diseases that eventually make you a statistic. I will hide out with my pots in my old age. Damn wars, violence, and the deliverers of death. Along with my cholesterol and blood pressure count, surely such proclaimed defiance must be included as a positive factor in any objective diagnosis of my present health.

The young must make sense of their lives, give direction and purpose to their future. Americans trivialize this need and reduce it to a resumé adjunct to pursuing a career strategy. Leading a meaningful life is not usually regarded as a subject worthy of the same self-conscious application of attention as achieving employment compensated by ever increasing income. In this sense, success can indeed be calibrated and defined by a bank account. Young John Ruskin, in nineteenth century England, had a different problem. Should he go into the ministry or pursue his intellectual and aesthetic interests? In a wonderful biography of Ruskin, "The Wider Sea: A Life of John Ruskin" by John Dixon Hunt, that I am currently reading, his answer underscores the complexity of the final decision:

"…does the pursuit of any art or science, for the mere sake of the resultant beauty or knowledge, tend to forward this end? That such pursuits are beneficial and ennobling to our nature is self-evident, but have we leisure for them in our perilous circumstances? Is it a time to be spelling of letters, or touching of strings, counting stars or crystallizing dewdrops, while the earth is failing under our feet, and our fellows are departing every instant into eternal pain?"

Dear young John did not have to worry about sustaining himself through employment. His parents were wealthy and most indulgent. But his options were real and important for him. How do you choose a life in art over the imperatives of rescuing humanity for spiritual salvation or attending to the ills of the afflicted, much less the vulgar pursuits of making money? How do you, Christa, justify your decision to make your life in art? You are still young enough to change your mind. A final commitment, made in youth, to a lifetime pursuit, does not only explain what you are going to do with your time and energy over a lifetime, it defines your very character and personhood.

War is coming, does your wheel speed up with increased agitation? I read in the Los Angeles Times newspaper this morning about:

"Sam Hamill - author of 13 volumes of poetry, pacifist ex-Marine, Buddhist, craggy white-haired introvert - once had a life he liked. It was lived in private. Then First Lady Laura Bush, in mid-January, invited him to take part in a White House symposium called "Poetry and the American Voice..."

Hamill, opposed to war with Iraq, organized an internet response of poets that resulted in hundreds of anti-war poems. The White House canceled the entire event. The outpouring by e-mail, which came from some of the most distinguished poets in the land, will be sent to the United States Congress. Poetry readings of these poems are spreading across the country. This newspaper column, written by the journalist, Tomas Alex Tizon, was on the first page of a major American metropolitan newspaper. Tizon provided a sensitive insight in the article:

"It's generally accepted that poetry, in this sprint-paced, digital age, no longer appeals to the masses as it once did. Reading poetry requires contemplation; it is an act of stopping and reflecting, neither of which, to many Americans, holds priority over climbing the corporate ladder or developing buns of steel."

The First Lady, wife of the most powerful man in the world, canceled her plans for the conference, retreating from the unarmed army of poets. Tizon reminds us, despite the feeble sales of poetry and their marginalized status, that another poet, Percy Bysshe Shelley once declared that "poets are the unacknowledged legislators of the world".

Is this all nonsense? Should I know better? That poets and potters, not by temperament or ambition, but by the power of their art and sensibility, can be cultural and moral leaders? I do not know your politics. It doesn't matter. Morality is not determined or defined by membership in a political party. If the common response to issues of peace and human welfare are determined solely by membership in one particular race, nation, political party, ethnic group or religion, the world is doomed to continue centuries of death and destruction. Morality demands the superiority of virtue over allegiance to self-interest or group identity. Blind loyalty, to any cause or group, however noble the intent or however noble the group would appear, becomes the handmaiden of moral surrender. Ultimately, if the world is to survive and flourish, the remote and unknown stranger or foreigner must have as great a claim for your love and compassion as the most intimate loved one or family, or fellow citizen, or member of the same religious faith.

At this point, I simply do not know if the human species is constitutionally capable of surmounting their hatreds and insecurities and embracing all members and groups within the species. My reservations indicate the natural conservatism of old age regarding human nature, based on a lifetime auditing the daily atrocities that unfortunately provide abundant documentation for pessimism. Despite what I have witnessed, with some embarrassment I must confess that I simply cannot bear the thought that hands capable of creating a beautiful piece of pottery would be equally capable of killing another human being. I am a very simple and naive man.

We have not been given sufficient opportunity in this new century for the escapism of hope. This century opened with the crisis in our democracy where five members of the U.S. Supreme Court decided that the man who received fewer votes would be the next President; 9/11 and the greatest loss of life in violence on American soil since the Civil War; endemic plague of Aids sweeping the world with no cure in sight; business executives, bloated with huge salaries, corrupting corporations that collapse under the weight of their sheer greed and dishonesty; Wall Street crashes, taking pension funds and life savings of many in the middle class with it. Still no breathing room, with the nation divided over war and estranged from many of our European allies.

How unlike the beginning of the 20th Century, where Alexander Scriabin, the Russian composer, would devote himself to composing "Prometheus, Poem of Fire" in 1910. According to the CD program notes of Hugh Macdonald, this symphonic poem was:

"A single-movement orchestral work with parts for solo piano and wordless chorus, it is one of those remarkable masterpieces from the feverish years before

World War I, when art still aspired to the highest goals and when a grand cosmic vision was still an ideal and not an absurdity. Scriabin's vision was of world transformation through the mystical agency of his own creativity; his music was to usher in the millennium, when his divine authority would be revealed. He died in 1915 with his dreams unfulfilled."

Artists cannot have grand visions if our generals command the nation's destiny. Battlefields lead to 'lost generations', not a transformation through creativity. How do we wean adolescents from drugs if our ideals become absurdities and have no basis in reality. Often great tragic art can emerge from the dark pit of war, but we all become casualties of despair if art cannot ultimately affirm a future.

You have notable artist ancestors of your own gender in Northern California. Lillian Palmer, at the beginning of the 20th century, worked in San Jose and San Francisco. According to Kenneth R. Trapp, in his book, "The Arts and Crafts Movement in California: Living The Good Life", Palmer is described as follows:

"One of the earliest recorded workers in metals after the earthquake was Lillian Palmer, who lived in San Jose. Ignoring the gendered roles that obtained in that period, Palmer not only designed pieces but made them as well. Originally attracted to metalwork as a recreation, by 1907 Palmer was devoting herself full time to work in copper, lead, and brass... Palmer's lack of formal training in metalworking proved an advantage, for she was not encumbered by tradition or doctrine. She discovered that she could manipulate lead into an upright form and then hammer into it relief and repousse decorations, much as in copperwork. With a spirited inventiveness, she introduced beach pebbles as decorative elements, just as workers in precious metals and jewelry would use gems to add color and ornamentation. From what we can surmise from the meager literature, Palmer prospered sufficiently after being featured in the San Francisco Call of April 28, 1907, to enable her to study metal crafting in Vienna... With the opening of her art-metal shop in San Francisco in 1910, Palmer concentrated on making lamps and lighting fixtures designed for the new electrical age."

Christa, you have friends. Go forth with our sponsorship and support. You are early in this century and it still harbors hope. The future belongs to you. May you and your pottery find refuge and acceptance in the coming years. I leave you soon to search for the historical remnants of William Morris in England. Make your pottery the manifesto of your ideals and hopes.

Take care.
Your friend,

PS I leave you with some lines from a Sam Hamill poem

To Bill and Chris

I never wanted
a cell phone or electronic
mail, a Cadillac
or a limousine to cruise
the Information Highway.

A dusty back road
through obdurate relics of
civilization
is where I've built my retreat.
Give me a California

Job Drawer, a press
I can ink by hand, cotton
fiber paper made
by hand in France, Italy
or Japan, and let me be.

I like the feel of
the poem as it takes shape
in my hands, the smell
of damp paper, oil, type wash,
the hum and clunk of the press.

Technology is,
of itself, neither good nor
evil, but bequeaths
and reveals what's in the heart
already...

Fifteen

May 13, 2003

Dear Christa,

I have returned. Over two weeks in Britain with daily sun and blue skies only to be greeted by rain on return to Southern California. The hazards of generalization, although documented by past experience and necessary for planning purposes, can lead to surprising discrepancies and the upheaval of safe assumptions. It was the longest non-raining Spring period on record in England and Scotland. Our top coats remained in baggage and umbrellas stored unfurled. Pleased to hear that your own parallel trip to England, to visit friends and attend a wedding, by your recent account, went well. We share a common affection and fond memories of the place spread over many years. I came back with a few pots, several antique and contemporary etchings, and one splendid antique English watercolour. Fresh memories soon fade, crowded in too small a place and time; houses, interiors and art merging and blurred, sorted out by the guidebooks that returned with me, introducing me to what I have just experienced.

Arrived in the train station in Edinburgh from Cambridge, attempted to get a taxi, puzzled by a long line of people in similar need, no taxis in sight. Found out later, after a long walk pulling heavy baggage down busy sidewalks, that a peace demonstration had tied up traffic in central Edinburgh. This personal inconvenience, early in the trip, provided a minor historical reference for the daily newspaper and television accounts of the ongoing reports of death and destruction in the war in Iraq. Our cultural values neatly coincide with our military objectives, the oil wells are saved and the museums are looted, the heritage and legacy of this rich civilization are lost but the oil will flow. Going on holiday during war cannot be defended, only rationalized. There are simply not sufficient periods of peace for me to enjoy my self-indulgent excursions without the nagging distractions of global tragedy. I must train myself to view real war and similar atrocities as I would the theater. When the curtain comes down, a brief critique, and then on to other entertainments.

Two living heroes sustain me, Nelson Mandela and Vaclav Havel. One a lawyer, the other an artist, both victims of injustice who eventually triumphed and liberated their people; not through superior weaponry and victory on the battlefield, but through their moral courage and vision. Havel, in a statement published in "The New York Review of Books", September 23, 1999, spoke of a different kind of dictatorship than that of Saddam Hussein, one that in my view poses an even greater danger:

"The dictatorship of money, of profit, of constant economic growth, and the necessity, flowing from all that, of plundering the earth without regard for what will be left in a few decades, along with everything else related to the materialistic obsessions of this world, from the flourishing of selfishness to the need to evade personal responsibility by becoming part of the herd, and the general inability of human conscience to keep pace with the inventions of reason, right up to the alienation created by the sheer size of modern institutions - all of these are phenomena that cannot effectively be confronted except through a new moral effort, that is, through a transformation of the spirit and the human relationship to life and the world."

I always feel an obligation about this time in my letters to initiate some kind of pottery shop talk in order to justify my communications to this potter who is willing to take the time to read them. But I think you know how I feel about this. Everything - nature, war, gardens, ethics, even the weather, is all about pottery. Pottery is about life. Pottery belongs to what John Ruskin said, "There is no wealth but life". Pottery is not a special event. Pottery is not special. It is as ordinary and remarkable as the other intimate residents of my home encountered in my daily domestic life. I do not need to mystify pottery or deify potters. You are both ordinary and remarkable too, focused to do one task supremely well. I would not construct a hierarchy and put you ahead of the maker of my furniture or the artisan who created my stained glass window whose work I also visit each day. I am devoted to all of you.

To isolate pottery and potters to matters of technique and glazing formulas, the objects themselves, or the eccentricities of potter personalities, without the cultural context or complexity of the motivating aesthetic or the experiential richness of those of us lucky enough to cohabit the same site, reduces the meaning and value of pottery to just more commercial commodities for consumer consideration in the glutted marketplace. The gallery and museum are not really decent places to view art. Art specially designed for those places is essentially dishonest; sensational objects designed to attract attention by their vulgar novelty. I can spot them a mile away. When I purchase art in a gallery, I rescue that object and give it a home. I mean that literally.

To understand the stained glass windows, wallpapers, and tapestries of William Morris, you must understand the aesthetic of John Ruskin. As we know, Ruskin never made stained glass windows, wall paper or tapestries. Why did Morris bother with Ruskin? To understand William Morris and John Ruskin, two privileged members of the English upper class, you have to understand why they organized seminars and presented lectures to industrial workers, even though those workers could not afford to travel to Italy with Ruskin or buy the wares of Morris. Havel would understand, it was to share, "… that transformation of the spirit and the human relationship to life and the world". That is what you do for me, Christa; you help me understand and experience, through your pottery, 'the transformation of the spirit and the human relationship to life'. We are all ordinary and remarkable, and we are all eligible for that transformation.

Part of our trip was on an 'Arts and Crafts Tour of England' sponsored by the Roycroft Foundation in East Aurora, New York. We went to a few museums but the genius of Morris and his friends was best demonstrated in the homes we visited on our tour. I learned something about the organization of pottery during this exploration. I tended to place my pottery at full attention, side-by-side in strict rows of military formation on the deep shelves in various rooms. In many of the homes we visited ceramics were clustered, overlapping with the taller vases in the back. This was a natural and unpretentious placement, appropriate in their informal and intimate arrangement in private lifespace. Needless to say I have created new compositions with pottery after the trip.

First stop on the itinerary was a natural one, Brantwood, the home of John Ruskin on the shore of Coniston Water in the lovely Lake District. The eccentric Ruskin bought the house unseen, partly to get away from his parents. This house commands magnificent views of the lake and surrounding countryside. The house is filled with his drawings and watercolours. Ruskin is often underestimated as an artist, yet the artworks present in the house attest to his great talent. John Julius Norwich aptly summarizes Ruskin in "Preserving A Visionary's Lake District Retreat":

"He had identified architecture with morality, had championed J.M.W. Turner and the Pre-Raphaelite Brotherhood and had led his own personal crusade against the worst horrors of the Industrial Revolution. He was seen variously as a teacher, a prophet, a saint and a dangerous revolutionary."

We then journeyed to Blackwell, designed by M.H. Baillie Scott. Scott is dear to my heart. He is best known for cottage houses in southern British garden suburbs, and his preferred clientele, he described as "… people with artistic aspirations but modest incomes". That pretty well describes me. He was involved in all aspects of interior design, including furniture and fabrics. There are some beautiful William De Morgan ceramic bowls and tiles with lustre glaze here. Baillie Scott preferred to work with local craftspeople who contributed to his designs.

Christa, have you ever thought of joining or forming some alliance with other local designers, artists, architects, interior decorators, furniture makers, etc. in offering prospective clients an integrated design of both structure and interior? Remember Candace Wheeler in New York a few letters ago, who teamed up with Louis Tiffany and others to offer a total package. This is of course what William Morris did in England. Is this practical today? There would have to be some consensus about overall design approach, and people or developers would have to be able to afford this combined service. What would our suburbs and cities look like now if this approach had been taken when the housing tracts spread out after World War II. Is it too late? Are good design and beautiful things still reserved for the very rich? Just brainstorming.

Next stop was the Cheltenham Museum, a small regional museum with a very fine Arts & Craft display. Mary Greensted, director and author of several books on the arts and crafts of the Cotswolds, led us through the exhibition. Greensted points out, in her book co-edited with Annette Carruthers, "Simplicity or Splendor: Arts and Crafts Living: Objects from the Cheltenham Collections", that:

"William Morris in his lecture to an audience of pottery students and manufacturers at Burslem Town Hall, Stoke-on-Trent in 1881, gave his philosophy as far as pottery was concerned. A pot should be individual, '...you must give it qualities besides those which made it for ordinary use, true to its material and hand-painted'."

Greensted and Carruthers led an interesting discussion of the impact of the Arts and Crafts movement on Modernism, their eventual successor. Traits that were similar:

"... interest in the population as a whole, rather those of an elite who had hitherto been the consumers of art and design, indicates a concern for social morality, and in turn leads on to the idea of good design being socially improving. Truth to the way an object has been made or to the materials of its construction was considered an essential... Adherence to these principles would bring about a 'transformation of consciousness', improving the lives of the users of designed goods... "

Greensted and Carruthers identify the aspects of Arts and Crafts that Modernism rejected. They include the rejection of traditional craft skills, approval of technology, and a decorative style that forsakes historical references for abstraction. Mass production of standardized objects replaced the hand-made object, with the optimistic embrace of a future where massive distribution would bring an international triumph in good design for everyone, leaving behind the provincial vernacular of the local culture. Tell me Christa, how long can contemporary American studio potters continue to go against the grain?

One interesting attempt to reach a compromise is Highland Stoneware in Lochinver, Scotland. David Grant, graduate in ceramics from the Royal College of Art, founded this pottery about twenty-five years ago. The aim was to achieve the quality of studio pottery but use industrial techniques. Most of it is domestic ware, some tiles, special one of a kind pieces, commemorative and ceramic jewelry. Two groups divide the work, 'makers' who throw the pots, and 'decorators' who hand paint all the work. Variation rather than absolute replication is encouraged, visiting artists come to this remote fishing village in the north Highlands, and potters are encouraged to visit other potteries and try new ideas and designs. According to Malcolm Haslam, author of "Highland Stoneware: The First Twenty-Five Years of a Scottish Pottery":

"The original direction was to make tableware with the ceramic qualities of studio-pottery, and the manufacture of practical ware is likely to remain a major activity of the company. But the artistic merit of Highland Stoneware has been so refined and developed that the product has outstripped much of the studio-pottery made in Britain today in terms of ceramic quality. Collectors have begun to buy individual pieces specially decorated for exhibitions, and probably more of these will be made in the future. It has been widely recognized that the policy of allowing decorators ample freedom of expression encourages the variation and innovation that collectors enjoy, and David Grant has recently been trying to introduce more creative freedom into the making as well as the decorating of Highland Stoneware, putting more emphasis on throwing."

Almost all the throwers and decorators studied ceramics and graduated from Schools of Art before working at Highland. Christa, would these people be accepted by studio potters as full colleagues? Is there a hierarchical ranking within the existing pottery world that insists that the shared collaboration and impressive production results make them lesser potters? At what point on the continuum does collaboration on design and execution reduce the prestige of the individual potter or the artistic significance of the pottery? As I recall, Picasso never threw his own pots or made his own plates. Are the worlds of industrial pottery and studio pottery two different worlds that cannot be bridged? There are almost always two names on most of my antique English prints - the engraver and the original artist. We know that many of the famous painters in Western art had workshops where apprentices did much of the painting, the old masters designing the composition and adding the distinctive finishing touches. One name only of course appears on the canvas.

What permits some art media to be a collaborative event and others an individual one? Making a film is such an example, the long string of credits at the end of the film give ample proof of the collaborative effort. I love the theater for that reason, all actors, at the same time, usually hand-in-hand, receive the applause of the audience at the end of the performance. Maybe the set directors and stage hands should be on stage too to receive the applause and gratitude. I am told that the City Hall in Stockholm has the usual cornerstone that ordinarily celebrates important civic dignitaries, but this plaque instead announces the names of the carpenters, masons and artisans that actually built that building. Who gets the credit might say more about our culture than the cultural products themselves. I guess it wouldn't be practical for you to scratch on the bottom of your vases the names of all the mentors and other potters that have influenced and contributed to your work.

I recently attended a very thoughtful contemporary play, "Ten Unknowns" by Jon Robin Baitz. Stacy Keach, in a commanding performance, plays an old painter, down and out in exile in Mexico. Important in his earlier days in New York, the abstract expressionists took over and he fled, rendered obsolete by the sea change in fashion and new trends in the New York gallery scene. Bitter and mostly drunk, he still appears to be painting, canvases stacked on stage as noteworthy props. A young apprentice is sent by the old artist's New York agent to look him over and prepare for a comeback exhibition. The old painter keeps him busy with studio chores. We later learn that the old man, burnt out, sits and talks while the young apprentice paints the canvas. The young man is angry, responsible for the paintings and yet receiving no credit. Keach explodes with wrath, insisting that it is his visions, themes, and life issues that he narrates and explains that allows this young man to hold the paintbrush and dab the canvas. He insists he is still the artist - the hollow young man has only technique - while he has the heart and soul to guide the content. Maybe Keach and the young man should have continued their association, with two signatures on the canvas.

This is a variation on our earlier discussion. Authors usually thank their friends and relatives in the preface for the support and help they received in writing the book. In fiction one can trace the influences of previous authors on their style. To the degree that all fiction is biographical, perhaps one should include inventories of all the memorable beings encountered in life that eventually end up in some form on the page as the borrowed characters of the story. In academic writing, one is supposed to provide a footnote and acknowledgment for direct input from another source. The name for not doing so is something invidious called plagiarism.

The modes of reproduction of the cultural products of others has been recently enhanced by various electronic devices and the computer. Someday I might move a mouse or press a button and out of some electronic kiln will pop a Christa Assad vase, made to order to suit my specifications. Boundary lines are blurring, and what is an 'original' and what is a fake or reproduction does not seem so simple anymore. If imitation is the highest form of flattery, exact dupli-cation of sound, image or object might be the most passionate form of approval. Actors in films can now be contrived on the computer screen, a special effect that does not require compensation to a real human being. Do they have an ethi-cal duty to confess to the audience what actors are real and what actors are computer creations? Digital cameras will soon put film developers out of busi-ness. We don't need middle brokers anymore - we can make our own perfect copies of sound, image and object. If a computer can now beat the World Chess Master, how long will it be before the first computer claims the creation of an original pot? What a brave new world.

Patrick Lyndon, in an article in the April 2003 issue of the British periodical, 'Prospect' entitled "Unoriginal Art", proposes that smaller art museums and galleries should frame and display copies of original masterworks, since they cannot afford to buy them. He argues:

"Why aren't copies of great paintings shown in the public art galleries that lack them? Generally, two reasons are given. First, it is said, faithful copies cannot be made. But faithful copes can be made - and indeed have been made by artists and forgers, which experts can't distinguish from the originals... The second reason given is that full appreciation of a painting depends on the belief that it is the original specimen touched by the artist's own hands. One conceded that full appreciation of a holy relic or a tailor-made suit depends on such a belief. However, in terms of artistic communication, the first specimen is of value only to its owner or a specialist antiquarian. It is the copies that count. Is a painting, like a piece of the true cross, valuable only because of its sacredness? Or is it an artistic communication, detachable from its original handiwork? The art world must believe the former, otherwise why the huge prices for the origi-nals?"

Rodmarton Manor was commissioned by a rich stockbroker early in the 20th century. Ernest Barnsley designed the house in the English Arts and Crafts style, his brother Sidney designed and made much of the furniture. The village of Rodmarton supplied the materials and craftspeople from the village did most of the work by hand with little or no use of machinery. Simon Biddulph, grandson of the original owner, provided the text for the publication, "Rodmarton Manor: The English Arts and Crafts movement at its best is here". He quotes Sir William Rothenstein who celebrates the fact that the local blacksmith, carpenters and masons did the work on the manor.

"Stone was quarried and dressed, trees felled and adzed, while ironwork, window frames, door hinges, garden gates, fire irons - all these were given over to the Rodmarton smithy... The result is a triumph of modern craftsmanship... for here is proof positive that given the opportunity, the old skill and poetry still live under the crust of neglect which covers them... It is not the museums and picture galleries, but this practical encouragement, and the training that active work gives, that could bring back prosperity and skill to our villages."

Where is the 'old skill and poetry' today. What would happen if you and fellow artists tried to organize a similar project in San Francisco? An original structure with an original interior made with local craftspeople and local resources, designed to represent the essence of location and use. Why have 'laborsaving' technologies become so important when so many people are unemployed? How can the cost of labor be balanced by the creativity of the human hand? John Ruskin, whom I re-visited recently, insisted, "Manmade articles should reveal rather than seek to disguise their origins; individuality and roughness were preferable to perfection and standardization." What would the modern consumer think of that? I am told that the main reason farmers cannot stop the use of pesticides is that organic fruit and vegetables might have blemishes and imperfections that would offend the shopper in the grocery store. When did the aesthetic of the modern world begin to value mechanical perfection over the genius of human imperfection? Who profited and what have we lost?

Two important homes in one day, Wightwick Manor in the morning and Kelmscott Manor, the home of William Morris, in the afternoon. We move through the rooms rather quickly, with guides talking and so much to view, attempted unsuccessfully to take pictures through the lens of my eyes for permanent storage in my memory bank. Families lived in these houses, children grew up here, gardens surrounded them. The pedestrian accoutrements of family life co-exist with the sublime beauty of the furniture, wall coverings, carpets, stained glass, paintings and pottery of William Morris and his Pre-Raphaelite friends. The kitchen and the bathrooms were once used, the washstand in the visitors bathroom at Wightwick Manor has 'Tulip and Trellis' tiles designed by Morris in 1870 and made by the De Morgan pottery in the 1880s. To sit on the toilet in your own home and view great art must indeed be the very greatest luxury anyone could ever imagine. The profane and sacred rituals of daily life, succeeding generations of the same family, homes periodically restored or altered, paintings and photographs of young children that suddenly become old people, all in one glimpse, on the same shelf or wall, the durability of art and the durability of families.

As Brantwood was the inner sanctum of Ruskin, Kelmscott constitutes the conclusion of the pilgrimage in the search for William Morris. We paused in his bedroom, at the front of the bed where he died, bed-hangings and valances designed by his daughter, May. The embroidery on the bedcover created by May displayed her great skill and art. This ancient country home had melancholy origins for Morris; his attempt to remove the passionate love affair of his wife, Jane, and the painter Rossetti from possible scandal in London to the discreet shelter of the rural countryside. He allowed Rossetti to live there with Jane, escaped to Iceland twice, kept busy in London. Even after Rossetti finally left after a nervous breakdown, Kelmscott remained largely unattainable for a chronically energetic and overworked Morris. Bouts of inactivity or leisure in a country house was simply not part of his temperament. Yet he yearned to be there, as Jan Marsh described in "William Morris: Art And Kelmscott":

"Kelmscott Manor was somewhere William Morris wanted to be, but, mostly could not be: an unattainable ideal, in fact - always desired, never permanently achieved. 'I confess I sigh for Kelmscott', he wrote to Jane in the later seventies."

Aside from Kelmscott, more memorable than the huge manor houses in its impact on me, was Little Holland House. One remarkable man, Frank Reginald Dickinson (1874-1961) designed and built his dream house. Born of poor working class parents, unable to afford an education, he went to work for Royal Doulton Pottery, not as a potter but with their ceramic sanitation pipes department. Frank was inspired by John Ruskin and William Morris, and determined to get the funds and build his own house. Not trained as an architect, but with the help of his brother and a loan from a Mutual Building Society, he proceeded to build. A small house, built in the rural countryside outside London, now surrounded by roads and houses. He and his bride, Florence, who sacrificed her wedding trousseau to purchase the green slate to roof the house, spent their honeymoon cleaning and staining the floors. Dickinson designed and built most of the furniture - working at night in his parents' cellar. He painted murals on the walls, carved scenes in wood, painted pictures for the walls, even made a silver coffee pot and the silver tea-set for his beloved wife to mark their 25th Wedding Anniversary. This uneducated Renaissance man also created the copperwork on the fireplace, incorporating quotations that celebrated the working man and stanzas from the poems of Longfellow and Coleridge into his paintings and woodwork.

There is no one so dangerous and powerful as one who receives empowerment from the wisdom of others and seeks to prove its validity in their own lives by actually living out that wisdom. Dickinson perhaps never became a complete master of any of his endeavours, but he and his wife created a modest home that personified the Arts and Crafts principles. Frank Dickinson wrote an account of the building of Little Holland House, unpublished but available through the London Borough of Sutton, which bought the house in 1972 and maintain it today. Dickinson proclaims his commitment:

"There would have been little difficulty in securing an ordinary house in the usual way, with very much less money and labour, but I wanted a very particular house, a house that stood up by itself, without the help of its neighbour; a house with beautiful things inside, a house with a large garden, with fruit trees and a nice lawn. Above all, I wanted peace, pure air to breathe, the scent of flowers and the songs of birds. I also wanted things in my house that an artist and craftsman desires, and which the usual builder cannot supply or understand."

How far should I take this do-it-yourself approach of Dickinson? As a collector, I could save a lot of money if I purchased some clay and a wheel. My 'folk art' might look primitive, but as the Grandpa Moses of the ceramic world, its wobbly form and pathetic condition might even be considered charming. On the other hand, maybe we do need specialist potters that we subsidize. The idea of excellence is essentially elitist, difficult for a populist like me to accept. I do know I would never buy any pot I would make, probably couldn't even give it away to family members.

In defiance of my earlier discussion, I have decided to take full credit for the authorship of this letter. I don't owe anybody anything. No ambiguities here. The authors and sources I credited here were merely recipients of my generosity. Even John Ruskin and William Morris grabbed too much of the credit. I had thought of all their ideas, they just beat me to it. Whatever the biologists say about our genes, it is very important for humans to take credit, even more so for artists. I don't believe in cloning, people or art. Stick to the original. No computer could possibly make up these letters. A hint, Christa: some potters in history have written their signatures on the visible side of the vase, not the bottom. Go for it!

Just back and I received a brochure announcing a conference: "In Full Flower: The Arts and Crafts Movement in the San Francisco Bay Area". Occurs next month, June 19-22. Great people participating, authors of many of the books I have read regarding the arts and crafts of California. What is it about the Arts and Crafts movement that continues to make it so meaningful to so many? The life of the retired professor and active collector is so exhausting. Judy made conference and airline reservations on the internet. Maybe we can get a chance to have lunch or dinner during that time. Take care - I hope things are going well for you.

Your friend,

Richard

Sixteen

June 23, 2003

Dear Christa,

Very busy putting the last plants in the ground before the heat of summer. Observing the long line of people waiting for the morning opening of the Spring sale at the arboretum and Huntington Gardens reinforces my hopes for the future of human civilization. What a harmless and pleasant endeavor, what a wonderful result to share with others. I have never met angry or hostile people in a garden. Many have brought their children's red play wagons and various kinds of carts to carry the plants. They scurry from booth to booth, multitudes of people seeking some favorite or rare plant for that particular spot in their garden. I move with them from the succulents to the perennial areas, then on to the shade plants, trying to keep in mind the few empty corners left in my garden, but inevitably buying too many plants for the sun when I really need more plants for the shade. I pick out the small potted plants, optimistic about their future growth once in the ground. Others lug huge containers with fully grown plants, impatiently seeking instant rehabilitation of their garden. We are for the most part amateur gardeners, asking each other and other nearby strangers about the needs and characteristics of unknown plants that excite our interest. The amateur is not highly regarded in most endeavors in our society, although others are dependent on us for their profit. Can you tell an amateur pot from a professional one?

How do you feel about amateur potters? Paul Greenhalgh, in his book, "The Persistence of Craft", explains his mixed feelings about the amateur in the crafts:

" A central issue throughout the century, and one which is still vibrantly current, is that of the relationship of the professional with the vast numbers of amateur craftspeople. Understood as those groups who engage with some form of making on a part-time, non-specialist or hobbyist level, amateurism is an important element in all the arts. There is nothing pejorative in describing areas of practice amateur, of course. The enthusiasm and commitment of those who

97

engage physically with the arts is vital to their maintenance and dissemination. But in many ways the amateur sphere in the crafts has come to symbolize the whole. Craft as a word does not immediately and automatically conjure up an image of works of high excellence displayed in marbled halls; it is as likely to materialize images of wooden stalls crammed with baskets, pots and jars of jam under a canvas awning. Craft has been portrayed as a pleasurable way of filling time, or alternatively as a subsistence practice that is done alongside other things."

Greenhalgh goes on to discuss the 19th century ideas of John Ruskin that the making of crafts was in itself the sign of a humane society and therapeutic for all engaged in the autonomous craft activity. Greenhalgh concludes this discussion with his reservations that amateur craftspeople, pleased with their own products, fail to appreciate and purchase the work of professional craftspeople and have vastly different attitudes and purposes.

"In an affirmation of process over product, amateur craft is to do with the need to physically engage with things in an overly pre-packaged world. It is a vital element in any healthy society, but it is not the same thing as the obsessive, intense search that is central to the professional sphere. The former is to do with injection of the subjective self into objective phenomena, the latter is to do with the objectification of subjective impulses. The former strives for locality and the latter universality of consciousness. The real difference is in the way the work is situated, and in the research conducted."

I am an amateur collector. I do not even attend estate sales or auctions. I am insecure and indifferent about competing, and lack complete knowledge about one single specialized area of pottery or porcelain. I have big books on these things, but I tend to read all sections with the same amount of interest and intensity. I do not have the passion to own all the examples of any one kind of thing. I do not need to establish a monopoly or dominate a single category of pottery. I do not particularly value great rarity. I can't afford to develop that appetite. I value the well circulated virtues of the vernacular pot and the honest creative inventions of the serious potter. Size and elaboration are not necessary to capture my interest. The porcelain and pottery historically created for European aristocracy match their capacity for excess; decorations in rococo fantasies of color and form that justified the cost and projected their chronic indulgence. The great artistry of the result does not finally make them attractive to me.

I am not a pottery groupie. I do not have a personal relationship with a potter. I do enjoy a good conversation at the time of purchase if they are not too busy and seem interested. I do not wish to look over the shoulder of the potter, trying to uncover the particular techniques of the wheel. I am not interested in glaze recipes. What the potter does at the wheel, which I deeply respect, should remain a private act of the creative process. Perhaps the egoism of the collector involves the sense that we can look at the final product of that solitary creative experience and know if the integrity is evident in the character of the pot. It is the pottery I wish to encounter, and it is the pottery that fascinates me.

I am interested in the occasional manifesto or statement of the potter. Sometimes I am pleased with the sensitive insight or aesthetic and intellectual depth of the statement. I guess I need to believe that the best pots are made by the smartest potters. I do not wish to know too much about this, like all sacred belief systems, love of pottery ultimately requires mystery. As collector, I remain an outsider, implicitly believing that the impact of the collection as a total experience remains as aesthetically memorable as any individual pot within that collection. Tell me, Christa, do potters generally respect pottery outside their own tradition and personal style? Are collectors more tolerant of ceramic diversity of style than potters?

I do not know other collectors nor do I belong to any association of collectors. The people that know me do not collect pots. They are amused by my eccentric hobby. None of the homes of my relatives or friends have pots, maybe one or two vases to hold flowers. I seriously doubt if there are any other pottery collectors in Glendora. I was not born in a house of pots. I did not know a potter until I met my ceramics instructor at the university. The experience of making pottery did not excite me. I never took a pottery course again. I did not begin to collect pots until well into middle age. In my youth I collected stamps, certainly more convenient in taking up less space, and, unlike pottery, they collect little dust. Perhaps this profile of the anonymous and amateur collector is not very interesting or even typical. I do not know the research literature, if it exists, on pottery collectors and have no intention of finding or reading it. I do not need pottery to feel self-important or to advertise myself to friends or neighbors. Frankly I haven't met too many people that are interested or impressed with my pottery collection. They largely want to know the potential resale value of them on eBay. Usually when they visit me they don't spend much time looking at my pottery. I, on the other hand, spend a lot of my time looking at my pottery.

Unlike my former academic posture of supposed objectivity and neutrality, as a collector I can freely proclaim my biases without shame. I do not have to be fair and balanced in my appraisal of a potential pot, but rather activate my prejudices as the very basis for judgment. Without shame I declare the glorious limitations of arbitrary choice. I do not wish pottery to attain the status of the historical urinal or the more contemporary soiled British bed as seminal examples of modernist art. I do not want to sponsor the dubious products of gallery hustlers who want to find some mode of expression that demands the aesthetic denial of pottery as craft for the more sensational and profitable opportunities of pottery as 'art'. I do not want to be on the cutting edge of the calculated promotion of the potter/artist as eccentric radical and revolutionary. In the commercialized art world today artistic 'radicalism' is the privileged norm and often rewarded. True radicalism cannot be made up to increase gallery sales. It is never a calculated behavior in any field, but the normal condition of an ethical or aesthetic visionary who cannot accept the corrupt conventions of common practice. It is the antagonistic response of others who support that corrupt or conventional practice, in opposition to the dissenting behavior, that creates the radical. The attainment of the status of radical is not the purpose for the behavior. Nelson Mandela would have preferred the daily routine of his law practice and home to dinner with his family every night rather then twenty-eight years in an island prison.

I just don't believe some of the stuff I see posing as art can indeed be the extended products of a complex and subtle analysis of the corrupt or outmoded conventions of the powerful potters of the past. I do not wish to subsidize potters who want to join the sex-drugs-rock & roll media driven entertainment world that poses for culture in this society today. I do not wish to support those shards of clay, lumps of piled or cooked earth, whatever, that represent the forces of anti-pottery. There is so little in our constructed world today that can attain to the refined aesthetic of art, why should one deliberately create art as anti-art? In summary, I don't need potters trying to entertain me with absurd results that are supposed to represent the ironic absurdity of life but remain isolated in their absurdity because they are obvious and trivial. Lessons about human absurdity or pottery as critical commentary on past traditions require a sublime profundity and great talent.

I review the last few paragraphs and feel a bit uneasy. I do not wish to denigrate serious artists who find clay a suitable medium for explorations of abstract form. But I am not ready to acknowledge that my need for ceramic narrative or potential function is either reactionary or symptomatic of a personal pathology. What can be viewed as sentimental references to previous traditions can be a refined insight and disciplined reflection on the life cycle of the individual or culture. I too enjoy ironic statements and black humor. I have already confessed in previous letters that I prefer foreign films with indeterminate endings. My MA thesis was on collage, the assemblage of the waste products of industrial society to create new art. I am being defensive, trying to prove my aesthetic sophistication to you, at the same time I hesitate to endorse much of contemporary practice in the arts. I must remain humble, it is the proper posture of the amateur. Experts and specialists can provide cosmic proclamations and sponsor the latest gallery sensation. I can demonstrate my self-conscious preferences with those pots I purchase and invite into my home as permanent residents.

Susan Peterson, in her book, "Contemporary Ceramics" describes the background of my self-selected placement:

"Artists for whom symbolism and narration are important make huge efforts to find the best way to project ideas for the viewer. Some symbols are clearly spelled out, others are hidden in the cloak of form. Story-telling as a means of giving information through clay can be graphic or conceptual, ancient or contemporary; narrative ceramics are found throughout history, from the earliest works discovered in archaeological digs or exhibited in museums to the creations of the present day."

In partial defense of my ceramic taste, I view pots on my shelves that are abstract forms with a variety of glazes that have abstract designs or only the glaze itself. Admittedly, for the most part, they retain at least the outline of the potential container. It is simply as far off the path as I wish to go in my own ceramic journey. The attempt of some potters/artists to get on the 'fine art' bandwagon can be a reactive stance. Why the lack of self-confidence on the part of potters? Are there not inherent virtues and embedded integrity in the craft of pottery. Why aren't the painters attempting to emulate the virtues of the potter? Considering the state of painting today, this reverse transfusion of influence could be of great value.

I might as well provide a complete confession. I know you will never take anything I say seriously again but here it is, I prefer paintings that have frames. All my etchings and paintings have frames. I don't think the Guggenheim Museum in Bilbao had any paintings with frames. So here I am, hopelessly locked in obsolete references, remembering my youth as an art student, then appreciating the radical contribution of the French impressionists in their revolt against the stale convention of the official French academy and salon. My avant garde youth stopped somewhere around Andy Warhol. So I am a hopeless old man, living out my last days with framed pictures and container pots. I viewed the Tony Awards the other night. They have a category for 'revivals', plays brought back from the past, still relevant, still with meaning, still durable and of value. I think art works that way, only unofficially. My heirs will be ready for some future ceramic 'revival' if they hold on to my stuff long enough. Unfortunately, ultimate vindication will occur long after my demise. I am feeling better now. Forget the defensive comments of previous paragraphs.

What a contradiction! I celebrate my own outlaw status as a life long icono-clast yet refuse to acknowledge the creative force of outlaw artists that defy the calcified canons of their art or craft. How do I make sense of this? I guess the bottom line is quality. As an institutional outlaw, creating and teaching interdisciplinary curricula beyond disciplinary compartments, I continued to hone my craft, the pedagogical and intellectual skills tested and refined for over forty years in the classroom. I resisted the traditional curriculum because it was composed of the dry summaries of previous investigations by specialists that did not allow the dialectical exploration of the central issues of the human condition by students. The rigorous, analytical and critical discussion of ideas was not permitted. Students were simply judged not qualified to make sense of things. Despite my controversial status at the university, I was selected by a panel of my peers as 'professor of the year' in recognition of my efforts.

Again Paul Greenhalgh can be of help here. In his discussion of the question of quality, he states:

" A sense of decline in standards was promulgated; the idea was abroad that craftspeople across the media had somehow lost the plot, that they had feebly given up a higher heritage in order to wallow in one of several lower ones. Writers railed on about the need to 'return to' or 'rediscover' quality in technique and idea. Two evil places were identified as the abodes of failing craftspeople: the abyss of commercialism, in which makers sacrificed all to make a living; and (worse) the ghetto of bourgeois individualism, where they gave up the specific heritage of their disciplines to embrace a generalized and debased form of Fine Art practice. Skill was - and is - associated with the idea of quality. Skill has had a very mixed press within Modernist culture. Often interpreted as the perfection of mechanical techniques, it has been derided as limiting the potential of the mind to generate a truly liberated poetic vision. Skill has been associated with the measurable aspects of visual culture, a thing invented by academics and guilds to provide benchmarks and standards. While many defenders of the notion of skill in the visual arts have denied these limiting definitions, it remains a phenomenon marginalized by its apparent anti-cerebral intent. Craft and skill have often been used as interchangeable terms and this has undoubtedly under-mined the status of craft as a Modernist activity."

Greenhalgh concludes this discussion of quality in the crafts with comments I basically support and that reinforce my suspicions about much of what I see called craft in prestigious galleries.

"Quality is not to do with immutable models of value. It simply implies that any fabricated phenomenon, any thought, object, physical action, speech, or any other thing that is made, has the potential to be in a better or a worse condition. Quality denotes the constituency of a thing and confirms that it has this propensity, rather than being merely different from other things or its own previous condition. Quality is an a priori condition of art. Art is the realization that material has the potential to be raised into a higher state. None of us should tolerate the absence of quality."

Greenhalgh does not attempt to actually define the standards of quality here. Christa, I am sure you must have ideas about quality in pottery. Does it matter if an abstract expressionist painter drips or spills paint as a bravado example of the wide repertoire of talent, or drip-paints out of desperation because they lack the drafting skills to do otherwise? Should I demand a prerequisite demonstration of drawing skill before I permit the unbridled creativity of unrecognizable worlds? Should I demand a pot from the aspiring potter/artist before I can accept shapes and forms that could not hold my morning coffee or a bouquet of flowers? I am not even going to try some absolute or authoritative definition of quality regarding pottery. Exactitude and expression, precision and passion, discipline and freedom, originality and tradition, stability and surprise, economy and elaboration, elegance and humor, innovation and continuity; all potential virtues, possible in infinite combinations. I marvel at the little ceramic orange provided by my granddaughter that sits on my bedroom dresser. The message on the side of the orange, "To Grandpa with Love", makes it the most valuable ceramic object in the house. The assignment of value and quality cannot be finally agreed upon. The recognition of quality in pottery, like the presence of pornography, becomes apparent when viewed but unconvincing when described.

Originality is not only being the first one to do something, it is doing it better than anyone else has ever done it. The excellence of the individual result provides its particular uniqueness. The pathologies of the private personality of the potter deserve the attention of the latest medication and professional therapist, it is not the basis of the potter's art. I call this the Van Gogh ear problem; within the cocoon of popular culture, individuals mistakenly credit sexual dysfunction, emotional instability or drug addiction as the inspiration and source of art. Self-destruction more often displays instability rather than aesthetic sensitivity. Spontaneous expression is not often the messenger of great meaning or significance. Extensive experience and dedicated practice finally allow the uninterrupted flow of mastery. The arrogance of not only sharing your object with others but putting a price tag on it and getting others to purchase it implies that your private catharsis in clay is worth something to others. That conceit surely should represent a very special person and pot. Excellence is rarely an accident or a surprise. I do not want the potter to be more interesting or excellent than the pot.

How can I celebrate the amateur, who will never achieve the supreme quality of the professional, yet rail against the professional who, in experimenting with creativity, achieves tentative and inferior results? I value the courageous curiosity and audacity of the amateur, yet would restrain the professional to areas they know best, only permitted to produce finished products for my future collection. Complete containers of mastery, nothing less. For the amateur, tentative explorations without final results, ambiguous explorations on a life-long pilgrimage; for the professional, classic and durable objects that can only accrue in value. I am not going to try to talk myself out of this discrepancy, just think about it some more.

Both amateur and professional are capable of quality because quality has something to do with character and intention as well as result. I paid respect and tribute to the flawed struggles of my students in their hesitant approximations. I forgave youth most indiscretions. I find it difficult to credit the mature professional, particularly if they are successful and personally profit from their talent. I suspect the successful pot is part of the maneuver, the finished object as the strategy of calculated ambition. The successful icon or object as cultural commodity provide superior sales. The calibration of the quality of films with their box office sales is not an indication of quality but it surely motivates film as product. What motivates pots as product? I suspect success in the culture often has nothing to do with quality or excellence. It is a major prejudice of mine. It is often unfair, but persists in my nature. I must share blame with this culture, which has provided me with so many examples to reinforce my bias. My collection is not filled with amateur pots but professional ones. I do collect the resumés of potters, I do expect numerous citations of exhibitions and honors. I do demand much of them. I cannot reconcile all these thoughts and feelings. I can only take comfort in the thoughts of Ralph Waldo Emerson in his essay, "Self-Reliance":

"A foolish consistency is the hobgoblin of little minds, adored by little statesmen and philosophers and divines. With consistency a great soul has simply nothing to do. He may as well concern himself with his shadow on the wall. Out upon your guarded lips! Sew them up with packthread, do. Else if you would be a man speak what you think to-day in words as hard as cannon balls, and tomorrow speak what to-morrow thinks in hard words again, though it contradict every thing you said to-day. Ah, then, exclaim the aged ladies, you shall be sure to be misunderstood! Misunderstood! It is a right fool's word. Is it so bad then to be misunderstood?"

Emerson is a long time friend of mine and the generalist. His essay, "The American Scholar" was required reading in the interdisciplinary program I led at the university. Emerson, who never taught at a university, urged the inclusive development of a general intelligence:

"The scholar is that man who must take up into himself all the ability of the time, all the contributions of the past, all the hopes of the future. He must be a university of knowledges. If there be one lesson more than another which should pierce his ear, it is, The world is nothing, the man is all; in yourself is the law of all nature, and you know not yet how a globule of sap ascends; in yourself slumbers the whole of Reason; it is for you to know all, it is for you to dare all."

Without getting too self-conscious, even these words on the page must be exposed as amateur efforts. I am not a professional writer, never been compensated for past efforts, published only in a few pedantic and obscure academic journals. I have been writing my whole life, delivered papers to national and international conferences; employed language as speaker, consultant, teacher and employ language as social being. Do I deserve some consideration or clemency because of my humble status? Surely I must demonstrate some traits of refined wisdom. Does the love of language and ideas compensate for the absence of professional polish? All the references and quotations from books and periodicals are obtained from my library shelves. I would never go to the library for research for these letters. This correspondence must be hand-crafted, from the materials available within my domestic site. I work from my house. I wouldn't cheat. Amateurs have standards too.

The amateur cannot be duplicated or franchised. Voices independent of official sponsors and career insecurities, they are idiosyncratic spirits that form multiple voices. First person voices that are not embarrassed by the naivete and romance of their passionate pursuits. Innocence and idealism are often the sweet partners of amateur explorations. Without resumé or public office, refreshing honesty untethered by institutional placement can lead to insights that challenge more official conventions. Historically, amateurs were the 'folk' that professionals taped and recorded for prosperity. The authentic provincialism of indigenous communities represent and preserve local culture and regional history. These democratic variations and diversity of folk that sing, dance, tell stories, and create pots without self-conscious guile create communities and culture. Their contributions provide the resources for professional composers, musicians, artists and craftspeople to emulate, absorb and integrate in their own work. For the amateur, the passions of discovery are not segmented by the time of day;

their curiosity not bound by the limitations of a job description. Their art, their homes and their life are inseparable.

We amateurs are many things. We sing our multiple identities. We are generalists, laypersons, citizens of the republic, collectors of cultural artifacts, public intellectuals, active learners, celebrated in the rhetoric of this democratic society; yet in practice denigrated in culturally toxic terms as dilettante, journeyman, hobbyist, jack-of-all trades, utility infielder in late innings; without complete authority and expertise; seeking patterns of interdependence in a society that values isolated expertise; crossing boundary lines in subversive strategies to communicate with communities that do not resemble our own origins or identity. Dare I speak to potters without the film of clay on my fingers, dare I reach across the decades to the young woman potter only briefly introduced? What effrontery, what gall, my amateur status can only earn contempt. I invade foreign taxonomies, unknown territory controlled by specialists, and I occupy them with my energy and curiosity. I retreat only when I have appropriated meaning, connected subject to context, and questioned insular authority. I bring exotic gifts from other worlds into the domain of the master potter. In return, you provide the sublime excellence of your refined craft. I think it is a fair exchange.

Your amateur friend,

Richard

Seventeen

July 9, 2003

Dear Christa,

We have much to celebrate. I was so pleased to share your company in two recent events. In the July 2 issue of the San Francisco Chronicle newspaper, reporter Angelica Pence wove my correspondence to you in the story about your ceramic achievements. I do not intend to retract any part of her quotation of my thoughts regarding this outstanding young potter whose work "…was strong, restrained, disciplined and subtle".

Your printed comments do indeed reflect your serious commitment, "Just as scales provide a vocabulary with which musicians can speak to each other, there are rules to making functional pots. I like to think that my work reflects a system of parts that strike a chord. Clarity, as well as harmony, is essential in the attachment of handles, the fit of lids (and the) curve of spouts."

I am grateful that my comments as the concluding statement in the article reinforces the substance of your thoughts that a vessel should be as useful as it is beautiful.

"Christa is working within a tradition (where) the pot still acts as a container, a functional object," he says. "That is a tradition that is not hot or trendy, but it's a persistent tradition. It's a noble tradition."

While it seems a bit impertinent to quote myself in this letter, I will permit myself the indulgence on this occasion. As collector, I intend to ultimately claim some authority on the ceramic excellence of Christa Assad. I too enjoyed the validation that came with the publication of my words.

The second shared triumph came at your recent work at Anderson Ranch. Imagine my surprise when I received a telephone call from a Glendora Police Sergeant who attended your ceramic workshop there. He related his great appreciation for your instruction. He also described your lecture/presentation to the entire community where you used my letters as the background for your talk. He came over to the house and I gave him a personal tour of the collection. He intends to retire shortly after thirty years on the force and devote himself full time to making pottery. I was quite pleased when you filled in details of your presentation and the positive response of people. Your faith in the value of these letters and your willingness to use them in an event important to your reputation and future did not go unnoticed. One central purpose of my letters, aside from the invaluable wisdom you regularly receive, was served in your presentation. That purpose involves the support for the continued success of your efforts as a potter. In addition, my letters help me to focus and clarify my own disposition and attitude as a collector. Lastly, for other interested people that might eventually read them, the letters attempt to explore and understand the cultural context and aesthetic principles represented in the struggle of potters to achieve contemporary standing and recognition. This is based on my given assumptions that potters, as craftspeople and artists, are fully capable of engaging the central aesthetic issues of our time, and that the conscious self-placement of the potter in relationship to those ideas is finally reflected in the quality of the pottery. I am totally untroubled that the reader might start and end this experience with completely different and even conflicting thoughts that contrast with my own.

You are not the only wonderful potter I know. During my annual visits to the Ojai Music Festival, I encountered Frank Massarella, owner of Firehouse Pottery in Ojai. Frank went to UCLA, apprenticed in all aspects of production pottery, came to Ojai and purchased an old fire house that is now his studio and gallery. He invites other distinguished potters to exhibit their work in the gallery. Frank and you share many hopes, worries and ambitions. He is determined to do serious and creative pottery, pay his bills and maintain the business. This reminds me of a determined young potter in San Francisco. As an outsider, I assume that all potters know each other and, like police and firemen, you all go bowling together, share the fruits of the backyard barbecue, have your secret language, recognize each other in a crowd, and interbreed to maintain group solidarity. But in case I am mistaken about any of this, and you don't know him, I sent him a copy of the article in the Chronicle and bragged about you to him.

I first became aware of Elaine and Tom Coleman at the Firehouse Gallery. Their pottery was on display, some they did together, some Tom did by himself. Along with the pottery, copies of a book, "Mud-Pie Dilemma: A Master Potter's Struggle To Make Art and Ends Meet" by John Nance, described the ceramic struggles of the Colemans. What made this book special was that this book was the second edition, with a closing chapter, 'Twenty-Five Years Later' describing the Coleman fortunes a quarter of a century after the first edition was published. The first edition involves Tom Coleman getting ready for a show that was to open in Seattle in 1977. He was 32 years old at that time, the same age as you are today. The narration is an honest observation of the daily struggles of the Colemans, with appropriate swear words and Tom's love of an occasional beer fully reported. Maybe making pots is like making sausage and making laws, really ugly to see and better not observed by customers, citizens and clients. Nance reports:

"Coleman started reducing the upper thickness. His right hand seemed to float on the outside, tips of index finger and thumb grazing the clay while the other fingers occasionally squeezed a palmed sponge. This released streaks of water that widened into dark bands as they encircled the bowl. Coleman's left hand was completing a pass inside when an overhead light dimmed for a moment...an electric power fluctuation. The wheel twitched, the thin wall of clay wavered - possibly snagging on a fingertip or knuckle - and produced two barely perceptible slumps, first in the bowl and then in Coleman's shoulders. 'Damn it!' he yelled and sat silent. After more curses, he horse-laughed and slapped the crippled pot flat and then into a mound."

I want a full confession of your behavior at the wheel. Do you curse when the wall of a pot crumbles? Are you so good that nothing bad ever happens? Do you sweat a lot when you work at the wheel? It occurred to me that some celebrity potter could do deodorant commercials and make a fortune, analogous to the smiling basketball player and his magic tennis shoes. Is the mastery of the excellent potter obvious at the wheel? What do you think of when you're throwing a pot? Maybe its my ageing bladder, but it just occurred to me that you can't stop in the middle of throwing a pot and go to the bathroom. Well, can you? What about those great moments when everything works right and that soft, wet and wonderful object, so tender and fragile that a bump will destroy it, sits there in front of you in all its majesty? Do you know? Do you experience the profound joy of that moment, the culmination and triumph of the just completed pot? Surely this creative act forms the very rhythm of your life as a potter? I dimly remember those feelings from my artist days as a youth and now feel a twinge of envy.

The full richness and terror of ordinary life for a potter is all on the page in "Mud-Pie Dilemma". Tom's health is not so good, he is not making a lot of money, doesn't have time to travel except to shows, fairs, galleries that simply drain him of energy. On top of all that, the essential struggle to get away from production stuff to really creative stuff is present every day.

"Oh sure - I'd love to make some pots just for myself. Now these I'm making will be good, but to make things strictly for me, well, hell, now that would really be something. But hardly anybody gets to do that.' What would he make? 'I don't know. I'd take a year at least, like a sabbatical. No telling what I'd do - test myself, I imagine, try some new things. I do some of that now, but I make only small discoveries, important just to me, like how far to push this clay or what that glaze will do. Sure I'd love to have a year without shows and sales and all the stuff that pays the bills.' He paused, then added, 'I don't mean our functional stuff isn't good - it is - but I've done all that for years, over and over and over. I can do some of that stuff and watch TV at the same time. It's true, I do.' So why not do more experimental work? 'I've tried, but you've got to be free and loose. You need lots of time to just experiment and play around. We've got too many bills for that.'"

How do you rationalize or justify your own creativity and experimentation? After paying the mortgage or gas bill, maybe one or two pots that try something new? The best of all worlds is to have your daily work match your own aesthetic dreams and standards, when each day's work is not a compromise, but on your own terms. How many potters reach that exalted state when this is possible for them? How do you react when people buy the production stuff in preference to your own favored pot? I remember when I visited the home/studio of Mary Fox, a great potter in British Columbia, Canada. Actually I woke her up some time in the morning by knocking on the door (collectors are desperate people!) and she good-naturedly showed me her recent work. I immediately reacted to a plump yellow bowl but she sort of nudged me, said something about that being her 'bread and butter stuff', and pointed me toward a stunning vase with a tapering shape that was anchored in a small base. Her pride in that vase was evident, and it became my proud possession. I of course take full credit for the choice when visitors review my collection.

I am beginning to understand the drama of the countdown to triumph or tragedy - the fateful results of that crucible of fire - the avenging angel that the kiln represents in the life of the potter. Whatever the talent or technique employed by the potter - the kiln can destroy the products of their genius with arbitrary caprice. It represents the great gamble and risk - the hours of toil and the achievements at the wheel, the delicate form and subtle decoration, all placed in the kiln in the ultimate mystery that cannot give assurance or warranty. Whatever the advanced technology of the kiln, however experienced the potter, there is no safe petition to protect pots from the harsh and extreme torture that blasts them with searing flame. No pot is safe, no pot has a future until rescued from that hell box, cooling in fragments, cracked or joyfully whole.

I know of no other art or craft where the artisan is forced to surrender their work to such a crucial and severe test. There must be secret ceremonies, perhaps derived from various religious traditions, good luck charms, some gestures or chant just before placing those objects at the mercy of the fury of that fire god or just before the kiln door is opened to reveal heartache or joy. Some emerging ceramic theology must explain the shattered and heat mutilated results as appropriate punishment for a sinful life full of misdeeds. Perhaps a series of good works, alms for charity or regular payments to alleviate some far off foreign misery would reduce the casualty rate of the kiln. Even the very word kiln terrifies me, this active and murderous beast which retaliates without reason or excuse with fatal malice. There probably should be some corresponding celebration, perhaps with music and dance, after the kiln door is opened and the contents are marvelously intact and glorious. I would recommend 'Also sprach Zarathustra' by Richard Strauss as a possible choice. It did wonders for the film '2001'. Obviously a good California wine would add to the gaiety. If the results are really good (and I'm invited to the kiln opening), I would suggest a superior single-malt Scotch whiskey.

The kiln does not make informed judgments about the quality of the pots within its control in determining their fate. Nor I fear does it take into account the virtues and moral conduct of potters who surrender their precious ceramic children to the fire within. Maybe the construction of the pot and the placement has something to do with the outcome, but nothing is promised and the results can be very unfair. While no standardized justice can exist or be established, the drama of the kiln firing does provide adventure and creative tension to the humdrum lives of the potter. The ceramic gods must be crazy however, to allow so many bad pots to survive and to destroy so many good ones. Quality is rare, and the odds of creating the excellent pot does not end at the wheel. If you could reduce the mortality rate and find a safe way, you would also be ending that historical tradition of trial by fire that seems to me to be integral to the pain and joy that all good potters deserve.

Tom Coleman describes his reaction after opening the kiln:

"Think of the hours of work in there. Man, I tell you I didn't sleep all night - not a bit; laid there thinking about this kiln. I got up, came out here so damned keyed up I worked like a madman - over-dosed on tension or something - and decorated more pots in one day than ever in my life. Goin' crazy!... Babbling with delight, he was not disturbed by the pieces lost in the firing and said that such a high percentage appeared to have succeeded that he could not be upset... He showed me the pieces and said, 'I really like that pot, biggest one I ever made... oh well, sometimes you just lose 'em - hope you don't lose a lot. I just wish some people realized how hard this is. They just don't realize."

I know you can control and create the shape or form of the pot and take full credit for the success. But, honestly, don't you have to give the kiln at least partial credit for the results of the glaze? Is it entirely the results of your planned design, predictable and precise? Don't you just luck out sometimes, when the kiln becomes the co-author of unexpected and delightful results? Can you plan the surprise and give the kiln some choices in outcome or do you want to control everything? Can a good kiln make a potter look good? The use of glaze reveals the temperament of the potter more than anything else. From sensuous and spectacular rainbows of color to subdued subtlety - it exposes the nature of both pot and potter. The refined classical restraint that refuses decoration beyond the thin film of the glaze - what a decision! Does some incised design or portrayal of natural form represent sentimental excess? Could an argument be made that only when you actually draw and paint on the clay do you most resemble the fine arts of painting and drawing? I can embrace multiple traditions, but the intentions of the differing potters are aesthetically profound in their contrasting dissimilarity.

The existential issues of the mud-pie dilemma challenge every potter. They are not limited solely to activity at the wheel. How do you combine and balance the solitary hours at the wheel with loving and responsible relationships with family and a primary partner? How can you make your pottery productive and profitable while still aspiring to excellence? How do you compete with the glut of amateur and commercially savvy potters who cater to the lowest popular taste with their ceramic soap dispensers and pretty floral pots? How do you maintain your dignity and integrity and still hustle the galleries, collectors, and walk-in customers? How do you struggle to get better and better when it might appear that no one else even seems to notice and no one else seems to give a damn?

Twenty-five years later, in the last chapter, the photographs in the book show an older, more weathered Tom Coleman, still working with great intensity and determination, successful but wanting to risk possible rejection and failure by making that final effort to reach the very pinnacle of his art. Where do you want to be in twenty-five years, Christa? Do you have a plan? What will your pots look like then? Who tells you when you have achieved that final excellence? Will it still be fun, still exciting? Is there much room at the top? I am amazed at the sheer duration, the extreme longevity of many creative potters. Be it Beatrice Woods or Otto Heino, it seems that their lives were extended just to allow them to complete their life's work. Is there some nutritional or medicinal value in the dynamic life of the creative potter?

I read about potters, and meet them at their studios. I respect those potters who aspire to reach the full potential of their ability to create memorable art. I sense that this effort can never be fully realized because the obsession with excellence is necessary to do work that inevitably, no matter how good, always falls just short of that perfection. The excellent potter is never completely satisfied, however others might enthusiastically embrace their work.

I compare the commitment of Tom Coleman, Mary Fox, Frank Massarella, others, and certainly you, Christa Assad, with the tawdry display of much of so called 'fine art' in galleries today. Julian Spalding, critic, author, and former director of the Glasgow Museums and Galleries, recently wrote in his book, "The Eclipse of Art: Tackling the Crisis in Art Today":

"It is often maintained by the pundits of modern art that a urinal, or an ashtray or an unmade bed can legitimately mean what anyone looking at it wants it to mean. But the public are right to ask where is the art in that? They know perfectly well that they have no choice but to think their own thoughts when looking at such 'found objects' because it is impossible to feel about them, because they have not been changed by the artist in any way. They are still a urinal, an ashtray or an unmade bed, whether they are in an art gallery or not. The audience, far from being engaged in a debate, is in fact left totally at sea… You can debate whether something is art or not until the cows come home (or get sliced up) but art is not a language of debate. It is at once less than a language and more than a craft. Art is a language of expression and it manifests itself through craft."

If you accept the explanation of art that Spalding offers, then pottery can become art and the potter can become the artist. Spalding's insistence on the importance of craft in making art defies the art market today. The challenge for pottery is to successfully argue that the functional pot also contains aesthetic properties, a subtle language of form and decoration that enhances both function and statement. As with great paintings and sculpture, repeated trips to visit the same pot can still further inform and enhance you, still show you things that are only revealed after much time, patience and disciplined viewing. Great art has so many subtle secrets, so do many of my pots. I intend to be deserving of their gifts by paying very close attention to them.

I want to come full circle in this letter. Celebration is still in order. I can't think of a better way than giving you the last word. You might recognize the following quotation since I retrieved it from your website. It appears to me that it constitutes at least a part of your answer to 'A Master Potter's Struggle to Make Art and Ends Meet'.

"Making pots provides a few very important things for me: discipline, including regular physical and mental exercise; a measure of creativity and productivity; and a role in history as artisan. The choice to pursue potting as a profession came as a bit of a surprise to me at first, but now seems the ideal solution to the puzzle of life. It satisfies the athlete, the academic, and the connoisseur in me alike. I can be my own boss, make my own inventory, and connect with those who buy and use my work. Along with the rewards, there are many lessons to be learned in patience, cooperation, and loss."

Bravo, dear friend,

Richard

Eighteen

Aug. 11, 2003

Dear Christa,

Is the glass (or pot) half-empty or half-full? Do we live in the best of times or the worst of times? Or do we agree with Dickens that both conditions exist at the same time? Is this the time to return to some tried and true values or is this the time to overthrow corrupt institutions and customs that represent the past? Have we lost our way or have we tolerated conformity for too long? Do we overthrow authority in our culture or do we restore the traditional rules? Are the standards for good pottery the same as for a good society?

I am receiving too many negative messages, most of them depressing. The newspapers and TV share and divide attention between the domestic homicides in our American cities, which appear normal and commonplace in their daily regularity, and the greater mystery overseas of attacks on uniformed victims by believers of foreign faiths with unknown grievances. Popular journalism, efficiently disseminated to my home each day, provides vivid images and words that portray bloodied bodies and frightened, angry people on the edge of disaster. I feel the need to hide out and take refuge but as a matter of conscience I cannot break away from the daily narration of human crimes and failed civilization. Does making pottery in bad times make sense? How do you justify ceramic indulgence when it might distract you from greater human needs? If people need bread, why give them clay? Shouldn't all potters abandon their wheels and join the army or the Peace Corps?

Collectors are conservative in that they need security and stability to maintain and preserve their precious hoard of loved objects. There is some inherent belief or illusion in historical continuity or we would not seek to conserve objects beyond their immediate time and use. We hope that the future custodians of our wares will replicate our own passion in perpetuating our possessions. I place an antique vase next to a contemporary one, pleased at the juxtaposition of longevity and promising future. Why do I collect both the old and new? How can I justify obsolete or passé aesthetic expressions sitting next to modern and experimental ones? This leads me to a late-life crisis regarding my basic temperament and world view. My preferred self-description would assure the profile of a progressive and dynamic person, embracing new experiences and ideas while still appreciating the past traditions that stabilize our lives. But this grumpy old man is not so sure of that self-serving advertisement. I need to pull a particular rabbit out of the hat - politically and socially progressive but culturally conservative in regard to much contemporary artistic production. I'm just not sure I can pull this off.

I hesitate to join Jacques Barzun, another grumpy old man, as he laments the decline of Western civilization in his recent book, "From Dawn to Decadence - 500 Years of Western Cultural Life". Here truly is an integrated conservatism in action as the end of the book takes us to our present reality - and concludes with both whine and whimper. Barzun explains the impact of war on the artist:

"They represented on canvas or in stone, wood, or metal human beings in dehumanized form - body parts twisted, amputated, emaciated, background and accessories revolting, coloring and texture mortuary. At one exhibition in New York the artist produced the ultimate model by painting his body green and lying nude in an open coffin. Since then an English painter has chosen as his medium excrement. They have a good pretext for their offerings in the physical and moral destruction of war. No imagining of disfigured faces and torn bodies and ruined landscapes could rival what firepower does ... "

I do not know if you feel the need for political and artistic protest, but you could possibly emulate the English painter described by Barzun and substitute excrement for clay and truly provide a stunning statement. I assume that excrement does not have the resilience to withstand the kiln but don't know if it has been tried. I fully expect you to give me full credit if you attempt this innovative experiment. It is after all a short sequence from mud to clay to excrement, the hands of the rebellious potter plunge into the material regardless. I remember long ago when my two infant sons emptied their diapers and made a beautiful mural on the exterior of the house in the backyard. The sun proved to be a remarkable adhesive, quite difficult to remove. My own experience in this episode does not inspire me to collect excrement art, although many pots I have rejected in the past often look like they were, or should have been, made of that substance.

Barzun goes on to describe the impact of war on the nature and quality of art:

"Given the several ways of modernist art it is logical to conclude that the production of things to see and read is not a rare or special gift. It is populistically distributed to all or nearly all. For one thing, some of the genres such as Found Art do not require long study or much practice. For another, the unimportance of subject matter eliminates the need for psychological or other truth in the work. In other words, the demand for genius has died out."

Here I tend to agree with Barzun that wars produce art in all media that is often cynical and without hope, conveying a death-wish for the very art form that preceded them in their shattered rejection of past practice. I also agree that the elimination of subject matter can also mean the elimination of meaning.

Barzun, inherently suspicious of the welfare state, which has included the emancipation of women, racial minorities and the working class with rights that include pensions for the elderly and health benefits for all, decides that much of the egalitarian reform of the last century was unwise and integral to the current state of decadence:

"The late 20thC welfare states of the West are not Communist Russia or Seville in the 16thC, but some of the aims and devices are not unlike. The desire for security on the part of the population is the same, coupled though it is with a desire for freedom. This combination . . . is self-contradictory and probably unworkable."

So I cannot join Barzun in his all encompassing indictment of modern life, but stop at the artist's studio door, nodding with him about much of what happens inside that room, and wondering if my aesthetic agreement there provides support for political ideologies I do not favor elsewhere. Of course I want freedom for all, potters included, but I also want order and stability. I really want and expect people to voluntarily impose on themselves the iron cage of regulated freedom, with the state controlling the plundering corporations against excessive profit and exploitation. I want potters to explore and experiment, but to have the good taste to restrain themselves. I want to be surprised but not shocked. God, is it possible I am conventional after all?! The basis of humor is the ability to laugh at oneself. I have a highly developed sense of humor. I fear I would police the human soul and imagination every bit as severely as my puritan ancestors or the political and cultural reactionaries that now dominate our society. What is liberal and progressive in my oppressive platform is the insistence that this discipline be voluntary and self-imposed. I am temporarily ashamed but hope to recover in the next few paragraphs.

I tend to read a dozen books at one time, seeking patterns and meaning in the active integration with other sources and previous knowledge. Another history, another book, weaves a story that does not end with pessimism and decadence for the author. Paul Rice, in "British Studio Ceramics" surveys the history of British studio ceramics since about 1900. I know that you have spent considerable time in England and are very familiar with ceramics there. Rice is a native American who has lived in England for several decades and has written several books on British ceramics. He claims that, although London was never the centre of modern art in the same way as Paris or New York, Britain led the world for much of the twentieth century in studio ceramics.

Rice credits two reasons for this ceramic prominence - one is the long historical ceramic tradition going back in Britain to medieval times, the other reason is Bernard Leach. He looms like a giant over the ceramic landscape, and as with all giants, attempts to topple him were persistent. He has remained to this day the essential reference point to emulate or to repudiate. He cannot be ignored. As Rice reminds us:

"His influence on modern ceramics parallels and even exceeds that of Pablo Picasso on modern painting. Leach's pots, ideas, books and students have left their mark on every corner of the ceramic world."

Rice sponsors a discussion about pricing pots. Although his subject is Richard Batterham, the issues are there for every potter.

"Initially, Batterham's work was made in large quantity and sold at low prices as domestic ware in craft shops and smart kitchen shops. Over the years, he has reduced production and included more 'individual' pots at somewhat higher prices. While this has obviously meant less dinner plates and more large pots, the nature of his work is fundamentally unaltered."

In this discussion Rice remarks that:

"The difference between an 'individual' potter, Hans Coper, for example, who makes many similar pots in refining a shape and a 'repetition' potter, such as Batterham, is not as great as is often supposed. Whether one labels pots as domestic ware or individual pots is unimportant. All that really matters is the life and quality they have."

Do all potters start off as humble 'repetition' potters making stacks of domestic ware? And slowly work yourself up to that dramatic risk of doing far less work for far more money? Is the big difference, aside from ego and ambition, the fact that some potters are graduates of prestigious university departments or art schools, mentored by famous potters, while others start as humble apprentices in somebody's studio? I would like to think, at that crucial moment of the business transaction - to buy or not to buy, that I am far more impressed with the quality of the pot rather than the modest price. There are difficult merchandising questions for both buyer and seller. Perhaps a scale should be installed in the gallery and pottery sold by the pound. Small pots, except for those by very famous potters, tend to cost less. I have talked to a few potters who are frustrated that other potters, perhaps at an adjoining booth at some pottery fair or show, somehow get a far higher price for pots they insist are not any better than their own. I do have some standards - I will not purchase a pot I do not like - no matter the bargain price. Now, due both to my modest financial situation and the few remaining spaces left on my shelves, I am selective in adding only quality pots to my collection. When do potters raise their prices? Is the quality of the pot and the increasing reputation of the potter the basis for increased price? Or is it all a bluff? Raise prices, cut down on production and hope people will be so impressed with the high prices that they will also be impressed with the pottery? As a collector, I do hope that my enthusiastic appraisal of your pottery in these letters will not be the cause for you to further raise your prices. There must be some consumer psychology behind all this. Perhaps you should consult people who manufacture and sell footwear or fast food hamburgers to discover the successful marketing principles involved.

I do expect my potters to outperform stocks and bonds - no downward fluctuation, please - steady and sure accrual of worth as potters and the value of their pots mature over time. It is morbid to relate, but it appears that your future demise, after a lengthy and successful career, of course, will provide the big spike in increased value for your pots. Despite all that, I do sincerely wish you a very long and productive life. At my age, I will appear in the obituaries far sooner than the precious young potters represented in my collection. What determines the prices at estate sales? Oh, well, I won't have to worry about that; Judy will have to sort that out.

I suspect most potters trying to make a living have done and are still doing both 'repetition' and 'individual' pottery. To label some ceramic objects 'domestic ware' while others are called 'art pottery' seems a terrible fall from grace and obviously contains much cultural prejudice. When you place a Picasso or Matisse in your living room over the fireplace or sofa, doesn't that become 'domestic ware'? The furniture of Stickley and the Greene brothers that formed the dining room set, the wallpaper of William Morris that covered the walls of manor houses and most of the rooms in my own home are precious possessions in museums; all these things are artifacts of the domestic site. This discussion becomes as mysterious as when I seek to determine when food becomes cuisine.

It must have more meaning than simply the higher prices and reduced portions when advertised in that manner on the restaurant menu or in the yellow pages. I wonder if this chronic and historical undervaluing of the so-called domestic or decorative arts in America has to do with the home as the traditional site (or prison) of women. I fully agree with Rice when he states:

"Devotees of the 'fine arts' argue that ceramics is a minor art form that lacks the profundity of painting or sculpture. I would refute that. Great works of art in almost any medium are infinitely profound and any lack is in our ability to see and feel what is there. No such problem exists in the East where ceramics are considered to be at least as important as any other art form."

I will be leaving you now. As a retired person who can schedule each day by whim, without imposed appointments or exactly timed duties, I contrive each day in an ad-hoc pattern to suit myself. Cleaning out the fish pond in the morning, working in the garden, dusting pottery and furniture, vacuuming carpets and mopping tile floors, adding some lines to this letter to you, perhaps a brief nap after lunch, spells of classical music and reading in the afternoon, a much deserved shot of Scotch at 4 o'clock (sometimes I cheat, about 3:45), a foreign film on DVD in the evening. A daily, somewhat bizarre combination of routine and pedestrian household chores interspaced and broken by periodic encounters with the sublime evidence of human genius and civilization. All waking hours, whatever the task at hand, are suitable for meditation and reflection. At times I have abruptly stopped some mundane activity and hurried to the computer to add a thought or two to one of my letters. Writing my thoughts on the computer screen and their eventual circulation to you make them seem more important.

Whatever Barzun might say, "From Dawn to Decadence" will never describe the character of my day or the evolution of your pottery.

Take care, your friend,

Richard

Nineteen

August 23, 2003

Dear Christa,

August is the cruellest month of all in Southern California. This August is living up to that reputation. The sheer heat discourages my departure through the front door. Regardless of my public policy position regarding the conservation of energy, the thermostat in the hallway remains fixed and the faint hum of the air conditioner outside reassures the continuation of civilization inside. I do not know if snow in other weather zones has the same restraining capacity. Cabin fever can be the experience shared by both climates. I love my home but prefer the accessibility of other options. Do potters have the same occupational hazards as bakers? Do you feel the heat from the kiln? Don't you ever wish you had taken up ice sculpture?

I must remind myself that people travel from distant lands to luxuriate in this heat and broil themselves on the sand to achieve a bronze skin that can only lead to an increased possibility of wrinkles and cancer. People who work near the kiln must be somewhat like those people who work in laundry and dry cleaning establishments. If you know that the heat is going to be unrelieved and with no possibility of escape, it must then somehow become tolerable. I once worked in a supermarket when a young student. The owners resisted air-conditioning, then just becoming available, with the overheard remark that the workers' comfort would be an unacceptable cost. People born in a certain climate must have a natural ability to cope with it. I am not sure that we are all that adaptable. Global warming should certainly test that. I do want your pottery to cool before you give it to me. I enjoy the cool, sometimes cold, smooth surface of the pot and assume that it could have never have been otherwise. People are very warm to the touch. Maybe that's the reason they don't last as long as pottery.

Do you ever hit a dry spell in your creative energy? Times when manipulating that clay becomes sheer drudgery? How do you trick yourself in getting through this ebb in effort and morale? When it becomes just work, how often do you dare to escape? I celebrate my own self-discipline, that voluntary misery whose discomfort has to be rationalized as an incremental investment in the future or the possibilities of a pleasant after-life. Americans have considerably less vacation time than all other industrialized, democratic countries. Europeans enjoy paid holidays of about six weeks of the year, Americans get maybe one week. There is no mass protest. We have nothing better to do with our time. I am not sure a culture that does not have a joyful aesthetic for life can have a meaningful aesthetic for ceramics.

Ellen Goodman, in the 'The Washington Post' section of the British "Guardian Weekly" newspaper (Aug.20, '03), provides her opinion:

"Americans have always been a touch suspicious of leisure. Our Puritan patriarchs not only famously regarded idle hands as the devil's workshop, they believed the grindstone cleared the path to salvation. We've long been wary of both the idle rich and the idle poor as threats to our democracy... Now we arrive at the summer of the incredible shrinking American vacation. It's predicted that we'll take 10 percent less time off than last year and last year was no week at the beach. Americans have notoriously fewer vacation days than workers in any other industrialized country. ... Americans do have a stunning capacity for turning everything into work."

The few free hours are spent with various forms of passive commercial entertainment. This cannot constitute culture, rather it is an escape from work and culture. It is a sedative for the over-worked and insecure American middle class who are just one illness or job layoff from destitution and poverty. European taxpayers subsidize culture because they value it; their museums, symphony orchestras, theater, art. Culture is essentially a public and civic activity, thus diminished in America where the private sector is all privileged and powerful. State support allows serious artists in all fields of creative endeavor to transcend the immediate need for profit and acceptance in the marketplace.

My conviction that entertainment can never constitute culture can only get me in trouble. I cannot forsake the great mass of my fellow humanity; I want them fed, housed, and educated. My values and politics demand public policy that will achieve those goals. But I must separate myself from most of them - and seek a more refined culture. Many whose company I join and keep in that search are cultural elitists and political reactionaries. Matthew Arnold is a wonderful example of my current predicament. His classic essay, "Culture and Anarchy", is a text that contemporary American conservatives dearly love. Arnold had much to say about culture in England in the 19th century. I find it perplexing why the American right wing is so infatuated with Arnold. Much of what he declares is in direct contradiction to their politics:

"The idea of our strong individualism, our hatred of all limits to the unrestrained swing of the individual's personality, our maxim of 'every man for himself.' The idea of perfection as a harmonious expansion of human nature is at variance with our want of flexibility, with inaptitude for seeing more than one side of a thing, with our intense energetic absorption in the particular pursuit we happen to be following ... Faith in machinery is, I said, our besetting danger; often in machinery most absurdly disproportioned to the end which this machinery, if it is to do any good at all, is to serve; but always in machinery, as if it had a value in and for itself. What is freedom but machinery? What are railroads but machinery? What is population but machinery? What are railroads but machinery? What is wealth but machinery? What are religious organizations but machinery?"

This rhetoric would hardly please the individualism, religious fundamentalism, and corporate power that presently control the politics of America. To make matters worse, he locates the final authority to determine standards in the centralized power of the state. What do they see in Arnold that causes them to celebrate him? The answer is that Arnold seeks a central authority to determine standards of culture, a single standard for all. Here he hopes to avoid the anarchy he saw in an England where the middle class and working class were demanding their rights and challenging the traditional agencies of the aristocracy and upper class. Some Americans view the emancipation in the last few decades of women and minorities as causing similar problems. The anarchy of multiculturalism and the escape of women from their domestic residence threatens the sacred domain of the family and the Western classical tradition. They recoil at the inclusion of texts by women and non-Western sources in the great 'canon' of traditional classics in our universities and see this as the dilution of our Western European traditions, and so they rally around the flag and Arnold.

Arnold defines culture as the...

"...pursuit of our total perfection by means of getting to know, on all the matters which most concern us, the best which has been thought and said in the world, and, through this knowledge, turning a stream of fresh and free thought upon our stock notions and habits, which we now follow staunchly but mechanically..."

We arrive at a quandary. The very definition of democracy implies diversity. Some would claim that democratic diversity only works in a heterogeneous society, where the racial and cultural similarities allow differences in opinion. How do we nurture and support cultural and political differences in a multicultural society where differences fragment and isolate us in separate communities? Tell me Christa, how can an 'Assad' and 'Jacobs' come together in agreement when our origins would not find us at the same site? Do the descendants of Leach and Voulkos co-exist or does one side have to triumph in order to establish stability and authority in ceramics?

Why should this be of concern to potters? If you want to achieve excellence, how do you predetermine what that excellence will look like? To paraphrase Arnold, what is the best that has been thought, said and created in ceramics? I assume you know when a pot achieves this level, and I assume that not every pot attains it. If I asked you to describe what the perfect pot would look like, would that description allow for only one answer, one perfect pot that in its specifics would not allow any pot that looked differently to achieve that same status? Do you seek to validate only one cultural tradition and one aesthetic when you declare the perfect pot? Do you cancel and nullify all potters who posses other definitions of perfection? The declaration of that template of perfection can be the most extreme form of intolerance. And yet, how can we strive for excellence without arbitrarily determining its content? Are the culture wars in ceramics as fierce and deadly as they are in the general culture? Does the authority of an aesthetic viewpoint have to posses absolute and monolithic authority to be creditable and valid?

The very title of the book, "Great Pots: Contemporary Ceramics From Function to Fantasy" by Ulysses Grant Dietz would imply that the definition of a great pot, the best pot, the superior pot, is available to Dietz. In the 'Foreword', Mary Sue Sweeney Price, the Director of The Newark Museum which forms the basis of the book, defines a very generous and democratic criterion for selection to the museum collection:

"From its founding in 1909, The Newark Museum has intentionally collected objects traditionally viewed as typical, even ordinary. Masterpieces were also collected, but - especially in the decorative arts - it was understood that masterpieces are far removed from the reality of most people and that typical, often common, examples of material culture can more eloquently express the way in which objects and everyday life interact in human culture."

This statement resonates of course with Morris and others in the Arts and Crafts movement. My humor in describing my own collection - 'The Richard C. Jacobs Collection of Medium Priced Art' tries to achieve the same effect. No trophies or masterpieces but objects in my everyday life that interact with me.

I think Arnold would be very upset at the sheer anarchy of my collection - $15.00 museum replicas, an 1875 Swedish plate worth about $1,000, an anonymous pot from a tribe in the Amazon rain forest, a Chinese mythological figure that once adorned an antique roof, etc., etc., all housed together, with no object in charge, all co-existing in a spirited aesthetic discourse, with no clear winner.

Dietz offers definite ideas about the excellent pot. At the beginning of the book there is a full page picture on the left side of a small cylindrical bowl. He starts the book and his discussion about a pot created by Ruth Kenly:

"This is a great pot. We no longer know who Ruth Kenly is. We know nothing of her training as a potter, or what influenced her craft. We know only that she lived in Short Hills, New Jersey, and that this bowl won first prize in the craft division of an arts festival held at The Newark Museum in 1959. We also know that the slip decoration was inspired by a pattern left on a window after her dog had licked it. We paid Mrs. Kenly $12.00 for the bowl in June 1959."

At this point, you must join me in total bewilderment. I look again at the picture of that small round pot. Trying to understand the enthusiasm of Dietz, I wonder and worry about how many times maybe I have walked by similar 'great pots' in galleries, ignoring their obvious beauty and failing to acquire them for eventual recognition and possible inclusion in some future book about great pots.

Dietz tries to be helpful - he starts to describe the glories of this pot:

"A first-rate pot need not be an 'important' pot. This pot deserves careful study because of the remarkable finesse with which the rich, grainy Steiner body is brought up to a smooth, perfect, thin wall. The slight outward flare toward the base and the sharply undercut foot show a master's control of the medium. It is a wonderful, satisfying shape, not too heavy and not too light. It is a joy to hold in one's hand. Ruth Kenly knew how to throw. She also knew how to glaze, and how to decorate a piece in a way that was elegant, balanced and harmonious. The silky mauve and blue slip with which the decoration is applied complement beautifully the rusty brown of the ground. The bold yet delicate brushstrokes of the calligraphic decoration are graceful and deftly poised between rim and base. It seems effortless, and yet it is achieved with an expert precision rare for an amateur potter."

Christa, I am really paying attention, looking back and forth across the open book and double pages of picture and text. I think I see what Dietz is talking about but not at all certain if I would ever have the same reaction and assessment if I didn't have his words to guide me. I resolve to have Dietz go with me on all future excursions to purchase pottery. Does Dietz agree with Arnold, that there is a single authority that can determine the best in culture? Or in pottery? Is he that very authority? Remember he didn't start the discussion with, "This is a great pot for me" or "It is my opinion, based on my own preferences, that this is a great pot." He said flatly, "This is a great pot." As the reader, and a small time collector, I do not have his permission to disagree. It must be a great pot.

Dietz continues the discussion, trying to win me over.

"While most museums and most collectors of contemporary ceramics might not look twice at Ruth Kenly's little pot from 1959, I hold it up to you as a work to be celebrated. It represents beauty, utility and wisdom. It does not startle or provoke, but it does give pleasure if one takes the time to look. It shows a love and understanding of clay and glaze, an intense personal interaction with the medium. It may not answer today's taste for the grand and the flamboyant, for the bold statement or the large gesture. Mrs. Kenly's bowl is modest, but even so it demands that we respect its greatness. It is everything a great pot should be, and the lesson it teaches can be applied to every piece discussed in this essay. The qualities of beauty, utility and wisdom found in Mrs. Kenly's small pot are the three broadest themes of this book and I want to proceed with an example of each."

To be fair to Dietz, he goes on in the book to discuss these three ideas of ceramic excellence, beauty, utility and wisdom, and provide wonderful photographs of stunning pottery. He makes an interesting point in discussing beauty, illustrated by a picture of a Glen Lukens plate:

"Unlike 'fine art' art, a beautiful vessel can be an end and not just a means. Beauty is enough. Surface, form and technique are both necessary and sufficient for a beautiful pot. Utility is not necessarily excluded by beauty, nor is wisdom. But the self-sufficiency of beauty sometimes leaves no room (because there is no need) for anything else."

His final statement in the conclusion of the book compares the pottery of Ruth Kenly and Andrew Lord - two very different potters - and he concludes that both created great pots, with completely different results. I look at the picture of Lord's vase - with a tortured surface, punctured holes, clay twisted. Dietz describes him as a 'hip modern artist' and his vase as having…

"…subtle and lustrous surface … as delicate and sensual as the shimmering taffeta of a Worth evening gown."

It is evident that for Dietz there is no single standard and no single result that is the exclusive monopoly of a great pot. The astonishing variety of pottery in the book indeed does range 'from function to fantasy' as the author promised in the title.

This takes me back to "Culture and Anarchy" and an essay by Gerald Graff, 'Arnold, Reason, and Common Culture', that accompanied Arnold's essay in the same volume. I know Graff from previous books, he would be a natural adversary of Arnold and his current allies.

"What seems important is not that Americans find 'a common identity' whatever that may mean, but that they learn to differ fundamentally with one another without always being on the brink of violence. For this reason, it would be more fruitful to shelve the present hand-wringing about common culture and begin talking about how to create a common debate about culture. We can hardly conceive such an alternative, however, as long as …we equate debate and conflict with disintegration."

Perhaps art, and in particular, ceramics, can be the agents of this common debate. The genius of the human imagination cannot be nullified by a demand for a single result. The inherent relativism of an aesthetic lies in the recognition, however begrudged, that art foreign to your own taste and talent can still achieve greatness. Aesthetic anarchy is not dangerous nor a threat to our stability. I do not have to take a partisan position, but enjoy the experience of good pottery even, on occasion, great pottery. I do not flinch from private preferences, knowing that my prejudices are not harmful to others, they simply determine what I purchase and place in my home for myself. I would never think of imposing my views on others. It must be modesty, but I don't think I could claim to know what is a great pot, except when I entered that gallery near Fisherman's Wharf in San Francisco about a year ago, I thought I saw a few great pots. The definition of 'taste' overcomes the definition of a single standard. I find it difficult to understand why this is so unsatisfying to Arnold and his modern friends.

Great pots and great art are still possible in a consumer society where the popular taste for a more trivial entertainment dominate. We have the grotesque summer movie, with spectacular violence achieved through special effects, and we have the small independent film that searches for insight and wisdom in the human predicament. I know that, in most cases, the results at the box office favor the movie whose script and plot resemble a comic strip. Yet there is that occasional film, that small foreign or independent movie that somehow catches on and defies the odds. My search for excellence is not inherently elitist or undemocratic. Great art can spring from modest circumstances and humble origins. Wisdom and beauty are available in this culture. The decision to seek excellence is dependent upon a vibrant culture of art, a vigorous education for youth that celebrates and explores the arts, and a society and state that support the arts at the very center of life for its citizens.

I look forward to a trip to Alaska at the end of the month. The contrast of another weather extreme will be welcomed only because it promises relief from the heat. I will not remember that statement because I am sure to complain about the cold. I will be bringing back artifacts as usual. They will not be of all the same kind, and the anarchy of my unruly and motley collection will only be enhanced.

Take care, your friend,

Richard

Twenty

October 12, 2003

Dear Christa,

Barney Hehn died the other day. His daughter called last night to invite me to the service on Friday. He was a old man, walked with the aid of a cane. He had a bad stroke about a year ago. Barney used to come to city council meetings, not because he had nothing else to do but because Barney really cared about his community and he was not afraid to speak out. This was really courageous of him, because he spoke truth to power in a town where a small clique controls everything and tries to intimidate everyone. He had dared to be supportive of my efforts as a city council member to control development, preserve the foothills and save the oak trees. This was considered treason by the developers who own the town and city hall. They spent a half million dollars to recall me and my two colleagues on the council. So current events in California really resonate with me. Watching TV and reading the newspapers regarding the issues and candidates in the recall election for governor revives that far more intense and painful experience in my own life a short time ago.

One important lesson learned the hard way: civic virtue can be an insurmountable handicap in politics. A far better indicator of political success, on any level, would be the size of your wallet and the wealth of your supporters. Tell me, Christa, do the best potters always become the most successful, or is it often just like politics, who you know and what artistic principles you are willing to jettison to get ahead actually can be the more reliable indicator of success? The attainment of public notoriety is often mistaken for character and commitment in our society. What a lost opportunity for me. Just think of the size and value of my pottery collection had I only gone along with the boys at the local country club. Perhaps you should not associate with a loser. I will understand.

My cottage becomes my citadel, the fence barely defends my garden and only the thin walls of the house protect my private existence and acquired treasures. I will hole up here for now, then join Barney someday in heavenly discussions of the inadequacies of trash collection and the ubiquity of the notorious pothole.

The importance of my home as individual fortress against a hostile world appears to contradict my proclamations of communal cooperation and interdependent responsibilities to achieve a just society. I found help in understanding this discrepancy in "The Poetics of Space: The Classic Look At How We Experience Intimate Places" by Gaston Bachelard. In his comments in the foreword, John R. Stilgoe summarizes Bachelard's views regarding the house:

"...the house is a nest for dreaming, a shelter for imagining... To imagine living in a seashell, to live withdrawn into one's shell, is to accept solitude - and to embrace, even if momentarily, the whole concept and tradition of miniature, of shrinking enough to be contained in something as tiny as a seashell, a doll's house, an enchanted cottage."

This idea is very attractive for me just now. Modest dimensions that require a brief walk through the limited boundaries of a few compact rooms; aesthetic precision that determines placement and domestic order; images and objects that co-exist and communicate in many cultural languages; all within my own 'enchanted cottage'. I can withstand everything that happens elsewhere, I am truly protected by my property and pottery. All my artifacts are grateful, they have my loyalty. I live with my friend and wife (the same person) in a world we co-created. You must consider these thoughts directly from Bachelard:

"...the house is one of the greatest powers of integration for the thoughts, memories and dreams of mankind. The binding principle in this integration is the daydream. Past, present and future give the house different dynamisms, which often interfere, at times opposing, at others, stimulating one another. In the life of a man, the house thrusts aside contingencies, its councils of continuity are unceasing. Without it, man would be a dispersed being. It maintains him through the storms of the heavens and through those of life. It is body and soul. It is the human being's first world. Before he is 'cast into the world,' as claimed by certain hasty meta-physics, man is laid in the cradle of the house. And always, in our daydreams, the house is a large cradle. A concrete metaphysics cannot neglect this fact, this simple fact, all the more, since this fact is a value, an important value, to which we return in our daydreaming. Being is already a value. Life begins well, it begins enclosed, protected, all warm in the bosom of the house."

How did Bachelard find out about my childhood? Memories of that small house on the dead-end street, the closet near the front door, the escape from reality when I slipped inside unnoticed, closed the door and sat on the floor and stared though the octagonal amber glass window, not needing to see anything on the other side but having a focus for the concentrated daydreams of my isolated childhood. What constitutes that inner sanctum for you Christa, that safe retreat that most of us call home? I suppose that most secure people would charge that the only real refuge is the internal fortitude to sustain all other loss. Pottery will break, the William Morris wallpaper will eventually fade, stucco walls crumble, termites descend on the rest. Regardless, I confess my dependence on my house, on my pottery to sustain and protect me. Here I will make my last stand. I do not require warranties of infinity or immortality to place hope and value within the domestic realm that now sustains my life and daydreams.

I accept multiple definitions of family and respect love and union between every conceivable combination of human beings. Still I am witness to a rather remarkable event. My youngest son, Sean, with his wife and baby daughter, purchased a corner house on the same block as my own. They join my other son, daughter-in-law and two grandchildren who live next door to us. The Jacobs compound, although not quite completely connected, now occupies three of the four corners of our suburban block. We actually seem to like each other. Whatever the sociological literature about the fragmentation of the modern American family, the Jacobs clan is gathering as a traditional extended family at the same site in the same neighborhood. The grandchildren will walk to the same elementary school where their fathers went to school. This might be considered normal in some places in the world, but is extraordinarily rare in the transient dormitory communities of Southern California where instant communities of immigrants from elsewhere have abbreviated local histories. I wonder why my sons, as most normal grown children are wont, do not indict me for all the miseries of their youth and credit me for all their present deficiencies. Obviously we are not a modern family in the full range of possible pathologies. I privately celebrate their positive traits, assume that they are obviously inherited from my own persona and take no blame for the rest.

What about this discussion so far? What about my ramblings about home and family. How can I connect this to the potter's wheel? For William Morris the home was the center of human civilization and artistic culture. We both know his famous injunction, "Have nothing in your house that you do not know to be useful or believe to be beautiful". We know that his utopian hopes for human justice were located within the home, "I have more than ever at my heart the importance for people of living in beautiful places; I mean the sort of beauty which would be attainable by all, if people could but begin to long for it." As Nikolaus Pevsner observed, "We owe it to William Morris that an ordinary man's dwelling house has once more become a worthy object of the architect's thought, and a chair, a wallpaper, or a vase a worthy object of the artist's imagination."

Am I claiming the power of your pottery to enchant my home and exercise some magic spell over its occupants that results in fantastic happiness and well-being? If I could only prove this, I know it would greatly increase your gallery sales. Are potters the tricksters or shamans of our modern world? Do you deliberately design and create that mysterious influence that radiates from your pottery and changes the very nature of domestic space? Do you rub in some mystical potion in the clay, fire and fix it in the object, place its compelling power unsuspected in the very rooms where we live? Does the kiln god watch over your studio? Are potters modern witch doctors who can implicitly promise the miraculous healing of body and soul through the purchase of their pottery? Only William Morris and I could possibly believe in that. What claims can a potter dare to make about the healing powers of the pot? Do your pots help heal the wounds of your own heart and soul?

A quick transition from innocent celebrations of home and family to the sordid theories of "The Culture of Collecting". Oh, they were right about the French, their culture permeated with outlandish displays of sexuality that leave them unashamed. At least the Americans so suppress their sexuality that it all becomes obscene when made public; the dirty-minded French outrageously assume that what is normal and natural cannot be vulgar, it can only be perverted. Jean Baudrillard has gone too far. I take what he said personally. In his opening essay in the anthology edited by John Elsner and Roger Cardinal, entitled "The System of Collecting" Baudrillard attacks me and exposes my latent sexual perversion:

"If it is true that, in terms of object choices, perversion manifests itself most classically in the form of fetishism, we can hardly overlook the fact that, throughout the system, the passion for, and possession of, an object are conditioned by comparable purposes and modalities, and can indeed be seen as what I would call a discreet variety of sexual perversion. Indeed, just as possession is coloured by the discontinuity of the series (be it real or virtual) and by the targeting of just one privileged term, so sexual perversion consists in the inability to grasp the partner, the supposed object of desire, as that singular totality we call a person. Instead, it is only able to operate discontinuously, reducing the partner to an abstract set… Henceforth she is reduced to a set whose separate signifying elements are one by one ticked off by desire, and whose true signified is no longer the beloved, the subject himself. For it is the subject, the epitome of narcissistic self-engrossment, who collects and eroticizes his own being, evading the amorous embrace to create a closed dialogue with himself."

After reading Baudrillard, seeking to develop a more foreign and sophisticated orientation, I look again at my pottery. Does that angled spout, that long erect neck of the vase speak of an erotic tribute to a lover or an unresolved relationship with a father? The bulging bowl the pregnant promise of ceramic fertility? The lidded opening a modest and yet tempting opportunity? In this case, scholarship has delivered far more titillating reporting than the supermarket tabloids. I must admit this commentary arouses a new interest in the erotic shapes that seek to seduce me as they lay waiting for me on my shelves. Baudrillard must be right, all these clay shapes and forms, all manifestations of the sexual apparatus of male and female, why didn't I see it before? But if the collector is guilty of "a discreet variety of sexual perversion", what about the pornographer/potter who created the form in the first place? Don't worry, Christa, I won't turn you in but you have got to clean up your act. I now look at your pottery with some hidden embarrassment as a source of adult entertainment, capable of being enjoyed while going undetected by my wife and family members. I protest, yet cannot challenge Baudrillard, conceding that his bibliography must be longer than mine. Even so, I agree with Freud, sometimes a cigar is just a cigar.

In a chapter called 'Body Language' in the book "The Art of Contemporary American Pottery", Kevin A. Hluch further exposes the sensual dance of the potter at play:

"Potters often use the word skin while discussing the surface qualities of some pots… Moist clay accentuates that feeling of fleshiness that is eminently pleasing to both the eye and hand… These kinds of soft glazes, coupled with the softly rounded shape of a pottery form, certainly speak tellingly to the hand as well as the mind. This observation also suggests a level of understanding and, on occasion, overt eroticism in pottery. This is an element not often detailed but, nonetheless, is one of its most important. Indeed, perhaps the most compelling reason for the popularity in handling plastic clay lies in its soft, ductile, sensual quality. With the addition of water it becomes even more seductive due to its slipperiness. Without water for lubrication, it would be impossible to throw clay on the wheel. The analogy to reproductive activity is not easily dismissed or ignored."

The very names of portions of the vase reflect the human figure, from the mouth of the pot at the top to the foot at the bottom. I do have trouble with the need to attach neurotic dysfunctions to the sensuous aspects of art, for collector and potter. An aesthetics without sensuality would remove the human dimension. Perhaps pottery more than any other art medium provides intimacy; in the nature of materials, in the act of creation, in the shape and feel of the object, and in the private function of pot and person in personal space.

There is a far more innocent and rewarding motivation for me than what Baudrillard offers. It is the sense of wonder. Many authors restrict this capacity to childhood, warning of its declining possibilities as we age. I don't accept this. For the old, the sense of wonder is not a symptom of senility, but the committed defiance of an on-going engagement with life. I have never lost it. Adam Bresnick, in an article entitled "Surprises of the Soul" reviewed a book by Philip Fisher, "Wonder, The Rainbow, And The Aesthetics Of Rare Experiences" in The Times Literary Supplement, December 24, 1999. Bresnick describes Fisher's approach:

"In his campaign to enshrine wonder as the essential emotion of the aesthetic experience, Fisher enlists as his allies Plato's Socrates, who famously claimed in the Meno that 'Wonder is the only beginning of philosophy', and Descartes, who argued in the "Discourse on Method" that wonder is the first of the passions, 'sudden surprise of the soul' beyond any notion of interest. In keeping with Plato and Descartes, Fisher describes wonder as 'The hospitality of the mind or soul to newness', an opening of our senses to the objects of the world that results in a kind of gripped mental alacrity. Wonder allows the mind to feel itself anew again; it rejuvenates the spirit deadened by quotidian experience. For Fisher, as for the philosophical tradition he summons, it is the role of art, science and criticism to restore to our minds the wonder that initially sparks mental activity."

Pottery is wonderful - it is the source of endless wonder. I once asked a question at a seminar at the Ojai Music Festival. The expert speaker completely misunderstood my question. I asked him about the possible handicap of bringing complete knowledge to the performance of music. Seeking to dismiss me, he quickly replied that knowing little about music need not be a detriment. I was of course inquiring about the danger of knowing too much, not too little. Perhaps he interpreted my question as a personal challenge and could not bear to discuss the issue. I too bring multiple references that form a moveable context to generic or general discussions. Some would say that all this intellectual baggage detracts from the immediate encounter with art and the opportunities for wonder. Does art have to be a surprise of the mind as well as a 'surprise of the soul'? Fisher apparently thinks so, "For wonder there must be no element of memory in the experience." I have heard that artists often know less about the intellectual history of their medium than others. You either know about it or you do it. The same idea has been used against teachers. Tell me, Christa, are there any 'surprises of the soul' left when you observe the results of your efforts? After all the pots you have made, can wonder still fill you with awe when you remove the pot from the wheel or kiln? Wonder is an explicit experience, as is the sensuality of beauty. Together they form a mighty alliance.

I stand revealed. Failed politician and apparent sexual pervert, family man and old man-child of wonder, collector of pots and friend of potters. This is my twentieth letter to a young potter. The issues are not yet exhausted. My curiosity requires further exploration. Take care.

Your Friend,

Richard

Twenty-one

October 23, 2003

Dear Christa,

Fall is confirmed on the calendar but not yet experienced in the weather. A belated blast of daily heat defies the logic of the seasons. Fall is a good time for us - announcements of craft, antiques and pottery shows arrive in the mail, opening of the new Gehry concert hall and the Philharmonic season in Los Angeles, new plays and new theater seasons. The best films are released in the fall, in order to qualify for consideration for academy awards early in the next year. We make a series of voluntary commitments that oblige afternoon attendance at matinees well into the next year. We are modest but loyal patrons of the arts. We experience a seamless integration of our daily lives with creative gifts of profound beauty and subtle meaning. The state has severely cut support for the arts, and I now receive telephone calls asking for support, beyond the price of subscription, that for the most part I sadly cannot satisfy. It is perplexing - why great art can be traced back to the prehistoric cave, yet so few today seem to require its presence in their lives. I think how many pots the cost of just one Hummer would obtain, how many potters would be supported by that great sacrifice, with the added benefits of reducing toxic fumes and lowering energy consumption. I insist that my aesthetic appetites and needs are basic and essential to my nature, fundamental to my welfare. How did civilization come to be regarded as a frill?

I know that letter writing is an archaic medium. Why don't I chat with you on the internet? Cordless conversations on a portable cell phone? Wireless wisdom expendable and immediately forgotten? Instant contact that informs without reflection, functional communications that do not justify or leave an historical trace. I compromise the purity of my obsolete art by using the computer as word processor, embarrassed by the unreadable abstractions of my left-hand scrawl, needing the corrections of a spelling check, the slow evolution of the text by revision and refinement over time.

Gay Daly, in her book, "Pre-Raphaelites In Love" points out the invaluable virtues of letter writing for later consideration by others:

"No one will know us as we can know these Victorians; telephone calls are words cast into the wind. Then, everything was set down on paper, even the most casual invitation. Such wealth of material is a biographer's dream. ...I still felt privileged to be able to read immediate accounts of these women's thoughts, plans, hopes, dreams, and disappointments. There is a special pleasure, a sense of connection, in holding in one's hands the same leaf of stationery that the letter writer picked up a hundred years ago as she pulled up a chair to the secretary in her sitting room, a sharpened quill and a pot of ink at her side. Letters yield a myriad of small, quiet clues that carry one beyond the words."

Letters are an amateur's effort, sharing the mundane with those uncritical friends who welcome personal news. Only later, after the person has long since become unavailable, do these comments reveal not only private events and behavior, but the very spirit and fabric of the time. The genre of correspondence is an autobiography that reflects an implicit display of self-confidence. It is difficult to avoid yourself as the subject worthy of discussion.

Does the potter hide behind the pot, otherwise inarticulate? Would you resort to the lump of clay if words could better express your feelings? Are potters satisfied to have their pots become the narrative of their lives? If I decide to collect both pots and letters, who will I finally better understand and know, the potter or the letter writer? Some people need the words as preface to the pot, some people need the pots to better understand the words that might come after. I catch myself sometimes rushing to the wall to read the title before viewing the painting, hoping one describes the other. Art should not need a prior code to decipher meaning. I prefer to see the pot first, then investigate the potter if warranted. I could like you even if I didn't like your pots, I could like your pots but not like you, but I don't think I could like your pots just because I liked you. Pots assume lives of their own, perhaps personal letters remain more attached and derivative of the writer. Are the words of the potter, critic, and collector the friendly ally of the potter or do words just get in the way? I can look at my pots, experience them, and do not need words. But words inevitably come to me, they burnish the pot, and explain perhaps too much. I love words and pots. I cannot decide or choose what I love the most. Both are therapeutic for me.

This book, "Pre-Raphaelites In Love", an account of the women, often models from lower class origins, who posed, slept, and sometimes married those young nineteenth century British artists, who became known as the Pre-Raphaelites, makes an engrossing read. After the fact, these women are now being rediscovered as talented and contributing individuals in their own right. Artists were not really respectable then, highly suspect and yet richly envied by the upper classes because they were permitted excessive behavior in true romantic style in ways that could be ruinous for men of property and propriety. The price of respectability for the successful artist was very high. You had to keep doing the one thing that brought you success in the first place. William Holman Hunt and John Everett Millais, two of the most famous artists of this briefly celebrated school, were good friends. According to the author, Hunt confronts Millais about his acceptance and good fortune:

"Hunt had accused Millais of descending into the popular mire where the money flowed so quickly, but Millais defended himself quite eloquently: 'You argue that if I paint for the passing fashion of the day my reputation some centuries hence will not be what my powers would secure for me if I did more ambitious work. I don't agree. A painter must work for the taste of his own day. How does he know what people will like two or three hundred years hence? I maintain that a man should hold up the mirror to his own times. I want proof that the people of my day enjoy my work, and how can I get this better than by finding people willing to give me money for my productions, and that I win honours from contemporaries. What good would recognition of my labours hundreds of years hence do me? I should be dead, buried, and crumbled into dust."

Gay Daly immediately adds that she sees merit in his view. Millais tried to persuade his friend that he had to " ...keep cranking out portraits in order to survive." This discussion represents a central issue I have referred to in previous letters. Millais was finally, just before his own death, voted in as President of the Royal Academy. The bohemian prodigy came full circle. It is one thing, for the ambitious artist/potter, to want acceptance from a potential lover or a circle of dependable friends, and another to desire the fatal acceptance of commercial success.

I read with great interest, usually in obituaries, about a recently expired actor or artist, given the ultimate compliment, that he or she was 'an actor's actor' or a 'writer's writer'. What does that mean? That this person was a master in her art, a superb and serious performer who had the respect of her peers, whose excellence did not cater to the public and did not result in a spectacular career. Would you like to be called a 'potter's potter'? Perhaps I am too severe and demanding of my artists. Who can wait or witness the eventual fame if one has been reduced to " ...dead, buried, and crumbled into dust"? As someone just short of that final condition, I do understand the natural urge for the experience of lived success rather than the more problematic assessment that might come unenjoyed later. I understand the sentiment to acquire an immortality that depends less on the disposition of God and more on the ratification of historical fame by the embrace of public acclaim and by the expert critics of the culture. Millais certainly experienced all that, but the Pre-Raphaelites were quickly replaced:

"The young men who formed the Pre-Raphaelite Brotherhood in 1848 meant to mount an aesthetic revolution that would change the history of painting forever, but in this they failed; the Impressionists across the channel superseded them within their lifetimes."

As Daly mentions in the Prologue, her own interest as a little girl in these romantic portraits of "…big dreaming ladies with the masses of rippling, shimmering hair, black or red-gold" were ridiculed by the later verdict of the culture regarding these paintings as "…embarrassing, fit only for greeting cards". If one's artistic reputation, as well as physical body, can be so easily rendered into dust, "dead and buried", what should be the primary motivation and hoped for result of artistic effort? One could argue that all this doesn't matter, you just need to go to the wheel each morning and put in a day's work, all that follows cannot be determined beforehand. But surely intention does determine the nature and result of production. There is a different pretension between the repetitious duplication of domestic ware for the dinner table and that single pot that represents the height of your skill and talent. What is it to be? I assume one does not go to art school or the university in order to develop the skill to produce a dinner plate in endless copies. But if you could find the formula for ceramic success, acclaimed and rewarded with material success, I would understand and forgive you your good fortune. Just don't buy a Hummer with your great surplus of cash. Maybe just earning a living for a potter is enough of a rare triumph that all these other critical questions and issues become unfair.

Please do not underestimate my own particular prejudice. I don't think I could buy a pot if I knew that the potter owned a Hummer. My use of this example is not a rhetorical or humorous device, rather a deeply held polemical one. In the same sense I would not buy a pot from a racist bigot. I would never buy a great pot from a bad person or a person indifferent to bad things that might result from their behavior. It might be dangerous for me to get to know potters too well. I don't think I could continue to respect a pot I had already purchased if I found out that the potter was dishonest or hateful. Can bad people make good pots? I know this is guilt by association. The pot is completely innocent, isn't it? The German film director, Leni Riefenstahl died recently. I remember years ago seeing her films about the Berlin Olympics of 1936 and her Nazi propaganda film, 'Triumph of the Will', a magnificently constructed and yet terrifying tribute to Adolf Hitler. In this kind of situation, I must deny myself the artistic greatness of the artifact because my patronage would commercially enhance the evil intentions of the artist and her sponsors. I would never buy a poorly made pot just because the potter was a good person, as a gesture of support or empathy. I might suggest a change in vocation or provide a free dinner, but no insincere charity would allow placement of that mediocre pot in my collection.

A potter might retort and ask if bad people who are collectors deserve great pots. How about the collectors who knowingly hoard plundered art taken from the Jews of Europe by the Nazis or who welcome the new additions stolen from the museums of Iraq? If all the art taken by force through history were returned, particularly that robbed from the non-Western world, the rooms of our museums and the shelves of private collectors would be emptied. I am not going to respond; I am beginning to feel defensive. In my heart I know I am a worthy custodian of pottery, there could be no basis for disqualification or rejection of my offer of shelter and safety.

John Dewey has been a life-long friend and mentor. I went to a progressive elementary school founded on his educational theories, where in the middle of a metropolitan area, we children fed and cared for small animals, worked in our garden, wrote a school constitution, authored plays about the westward movement and the California missions, made the costumes and acted out our dramas. We cut, hammered, sewed, danced, sang, painted and glued our way through the curriculum. It was learning by doing, by making active learning a series of social experiences in the classroom community. We created and constructed our knowledge. Later, as a teacher, I continued to practice the tenets of Dewey's pedagogy, sponsoring interactive exchanges and activities that encouraged informed interpretations of ideas and themes by the students. I know I am not supposed to do this - I am retired, have lost my authority, you are very busy - but, if I had my way, I would assign you and every other potter his remarkable book, "Art As Experience".

Dewey squarely defines the problem, "…that of recovering the continuity of aesthetic experience with normal processes of living". This idea is very important for potters. The cultural bias that separates craft from art and art from life revolves around this problem. In the first chapter, "The Live Creature" Dewey explores further:

"When artistic objects are separated from both conditions of origin and operation in experience, a wall is built around them that renders almost opaque their general significance, with which aesthetic theory deals. Art is remitted to a separate realm, where it is cut off from that association with the materials and aims of every other form of human effort, undergoing, and achievement. A primary task is thus imposed upon one who undertakes to write upon the philosophy of the fine arts. This task is to restore continuity between the refined and intensified forms of experience that are works of art and the everyday events, doings, and sufferings that are universally recognized to constitute experience."

Dewey is the essential American democrat in every aspect of his thinking. There is an American civilization, and Emerson, Whitman, and Dewey personify that inclusive and generous spirit that includes the reality of all of us as the basis for the common experience of significant and profound art. Pottery is a vital bridge, a part of the connecting tissue that enhances the home, provides dual opportunities for potential function and potential art, infused with aesthetic capacity, yet humbly accepting a domestic chore as integral to its existence and central to our experience. Pottery is graced by Dewey's thoughts and implicit support.

Another local inspiration for the integration of community life and great art is the new Frank Gehry Disney Concert Hall in Los Angeles. As long-time subscribers, Judy and I were provided a tour of the building just before it opened. I did have reservations about the Guggenheim Museum in Bilboa, so striking in exterior and interior that no other visual art can compete. Another immature remnant of a younger Gehry, a need for that huge and awful Koon dog made of mud and flowers outside the Bilbao building. His need for funky putdowns is leading to a dubious and clumsy looking flower/fountain made of bits and pieces of broken Delft pottery, and, according to reports, a not yet installed giant bow tie in the soaring lobby of the new concert hall. My full reaction to the concert hall must wait for my first concert next month. I expect that the audio magnificence of music will be enhanced in the concert hall, unlike the visual distraction of museum art competing with the undulating and chaotic interior contours of the Guggenheim. My reaction to the concert hall, although containing similar elements to the Bilbao Guggenheim, was quite different. This concert hall building is not just a novelty, but a thrilling icon that expands the range and possibilities of modern architecture. It will change, particularly for out-of-towners, the personality and perception of Los Angeles. I am not changing the subject from the previous paragraph. I brought up Gehry here for another reason, because he, like Dewey, has democratic impulses. He designed the concert hall to be a public space, available to the city, a public gathering place that he calls "a living room for the city". A lovely garden around the building becomes an urban park, accessible to both concert goers and the downtown workaday lunch crowd. Gehry creates public space enhanced by a communal aesthetic, Morris celebrated private space enhanced by a domestic aesthetic, both are available and accessible, to be experienced by the great mass of us who have no special privilege or power.

Dewey sustains me. He provides after-the-fact confirmation that my own thoughts and feelings are normal and did not originate in some organic eccentricity. Read his words about fine art and everyday living:

"Life is compartmentalized and the institutionalized compartments are classified as high and as low; their values as profane and spiritual, as material and ideal. Interests are related to one another externally and mechanically, through a system of checks and balances. Since religion, morals, politics, business has each its own compartment, within which it is fitting each should remain, art, too, must have its peculiar and private realm. Compartmentalization of occupations and interests brings about separation of that mode of activity commonly called 'practice' from insight, of imagination from executive doing, of significant purpose from work, of emotion from thought and doing. Each of these has, too, its own place in which it must abide. Those who write the anatomy of experience then suppose that these divisions inhere in the very constitution of human nature."

Dewey is summarizing the fate of craft, and thus the fate of ceramics in our society. Dewey is summarizing the fate of our lives and thus the fate of our existence. We must repair what has been rent by the fragmentation and specialization of hierarchies of cultural prejudice. When I am out in my garden, is it just a lesson in botany? An aesthetic revelation of form and color? The biology of observed insects, birds and butterflies? Am I a refined naturalist? Landscape designer? Or does the dirt on my fingers and clothes indicate just a common laborer? If the potter wore a tie or suit while working the wheel could he or she claim executive status? What determines if your pot is high or low art is not your pot, it is the bias of a culture that denigrates or celebrates one kind of making over another. In Japan you might eventually earn the high distinction of 'National Treasure'. Here it is more difficult for reasons that Dewey explains on every page of this important book.

I know I should not quote too much, just paraphrase. I shall try, because I cannot reproduce the book here. Dewey states that art is a process of doing or making. He carefully includes the molding of clay in the list of potential art. He further defines potential art as something to do with physical material, use of tools, and the result as something visible. He then states, on the same page, that "Craftsmanship to be artistic in the final sense must be 'loving'; it must care deeply for the subject matter upon which skill is exercised." What does he mean by this? I want to stop a minute and think about it. Technique is not enough, the potter must be 'loving'. He adds that passion is not enough. It is your qualities, not the pots, that he is now talking about. The qualities of the potter result in the qualities of the pot. An artist, Dewey maintains, is not only gifted in technical execution but an "unusual sensitivity to the qualities of things".

I assume most people would not be satisfied with this, not only because I have failed to include his entire argument but because we don't usually do too well with 'qualities'. Americans tend to measure the world and its value by the quantity of things. It is a convenient tendency given our great affluence. Dewey would not allow you to be automatic at the wheel, no matter your technical skill, nor would he approve of a caprice born of pure emotion.

I assume that you, Christa, the one after all with the actual experience of making, would have much to say to me and Dewey about these qualities of the potter that result not only in a crafted object but in art. Perhaps you could even describe, modestly of course, qualities that you possess or seek to possess that are generic to this discussion with Dewey. In the book, "Made Of Clay: Ceramics of British Columbia" in a section edited by Deborah Tibbel, the makers of pottery speak and hint at some of these qualities. Susanne Ashmore ends her statement with:

"In my work, I am interested in paring down, eliminating, so that the result is simple, quiet, a presence. My voice."

Lesley G. Beardsley talks about the ability of clay to be…

" … a wonderful medium for expressing inner visions. It never fails to excite me and inspire creative ideas."

You will notice that your colleagues are speaking of qualities. It is quite possible for potters to do this. Penny Birnbaum states:

"There is a basic resonance with clay in each person - it seems to be the primary mark making medium. I enjoy the parallels with mythical acts of creation, simultaneous with the experience that it is hard to be pretentious in clay. Technically as well as artistically, I don't think it's possible to know all about it in one lifetime, so I can go on learning and experimenting for the rest of my life and never do the same thing twice."

I just came across another that I must share. Linda Doherty declares:

"Clay arouses the senses. Form reveals life experience. And fire gives each piece spirit."

The final voice, from another source, Christa Assad:

"Along with the rewards, there are many lessons to be learned in patience, co-operation and loss."

As this brief sample indicates, potters who aspire to be artists, can both make art and explain it. I assume this is because they are serious and reflective about purpose and intention. Both integrity and intelligence provide mission and direction. In searching for these qualities, I am not looking for final, single or correct quality. That is the paradox. A philosophy of aesthetic, according to Dewey, accepts the uncertainty, doubt and mystery of life, and "… turns that experience upon itself to deepen and intensify its own qualities - to imagination and art."

I find myself collecting and reading books about the nineteenth century. Why do I seem to have a romance with that century? I have a few objects from that time in my collection. I had assumed that the reason was that I could not afford objects from earlier centuries. Now I am not so sure. In England at that time one could take either of the two opposing views and still be hopeful; that the industrial revolution and the advance of technology would liberate the masses of humankind, or the opposite, that human beings could create utopian societies that controlled technology for the superior purposes of a common culture. We've found out since that both sides were sadly mistaken. I don't think the current dominance of corporate and consumer greed even requires a normative value beyond its own appetite. The power and wealth of the few today, so unchallenged, need no excuse or apology, no cosmetic camouflage of idealism or altruism to defend themselves. They easily co-exist in the world with war and poverty, hunger and deprivation of the multitudes, without embarrassment. There are a few contemporary potters and their pots, yourself included, that hedge my enthusiasm for that backward journey. I think I will return to my garden, walk the rooms of my collection, fantasize about the personal hospitality of the 19th century, and wait for fall to become real.

Take care - I hope everything is going well for you.

Richard

Twenty-two

November 24, 2003

Dear Christa,

California is my home. I was born in Southern California and possess a life-long and abiding sentimentality about this region. I am aware, Christa, that you are comparatively a rather recent immigrant, but rest assured I fully accept your residency. Concern about the hordes of people that have entered and remained in my paradise during my lifetime revolves around the environmental degradation that inevitability accompanies this reality. I do not know the progressive and enlightened solution to this paradox - economic prosperity invites further population density - economic depression encourages a welcome exodus. This familiar locale has been the geography of my entire existence. Aside from a brief residence in England and multiple excursions as a tourist, I return and remain an anchored native of one site, my birth certificate and resumé confirm the parochialism of personal history. The characteristics of my local identity and regional personality are obvious to others but unknown to me. I must have a Californian accent, assume that my behavior must be amusing or obnoxious depending on how foreigners from other worlds assess my typical California style. This embarrassing confession reduces my cosmic perspective to a provincial ethnocentrism. I cannot help it. I will never attain true sophistication.

Joan Didion does not share my enchantment with this state. A child of several generations of Californians, she abandoned California years ago for that citadel of east coast hostility toward everything precious to me, New York. This brilliant traitor to my homeland wrote a book recently, "Where I Was From". I have not read the book, but read a review about it in 'The New York Review of Books' of December 4, 2003 by Diane Johnson. I also observed Didion on at least two TV talk shows in which she discussed her thoughts and the book. Perhaps, as a California chauvinist and as protest, I should cancel my subscription to that horrid New York publication. Didion, as quoted by Johnson, charges both America and California with the same generic crimes:

"There was never just the golden dream of riches and bountiful nature, but always a scene of exploitation and false promises, indifference and ruthlessness, a kind of hollow core".

Johnson discusses Didion's central premise, this American mythology as exemplified in California history, with the heroic crossing across the western wilderness, greedy gold miners and prostitutes, the early ancestors of generations of pioneer family respectability, later failed farmers from the Midwest, the common trek across the western wilderness, finally to the golden state and the promised land. Here freedom and opportunity to become rich met the contrasting reality of...

" ...mistrust of government while feeding at the troughs of public works and agricultural subsidies; unchecked commercial exploitation of natural resources in the very footsteps of John Muir; the decline of education from a place near the top of the nation to somewhere near that of Mississippi; apathy, increasing rates of crime, and crime's related social problems."

This depiction of California by Didion is not the one historically portrayed by the State Chamber of Commerce, as seen on the collectible posters of citrus groves recovered from old fruit boxes, the railroad posters that attracted thousands here before World War II, or by the annually televised football game from the Rose Bowl. Viewers gazed at a land bathed in the warm sun, backed by a range of towering mountains, made even more inviting and painful to the remote audience exiled to the frozen wasteland of the remainder of the nation. The state has the fifth or sixth biggest economy in the world, an action movie hero for governor, teetering on bankruptcy, nothing can diminish my pride.

We cannot afford to remember our entire history in California. Accurate memories would be too damning, too embarrassing. Brian Fagan, in his book, "Before California", as reviewed by Donald Johanson in the Los Angeles Times Book Review of November 23, 2003, reveals the massacre of the indigenous people:

"Almost nothing of the ancient California world remains, Fagan laments, pointing out that in the 16th century there was an estimated population of 310,000 native people, speaking some 60 languages. Each society was rich in tradition, oral history and culture, nearly all of which are now gone forever. Once California was 'discovered' by Europeans, the decimation of its indigenous peoples was relentless. By 1900 only about 20,000 California Indians remained."

The mythology of the dominant or occupying power is the one represented in the school textbooks. I remember during my childhood the numerous elementary school lessons on the California Missions, with happy Indians busy with their chores, if not civilized, at least domesticated and content. There was the exciting added possibility of an eventual heaven pending the decision by European councils to determine if these pagan savages could possibly possess souls. Exploitation and colonialization were not concepts or thoughts introduced in these classroom lessons. How could an elementary school lesson be political? How could dear Miss Klein, that stout spinster teacher of mine in the fifth grade, be a political agent of the state?

One criteria of what constitutes art is that it is capable of a cultural and political viewpoint. Some might use the same evidence to denounce art consciously contrived for that purpose. Samuel Goldwyn, the owner of a movie studio and producer of Hollywood films, declared that if people want to send a message, they should use Western Union, not the medium of film. Is pottery capable of a political point of view? Does pottery send a particular message that promotes the world view and mentality of a specific person at a point in time? I assume many would deny or refute this possibility or opportunity. How could a pitcher, bowl or vase have a point of view? A voice that asserts and projects the views of its maker and cultural sponsor? When reading "Made in California: Art, Image, and Identity, 1900 - 2000" the volume published in conjunction with the Los Angeles County Museum of Art's ambitious exhibition of art in California in social and cultural context, a statement by Sheri Bernstein, in a section entitled 'Contested Eden 1920 - 1940, I came upon this brief passage:

"… there was a 'vogue for things Mexican' that pervaded many facets of cultural production in California. 'Things Mexican' ranged from artwork by Maxine Albro, one of the many creative figures who traveled to Mexico and interacted with Mexican artists in California to Bauer Pottery's El Chico and La Linda dishware lines. It is perhaps not surprising that commercial ceramists and textile designers served up easily digestible, stereotypical images of Old Mexico to modern consumers."

Ideology in a teapot? For centuries function dictated form, but now the post-modern teapot can provide a range of messages. Richard Notkin, quoted by Rebecca Niederlander, in "Color and Fire: Defining Moments in Studio Ceramics, 1950 - 2000" testifies to this ability:

"Although my work since 1983 has consisted almost entirely of teapots, I consider myself a sculptor with a strong commitment to social commentary. My chosen medium - the material I love to work with - is clay. The vessel is the primary 'canvas' for the ceramic artist, the most complex of vessels, consisting of body, handle, spout, lid, and knob. This allows me the widest latitude in juxtaposing the many images I use to set up my narrative pieces."

Judy Chicago, a leader in the women's art movement and working in California at the 'Womanhouse', created and exhibited 'The Dinner Party', thirty-nine ceramic place settings honoring creative women in history with graphic representations of female genital imagery that provoked great controversy. The dining room table, previous site of the family china, the pride of middle class families and social occasions, porcelain finery adorned with handpainted periwinkles, became the platform for a feminist manifesto that gave biographical names to the ceramic landscapes of the vulva. This effort might represent the most militant use of clay in modern times to challenge and confront the conventions of sexist culture. Clay could indeed become political, provocative and powerful.

Robert Arenson, in the Bay Area with a pop culture attitude that produced ceramic self portraits: open shirt, hairy chest and pot belly, beer bottle and marijuana plant on the crumbling pedestal below. Rebelling against traditions, Arenson and his followers pursued humorous and vulgar expressions of defiance that severed any connection with the functional, crafted container. Cultural revolutions inspired by outsider renegades discovered clay as a most suitable material for incendiary statements. California was indeed on the ceramic cutting edge. Did those ceramicists who determined to continue functional pottery lack the social conscience or political commitment to activate their craft for progressive political causes or satirical attacks on the powerful? Christa, wouldn't it be more fun to be a cultural outlaw, a bohemian eccentric with excessive habits and addictions, creator of outrageous objects that offend and shock the staid respectability of those who could afford to buy them? Are you cleaving to ceramic tradition out of conscious conviction or a natural conformity?

I want to help you reply to that last question. Pottery contributes to the ceremonial and practical rituals of family life. Daily life enhanced by these ceramic objects within the home environment can become sacred and profound human events. The aesthetic significance of those resources enrich experience in that domestic space. The nature and purpose of that environment for potters is not just to provide decoration or handy props or utilitarian tools, it is to impact the very quality of life in the most intimate world possible for people; within that enclosed space which harbors their very lives. Sanctuary is an idea as well as that place we call home. The communion of people around a dining table has always been one of the major sites of active culture, communication and human civilization.

In California, trees document the successive waves of historical change. Trees here have not fared better than the indigenous people. Their eradication was the indicator of progress or disaster, depending on your point of view. First the vast groves of oak trees, natural to Southern California, present here when the Europeans arrived. I remember my parents had a very old and huge oak tree in their back garden when they lived in the foothills. It provided a great swath of shade for us in the hot summer weather. It was an important and prestigious tree in that community, pride of my father. Thousands of oak trees were and are still being cut down in Northern and Central California to plant grape vines. Some counties and cities are trying to initiate laws to protect and regulate them but much damage has already been done. In Southern California the oaks were cut down for citrus groves in the late 19th and early 20th centuries. Some oak groves still exist, mostly in parks. Due to greedy developers, Southern California, Los Angeles in particular, has very few parks. Later, after World War II, the next generation of trees, the citrus groves, once the very symbol of this part of the state, were largely cut down for the suburban tract homes that filled the land. In my community, when the last orange grove in town was being leveled, after civic protest, city officials agreed to plant a few orange trees in a small heritage park in the southern end of town, next to an old house they moved there. They are both museum pieces, representatives of history, not the present.

Even the tall spindly palm trees, planted along the parkways between sidewalk and street in Los Angeles during the first three decades of the 20th century are dying off, not being replaced. Their vigorous swaying on a windy day, fading memories of my childhood, made them look most unstable, with the heavy burst of palm fronds on the very top at the end of a long slender trunk. Do the images of trees planted in childhood memories evoke special meaning of place and time for others? They do for me.

Mike Davis, a dire prophet of a damaged and dangerous California, in his book, "Ecology of Fear: Los Angeles and the Imagination of Disaster", along with destructive fires and earthquakes, tells about the fate of trees in my area of Los Angeles County:

"In a 1956 report, for example, the Regional Planning Commission confirmed that all the remaining citrus orchards in the eastern San Gabriel Valley would soon be bulldozed and subdivided. The commission's only concern was that 'this transition to urban uses should be encouraged to take place in an orderly manner' to minimize the 'dead period' between land clearance and home construction… For a decade, meanwhile, at least one thousand citrus trees were bulldozed and burned every week. Between 1939 and 1970, agricultural acreage in Los Angeles County south of the San Gabriel Mountains (the richest farmland in the nation according to some agronomists) fell from 300,000 to less than 10,000 acres. One of the nation's most emblematic landscapes - the visual magnet that attracted hundreds of thousands of immigrants to Southern California - was systematically eradicated."

Davis, more celebrated for his earlier book, "City of Quartz", was criticized for "Ecology of Fear" by reviewers who thought he was too dramatic and inaccurate in his sensational treatment of all the potential threats to Southern California. This morning's Los Angeles Times informed me that this season's fires consumed more land and more buildings than any others on record. The Cedar fire in San Diego County alone scorched about 273,000 acres and destroyed 2,820 buildings. A belated vindication for Mike Davis and a troubling measure of future possibilities for a land living far beyond its natural endowment and overpopulated use.

I must anticipate the obvious critique. I am sure my own suburban home lot once contained oak trees, then citrus groves, now the housing tract and my home. A party to my own indictment, a small part of the problem, still seeking some sense of proportion and modest restraint. Over twenty-five years ago, I went to a commercial nursery, purchased trees and planted them around the home. They are exotic to the natural landscape, joining with the other waves of invaders who now occupy this changed and crowded land.

Is there some relationship between my love of trees and pots? Both face the same challenge. In this very practical and pragmatic society, trees and pottery need to justify their existence and value to survive. Both are endangered species. I once tried to save a grove of oak trees in my community by justifying their value: the lower temperatures by providing shade, the filtering and cleaning of air, reduced need for air conditioning, etc. I lost that struggle. The oak grove was destroyed. Pottery can pour beverages, hold food, receive liquids and hold flowers. So can plastic cups and plates from Wal-Mart. We must try to provide more convincing arguments. I love trees and pots for other reasons. I experience them. The sheer sensual beauty of a tree; the Jacaranda in my front garden where I sit on a bench in its soft shade, see and hear the movement of wind through the moving leaves, the sway of branches, the sunlight filtered through the leaves and branches. The creative form of the pot, elegant in its length and shape, cascades of colored glazes in subtle patterns, striking designs that represent natural or geometric origins. Why is that value not more convincing or conclusive in this society? What will happen to my trees and pottery after I am gone? Their

destiny should not depend on my partisan or personal support, but their intrinsic significance to any worthwhile quality of existence.

California has the poppy as state flower, the oak tree as state tree. Does it have a state pot? Could we identify some essential characteristics of the state pot? The state has a poet laureate, what about a state potter? We can find strong regional traits in a state like North Carolina, where generations of families have produced pottery and are still going strong. It might be possible to provide an outline of that typical North Carolina pot based on that long history. But California offers a more difficult task in this regard. As I understand it, indigenous tribes, particularly in Southern California, wove baskets rather than extensive use of clay pottery. I attended the exhibition, "California Pottery: From Missions to Modernism" at the Autry Museum of Western Heritage in Los Angeles several months ago, remember the show as a display of industrial pottery, with the bright flat colors of Bauer and Catalina Island pottery as the most enduring examples of California pottery ware. The most literal and romantic portrayal of California in clay were in the tiles where the romance of the missions and the sunny land-scapes were effectively projected. The RTK Studios in Ojai are continuing the tradition of tiles that contain images endemic to the California site and spirit. Perhaps this is a distinction not worth having. After all, William Morris turned down the opportunity of being Poet Laureate of England.

The extended family is gathering tomorrow for Thanksgiving, perhaps the most essentially American holiday of all. Motivated by family pressure, sense of obligation or voluntary attendance, the gathering of families happens. The two vegetarian members of the family, in silent protest at the exhibited carcass of the turkey, will consume an alternative diet. The turkey is past caring. This is an important celebration in my California, although apparently traced to an event a long time ago on the east coast. The gross historical error of indigenous natives in helping white settlers to survive that first winter does not detract from the event for us or enter the conversation at the dinner table.

Take care, your friend,

Richard

Twenty-three

December 28, 2003

Dear Christa,

I write this 23rd letter to you as the year is ending with one last holiday to endure, seeking some contrived thematic scheme to give form and purpose to the next 12 months. New calendars give a false optimism. Trips, plays and concerts, characteristic of my subscriber status, are ear-marked events scheduled on concrete dates. They provide a built-in continuity and confidence and guarantee the longevity of my personal existence for another year. Bad news is thankfully unexpected and presently unknown, absent from the twelve pages of the notated calendar. What can one hope for without inevitable disappointment? Is it possible that this next year will be the very first year without war or desperate poverty, at last my life-long hopes will deliver worldly results? No. I know, with old-age knowing, that I must reluctantly trim my resolutions to more realistic expectations. Great hope can make you look more foolish than extreme cynicism. The latter is more heavily documented in human history than the former.

I know this has been a very busy time of the year for you. The expenditure of energy within the compression of limited time must require great effort on your part. I assume that the making of pottery is spread throughout the year but the volume of exhibitions and sales might be more seasonal. Unlike other holiday shoppers or consumers, I do not purchase pottery for others, only for myself. The designation 'collector' offers the excuse for selfishness. I hope all your efforts are receiving due recognition and providing deserved satisfaction.

Christa, I have a real problem. I don't like white men. As a white man, this places me in an extremely alienated and isolated position. I know that my confession of prejudice weakens my forthcoming argument, namely that I don't like white men because they are narrow and aggressive, bigoted and stupid. I must edit my argument in a more elegant manner and regain the high ground. I am aware I did not originate this complaint, Michael Moore has his own concerns. I do not draw my inspiration from him, but rather from my own expe-

153

rience. Ronald Brownstein, in an article in this morning's Los Angeles Times, talks about the voting patterns of white men in recent elections. The discussion reinforces my disdain for white men. Brownstein traces the overwhelming support of white men for Bush to his aggressive use of force and blunt words, and quotes John Anzalone, a Democratic pollster, "He kind of runs a testosterone-driven White House, in terms of both the rhetoric and the dominant issue, which is war… It's a natural resonance with men, particularly white men."

This blood lust, second only to the lust for flesh, has moved from the battle-field to the art galleries. In another article the next day in the L.A. Times, William J. Kole of Associated Press writes under the headline, "From art house to slaughterhouse" about the aesthetic contributions of Hermann Nitsch, who has managed to integrate the manly pursuit of naked flesh with blood-soaked spectacle. "A naked man is lashed to a large wooden crucifix and slathered in the blood of a freshly slaughtered bull. A canvas is smeared with crimson oil paint and pig entrails that glisten sickeningly beneath a spotlight." Nitsch's work has been displayed at the New York Guggenheim, Metropolitan, and London's Tate Gallery. Naked models cavort in 'fleshfeasts' "… as butchers supervised by a veterinarian slaughtered and disemboweled a steer, and then (the naked actors) plunged with abandon into the bloody pulp." Surely this innovative, cutting edge demonstration of avant garde art successfully combines the allure of the brothel with the killer satisfactions of the battlefield. Only talk radio hosts could possibly claim greater credit for the celebration and promotion of masculine pride.

This is what John Dewey had in mind when, in "Art as Experience", he describes the social solidarity of the art experience:

"Expression strikes below the barriers that separate human beings from one another. Since art is the most universal form of language, since it is constituted, even apart from literature, by the common qualities of the public world, it is the most universal and freest form of communication. Every intense experience of friendship and affection completes itself artistically. The sense of communion generated by a work of art may take on a definitely religious quality. The union of men with one another is the source of the rites that from the time of archaic man to the present have commemorated the crises of birth, death, and marriage. Art is the extension of the power of rites and ceremonies to unite men, through a shared celebration, to all incidents and scenes of life. This office is the reward and seal of art. That art weds man and nature is a familiar fact. Art also renders man aware of their union with one another in origin and destiny."

Perhaps, if alive today, Dewey would not consider what I have described above as the progressive documentation of what he meant in those remarks originally delivered as the first William James Lecturer at Harvard in 1932. If I am wrong, just think of what the future holds for us. We will not need art museums and galleries, only field trips to the local abattoir and the more remote battlefield for aesthetic confirmation and experience.

I don't want to be unfair, but Christa, doesn't this discussion reveal your own dearth of imagination. I have been to your studio and gallery - staid ceramic objects arranged conventionally on shelf after shelf. Just think of the crowds and publicity if you hired naked people to throw blood and animal guts around the studio and on your pots and rub their bodies together in sheer ecstasy. I want full credit for this idea if you decide to go ahead with it. Christa, if you were only a man, all these ideas would occur naturally to you too.

Excuse me, I am getting a bit excited about this topic. I guess I underestimated my ageing but still macho persona. I now feel a heavy melancholy when I realize that it's too late for me to develop the appetite to take up hunting or stripping down car engines, too late to switch from PBS to NFL football on TV, too late to join Hugh Hefner at his pleasure palace, too late to watch NASCAR races with the screech and clash of colliding cars, too late for war, too late to be a real man. Thank God that those nice gay men who help heterosexual slobs organize their lives on that TV show haven't confessed yet any love of pottery. My public identity remains shaky. My interests in art, music and books fatally damage any possible claim to American manhood. It's just too late for a sex change or radical sexual reorientation, even an incremental modification such as Michael Jackson has attempted seems too ambitious. The culture just isn't helpful in my late-life identity crisis.

There is a possible upgrade for women happening in the culture. Women as warriors are having an experimental trial in Iraq. One woman even made celebrity war hero, although the story turned out to be lies concocted by Pentagon spin doctors. Women also achieved good box office in films such as 'Charley's Angels' and other flicks, with fighting and kicking that rivals the best efforts of men. You still need to look good naked or in a bikini to become a top action star. True liberation and promotion to the male big leagues will occur when you can deliver the same level of death and destruction as men. That's entertainment.

The nose and penis are always the first to go. Fortunately contemporary ceramics are replenishing the latter. A quick perusal of the classical collections of Greek and Roman sculpture confirm my observation. I have just finished "Sex Pots: Eroticism in Ceramics" by Paul Mathieu. I hide the book from my grandchildren and guests, bringing back warm memories of the surreptitious concealment of certain magazines and illustrations in my adolescence. I have obviously underestimated up to now just how exciting ceramics really can be. I browse the book, with the ceramic evidence of projected penis and dented vulva on countless objects across history and cultures. I do continue to be concerned about the future durability of contemporary works with potentially vulnerable appendages.

I fully appreciate the importance of pottery and clay objects in human ritual and the analogous references to the human body in the form and function of ceramic vessels that connect ceramics to human sexuality. Mathieu further explains this idea:

"... ceramic objects and human bodies remain basically interchangeable at the metaphorical level, but also through semantic analogies within forms and parts. Pottery forms are representations, abstractly, of human bodies. Through touch and direct contact, they are experienced intimately by bodies, and their inherent functions mimic as well as support bodily functions. This emphasis on tactile aspects, on physical touch, differentiates objects from images, which operate solely at the visual level."

According to Mathieu's book, much of the ceramic depiction of the male organ appears to be created by homosexual men. I do not know if this was always the case. Frankly I don't find the ceramic versions of female genitalia very erotic, mainly sort of silly. Images seem to offer more satisfying titillation than objects. Representations of naked genitalia, male or female, somehow lacks the subtlety to arouse. Private parts are trivialized to camp impersonations and pop culture cartoons. The problem with pop culture objects is that they cannot comprise satirical commentary. Whatever the manifestos or statements of the 'artist' might say about American commercial culture, the objects themselves just become more pop culture merchandise. It is a seamless integration due to the lack of artistry. One cannot create critical irrelevance if one has already embraced the subject of critique as a model. Self-conscious critique and the creation of crap, however clever or cute, does not constitute the excuse or change the result: it still leaves you with more crap.

Most of it cannot even attain the level of bad art. It is analogous to an anecdote told by Charles Rosen in his article, 'Culture on the Market' in the November 6, 2003 issue of the The New York Review of Books:

"The very elderly and supremely distinguished art historian Walter Friedlander once returned a paper to a student at the Institute of Fine Arts of New York University with the laconic remark that it was not good. The student asked Friedlander to tell him where it was wrong so he could correct it, and Friedlander replied sadly, 'It wasn't even wrong.' No doubt it has always been better to be right than wrong, and clearly better to be wrong than uninteresting or trivial."

True eroticism, like great art, is never uninteresting or trivial. I simply disagree with Mathieu, I think he is wrong when he states:

"The popular, low brow, kitschy and 'hobby' potential of ceramics objects to convey meaning is a fertile ground for makers everywhere, coming from the anonymous world of house ornaments, kitschy tourist souvenirs and gift wares, as well as various folk traditions worldwide..."

Popular and lowbrow ceramic objects do not convey meaning - that is why they are popular and lowbrow. Commentary and analysis about them might convey meaning but to add to the supply as commentary only supplements the ceramic trash already available. Folk traditions do not belong in the same category as the other cited examples. Whatever their earthy content, they are historically innocent within the envelope of their endemic culture. Only when they insult their historical traditions by making contemporary obscenities for tourists do they emulate their pop culture cousins. The modern pop culture trickster is making a joke. I don't laugh at jokes. Humor by definition contains wit. It is not present in sitcoms on TV, which is why they require laugh tracks as compensation. Nor is it present in much of the clay jokes assembled in the book. Most depictions are crudely crafted and obviously devised to promote a cheap laugh. Eroticism depends on only a partially fulfilled exposure. The dance of the seven veils did not begin with the nude Salome, adding the veils to provide increased suspense and arousal. The ancient world and modern burlesque understood this very basic principle of sustained erotic mystery.

Cultural and political victory today for men is based on the premise that you women have already won. We poor white men have retreated to talk radio, managed to capture the White House and Congress as defensive strategies representative of our current oppression and pained outrage. Poor us. Harvey Mansfield, a conservative scholar and apologist for conservative white men and their politics, has written an essay, "The Partial Eclipse of Manliness" in the July 17, 1998 issue of The Times Literary Supplement in which he comes up with the noble virtue of manliness. He does concede that, "Manliness is biased in favor of action. That is a severe criticism, when you think about it. One could even say that thinking is by itself a challenge to the superiority of manliness." But I know what Mansfield is really up to. It takes a white man to know a white man. Later in the article he adds up the attributes of manliness and decides women have considerably less of these qualities:

"Men through their manliness are more transcendent; women, without that advantage and that encumbrance, are better aware of what is left behind... the price of humanizing manliness, of raising it from quality to virtue, is allowing women to participate in it. It will not be equal participation, because, as Aristotle said, men find it easier to be courageous - and likewise, women find it easier to be moderate... For the most part, men will always have more manliness than women have, and it is up to both sexes, having faced that fact, to fashion this quality into virtue."

If I could only believe such nonsense I am sure it would bring great comfort. Perhaps I could even learn to enjoy pornographic pop ceramics. I might have to shift my correspondence to a man, someone to share sports stories and mutual lies about the conquest of countless women. I might even buy some rugged gas guzzler and go off-road. What to do with my pottery collection? It is a small price to pay. In the meantime, please let me know if you have ever met any nice white men. I need concrete evidence if I am to modify my present prejudice.

I hope the end of the old year finds you in the best of health and that you continue to contribute many, many beautiful pots to the world during the coming new year.

Your friend,

Richard

PS - Just thought of two exceptions before I mailed this letter - my two sons of course. Modesty forbids disclosing where they received their better qualities. They are both glorious failures, just as we raised them. They will never be rich or CEOs. They are educators, with social conscience and compassion that disqualify them from most work in this culture. I am so proud of them.

Twenty-four

January 28, 2004

Dear Christa,

I start each year with a birthday during January. This coincidence forms a neat and efficient calculation. I am not sure at what point I am expected to assign primary credit in my behavior to increased maturity or to the presumed erosion of the ageing process. As with most elderly people, I am not operationally aware of my condition, but I recognize the automatic deference paid to my old age. It can be more patronizing than the modes of tribute paid to the supposed afflictions of others but I do not complain. It is often a free pass and flat excuse that in earlier years I paid for with offended rejection of my iconoclastic spirit. The crediting of nonconformity to supposed senility is a small price to pay for the blanket forgiveness of strangers. The danger of being perceived harmless is that you soon become invisible. That fear of invisibility, not the impending sense of mortality, is the true dread of self-conscious old age. I am essentially healthy and happy, unaware of any serious infringement of my continued ability to enjoy the year ahead. I hope this moment finds you in similar straits, confident in your ceramic achievements and intensely active in your creative endeavors.

The heft of my bulky wallet surprises me. The number of business cards document my multiple memberships. Most are the necessary accoutrements of modern life, credit cards, automobile insurance, medical group identification, etc. A few announce membership in cultural organizations, museums, the county arboretum and such. I think of myself as a outsider, an independent loner who strives to maintain my autonomy by splendid isolation. Well, I just joined another group, the National Council on Education for the Ceramic Arts. I hope this move won't severely compromise my integrity. I am going to the coming conference in Indianapolis.

Before retirement I was a member of several academic organizations pertaining to interdisciplinary studies. I traveled to distant cities, often alone, straight to the hotel from the airport, choosing between competing seminars in small conference rooms. I would give a paper I had carefully prepared and researched containing the very essence of my wisdom and knowledge to an assembled group of a dozen or so attendees. They were mostly the same people I had seen in previous years, in different hotels in different cities. What am I getting into, Christa? I read somewhere that this is a big yearly conference, thousands of people. Why do potters go to these meetings? Is it important for your career? What kind of connections are most helpful? Will I meet people who share my interests? Will everybody seem to know each other but me? Maybe directly connecting with people is more important to me than I thought.

I would like to share my passion for ceramics with others. I would like interested people to visit my home and collection. I want them to value what I value. I do feel somewhat vulnerable. Maybe a serious potter or pottery expert would not be impressed with my collection. A rejection of my collection would constitute a rejection of me, a most significant part of me. Has your pottery ever been rejected? criticized by spoken or printed word? How do you cope with this? How do you know the difference between a constructive critique and rejection? Has this kind of response ever helped to make you a better potter? We are both represented by pots - by the ones you create and the ones that I collect. They are a window into our souls. If they are discounted, where does that leave us? You must face that test every time you exhibit and every time a potential consumer walks by your pots in your gallery. Do you ever overhear their comments? I can hide out with my pots in the privacy of my home. In contrast, your public pots must defend and advance your very welfare and reputation. How do you protect yourself? Maybe that is why potters stick together and assemble at places like Indianapolis, to commiserate on that cruel and uncaring world that has yet to fully embrace their beautiful pots.

Artists have often organized voluntary clubs and groups to gain solidarity and comfort in their creative pursuits. One such group in late 19th century America was The Tile Club, a short-lived small band of artists, many interested in the decorative arts. They actually painted few tiles, but highly valued the social interaction and painting excursions to the eastern seashore. Their in-house humour and affectations of Bohemian behavior did not conceal the fact that they were becoming established and successful as working illustrators and painters. Winslow Homer was eventually the most famous of the lot. In those days groups of artists were mostly fraternal affairs, with parties, dinners, and working studio spaces at their club headquarters in New York City. The club did not solely represent one style of painting, but was associated with the aesthetic movement in America. Oscar Wilde was hosted by the Tile Club during his lecture tour of America. In his book, "The Tile Club and the Aesthetic Movement in America", Ronald G. Pisano, describes the value of their association:

"In fact, the Tile club provided an important social forum for its members, from the time they returned from their extensive studies abroad, sophisticated but penniless, to the time they emerged a decade later as successful artists who could resume their ties to the continent... Through their mutual experience, perseverance, and most important, their art, they managed in one decade to establish a new and more cosmopolitan identity for American art, as well as a greater appreciation and respect for a new breed of American artist."

From what I could deduce from the book, friendships and social interaction were very important to the men involved in this club. The group was informal, no dues or officers, no by-laws or initiation fees. They did want to be exclusive, limiting the membership to twelve. They were serious artists who truly enjoyed each other's company and led a privileged life as well as a creative one.

What kind of company do you keep, Christa? The big formal organizations, like the NCECA must be useful in terms of your ceramic career. Do you belong to any informal group? Maybe a secret society of eccentric potters? You must, if necessary, make up some sensational stories just to keep me interested.

A very different sort of group was labeled "Bloomsbury". A bit later, and quite British. Formed by artists, writers and intellectuals, including of course Virginia Woolf, her sister, the painter Vanessa Bell, and her husband and art critic Clive Bell, Maynard Keynes, the economist, and the painter Duncan Grant, among others. The latter was the lover of Vanessa, and fathered their daughter Angelica, although he was primarily homosexual. Many of them, including Virginia, were intimate with both genders. You must admire, at least at a distance, their bisexual flexibility. It did allow for a marvelous circulation of friends and lovers among the group. I would imagine (that is really all I can do in this discussion) that the very height of sophistication would be the breakfast conversation between husband and wife regarding their recent lovers, some of whom they might discover they had inadvertently shared during the last fortnight.

A wonderful book, "Charleston: A Bloomsbury House and Garden", was written by Quentin Bell, the son of Clive and Vanessa, written in his old age, finished by his daughter, Virginia Nicholson, after his death. Quentin describes the house in the countryside that was the common meeting site of this informal group. Bloomsbury was not only an assorted cast of characters bound by family ties, lust, and mutual aesthetic interests, it was a place. That place was Charleston. The very personal statement of Virginia Nicholson in the preface of the book tells all:

"Above all, Charleston was a place where, for both children and adults, messy creativity was a way of life. My brother and sister and I grew up, as did Quentin and his siblings, with the conviction that Art was something everyone could do. Paint and clay, mud, glue and matches, were all endlessly available. Yet did the inhabitants of Charleston every really grow up? There is a wonderfully uninhibited, irreverent quality to the decoration of the house which is that of a child let loose to experiment and which is extraordinarily liberating. Part of the exhilaration that people experience from looking at the brilliantly colourful designs that covered the Charleston walls and furniture, comes from that sense of confidence and fearlessness. The Charleston artist did not deal with caution... Duncan and Vanessa were undaunted by such considerations. Their creative will never showed any signs of drying up, so if the table top decorations wore out, they could always just paint some new ones on top."

Each chapter of the book is identified by a room in the house, each chapter explores this individual room, with an extra chapter on the garden. Why this particular organization by Quentin Bell? Why not each chapter named after a famous friend and family member whose activities dominated the space? Why a history of each room? Can biography become a series of passages and placement within those domestic rooms? He fondly recalls childhood memories, discusses the fallibilities and strengths of those people he had loved, forgiven, and finally and fully accepted in their afterlife as his treasured memories. One tender story, told in discussing his father, displays his own humanity:

"The part Clive played in my life was that of a generous and amusing figure, and though his appearances were rare, he was always entertaining. I suppose he would have ranked as a rather poor father, but as I grew up he could be wonderfully sympathetic. I remember once after an exuberant party when, as happens when one is young on the morning after, I suffered from a moral hangover and felt deeply ashamed. I confessed to Clive that I was tortured by the memory of the utterly foolish things that I had said the night before. He smiled and said: 'Can you remember anything foolish that was said by any other guest?' I could not, and not only was I immediately comforted, but treasured the remark for the rest of my life."

How necessary is this sense of place, Christa? I have been in my house for over a quarter of a century. I know every square inch of the garden, a single weed the source of alarm immediately noticed and removed. I know every square inch of the interior, scanned each day in my journey through the rooms to conduct my visual survey of pots and prints. The cat carries inside a single leaf in her fur, left on the carpet, immediately discovered and removed. After much consideration, I move a pot from one shelf to another; as a more extreme measure it is transferred to another room. As a result, everything changes. I am unsettled, order then returns. It is the only small space in the world where I can enhance and impose harmony. If buried on the site as a pharaoh of old, all the artifacts that explain me would be available to some 30th century archeologist who dug in the ruins and found my bones and the shards of my pots. If the local health department would not complain, that indeed would be my fate.

Charleston did change over the years, the house deteriorated, the garden grew neglected, and people grew old and died. Poor Virginia hurried the process with a premature and deliberate death. Restoration of the property followed the eventual restoration of the reputations and contributions of the past occupants. A museum or gallery could never provide the human testimony that the rooms of this house provide. The creation of art was a domestic activity at Charleston. A professional academic or art critic, stranger to the house and their daily lives, can only provide a detached critique and arid analysis of the objects that were exported from the very rooms of their lives.

Richard Shone, in his book, "Bloomsbury Portraits" adds to the profile of family and friends who occupied Charleston:

"At the centre of their lives together were hard work and constant occupation. A chance visitor arriving at Charleston might reasonably have thought the house empty until, one by one, the inhabitants emerged from studio or library, from the pottery or a corner of the garden, to meet for an unhurried lunch or lingering tea. Then it was back to a History of the Roman Empire in French, to a still life in the studio or an evening landscape, to proof-reading or writing a review or, work over for the day, weeding or sewing or sitting in a deckchair to talk, cigarette smoke curling blue against the flint wall of the garden and floating over it with drifts of conversation and laughter."

Membership in a family is never voluntary and for some can be an unfortunate, even tragic occurrence. How rare and wonderful that the creativity and unique genius of each member of the family can be nurtured and supported by the others. I did not have that kind of youth. Did you Christa? This does not prevent eventual tragedy, it did not stop Virginia Woolf from putting those stones in her pockets and stepping into the water. It did not stop the violations of trust in the surreptitious trysts of their multiple sexual escapades.

I want to offer you another model, before you put down the pages of this letter and start joining or forming groups of potters desperate for company and solace. I recommend you give serious consideration - although it would require some adjustments in your personality and lifestyle - to the example of that 'mad potter of Biloxi', George Ohr. He had signs painted in front of his studio that proclaimed, "Get a Biloxi Souvenir, Before the Potter Dies, or Gets a Reputation". According to Bruce Watson, in the February 2004 issue of Smithsonian magazine, another sign announced, "Greatest Art Potter On The Earth". This eccentric, in a very intense creative period of ten years, 1895-1905, created thousands of pots:

"He made pitchers whose open tops resembled yawning mouths. He threw slim, multi-tiered vases with serpentine handles. He lovingly shaped bowls into symmetrical forms, then crumpled them as if to thumb his nose at the art world. He fired his works into kaleidoscopic colors that only a few years later would be called, fauve - for the 'wild' hues of Matisse and other Fauvists."

Ohr charged high prices for his pots - few people bought them. He stopped making pots, stored his entire collection, and spent the rest of his life '… enhancing his reputation as a loon.' He died and was forgotten. The story is one I am sure you know, as it is now the stuff of legend. A half-century after his death, an antique dealer from New Jersey travels to Biloxi, discovers the thousands of pots stored in the auto repair shop of one of Ohr's sons. He bought them all for practically nothing and took them back to New Jersey. Today George Ohr is hailed as a 'clay prophet' and 'the Picasso of art pottery'. Frank Gehry has designed a new museum for Ohr in Biloxi. I look at a photograph of Ohr in the Smithsonian article, he indeed looks mad, with a beard and moustache long and wild, with eyes looking sideways at the world.

Well, the inferences for you are obvious. I will understand if you can't pull off the beard, but do develop your own unique form of madness. I talked to Judy and my sons, and we would be willing to store all your pots for 50 years or more. I expect a very different appearance the next time I visit, and please, do something right away with your signs at your gallery/studio - maybe 'Mad Woman of Fisherman's Wharf - See the Loony Lady in Person Make Incredible Masterpieces'. Maybe you can try out your new persona at the NCECA conference in Indianapolis. I do try to give you practical advice as well as esoteric references to broaden your horizons.

Just a brief note before I leave you - I have a crisis of unimaginable proportions. I recently purchased a wonderful wood block print, placed in the very last remaining space on the walls of my small house. I have just one short shelf empty - soon all will be filled with pottery. What do I do? Help me Christa! How can I possibly justify the continued acquisition of pots and prints? Maybe I need to move, but big houses are so expensive and I do love this house so.

Add a second storey? I cannot dispose of any of them, not even the museum replicas - they are all family members now. Maybe I am the one that should emulate George Ohr and spend the rest of my days as the 'Mad Collector of Glendora', prowling the neighborhood with a long gray beard down to my knees, wearing my straw gardener's hat with the wide brim, taking a pot for a walk, mumbling to myself. I will join any group that promises immediate help and relief.

Your friend,

Richard

Twenty-five

February 20, 2004

Dear Christa,

This letter represents the 25th message I have sent you since the summer of 2002. It is both exciting and strange to know that excerpts will soon be published in a ceramic periodical. I need to avoid that knowledge while writing these letters. Contrived special effects that pander to potential audiences, loathsome in films according to my own prejudices, would not do well in these letters either. Christa, I am sure you are able to achieve that direct simplicity of intent and result at the potter's wheel. The economy of movement and the efficiency of meaning in the resulting object represent mastery. Yet I know that you can never be totally satisfied with the results. If you did produce the perfect pot, the search would be ended and you might stop making them. All human beings have the potential, if they find the right medium, to develop competence and express thought and feeling. Personal circumstances and the culture rarely provide that opportunity. As a one-time secondary school art teacher, this belief was my basis for teaching the arts in public school. I wonder at the state of their present condition in the curriculum.

The great liberation for the layperson is that experts profoundly disagree on the same thing. I do not have to choose between experts. They have achieved mastery and share the same bibliography, but often reach very different conclusions. This would lead one to believe that wisdom is not achieved through the sheer bulk of amassed knowledge, but through the engagement and experience of making meaning of that knowledge. The winning version is not the result of having the most complete information. I need only to find the ideology behind their conclusions and substitute my own. I have always preferred my own prejudice to that of the experts. The humility of the layperson is self-confessed incompleteness. The danger of the expert is the pretense of final authority. The buried presuppositions of the expert can be located. Informed bias does not necessarily contain a more complex virtue or wisdom than uninformed igno-

rance. Both can lead to deeply mistaken summaries and tragic human consequences. I have never petitioned an expert in any field to tell me how to live and
what to live for, although their commentary can form a useful resource. Only
art can convert me, transform me. Artists can never be experts. Unlike experts,
it is what artists don't know that demands they create in order to try to know the
unknowable - and their magnificent failures are called art.

This brings me to M.C. Richards, a beloved icon to the ceramics field and
the author of the classic book, "Centering: In Pottery, Poetry, and the Person".
Her books appeared in the early 1960s, never out of print, still relevant. This is
proved by the theme for the future 2005 Baltimore conference of the National
Council on Education for the Ceramic Arts (NCECA), inspired by the words of
M.C. Richards, "Freedom is presence not absence. Centering is the act of bringing in not leaving out. It is brought about not by force but by coordination."

M.C. Richards is direct and honest, yet her thoughts are often abstract and
general, needing thoughtful individual consideration, response and application
from the reader. She demands much from those who seek her advice:

"By accepting suffering, we may relate more to others, developing compassion. By grace we may become free. And best of all we may find our sense of
humor enormously expanded through the warmth of our heart center, that deepest crossing point."

Nor does she dispense advice and wisdom from a superior perch on high:

"In my own efforts, I become weak, discouraged, exhausted, angry, frustrated,
unhappy, and confused. But someone within me is resolute, and I try again.
Within us lives a merciful being who helps us to our feet however many times
we fall."

Richards employs the central metaphor of 'centering' to organize her ideas,
returning to the concrete reality of the potter's wheel and the very act of creating
pottery to ground her discussions. Richards was potter, poet and teacher. She
explains the power of this metaphor:

"Because I am a potter, I take my image, CENTERING, from the potter's
craft. A potter brings his clay into center on the potter's wheel, and then he
gives it whatever shape he wishes. There are wide correspondences to this
process. Such extensions of meaning I want to call attention to. For CENTER-
ING is my theme: how we may seek to bring the universe into a personal wholeness, and into the rich life which moves so mysteriously and decisively in our

bodies, manifesting in speech and gesture, materializing as force in the world the unifying energy of our perceptions."

I hesitate to provide critical comment, yet seek to place her contribution within my own self. I do not wish to diminish or lessen her value. I do not disagree with any particular thing she articulates and supports. On the contrary, the sweet spirit of the 1960s brings back a very optimistic and exciting time in my life. There are passages, beautifully expressed and virtuous in content, that now appear to me dated and anchored to a particular time in history. Much that was achieved then has since been sadly revoked or compromised. Much that was said then now seems naive and unrealistic. Perhaps these comments say more about me at this moment than Richards.

In retrospect, I think we both underestimated, in that innocent motivation to liberate all oppressed creatures, the determined commitment of the privileged and powerful to retain their advantage. We did not understand that destructive structures and practices that exploited people and destroyed the environment were systemic and functional, the normal behavior of an economic system that works efficiently to profit those who control the political process. We thought back then that if only their greed was exposed and explained - if the devastating effects of poverty and the destruction of the environment were made evident and public - that those responsible would be terribly embarrassed and ashamed, stop their evil practices and surrender power. Despite our hopeful rhetoric and all those peace marches, this ruling corporate elite has not been fundamentally displaced or overthrown in this society. It was the reforms that largely turned out to be temporary. It is the powerful that have endured.

Christa, can your activity as a potter provide you both therapy and profit? Are the thoughts of M.C. Richards simply too intense and overblown for the tight and disciplined schedule of studio production? Richards says that the craftsperson works from some inner vision. Is that idea simply too grand for the makers of 'mud-pies'? Did the flower power of that distant time of the 1960s that offered various evasions from cruel reality work any better than drugs and alcohol? You are at the birth site of that marvelous time, San Francisco, yet I cannot recall you in a tie-dye blouse or offering me a saliva soaked cigarette with that strange smell. Your resumé does not record residency in a commune. I doubt if you have ever even attended a love-in. Your belated arrival in San Francisco must be the excuse.

My notion of how you wild artists live has just been reinforced - I just saw the theatrical production of 'La Boheme', Baz Luhrmann's version of the Puccini classic. Luhrmann transferred the time of the play to Paris in the 1950s but the age old story is the same - artists (all men) drinking and carousing with wild women (models and mistresses). As a solid member of the respectable American middle class, I was both shocked and fascinated. We tolerate the sordid excesses of artists only because it comprises the chief source of our fantasy lives. Mimi, the heroine with uncertain morals, dies, of course, as did her sisters Camille and Anna Karenina on other occasions. The double standard flourishes in art and entertainment as well as in real life. Perhaps some day liberated women will produce a radically new production of La Boheme where the women are the artists and the men are the models and sex objects, and the man dies. I am not sure: would this represent progress in the culture? Brave men often died in duels and wars and came to other violent ends in 18th and 19th century operas and novels, while frail women either died from the physical sickness that inevitably accompanied their sins of passion or earned redemption by leaping off a bridge or under a train. It was the least they could do. We should search the contemporary novel and opera to discover how men and women currently die, it might open a window onto our present notions regarding gender roles. If today's women potters do not bleed from ravaged lungs or die from consumption, how do they pay for their sins and immoral conduct? The culture demands a reply.

M.C. Richards does connect the potter's wheel to the most significant manifestations of the human spirit. She does offer hope, and, to her credit, she does require each of us to make our own unique transformation. She taught some of us about pottery, she taught all of us much about living. She pays a moving tribute to the craftsperson in her book:

"The craftsman works from an immediate life sense. There is little reason in our culture to make pottery or furniture or fabric or jewelry by hand except out of an intuitive sense of one's own being and the being of others, and a love for the work. Surely there is no social or economic reason: no status, not much money, no security. The self-employed craftsman may labor on his own nature and upon his fibers and ores with a special kind of realism. Society needs the spirit of the craftsman throughout its procedures. For material prosperity and professional success, which are so much touted, often fall short of satisfying the person as much as he had been led to expect. There have been so many inner compromises, so many moments of falseness in the interests of expediency and the public image, that by the time the body is well dressed and housed and fed and delighted, the simple heart will have gone out of it. Working in the crafts can help to make a man bold in his honor, perhaps because he has very little else to lose!"

Paulus Berensohn evoked a loving reference to Richards in a recent article in

'The Studio Potter' (December, 2003). In his article, "Whatever We Touch Is Touching Us: Craft Art and a Deeper sense of Ecology", he wrote of their final days together before she died:

"At the end of her life, I made several trips to see her at Campill Village in Kimberton, Pennsylvania. She was frail, using a wheelchair, nevertheless preparing herself... looking forward. In one of her last poems, she writes herself into a fuller world where she will have no biography, where she hoped to 'backpack in the hereafter'. She lived life as the big art to the last. The morning of our final day together, just days before she died, I woke with an image that came with me from sleep. In it, I was wedging her ashes into clay."

M.C. Richards represents a generous and great spirit, still surging through the ceramic community. I look at that remarkable photograph of her on the back of the book, that dramatic visage, scarf wrapped around the neck, unkempt hair, wrinkled and worn face, probing eyes that see further than they can look. It was obvious from that picture that she had already experienced all that she was asking us to try. She believed that we were sustainable, as individuals and community, given the development of resources embedded in our own nature. M.C. Richards pledged on the page that awakening and regeneration were possible. We are so hungry for inspiration, we reach back to her, hoping that we can carry her thoughts into the future. Her words and pottery form a living legacy. I look forward to Baltimore.

I want to move for contrast to a solid and literal prose offered by Robin Hopper in "Functional Pottery: Form And Aesthetic in Pots of Purpose". Hopper offers a practical explanation of the nature of functional pottery; pots for eating, drinking, storage, pouring, cooking, rituals, and contemplation. Clear illustrations chart the differences and characteristics of each. The title of Part One of the book proudly proclaims ceramic intent, 'Made To Be Used'. I found two areas oddly missing in the book. He offers no exploration regarding the deviant heresy of non-functional clay work. He does not recognize their existence in this book. Although he claims in the title of the book to include the 'aesthetic in pots of purpose', I could not find this discussion in the book. His final chapter, where a powerful intellectual defense of traditional pottery could have taken place, entitled "Standards and Aesthetics" is less than two pages. I doubly regret this neglect because I strongly believe it is incumbent for serious writers and practitioners of functional pottery to make the case. My own pots, all capable of holding content, need this defense. The best that Hopper can do is to recommend on the very last page that those interested in aesthetics, "...read some or all of the books listed in the Bibliography, as this will give a much wider and more experienced view than mine in the understanding of aesthetic problems and solutions." Such modesty should result in modifying the title and promise of the book in the next edition. I am sure that the book, as claimed on the back cover, is most helpful for student potters as required reading in the ceramic departments of universities and colleges.

It is important to understand that the aesthetic of functional pottery cannot depend on their function alone. That form should follow function results in an anemic aesthetic that will not suffice. Function as an excuse for the deprivation of symbolic and metaphorical elaboration cannot satisfy me. Discussion of the techniques of construction or the differing demands in the design of spout, handle or lid depending on function do not in themselves constitute an aesthetic. The lack of a convincing aesthetic for functional pottery gives power to the argument that a craft by nature cannot have an aesthetic, only art can possess those qualities. Thus, some would say, pottery does not qualify as art. I expect better. M.C. Richards understood this and provided an aesthetic complexity that made potter, pot and collector dynamic actors in their individual identity and collective relationships. For her, potter and pot contain sacred and sensual elements that together form the transcendent aesthetic. In her vision, potters are tentative and struggling in the joyful suffering that constitutes the self-examined life, seated next to the whirling wheel, surrounded by the full richness of fantastic creations of clay.

The closest Hopper gets to this discussion is his brief exploration of pots for ritual and contemplation. Here he states:

"Objects that give off contemplative energy to those who are able to experience them can take almost any form, from a simple rice bowl to objects which are essentially sculptural. They can make you feel, think, and experience some sort of transcendence, akin to falling in love. Most pottery with this sort of built-in energy gets it from the care and attention to detail the maker works into the object, in concert with the happenings of the firing process, which can elevate the mundane into a meditative masterpiece. Even an object as simple as a mug can have this quality. Objects handmade in clay retain the qualities of touch and form put there by the maker. To hold such an object can be like holding the maker's unseen hand."

Not all potters can be poets. I welcome the diversity in temperament and talent because it promises a diversity in pottery. At the moment, given the variety in my own collection, I am prepared to agree with all possible positions, the promiscuity of my aesthetic philosophy required to justify the lack of a single viewpoint in my collection. That someone in total opposition to my preferred or personal viewpoint could produce a magnificent work of ceramic art testifies to the wisdom of my tolerance. I would gladly adopt standards if they did not exclude too many tempting objects on the gallery shelf. Besides, I could always point out, that crumpled dirty little vase for sale in the dark corner of a garage sale certainly looks like a George Ohr pot to me.

What are the differences between collectors and packrats? Is it that collectors lack the total commitment and energy to go beyond the tidy accumulation of their passionate objects of desire? True packrats would ultimately suffocate themselves in the things they love, achieve martyrdom by being crushed by the sheer weight of their prized possessions. On reflection, I am one of a lesser breed, although I cannot yet prove it. Unlike packrats, collectors have critical discernment that filters and rejects all possible candidates for possession down to a few quality objects. We have standards. I am trying to convince myself - and you.

I still collect, only a tiny space left, any day I could cross the barrier to an embarrassing pathology if my collection soon expands beyond reasonable space for it. I will just have to wait to see. Christa, you really wouldn't want me to deny myself one of your beautiful creations simply because that vase might occupy the very last empty, breathing space left in my home? Think of your guilt if it dropped from some dangerous height and fatally fractured my skull? Please, someone tell me when to stop. In the meantime I can only hope that a natural death comes before a voluntary withdrawal. I have just had a great revelation - it is not bankruptcy or death that should be the great fear for collectors, it is space: the awful fate of unoccupied space, narrowed, reduced and eventually eliminated. It is just not fair. I do not think that William Randolph Hearst ever had to worry about this tragic problem.

Do not show this letter to a professional therapist, seeking some well-intentioned help for me, I prefer to remain in my present condition and live dangerously. I might eventually even achieve some fame, though I would settle for notoriety. Mark Saltzman's new play, "Clutter" portrays the Collyer brothers, 'the world's most famous packrats'. According to this morning's L.A. Times (Feb.13,'04) and the review by Don Shirley:

"For nearly 40 years, the blue-blooded bachelors, Homer and Langley Collyer, filled their Harlem brownstone with 150 tons of clutter, eventually stacked to the ceiling. In 1947, an anonymous source informed the police that a body was on the premises. Officers soon found Homer's corpse, but two weeks - and a media frenzy - passed before Langley's cadaver was discovered under his own junk."

To be buried under a funeral pyre of beautiful pottery - even if unplanned and accidental - what a way to go! Judy provides the only restraint. How far can I persuade a reasonable person to go in our joint pursuit? We are still partners - not yet accomplices in some mad and excessive strategy to possess all the pots of the world. I seek to civilize my ceramic demons by voicing their siren songs. If you do not hear from me for several weeks, send the authorities to search the premises. Whatever they find, I have no regrets.

Your friend,

Richard

Twenty-six

April 20, 04

Dear Christa,

Spring is the most generous of all seasons. The garden right now is simply glorious. The first burst of bloom is extravagant, almost garish in its profusion. I do not know how long I can meet the expectations of Spring. I fear that the annual resurgence of my energy for renewal will not always be able to match the fantastic vitality of my garden. I traverse the year, welcoming some seasons more than others. Fall and spring provide the gifts and celebrations of a most beneficial existence. Fall slowly shutting down the ambitious growth and spectacular color of the garden, a quieting hush and slowing pace. The shadows come earlier in the day, a last invitation to visit the garden and prune the perennials. Fall is the time to invest in Spring, the best time in the year to plant, although most Southern Californians do not know it. I find winter and summer unkind each in their own way. The extremes of cold and heat inflict their particular discomfort and anxiety. Winter is less extreme here but my ability to avoid its chill and consequences also diminishes each year. Summer offers our most extreme weather. I stay inside this season, as if deep snow prevented my going outdoors.

Christa, it has been well over a month since I last wrote to you. I don't know if you have noticed the awful absence, but I do have a backlog of things to think about on these pages: the trip to Indianapolis and the NCECA Conference, North Carolina, particularly the Seagrove potteries and, beyond all that, the memorable daily events and experiences of my life, somehow unreported in the media and unrecorded except in these letters. These letters reflect my private thoughts, written in the privacy of my home. I am not required to write them, but acknowledge the pretense and hope that my thoughts might have some value through their circulation. You have generously encouraged this hope. I do not know if this need of mine for attention is a personal or universal need.

Once my behavior was a public performance, a larger than life dramatization in the classroom designed to enthrall and inspire the students. I would like to think that the public theatrics were projected from some inner virtues consistent with my personal self and provided educational and intellectual value. Christa - do you have a comfortable public persona? Also in your gallery? When doing workshops or giving talks? When you finally close the door of your apartment at the end of a long day or week, do you breathe a sigh of relief and shed your public persona? I was once considered - or so I was told more than once - to have possessed a dramatic charisma in my professional life, an intense presence capable of verbal fireworks that challenged and charged the students. I do not now display such charisma in my garden and my family would not expect or encourage such a performance at home. Why do we work so hard to get that kind of attention? What kind of attention do you really want, Christa? When is it most satisfying? Do you want them to pay attention to you or your pottery? Do you create the pottery to get the attention or is your pottery so good that the attention just happens as an inadvertent by-product?

Annette and Luc Vezin have something to say about this in their book, "The 20th Century Muse", in discussing the relationship of biography to the created work:

"In casting light on the muse who has contributed to the birth of a work, are we giving in to the temptation to reduce the mystery of creation to simple biography? The debate ... was taken up by Proust in his essay... 'On Art and Literature', in which he wrote: 'A book is the product of another me than the one we manifest in our habits, in society, or in our vices.' That idea is echoed today by the writer V.S. Naipaul. 'Everything valuable that I have to say is found in my books,' said the 2001 Nobel Prize winner for Literature while delivering a series of recollections on his childhood in Trinidad."

If potters agreed with Naipaul, why would they meet each year at NCECA and talk and listen to other potters? Why don't they just bring their pottery, be quiet, and let the pots do the talking? Is it possible that the potter could be a distraction from her pottery? Is the perfect aspiration that both potter and pots be admired and celebrated? How often does that happen? I think of M.C.Richards at this moment as one example. Is it a reflection on my humanity if I should, on occasion, like the pot more than the potter? All in all, without employing empirical research or statistical methodology, just sitting in the hotel lobby and observing more potters at one time than I had ever seen in all my life, I think I perceived a positive and fully functioning group of people. One speaker at a seminar bragged about the level of drinking and sexual escapades at these conferences. I did not observe this phenomenon nor was I approached or invited to such sexual experiences. I am now certain he was employing a sense of humour; it explains my exclusion.

North Carolina is a pottery collector's paradise. Seagrove's very existence and organization is structured to meet and engage all my ceramic passions and satisfy them. There must be almost a hundred studios/galleries within a twenty-minute ride in all directions from the city center. Judy and I were determined to fully exploit this marvelous opportunity. Armed with brochures and maps from the North Carolina Ceramic Center in Seagrove, we visited gallery after gallery in our rented car. City born and bred as I am, to actually drive on a dirt road was a dangerous and unwelcome adventure. I blissfully ignored the perils and drove down the rutted and pot-holed rustic lanes to the potential treasures awaiting me.

The ceramic origins of Seagrove and much of this region go back to the early pioneer settlement of the area. The families of potters represent many generations here. They have co-existed within a limited geography, often related by kinship, certainly by common history and experience. The vernacular tradition produced functional stoneware jugs, crocks, and pie plates for immediate use by neighbors and also merchants along the plank road running from Winston-Salem to Fayetteville. These working containers are the bedrock of this local tradition. Seagrove is a fascinating story of both tradition and innovation. This is in fact the name of the book edited by Douglas DeNatale, Jane Przybysz, and Jill Severn, "New Ways for Old Jugs: Tradition and Innovation at the Jugtown Pottery". DeNatale relates how Jugtown Pottery comprised an attempt in the early 1920s to revive traditional pottery in Moore County, North Carolina. Two prominent and sophisticated outsiders, Juliana Busbee and her husband, Jacques Busbee were responsible for this effort. They were not content to simply revive the 'folk' tradition but wanted to introduce the other ancient ceramic influences of China and Japan to these potters. This addition of grace and style would make the pottery more marketable to their bohemian friends in Greenwich Village, New York. This attempt to form an unlikely synthesis between remote traditions is essential to understanding the current anomalies of Seagrove. DeNatale further explains this idea:

"From the perspective of the potters, they were full collaborators in the creation of Jugtown and its pottery. And rightly so, for the potters' knowledge and skills acquired through their cultural upbringing contributed at least as much as the Busbees' artistic sensibility to the synthesis that was Jugtown. Where the Busbees decried the enthusiastic experimentation by area potteries with new glazes and forms, that creative, problem-solving impulse was an essential element of the very tradition they claimed to grasp; and it was this impulse Ben

Owen actively brought to the process of creating the oriental translations with Jacques. In retrospect, the fairest and most accurate evaluation of Jugtown's history in the life of Moore County must view the contribution of local ideas and aesthetics as an active force, not merely a resource that the Busbees mined."

As mentioned by DeNatale above, the Busbees employed a young local potter, Ben Owen. The history of the Owen family as potters goes back to the mid-19th century. Jacques took young Ben Owen to visit art schools and museums in Boston, Washington, New York, and New Orleans. Outside influences of historical and modern ceramics from diverse cultural sources were melded and synthesized by Ben Owen. Another branch of the extended family, who added an 's' to Owen for reasons not known to me, Melvin Owens and his family did not stray as far from local traditions and traditional pottery. The salesroom looks like it occupies the original home with a front porch on a modest wooden structure of long standing. Boyd Owens, son of Melvin and now the owner along with his wife, Nancy, who is the chief potter, told me with pride that the famous earthenware red glaze, original and still in use on decorative pieces was "… not store bought as some potters use around here but homemade".

In sharp contrast to this rustic scene, a short distance away we drove up to a handsome state-of-the-art two-storey structure that is the gallery and salesroom of Ben Owen III. Nearby work is being continued on a new residence for the Owen family. Huge outdoor kilns occupy another nearby space. Adjacent to the showroom is a museum of four generations of family pieces. Ben III continued the tradition of his grandfather, learning as a child playing with clay in the old man's pottery shop. He also continued another tradition from his grandfather - he left the area and acquired an education, graduating from East Carolina University with an arts degree in ceramics. He later traveled to Japan to study their ceramics techniques and tradition.

His wife, LoriAnn, welcomed Judy and me to the Gallery. The beautifully designed interior contained a varied representation of his work. We purchased a small vase with his layered Chinese Red glaze. Two different worlds, two very different orientations, all in the same extended family. Ben Owen III , like his grandfather, had bitten the apple, tasted the sweet flavor of forbidden worlds far away. I know it is foolish to simply contrast a sophisticated and eclectic approach with a 'folk' tradition. The Busbees had introduced and exposed many potters in the area to Asian pottery many years ago. All traditions, however ancient and insular, are embedded with the historical penetrations and invasions of multiple traditions, none are pure. But I must push the matter for the purposes of our investigation. How do you place value on the vernacular experience of ceramic practice that has been handed down in the family or region against the worldly sophistication of the 'educated' potter who has no allegiance to a single way of making things? What kind of a potter would you be, Christa, if your grandparents and your mother and father had taught you pottery from the time you learned to walk, and you stayed home in that single place, uncontaminated by formal education and training? Isn't innovation just the desperate strategy of isolated and culturally deprived strangers who have no cultural legacy or ceramic tradition and thus have no other ceramic choice but innovation? Can you borrow from these 'folk' traditions without shame, since it is not your family, not your region or culture, nor your world view? What is it that bonds all potters, regardless of site, history, or orientation? Are you all brothers and sisters, regardless of tradition or education? How do you achieve membership in a tradition if you are not a citizen of tradition? There are many outsiders, educated at fancy art schools and universities, now living in Seagrove, implicitly competing with the 'natives' for the pottery dollar of tourists and collectors. I wonder how they fit in, how they are accepted by those families whose ceramic legacy goes back hundreds of years? How would you feel toward the indigenous 'folk' potters if you lived in Seagrove? Please explain all these things to me, Christa.

Ben Owen answers a few of the questions just asked above. In an exhibition brochure from the Louise Wells Cameron Art Museum in Wilmington, North Carolina, entitled, "Ben Owen III: A Natural Influence", in an essay by Phyllis Blair Clark:

"… Ben had many options after graduating from college. I wondered then whether he would continue the clay traditions of his family or whether he would explore more contemporary avenues. His choice was to devote his life to the family pottery, but to incorporate his technical expertise and aesthetic awareness to make not only traditional ware, but also create one-of-a-kind pieces of great beauty and elegance."

Another voice who addressed this issue of the delicate synthesis of tradition and innovation is another fine potter I met in Seagrove, Fred Johnston. Fred Johnston shares a degree with you Christa, from Penn State University, an MFA in Ceramics. He remembers you from that time when you were an undergraduate there. On his website he states:

"My origins in clay are rooted in the southern folk pottery traditions of North Carolina. Growing up in the rural south has given me access to its colorful history and characters, which serves as a wellspring of ideas. Yet my work also draws from many cultures: Greek, Korean, Chinese, Pre-Columbian, European and Mimbres. The idea of dipping my ladle in many historical and cultural well-springs is an adventure, my journey. I question how I can extend the tradition of pottery. What can I contribute? I am not interested in pots that are mindless, shallow imitations and replications of the past. I believe in the idea of cross-fertilization and playfulness. The mixing and matching of different cultures, motifs and art styles are fertile ground, a place to cultivate."

Johnston ends his statement with a quote from Weston La Barre:

"Every era must write down its own ethical Baedeckers. But to know only one's tribe is to be primitive, and to know only one's own generation is mentally to remain always a child. We all need perspective in historic time and in ethnic space in order to assess, indeed even to sense, the naive quality of our own day. Imprisonment in the contemporary is the worst of all intellectual tyrannies."

I listen to Johnston and La Barre and want to be convinced. But I still have concerns and questions. Innovation has a good reputation now, often used today as camouflage for vulgar displays of very expensive non-art in very fashionable galleries. But tradition does not enjoy that kind of reputation. We give a free pass to indigenous pottery as a part of our pious and liberal politics of multicul-turalism, but to use that word in the art world to describe an artifact implies some invidious replication of obsolete visual vocabularies from the past. The artist is caught by the critic in sterile representations that cannot speak to our postmodern world. In short, it is generally used to insult the piece. How do people explain this contradiction? If you really respect a tradition, what gives you the right to modify or destroy it by what you do to it in your work? By using that tradition as an influence in your work, are you paying tribute to that work or correcting it? To be a real artist, more important than that, to be a successful one, do you have to repudiate and overthrow tradition as the price of admission?

It is better that I don't know the authors of the books I read. I would never attack the quality of a pot directly to the face of the potter on a visit to a gallery or studio. Like bombing a distant land far below from military aircraft, critiques are made easier by being depersonalized and separated from the intended victim. We do not want to witness the receipt of grievous injury, particularly if we are the agent of that devastation. Perhaps I should not mention a book that disap-pointed me but the title was so appealing. I would not like to deliberately hurt the author's feelings. I shudder when I scan the back pages of literary journals, where in letters to the editor, people viciously attack the authors of previous

179

articles, followed by the adjacent rejoinder of the offended and furious author of the article, denouncing each other in the most personal and vile terms. Yet, I do not think you can separate the artist from the failed artifact. For artists of any stripe and media, the pain of the received critique directed toward the object that bears her name is not less than an attack on her person. The precious artifact is indeed an extension of herself, the result of dedicated effort. Normally I do not have the stomach for this type of thing. That being said, I will test the sentiments above and discuss "Reverence: Renewing a Forgotten Virtue" by Paul Woodruff.

I have been thinking lately of trying to explain and identify the core of my attitude toward the objects that I collect. After some introspection, I thought that 'reverence' would best describe my feelings about pottery. I am essentially a secular personality and my collection contains few, if any artifacts that have explicitly religious connotations. Yet I still wanted to explore the idea of reverence, the ingredients of that term. I was pleased to find, about the same time I was mulling this over, a book that advertised a discussion about this very idea. Woodruff starts off by reassuring me that religion holds no monopoly on reverence. After that, he makes what I regard as an unnecessary and arbitrary statement that excludes objects made by humans as sources for reverence. He compounds this by saying:

"The principal object of reverence is Something that reminds us of human limitations. We speak of reverence to God, nature, and to ideals such as justice and truth."

In a further discussion, he relents a bit and allows music to be included. But the damage has been done. In my own view, it is the sublime creativity of the human spirit and the artifacts that celebrate that creativity that need to be the objects of reverence if we are to replace the greedy appetites of disposable consumerism and the violent competition for temporal power. He relents again, allowing this:

"For a lover of art, the Something might be a monument of ancient art, since this has passed out of our power to change without destroying."

I simply do not understand this special exception and his rationale for it. But the major offense awaited me toward the end of his book in a chapter called "Relativism". He makes a fundamental mistake in condemning relativism, defining it as having no standards, claiming that in relativism all positions have equal standing.

Woodruff's argument conceals his own presuppositions and orientation, pretending to be 'liberal' but in reality a closet absolutist and cultural conservative, seeking sources of reverence in that 'Something' that is really the final truth of exterior authority. A relativist insists on the use of critical intelligence and ethical sensitivity to define a just solution or the better argument, not reliance on the arbitrary authority of some fixed system, be it religion, the scientific method, Platonic ideals or the formal logic of professional philosophers. If Woodruff had his way, we would have to abandon reverence for great achievements of human culture for the supine posture of social deference and conformity. Critical appraisals of pottery and other art media, without resort to absolute standards, flourish and often reach consensus about the relative merits of art work. Human behavior, in a non-theocratic society, operates in much the same way. Standards evolve, often become law, and are modified through time because attitudes are not rigidly fixed by pretensions of a previous absolute Truth or governing authority.

Why do I take your time with this particular discussion? First of all, I really wanted some help with developing this idea of reverence as a key virtue for the collector. Some might argue that reverence for a piece of pottery is an overblown, if not overwrought, attempt to describe my deep attachment. Reverence in my case is not uncritical or sentimental. In the same sense that love between human beings co-exists and endures with the mutual realization of the fallibility and imperfection of the other, the pots in my collection are worthy of my reverence, whatever their varied condition or appearance. Each pot represents a human attempt to create something that enriches and elaborates the daily rituals and ceremonies required for us to exist and survive. I would claim that the dignity and love of human beings gathered in family and community is empowered through the grace and beauty of those objects of clay that serve as the accessories of the most fundamental experiences of humankind. The enhancement of the object in form, surface and decoration contain the unique genius of individual imagination, a gift that I humbly receive with reverence. I will defy the definition provided by that book. Respect for the potter, reverence for the pottery.

I envy the benign ageing process of the pot. It possesses an immortality far beyond my own limitations. A mere crack or chip endured over time, still the object endures. Aside from accident or malicious intent, pottery can span the centuries of human culture. Human beings as a species have a far more finite and limited warranty. I do not think we are well designed. Like a car with too many added computerized features that are always breaking down, our biological complexity is not sustainable. I do not wish to burden or bore others with the vicissitudes of my old age. When people in social situations ask someone my age 'how are you?', their expectation does not include a clinical inventory of bodily dysfunctions and disorders. Their obvious preference in this implicit protocol is for an automatic if dishonest 'fine', or a perfunctory 'OK'. It would be rude to do otherwise. I can now swallow four pills at once daily, each a different shape and color. I prick my finger twice a day, bleed on a test strip and keep a log of numbers that record the ups and downs of diabetes. I drink decaffeinated coffee to keep my blood pressure down, eat selectively to avoid high levels of cholesterol. I need to severely restrict common elements found in most food, sodium, sugar and fat. I have even taken the drastic steps of reducing my daily Scotch intake to one small glass at 4:00 p.m. and exercising on my stationary bicycle for 20 minutes each day. As a proud old man, I can still boast about the dependable regularity of my bowels. But enough is enough. I cannot expect you to tolerate such an abrupt transition from reveries about reverence to the vaunted condition of my bowels. I promise never to bring this matter up again. The human price of being self-conscious and awake in the world is to understand the predictable outcome of extended life. It cannot be a surprise.

It is springtime and my joyful embrace of pottery equals the vigor of blooms in the garden. It is good to be writing to you again.

Your friend,

Richard

Twenty-seven

May 9, 2004

Dear Christa,

My sanity and stability are dependent upon assumptions and pretensions of authority and control. I cannot control Iraq or the domestic policies of the White House but I can control my garden. I shape and trim the foliage, ruthlessly remove unwanted vegetation, mold the form of shrubbery to conform to the aesthetics of my personal preferences. Call it overcompensation for powerlessness elsewhere, but my garden is neat and trimmed, no branch or twig dares defy me and survive. My garden is an exterior room, with a collection of plants in a formation as controlled as the arrangement of my pottery in my interior rooms. I use nature as you use clay. I am routinely humbled by my pride of power. The garden can retaliate. I have been busy the last month helping in the gardens of my two sons. During my absence the plants initiated unauthorized growth and invited motley strangers into the garden. A friend once informed me that a weed was just an unwanted plant. I freely discriminate and ruthlessly remove these uninvited strangers. I have just completed the re-conquest of the front garden. I fear that this conquest is just as temporary as the armies that seek to occupy foreign lands.

Christa, how does your self-image shape your behavior? I have never been a procrastinator. It would be foolhardy to start doing it now. I am always on time, most often very early to arrive. No one has to tell me when to do my chores. I am responsible. I am an activist. I plan and schedule what happens to me. Ambitious extensions of my future in the far distance would now be unrealistic. I need to believe that my future, however limited in duration, is directly influenced by my present behavior and action. I assert that I make things happen in the future by what I plan and execute today. I do not wish for a critical response or a philosophical correction of this notion. If illusion, it does not become any less valuable. We must believe, even if a leap of faith is required, even if a contrived fiction becomes necessary, that we impact and shape our own destiny. We must think we make a difference.

You must have some overall plans, Christa, some grand scheme, that instructs your daily efforts. The old Soviet Union used to issue grand five-year or ten-year plans that mapped out the goals to be achieved by the nation. Of course their goals required the slavish obedience of all citizens and great sacrifice. It became a form of manipulation and dictatorial control of the masses. What is your ceramic five- or ten-year plan? I admire self-discipline. Is that the real illusion? We ultimately cannot control reality, however harsh we are in controlling ourselves. For example - you can control what happens at the potter's wheel but the kiln, that potential adversary of every potter, might capriciously destroy your best laid plans. Do you ever let go or give yourself a break from the routine and regime you have imposed on yourself? Those of us who claim to map out, in calculated and cunning ways our self-made destiny, are often as harsh on ourselves as that potential exterior authority that would arbitrarily remove our freedom to decide.

On behalf of the procrastinator, it might be said his reluctance to act is because he is so enjoying the present. That is the danger with people like us, so busy pushing our plans into future possibilities we forget to fully live in the present moment. That is the great gamble we take, to risk the immediate joys of living for the preparation for a future that remains highly problematic. If this attitude becomes a habit, the fruits of the future never appear to arrive, or if they do, never seem to satisfy. Whatever the results of yesterday's planning and efforts, one cannot stop long enough to really savor them. To push that point just a little further, one could say that the very basis of aesthetic experience is the ability to concentrate and focus in the immediate moment. One cannot be preoccupied when creating or engaging art. The stillness and stasis of time, stopped, paralyzed, frozen in the moment, allows me to look at my pottery with a level of engagement I never enjoyed in my 'active' years.

Anna Quindlen, a fine writer and novelist who has a regular column in Newsweek Magazine, had this to say in the May 17, 2004 issue, addressing college graduates:

"To the members of the class of 2004: putting a stop to this treadmill is like disarmament. Who dares to go first? A generation ago your parents, as a group, were known for wanting to give peace a chance in the world. Somehow we have raised a group that wants only a little peace in their own frantic lives. But peace is not what you see in the immediate future, for the world, for this nation or for yourselves. Instead, what stretches before you looks like a version of 'Survivor' in street clothes. Find the job. Find the mate. Scale the ladder. Have the baby. Make the deal. Make the birthday cake. The gym, the Gap, the lover, the decor, the cuisine. Who will win the contest? Perhaps it will be those of you brave enough to stop moving."

This attitude of repose is also necessary for intellectual work. As a teacher educator, I was always puzzled why public school teachers were so obsessive about getting the students to stop talking and be quiet. Most teachers don't know how to use that 'quiet' time when they get it. If you challenge students with knowledge as problematic rather than complete, you can offer open-ended questions that inspire them to consider the discrepancies and contradictions embedded in all human knowledge. Thus this space of silence does not represent a void, it becomes a rich and profound effort to develop disciplined analysis. A student of mine once paid me a great compliment, told me that the spacing of quiet between my remarks was the best part of my teaching. What he meant was that I left quiet spaces between comments to give students a chance to reflect, to think about what I had said. One cannot learn unless time is given for the making of personal meaning. Students are too often taught to memorize, not to think. Thinking takes time, why don't teachers schedule that in their lesson plans?

What should happen eventually to my pottery collection? Is it worthy enough to continue its existence beyond my own demise? I really have little choice in the matter. I have humorously suggested that Judy and her next husband will decide its fate. Or my sons will cash in the objects on eBay. How do you know if a collection is worthy of being maintained and kept whole after the demise of the collector? No one piece in my collection is a priceless museum item. But the collection as a whole, in its particular setting, does offer a tremendous diversity of antique and contemporary pottery from a number of countries and cultures. It is the placement and setting that is important and makes every collection unique. This is particularly true when that setting is a home. We are looking at both the art and the lives of the people that live there. In this case, they become the same thing. I embrace the term 'domestic ware' although it is intended to be a modest term that describes household goods used in everyday functions. I consider all the art in my house 'domestic ware'. In my life, both biography and pottery are now largely domestic events. Nicholas A. Basbanes understands what I mean. He states in his book about book collecting, "Among the Gently Mad: Strategies and Perspectives for the Book Hunter in the Twenty-First Century":

"What some bibliophiles regard as a specialty, I like to think of as a theme. What some call focus, I prefer to call context. Such fine distinctions may well be little more than matters of taste, since both argue strongly for the development of a central plan, yet they support my considered view that every collector is a storyteller, and every collection a form of narrative..."

Judy and I recently went with friends to an obscure museum in a Los Angeles suburb in the San Fernando Valley. J.B. Nethercutt, an heir to a cosmetics fortune, now ninety years old, built a vast and opulent showroom in which he has assembled one of the world's most outstanding collection of beautifully restored antique and classic automobiles. In addition, he has gathered a Mechanical Musical Instrument collection of nickelodeons, phonograph players, reproducing pianos and orchestrons and a mighty Wurlitzer theatre pipe organ. I do not have a vested interest in mechanical things, certainly not automobiles. But the superb craftsmanship and design of some of those automobiles was simply stunning. Two vast buildings, with a Grand Salon evoked the 1920s and 1930s, with automobiles that had been completely restored to every fine detail. I was pleased when the guide on the tour announced that Nethercutt characterized his collection as 'functional fine art'. This is a term that potters might very well borrow. He was right of course.

The examples of craftsmanship from a previous era might not be so evident today, given the pressure to produce standardized models for popular consumption. What about pottery, could we make the same statement as with automobiles - that the high level of previous craftsmanship of the past cannot be replicated today? Who today can match the efforts of Adelaide Alsop Robineau, the great American potter of the 19th century who put in over one thousand hours of work in creating a single vase, the intricate and elaborate lattice pattern organized around the motif of the scarab in her masterpiece, 'Apotheosis of the Toiler'? Does superb craftsmanship of that nature just take too much time for the current potter? Is that because today's potters don't have that level of skill or because it would be prohibitively expensive to invest that much time in one object? Or is it that modern aesthetics that call for a minimalistic or simple approach does not require all that work or time? Christa, if someone was willing to compensate you for the results, and you could spend a thousand hours creating one vase, what would it look like?

Could it be that I am an unsung prophet of my time? My love of crafts - the handmade object represents a deep commitment easily documented by a perusal of objects of wood, pewter, glass, metal and clay in my home. The Long Beach Museum of Art, a 53- year-old institution, housed in an old Craftsman-style home on a bluff hovering over the Pacific Ocean, has re-dedicated itself to craft and decorative art traditions. John Balzar, in an article in the Los Angeles Times of May 8, 2004, tells us the story of the revival of interest in crafts:

"For the first half of the 20th century, functional crafts, particularly furniture and architectural appointments, were part of the excitement of everyday life. Magazines and newspapers tantalized the nation with the virtues of distinctive styles of California living that emerged straight from craft workshops. Later, ceramists at Scripps College and elsewhere gave the region a national profile in the gallery crafts. During the years that followed, mass production, synthetic materials, saturation advertising, haste and who knows what else dealt crafts a staggering blow nationwide. But not a fatal one. In the last decade or two, the resurgence of crafts has been nothing short of remarkable, if the United States is considered as a whole. That includes both crafts with artistic ambitions and those old-fashioned and once disappearing practical crafts like blacksmithing, boot making, weaving and even the brewing of craft beers."

I have just finished reading a book that is often referenced as a significant statement in explaining and justifying ceramics as a major art form. Philip Rawson, former Dean of the School of Art and Design of Goldsmith's College, University of London, wrote a book about twenty years ago called "Ceramics". Rawson attempts to establish ceramics as an art form through investigating the essential ingredients of pottery. Wayne Higby, in his Foreword, makes a very good observation, speaking of Rawson:

"He recommends looking at the forms of pottery not just to classify them, but to read them as symbols analogous to sense experience. This recommendation has far-reaching implications since, in our society, critical awareness is primarily achieved by acquiring factual knowledge rather than by developing the resources of intuitive feeling. This emphasis on factual knowledge has isolated art from the general flow of Western culture by reserving it for a relatively small group of 'informed' individuals. The very fact that pottery is accessible to everyone by virtue of its immediate connection with human experience has disqualified it in the past as a major art form. Rawson introduces this accessibility factor as an important aesthetic consideration and implies that the power of pottery as art lies in its ability to communicate to a wide audience by expressing human sensuous life. He asks the reader to become more aware of emotional responses to pottery in order to give depth and clarity to learned perception."

These ideas are very appealing to me. It is the commonality of these household vessels that make their meaning as well as function significant. Rarity is advantageous for attaching monetary value but not necessarily for aesthetic or cultural significance. The 'fine' in 'fine arts' is often mistaken for the contrived prestige of the owner's wealth and the placement of the object within the affluence of that setting. Elaboration of detail necessary for ostentatious display cannot define what is 'fine' about art anymore than the bare object whose function has so determined outcome that grace and subtlety have been lost. Rawson best explains these ideas in his own words:

"Thus one of the prime reasons why ceramics is such an interesting art is that it fills the gap which now yawns between art and life as most people understand that relationship. To explain the meaning of ceramics can be, in a sense, to explore the historical roots of art as such. For whereas other arts, painting and sculpture in particular, have come for centuries now to resemble cut flowers, separated from the living plant which produced them, in the case of ceramics we are everywhere brought face to face with the root. This appears in the primal interweaving of matter, human action, and symbol that each pot represents. Inert clay, from the earth, is made into something which is directly and intimately related to active craft, to the processes of human survival, and to social and spiritual factors in the life of man, all at once. None of the elements is lost; all are reflected in some sort of balance in each successful work. This then becomes what one may call a 'transformation image', something undeniably material, weaving the evidence of its material nature in its visible and tangible forms and attributes, which at the same time contains so much projected into it from man's daily life and experience at all levels that it can seem to him almost like a projection of his bodily identity. It thus becomes an external testimony to his existence. By taking an existential back-step, so to speak, we are enabled to witness in humanity's pots a virtually unlimited variety of concrete realizations which uncover and authenticate his life and action in his world of meaning."

This is simply among the very best comments and thoughts about pottery I have ever encountered. These sentences are among the first in the book. But alas, Rawson does not in fact develop the uncovering or authenticating of the life and action of the potter or perceiver or their world of meaning. Nor does he investigate the social and spiritual factors that would form the context for pottery. Rawson chooses to devote almost the entire book to the attributes of the pots themselves, the techniques and symbolism of the form and character of the pot. He does achieve a weighty description of qualities of the pot that are convincing in making the case for ceramics as art. Perhaps I should not complain that he did not write the book, at least the complete book, I would have wanted him to write. Higby and Rawson promised me early in their work possibilities that I could not locate in the book. Rawson made a noble and largely successful effort to explore ceramics in as subtle and refined a manner as other fine art media enjoy. He does not connect the pot to the observers or communities who experience the pot as ritual, utensil, or aesthetic object. I guess I am asserting, without knowing if I have the authoritative support of professional aestheticians, that the aesthetics of art must ultimately include not only the object of art but the experience of that object. John Dewey is helpful here. In "Art As Experience" Dewey states:

"Language exists only when it is listened to as well as spoken. The hearer is an indispensable partner. The work of art is complete only as it works in the experience of others than the one who created it."

Elsewhere in the book Dewey further explores the importance of experience:

"For to perceive, a beholder must create his own experience. And his creation must include relations comparable to those which the original producer underwent. They are not the same in any literal sense. But with the perceiver, as with the artist, there must be an ordering of the elements of the whole that is in form, although not in details, the same as the process of organization the creator of the work consciously experienced. Without an act of recreation the object is not perceived as a work of art. The artist selected, simplified, clarified, abridged and condensed according to his interest. The beholder must go through these operations according to his point of view and interest. In both, an act of abstraction, that is of extraction of what is significant, takes place. In both, there is comprehension in its literal signification - that is, a gathering together of details and particulars physically scattered into an experienced whole. There is work done on the part of the percipient as there is on the part of the artist."

Rawson comes closest to this idea when he discusses the metaphorical suggestiveness of the pot. Here he talks about memory-traces, which he defines as based on our past experiences. The emotions evoked at the time of engagement form part of this memory trace. He does provide advice:

"If we are to understand the true significance of the formal units making up a pot, we must try to discover in ourselves appropriate memory-traces of our own, chains of vivid concrete experiences, to which, as we have seen, feeling may be the only key."

Another point of difference with Rawson, he offers many, many facts about pottery. I have always distrusted facts, I just don't think they are useful for most intellectual work. I particularly don't trust them as the basis for a fully developed aesthetics. Whatever biographers or critics might say, the totality of a life or a work of art can never be something as arid and clean as the facts about them. The preoccupation with facts is really what keeps most academics from becoming intellectuals (or artists). The experience of the engagement with art is not an objective and sequential review of the facts about that art object, the response is at best approximate and always interpretive. Facts do not just get in the way. I would maintain they distort the possibilities for a memorable encounter. Facts give the false promise of a single certainty. The most evident sign of a second rate intelligence is the search for a final truth, be it a religious fundamentalist or a pedantic academic. God and academia both seem to attract many souls who seek that salvation and security. Rawson does get it right in the last quotation stated above that 'feeling may be the only key'. But he either does not know how to talk about feelings or perhaps does not 'feel' that it is within his scholarly expertise.

One of my early intellectual heroes, C. Wright Mills in his landmark book "The Sociological Imagination" had this to say about the impact and effects of 'objective' facts on reasoning:

"It is not only information that they need - in this Age of Fact, information often dominates their attention and overwhelms their capacities to assimilate it. It is not only the skills of reason that they need - although their struggles to acquire these exhaust their limited moral energy. What they need, and what they feel they need, is a quality of mind that will help them to use information and to develop reason in order to achieve lucid summations of what is going on in the world and of what may be happening with themselves. It is this quality, I am going to contend, that journalists and scholars, artists and publics, scientists and editors are coming to expect of what may be called the sociological imagination... The sociological imagination enables us to grasp history and biography and the relations between the two within society."

Christa, are you willing to share the aesthetic definition of your pottery with the perceiver or collector? Do you mind if their appraisal or response is vastly different from your original aesthetic intentions? Are you the final authority in the official definition of your own pottery or can you be overruled or replaced by the aesthetic version of the pot by the perceiver? Could it even be possible that you would accept and modify your own assessment of your pottery by the evaluation of the critic or perceiver? My memory-traces are obviously different than yours, my life experiences are obviously different than yours, maybe we don't even see the same pot when we are looking at the same object.

I do not want to let go of this business with aesthetic experience. It is what I do each day. I might have even more practice with this than most potters. One helpful reference is offered by Louis Menand, Pulitizer-prize-winning author, in his book, "American Studies". In an essay entitled 'The Principles of Oliver Wendell Holmes', Menand discusses the contribution of this future Supreme Court justice and founder of the constitutional law of free speech. Holmes based his own understanding of the law not on abstract legal doctrines but rather human experience. Menand quotes Holmes: "The life of the law has not been logic; it has been experience". Then he further explains Holmes's idea:

"… [Holmes] does not say that there is no logic in the law. It only says that logic is not responsible for what is living in the law. The active ingredient in the compound, what puts the bones in the goose, is the thing called 'experience'. Holmes was using that word in a particular sense. He meant it as the name for everything that arises out of the interaction of the human organism with its environment: beliefs, sentiments, customs, values, policies, prejudices - what he called 'the felt necessities of the time'. Our word for it (in many ways less satisfactory) is 'culture'.

This comprises an inclusive and contextual approach to law, not the generalities and abstraction of theory but the concrete realities of human judgment. Another valuable aspect is Holmes' invention of the 'reasonable man'. Here the issue was civil liability for injury.

"The problem was what the basis for deciding that a particular act was negligent ought to be. Assuming that we want to make persons who act carelessly pay the cost of cleaning up their tortuous messes, how do we determine what sort of behavior counts as careless? How do we distinguish a tort from an accident, or from the permissible by-product of a socially desirable activity? One way of doing this would be to devise a series of general rules for conduct, violation of which would ipso facto constitute negligence; but this solution was obviously ruled out for Holmes by his contempt for the malleability of general rules. His alternative proposal was that we should do judicially what we all do anyway when we are confronted with a judgment call, which is to evaluate the conduct at issue by the lessons of experience ... Whose experience? The experience, Homes said of 'an intelligent and prudent member of the community'. He didn't mean by this a particularly intelligent and prudent person - a judge, for instance. He meant, precisely, a person who is neither particularly prudent nor particularly imprudent, an 'average member of the community' - in other words, a jury."

This is at the heart of my earlier comments about the very valuable contribution of Rawson. He defined the complexities of the pot. He constructed and codified the facts of the pot. I am looking for a protocol for the perception and experience of pottery. It might very well exist, but I haven't found it yet. Like Holmes, it must empower that 'average member of the community to appropriate and appreciate pottery within the context of past experience. That does not undervalue the importance of the pot. It remains the reference point. Indeed the encounter with a pot could encourage an extension and expansion of standards that enrich the frame of reference brought to the next ceramic experience. It is a democratic and liberal impulse. The citizen, not the political science professor, ultimately decides the fate of the republic. It is the same citizen who must make sense of that clay object on the table or shelf. How could we shape a strategy of observation that would help ensure a profound engagement? In my student days as an art major, there was a class called 'art appreciation' and a series of slides which required the memorization of name, date, place and one-word description of aesthetic approach. I wonder now how many of those artists from different cultures and historical periods really knew they were classicists, romantics or realists? We can do better for the aesthetics of pottery.

I am preparing for summer. I have recycled my short sleeved shirts to the front of the closet, recovered short pants and sandals from out-of-sight storage, braced for the hot weather. I must try to finish most garden chores before the full heat arrives. I hope this letter finds you in good health and spirits.

Take care. Your friend,

Richard

Twenty-eight

June 7, 2004

Dear Christa,

There is no happier surprise or greater expectation than the anticipated arrival of pottery by delivery. I received your pair of candlesticks a few days ago, complicated by my struggle to unwrap them because of frantic impatience. When fully revealed, they were simply marvelous. So stunned and excited, I first, to my embarrassment, set them upside down, I did confess this mishap to you on the telephone, insisting on a pure honesty in our relationship that I do not know I can continue, given my chronic mishaps. I held them by the natural light of the window, observed them, then placed them on the dining room table on the Celtic patterned tapestry runner, surrounded by the strict formation of the Arts and Crafts chairs. It will take a while to know them, but through our constant interaction we will soon become friends. I must go by them to get to the kitchen, they will be sentinels guarding this important household corridor. I will not be able to pass them without challenge or recognition.

Christa, I want to use words to engage your candlesticks. No grand inclusive theory will be activated with automatic standards. I don't want to evaluate your work, I want to experience it. The two candlesticks are identical, you obviously can plan and control the shape and glaze. They are robust in their full, round form, with a top platform for the candle, then a mid-bulge with a soft edge not quite rounded, flared at the bottom with a stable base. The top platform, greater in circumference than the rest, forms a white saucer with a raised rim for the candle, light green below, the glaze darkening as it forms an uneven and dense accumulation just below the middle girth, then dramatically darkens into a dark brown that anchors the candlestick. This great contrast ranges vertically from top to bottom in color, intensity and value. I truly enjoy each demarcation, especially the accumulation of glaze, threatening to spill down the remainder of the form, but holding back, at least for now, in scallops of thicker glaze. This represents, by design, the central irregularity in the otherwise highly disciplined object. A circular thin line of natural clay is visible at the very bottom. The result is solid and definite as the furniture in the room, with a profile of form that provides ultimate function with a flourish of contrast and interest that cannot be easily ignored. That is the best I can do with words right now. It helped. I can see more now. And I will have every opportunity to see yet more in the future. What a happy and fortunate breed, collectors! Dusting becomes a modest penance for such great benefits.

I already miss Edward W. Said. His recent premature death deprived us of a valuable intellectual guide to our world and to understanding literature as a window into that world. His commentary on the Middle East provided a rare and respected voice for the Arab and Palestinian perspective. A fine scholar and writer, he was able to integrate and synthesize culture, art and politics into a pattern of meaning that allowed those who have suffered historical colonization to reclaim their history and culture and give the rest of us reason to question the fortunate history of our own temporary dominance. He understood that the invasion of physical geography as political colonization was usually accompanied by the importation of cultural modes as intellectual colonization. Cultural forms emboldened and sponsored by superior weaponry and technology were implicitly judged to be superior in content and significance. We are still making that mistake today. Said became associated with a friend from a very different identity and perspective, Daniel Barenboim, musician and conductor. Barenboim was born into a Russian Jewish family that emigrated to Argentina. Said was born in Jerusalem into a Palestinian family, grew up in Cairo, eventually settled in the United States. It is important to note that they never fully agreed about the crucial issues in the Middle East, but they did experience friendship, co-sponsored reconciliation and worked together in a series of conversations captured in a small book, "Parallels and Paradoxes: Explorations in Music and Society". Edward Said knew how to connect his area, literature, to the central issues of the day. He stated:

"I've always thought that being a professional, whether it's a professional writer or professional specialist at something, is never enough. It's never quite satisfied me. One of the things that I believe, in my own case, that I do, and that perhaps distinguishes me from many of my colleagues, is that I feel I have an attitude toward what I do, which isn't very tied to questions of technique, expertise, or professionalism, to issues that are solely limited to the field of literature, but really try to go beyond into questions of the relationship between literature and society, between literature and politics, and so on."

In my view, ceramics will never be elevated to a fine art because of further refinement of isolated specialist knowledge, but rather through the efforts to connect ceramics to the core of human existence and human civilization. Who has tried to do that in the West? The aesthetic experience becomes functional and instrumental when the enrichment and illumination of daily life becomes internalized in the very fabric of that life. The health of the human spirit cannot have its temperature taken or scored by medical lab tests. All of us who have lived some extended time know by contrast and consequence the ennobling grace that art provides and, in its absence, the crushing grounding of life deprived of the transcendent possibilities of the human imagination. The Japanese knew that even a single piece of pottery placed in an interior space, as well as that modest and irregular container of tea, could provide that grace and spirit. Speaking of paradoxes, modest but profound life enhancing aesthetic resources are all around us; yet how rare and difficult it seems for most people to experience and celebrate them.

Barenboim, in his exchanges with Said, tries to explain the essential power and meaning of music:

"… if you study music in the deepest sense of the word - all the relationships, the interdependence of the notes, of the harmonies, of the rhythm, and the connection of all those elements with the speed; if you look at the essential unrepeatability of music, the fact that it is different every time because it comes in a different moment - you learn many things about the world, about nature, about human beings and human relations And therefore, it is, in many ways, the best school for life, really. And yet, at the same time, it is a means of escape from the world. And it is with this duality of music that we come to the paradox. How is it possible that something that can teach you so much about the world, about nature and the universe, and, for more religious people, about God - that something that is so clearly able to teach you so many things can serve as a means of escape from precisely those things?

What are the parallels with pottery? What can pottery teach us? Christa, you as the performer, as the professional potter, as with Barenboim as the professional musician, have the refined expertise to interpret the legacy of previous ceramic traditions. Barenboim, unlike the composer, has the added responsibility to create the sound intended in the score. You have no such restraint. Your restraints are self-imposed. Yet you accept the tradition of the container, there are no unwelcome holes in your vases where liquids can leak out. They do sit on the table, they do not fall over. Why do you impose such conventions? Perhaps you are more analogous with the composer as the primary creative agent. I still seek to find the commonalities of aesthetic experience across the arts. As the recipient of musical performances and pottery, I must acknowledge their profound differences. The performance of music is ephemeral sound that is immediate and leaves me, the pottery remains stationary and solid. They teach me different things and yet they co-exist and mingle in the sights and sounds of my house and find their way into my interior being where I cannot experience their further separation.

Others are not as friendly to Said and our search for context, connection and commonality. Peter Williams, in his article "A world of Delighted Imagining" in the Times Literary Supplement (TLS) of April 17, 1998, in discussing "The Aesthetics of Music" by Roger Scruton, commented:

"I resist anything that appears to put music second: music as gesture, language, expression, intonation, symbol, sign, embodiment, life, always as or like something else. Offense (in my terms) is likeliest to be given by attempts to 'situate music as taking place, so to speak, in a social and cultural setting' (Edward Said, Musical Elaborations), if 'cultural' means something politically narrow, for this approach has no interest in being faithful to music. I have never read anything of the situating kind that is free of shaky analysis, poor history, misprision of one kind of another."

I cannot agree with Williams. If placement within cultural context is a distraction, if music is '... a mode of experience complete in itself' as Williams concludes in the last paragraph of the article, then surely the experience of music by the audience must end with the sound of that music. I am not able to depart the concert hall with a memorized recording of Beethoven intact, I cannot replicate and hum the complete composition. According to Williams, I leave the concert hall empty of further possibilities until the next performance. My own version asserts that associations with biographical context and culture allow me to attach the musical performance to everything previously experienced. Aesthetic experiences form after-the-fact metaphors and summaries for the life already led. I do leave with the fortified inspiration and understanding of those basic affirmations that infuse and inform my life with meaning. A highly refined aesthetic as personal attribute is characterized by a highly refined capacity for self-conscious appropriation, placement, and integration. This is a creative and intellectual activity and process internal to the perceiver.

Pottery does not have a virgin birth. Nor does music or other art have the innocence of solitary origin. Christa, as artist your promiscuous intimacy with multiple influences reflect distinctive history and culture. You share the parenthood of the pot through this connection of biography and social situation. I do not think I should carry this particular metaphor further, I do not wish to give offense. Using you as agent, time and place leave forensic evidence in the creation of the object, sometimes obvious, often obscure and subtle. Use takes over often to further fashion the piece. The rich patina of old pottery, as with old furniture, results from extended use and exposed placement within a human community. It cannot be considered a thing in itself. I will not settle this matter here.

What is not prerequisite for me is the technical knowledge involved in the construction of the piece. I do not need to know the firing temperature of the kiln or the chemical mixture of the glaze, nor have the skill to throw a pot to engage the finished artifact with great benefit. It is the aesthetic engagement that is new and unique on each occasion. Even approaching the same pot daily, it is never quite the same. I am never exactly in the same condition, what has happened to me just before and since the last time I encountered the pot. The pot changes with the light, reveals portions once shaded; seems to shine with greater intensity, modesty abandoned and brazen in its beauty; then, depending on the time of day, withdraws, once again sublime in its continuing mystery. Still the pot belongs to families of relationships greater than itself. This community of intent and appearance remains general, you still need to stop and look at the individual pot for an experience that cannot be predicted by known class, category, or type.

Christa, the life of your pottery extends far beyond your act of creation. Do you care about their impact after they leave you? Since you are commemorated in the very property of the pot, does your performance last as long as the pot exists? You leave your mark on them, that stylized stamp and logo that advertises its maker. Do I prize the pot or the potter? Is it a more profound experience with the pot knowing you made it? Or should I convert to the position of Williams and claim the experience of the pot is independent of all else, including the biography, reputation, and extraneous intentions and circumstances of the maker?

I have not read fiction for many years. My past 'professional' reading at the university demanded more literal and instrumental dividends. This is now changing. I have just finished "The Cave" by Jose Saramago, the winner of the Nobel Prize for Literature in 1998. Translated from the Portuguese, the novel was written by an old man (Saramago was born in 1922) about an old man. No wonder I feel such affinity. But there is more. The chief protagonist is an elderly potter. What more could I ask for? This old potter, Cipriano Algor, lives with his daughter and her husband in a village near something called The Center, a huge conglomerate that includes shops, apartment blocks, offices and recreational zones. His son-in-law works as a security guard at The Center and is due to receive an apartment there where they can all live together. This would mean that Cipriano would have to give up his work. His pottery produced domestic ware for sale at The Center. They informed him his pottery is no longer wanted, none were buying it. People are buying plastic, it lasts longer and doesn't break. His daughter, Marta suggests they try to make ceramic dolls instead. The old man goes along with the idea. Saramago describes his ordeal as he tries to adjust his old pottery habits to this new product:

"From that day on, Cipriano Algor interrupted his work in the pottery only to eat and to sleep. His lack of experience of the necessary techniques meant that he mistook the proportions of plaster and water needed for making the mold piece, made everything worse by getting the wrong quantities of clay, water, and deflocculant to make a balanced mixture for the casting slip, and then poured the resulting mixture in far too quickly, thus creating air bubbles inside the mold. The first three days were spent making and unmaking, despairing over his mistakes, cursing his own clumsiness and trembling with joy whenever some delicate operation turned out well."

Saramago tenderly portrays this stubborn old man who is resisting shutting down his kiln and abandoning his life-long craft. The author plainly sympathizes with his chief character, in contrasting his simple and honest work with the impersonal machinery of this centralized corporation that controls and determines the lives of people in the region. His wife had died years earlier. He has a dog, 'Found', interest in a widow living nearby, his old house, his run-down kiln, and stacks of unwanted pottery. He is making his last stand and you feel the odds are against him.

Saramago turns out to be a very fascinating fellow. According to the article "Letter From Lisbon" in the Times Literary Supplement (TLS) of October 23, 1998, Saramago is a man of great independence:

"Jose Saramago, who at that point in his career ranked as only a mediocre writer of fiction, was already in the habit of saying no, and of stubbornly following his own, somewhat erratic course, which has led him to become one of the outstanding writers of the late twentieth century. Saramago, who has no kind words for global capitalism and is especially hostile towards the American economic and political system, would no doubt scoff at the Horatio Alger optimism that to this day still seems to inform and justify the capitalist creed, but he's the perfect example of a self-made man of letters, and in the deepest sense. For this is not simply the case of an author's native talent developing through hard work and gaining recognition through persistence; in Saramago, talent itself seems to be a product of patient forging."

Christa, do you have nightmares about what Ciprianio had to endure? What would happen if people just stopped buying your pottery? Could some new trendy ceramic style leave you behind? Or if clay was at last deemed an obsolete and unsuitable material? Would you change your entire approach to pottery, like poor Cipriano agreed to do, just in order to survive and find a market for your goods? How about Saramago's hostility toward globalism as sponsored by the US? How can the world honor an artist so unfriendly to this country? Was I disloyal and unpatriotic by purchasing this book and thereby supporting his message? Does aesthetics allow politics? Should an aesthetic experience answer my questions or give me new questions to ask? To make matters even worse, I did enjoy the book, glad I met Cipriano, and want to read more Saramago. I will never go to a Senior Citizen Center. This is my way of finding compatible contact. Even eccentrics need occasional company.

To return to the most important matter of this letter. Judy measured the platform on the candlesticks, unsatisfied with the small candles we had available. She came back with two candles of exactly the right size and height, with graduated rings, colored off-white and green, emulating the changing colors of the candlesticks, picking up the hue and intensity of colors in the tapestry runner. They flank a very nice dark green bowl, with a wide rim embossed and engraved with floral designs by John Denis Ransmeier, a North Carolina potter.

Our Christa Assad collection is growing. In fifty years you will need my permission to borrow them for a magnificent Assad Retrospective Exhibition that could well occupy an entire floor of the Smithsonian or other qualified museum or gallery. My garden is trimmed and pruned, my pots and shelves are dusted. My diabetes and cholesterol numbers are positive. I truly have found peace and joy. Have a good summer.

Your Friend,

Richard

Twenty-nine

June 20, 2004

Dear Christa,

I live a quiet, clean life in a quiet, clean suburb. I do not observe or experience poverty or violence in my neighborhood. When I work in the front garden in the morning hours, the occasional people I meet are neighbors walking or jogging for exercise, handsomely clothed with the appropriate apparel and shoes for this type of activity; thoughtful and decent individuals taking a dog for a walk, always with a small plastic bag in evident view for the removal of the animal's excrement; a friendly grandmother with a young grandson in a carriage, stopping by my garden so he can enjoy the bubbling sound and sight of the fountain, exchanging a few polite comments. There is no terrible drama in my life that bears any relationship to what I read or view as I monitor the remainder of the world. I do get dirty in the garden. I like to work close to the earth, on my knees weeding and trimming neat boundaries of blooming vegetation to match the curving edge of the paths. I immediately shower when I go inside, I also want to be neat and clean. I know it's superficial and limits my profundity, but I do associate aesthetic beauty with neat, quiet and clean things. I might even like rock and roll music if they would only play it softly.

I subscribe to periodicals that often provide me vicarious images of nightmare worlds. My resulting penance of anguished agitation is the only action I wish to take at this point in my life. No more barricades for me, no more losing crusades. I have paid my dues. It was the very last article in the June 24, 2004 issue of the The New York Review of Books that hurt me so, read in the early morning hours, still dark outside. I just finished reading it, just before I sat down and started writing this letter to you. Mark Danner describes, in "The Logic of Torture", the official policies that led to the torture of people at Abu Ghraib prison in Iraq:

"It has long since become clear that President Bush and his highest officials, as they confronted the world on September 11, 2001, and the days after, made a series of decisions about methods of warfare and interrogation… The effect of those decisions - among them, the decision to imprison indefinitely those seized in Afghanistan and elsewhere in the war on terror, the decision to designate those prisoners as 'unlawful combatants' and to withhold from them the protections of the Geneva Convention, and finally the decision to employ 'high pressure methods', to extract 'actionable intelligence' from them - was officially to transform the United States from a nation that did not torture to one that did."

Perhaps you will not consider this an act of friendship - sharing the following testimony with you. Please forgive this temporary unkindness. I must add the actual description of the torture, I want you to read this and possibly suffer for just a little while with me. I want you to bear witness with me. Damn it, Christa, if we are going to talk about pots and something called 'beauty', we need to understand that dark side of the human species, we need to somehow reconcile these irreconcilable things. Help me make sense of this. Isn't that what friendship is all about? The prisoner gives the following account of his treatment at Abu Ghraib prison:

"The first day they put me in a dark room and started hitting me in the head and stomach and legs. They made me raise my hands and sit on my knees. I was like that for four hours. Then the Interrogator came and he was looking at me while they were beating me. Then I stayed in this room for 5 days, naked with no clothes… They put handcuffs on my hand and they cuffed me high for 7 or 8 hours. And that caused a rupture to my right hand and I had a cut that was bleeding and had pus coming from it. They kept me this way on 24, 25 and 26 October. And in the following days, they also put a bag over my head, and of course, this whole time I was without clothes and without anything to sleep on. And one day in November, they started different type of punishment, where an American Police came in my room and put the bag over my head and cuffed my hands and he took me out of the room into the hallway. He started beating me, him and five other American Police. I could see their feet, only, from under the bag. A couple of those police they were female because I heard their voices and I saw two of the police that were hitting me before they put the bag over my head. One of them was wearing glasses. I couldn't read his name because he put tape over his name. Some of the things they did was make me sit down like a dog, and they would hold the string from the bag and they made me bark like a dog and they were laughing at me… One of the police was telling me in Arabic to crawl, so I crawled on my stomach and the police were spitting on me when I was crawling and hitting me…"

I deliberately left out his detailed account of the forced sexual manipulation of the genitals and the ramming of a baton up his rectum. I wanted to spare you, but it is also a matter of habit. We don't talk in public about violence, poverty and other kinds of obscenity in my community. Our religious and political sensibilities and concern for anything that might lead to the lowering of property values restrict our local conversations.

I know one possible response to this incident of prison torture. Maybe he was a real terrorist, maybe his friends were the ones who beheaded that American civilian yesterday. I just can't choose sides between barbarities. If one justifies the other, our world is lost. It might even eventually impact my clean, quiet neighborhood. I feel that all artists, all craftspeople, have a special obligation to know about the murderous cruelty embedded in the world. If you are going to try to create things of beauty, you need to know and appreciate that what you are bringing into the world will co-exist with terrible atrocities that take your breath away. This understanding has benefits - the agony of human brutality increases the need for art. It makes what you do even more significant as evidence that the human species is not inherently or entirely bad. But it also increases the sharpness of that contradiction, that perplexing and unresolved dilemma that does not provide final guidance regarding our very nature and our mixed capacity for creation and cruelty. The agents of destruction are competing with you. It seems to me, at least this morning, that maybe they are winning.

I was looking for good news when I picked up "On Beauty: And Being Just" by Elaine Scarry. She is a professor of aesthetics at Harvard University, author of previous books on similar subjects. Scarry delivered the essence of this slim volume as the Tanner Lectures in Human Values at Yale University. Beauty is reportedly making a comeback as a fit subject for scholarly study. She points out the arguments for the long held antagonism toward beauty:

"The political critique of beauty is composed of two distinct arguments. The first urges that beauty, by preoccupying our attention, distracts attention from wrong social arrangements. It makes us inattentive, and therefore eventually indifferent, to the project of bringing about arrangements that are just. The second argument holds that when we stare at something beautiful, make it an object of sustained regard, our act is destructive to the object. This argument is most often prompted when the gaze is directed toward a human face or form, but the case presumably applies equally when the beautiful thing is a mourning dove, or a trellis spilling over with sweet peas, or a book whose pages are being folded back for the first time. The complaint has given rise to a generalized discrediting of the act of 'looking', which is charged with 'reifying' the very object that appears to be the subject of admiration."

Scarry takes on these points and makes her critical case regarding these arguments. I do have a few problems with her overall discussion; the major frustration is that she never really defines beauty. How do you know it when you see it? I fear that the more common definition in our culture has more to do with something being 'pretty' rather than beautiful. I am not asking for a rigid inventory or laundry list of traits or properties we can call beautiful. I would be pleased to better understand the character, nature, and virtues of the beautiful, and the ensuing experience of the perceiver when beauty is encountered. The only reference to what constitutes beauty I could find was the identification of symmetry as the most singled out attribute over the centuries. So important is this idea of symmetry to her aesthetics that she makes it the basis for her central argument for the relationship of beauty and the virtue of justice:

"But what happens when we move from the sphere of aesthetics to the sphere of justice? Here symmetry remains key, particularly in accounts of distributive justice and fairness 'as a symmetry of everyone's relation to one another'. ...in periods when justice has been taken away, beautiful things (which do not rely on us to create them but come on their own and have been absent from a human community) hold steadily visible the manifest good of equality and balance."

One limitation to this notion of symmetry as the basis of beauty is that it is obviously restricted to certain cultural traditions. I returned to an earlier source quoted in my second letter to you almost two years ago to better understand a different tradition. Soetsu Yanagi, in his classic book, "The Unknown Craftsman: A Japanese Insight into Beauty", explains:

"For two thousand years or more Greece has dominated European art, hence the great antithesis between East and West in matters of beauty. In the field of ceramics, Western pots are almost always decorated with pattern. The beauty of the plain pot was almost unperceived, and shapes were rooted in symmetry. The ideal of Greek beauty hardly permits irregularity or asymmetry, for it was founded upon the symmetry of the human body. By contrast the Oriental found irregular beauty in nature outside the human form. From another angle, Western man may be said to be rational and Eastern man irrational; the scientific thinking of Europe is founded in rational thought. In the East the foundation is in the heart and its inspiration, in which Eastern man jumps to his conclusions on wings of intuition, whereas Occidental man arrives at his by a steady progression of intellectual steps. From this causation, man of the West brought about the age of the machine, while the man of the East is still largely dependent upon the hand."

While I am not totally comfortable with such gross and perhaps dated generalizations - for instance, one has to only look at today's electronic marvels from Japan - there are still profound cultural and historical differences regarding the very basis of understanding beauty. I have another more current reference. Yesterday Judy and I went to the Japanese American Cultural and Community Center in downtown Los Angeles to see a marvelous exhibition on "Contemporary Japanese Crafts". In the brochure accompanying the exhibition six principles underlying Japanese crafts are described. One of them is entitled:

"Deformation (The Beauty of Unevenness). Another important characteristic of Japanese crafts is the intentional introduction of deformation in the creation of bowls and the like. By destroying perfect shapes such as circles or squares, a form is revealed in which the beauty hidden behind the perfect, the beauty that cannot be breached through reason, is apparent. In this way a special Japanese artistic insight, which is not accessible via rational thought of the Western type, is expressed. Deformation as an expression of beauty can often be seen in tea utensils. Nowadays, however, such expression is not limited to tea utensils. More general displays of deformation can be found in crafts created as a means of self-expression by the artist."

Christa, where do you stand on this idea of beauty? Can you explain how your pottery displays your notions of beauty? I notice that all the ceramic shapes I have encountered in your work tend to be regular, almost geometrically balanced and symmetrical. Does that dependable balance in your work carry the claim that the world is also capable of that balance and harmony? Are you seeking to bring some small measure of these qualities to the world through your pottery? Do you and other artists possess the egotistical and extravagant belief that your art will change the world?

We have a modern Western approach involving the deliberate destruction of the orderly and regulated shape. I wonder if Peter Voulkos consciously gave credit to this Japanese idea in his evolving work? I am impressed that the Japanese ideals of superb craftsmanship and these ideas of irregularity or deformity co-exist. Both seem to flourish. Can they flourish in the same pot or tea cup? I think that Yanagi and Leach would say yes but I am not sure. Does it take great craftsmanship to provide memorable deformation and unevenness? I think most Westerners would assume that irregularity represents a release and liberation from something called craftsmanship.

I was not convinced by Scarry's argument on the relationship of beauty and justice. I wanted to be. Of course, I would offer myself as the exception and agree with Scarry that beauty works for me. It does bring peace and harmony to my world.

I did enjoy her brief definition of the relationship of the perceiver to the object:

"Beauty is, then, a compact, or contract between the beautiful being (a person or thing) and the perceiver. As the beautiful being confers on the perceiver the gift of life, so the perceiver confers on the beautiful being the gift of life. Each 'welcomes' the other: each - to return to the word's original meaning – 'come in accordance with the other's will'."

I also enjoyed her use of Iris Murdoch, another person I need to return to read, about the kind of 'radical decentering' that Scarry offers as proof of the impact of the beautiful on the perceiver. Murdoch talks of the relationship of ethics and its need for an altered consciousness that brings about unselfishness, objectivity and realism. This 'unselfing' is best brought about, according to Murdoch, by the encounter with the beautiful.

Still looking for good news, I finally found what I was looking for, a one page article in the June 2004 issue of the British publication, 'Prospect'. Beneath the top story heading, "Cultural Tourist", a smaller topic heading proclaimed "Clay Makes A Comeback". The discussion is initiated by an exhibition currently at the Tate Liverpool entitled, "A Secret History of Clay: From Gauguin to Gormley". According to this anonymous piece, Tate curator Simon Groom highlighted the wide spectrum of artists who found clay a significant medium:

"Chronologically from Gauguin to Gormley, but also geographically from the Russian Malevich to the founding father of American ceramic art, Peter Voulkos, leaders of almost every western art movement of the last 100 years have turned to this messy and humble material for new inspiration, sometimes in rebellion, sometimes in pursuit of recuperation."

The article promotes the aesthetic value of clay, citing as an example dialogue between experimental artist-potter Grayson Perry, recent winner of the Turner prize and Julian Stair, described as a "distinguished British potter known for his defense of traditional values". What looked like a confrontation of opposites found common agreement on the allure of clay. The article concluded with a tribute to clay I know you will appreciate, "… lovers of clay value above all its alliance with the human flesh, its frailty and unruliness and its intimation of mortality. In an age of anxiety, it is the material best suited to our fears and dreams."

In this same 'Prospect' article, in defending the idea that 'clay makes a comeback', the author cites the recent publication of Edmund de Waal's book, "20th Century Ceramics":

" …by its inclusive consideration of all works in clay, whether made industrially or in rural solitude, whether by artists or potters, he has significantly shifted not just our understanding of pots, but our picture of 20th-century art."

I had read this book a short time before, so I took it off the shelf and reviewed the contents. One of the joys of a long life as an active learner involves the page by page encounter of familiar references that are implicitly recognized and activated as a preexisting knowledge base. You do not have to have a single focus to achieve this, it is still possible to possess a general knowledge that forms a structure for the placement of new knowledge. This is not just information or facts. I cannot remember information in isolation. It must be attached to some idea, it must undergo an intellectual process when meaning and significance becomes evident to me. This is a rather mysterious process for me. If tested, I might not be able to regurgitate the item as a right answer, might not be able to spell or even pronounce its name, but I know the meaning and character of the item when I face it again.

Self-conscious appropriation, contextual placement and close scrutiny of new experiences and new knowledge constitutes the essence of critical intelligence. My own personal and eccentric way of knowing reminds me about an incident in my freshman college introductory psychology course. We were given an IQ Test, then instructed on the mathematics of self-scoring it. In those days, these IQ numbers provided an almost sacred and final determination of complexity and worth. I thought I did rather well on the test, but was unable to follow the instructions and execute the math to determine the score. Obviously this result was most disturbing, previewing a devastating score if I could ever figure out how to determine the test results. I did not raise my hand for help, stayed very quiet, and decided to remain in college anyway. Perhaps this experience is more typical for some: after all, I was an art major.

Edmund de Waal, an outstanding potter as well as author, attempts an inclusive overview of 20th century ceramics. He is critical about most commentary regarding ceramics. I found his comments on this subject valuable, aware of my status as amateur collector and correspondent, still struggling to make sense of these things in my informal, ad hoc letters to you.

"There was a paucity of critical writing about ceramics. The kinds of writing published fell into two kinds - either technical or commentaries on particular potters that were uncritical, if not adulatory. ...The technical literature was often more radical, reflecting the changing interests in techniques of glazing and firing... There were informed British and American critics who were prepared to take ceramics seriously, but few ceramics exhibitions gained the kind of coverage that even a first exhibition by a minor painter would achieve. This was partly due to a (mostly misguided) perception as to the inward-looking nature of the discipline. ... These were mostly far less interested in why potters were making pots than how, something reflected in the frequent presence as 'spectacle' of potters from Africa and South Asia at pottery festivals."

Of course I agree with him, it suits my purposes and interests. I am not concerned with the 'how', and often feel quite frustrated in finding so little about the 'why' in most publications regarding pottery. Do working potters read serious works about the history or aesthetics of pottery? I assume that the 'how to do it' manuals, publications, and demonstrations at workshops and conferences are so prevalent because they are so popular with potters. Is that the one distinguishing property of the serious ceramic artist over the humble potter? The ability to fashion a clay object within the articulated pretense of an aesthetic mission? As a former teacher educator, it was much the same way. There was a complete separation between theory and practice. The pedagogical research at the university level was not only ignored, it was held in active contempt by the classroom teacher. Anti-theoretical, verging on anti-intellectual, the classroom practitioner nevertheless was supposedly the guardian of the life of the mind for future generations. Is this analogous to the working potter, making a living, paying the bills, stocking the kiln, running a small business, meeting the public as clerk and salesperson; without the time, energy or interest in exploring abstract theories of distant strangers at the university? The ancient curse of my former profession - 'those who can, do - those who can't, teach'. How about – 'those who can, make pottery - those who can't, teach ceramics at the university?' I am unsympathetic with this point of view, just wondered if this type of bias exists in the ceramic world. De Waal alludes to this problem:

"The great majority of the ceramicists making 'disagreeable objects', work that sets out to 'challenge', were eventually lecturers in either art colleges or university art departments. This was true in Britain and Japan as much as in America. There was a growing gulf between the kinds of ceramics supported by the academy and the studio potters who were making their livings from functional pottery and to whom this kind of institutional support was not forthcoming."

In a strange way, all the loose ends in this letter come together in the last book cited in this letter, "The Middle Mind: Why Americans Don't Think For Themselves" by Curtis White. What makes it wonderful and strange is that the book has nothing to do with ceramics, does not mention ceramics, the author's stated background provides no indication he has any interest or expertise in ceramics. I really believe that the most profound and necessary response to the particular problems or issues in a specialized field do not come from the internal bibliography of that subject, even though these references know and cite each other, but the real insights and understanding come from exposure to outside sources that illuminate the subject without once directly referring to it. That is another indication of critical intelligence - the ability to connect and integrate those ideas that appear to have no prior relationship to each other. Inevitably, relationships become apparent that mutually strengthen understanding and allow the extraction of wisdom. I have just stated the credo of the generalist.

In a review of this book in the Guardian Weekly, Scott Stossel helps us understand how White defines the term embedded in the title of the book, the Middle Mind as:

" …the market-produced culture of entertainment - has usurped much of the individual's power to make meaningful aesthetic choices."

For White, the Middle Mind is not a location on the cultural-status hierarchy but rather capitalism's way of administering creativity out of harm's way. White reminds me of Dewey, a source I have cited previously in other letters, when he states that experience…

"…says something about the fact that the imagination is not only about creation; it is also about how we see and how we experience. We cannot create in a fresh and lively way while looking at our world from a stale (even if familiar and comforting) perspective. So, before the productive work of the imagination can begin, we must be outside of the familiar."

I might have to reconsider the assertion of Elaine Scarry about the relationship of beauty and justice. White provides definite support for her position:

"I would still maintain, unlikely though it is, that imagination and thought, art and philosophy, are the things we urgently need if we are ever to confront the performative logic, the imperatives to efficiency and domination of our culture.

I would go even further. Reawakening the imagination and a capacity for thought is a spiritual and perhaps even a mystical procedure. This has nothing to do with the crisis of rising or falling church attendance at the corner Presbyterian church. Our spiritual crisis is human, historical, and social. What, we need to ask, is the spiritual content of a concept like justice? Ultimately, our crisis of the imagination is a crisis of spirit related to Henry James' notion of a moral individual. For James, the moral individual is 'richly responsible and richly aware'. But how is it possible to be aware and responsible in a society that prohibits understanding and grants all responsibility to governmental and commercial institutions?"

White is something of a radical, with acute criticism of the conventional structures in our culture:

"Let art out of the museum and out of the university. Deinstitutionalize it. Take off the straitjacket of philanthropic support. Defeat the corporate ownership of what little imagination we have."

White, like Scarry, sees art as powerful, impacting society, providing stability and insight.

Christa, going back to my original mood at the beginning of the letter, could we do an empirical study of the guards and interrogators at Abu Ghraib prison? Find out what kind of art they appreciate, compare it with groups of do-gooders who hopefully buy a great deal of pottery and love art, then provide remedial rehabilitation for the prison torturers through an art appreciation course or a pottery workshop? I remember Hermann Goring, the Nazi war criminal who amassed a treasure trove of magnificent art looted from those he conquered. I heard he had exquisite taste in art. Despite all this, I will continue to take these ideas about the healing powers of art seriously because it makes me feel better. I will accept pottery as my salvation even if it turns out to be a fraudulent placebo. How ironic, I have discovered in a material media placed in a temporal setting the means to escape an awful reality.

Still looking for good news, I will cite yet another example from White:

"The problem that art helps us face, and great art helps us face best, is the problem of creating social stability without creating a state of administered conformity. In other words, art helps us to think what it would mean to live together as a whole and yet be fully human as individuals."

There is another problem I see here, Christa. Don't you and other potters identify with the populist notion of providing functional containers and domestic ware for average folks? How can you approve of their taste when they purchase one of your pieces when, at least according to White, the prevalent mode among Americans is a taste for mediocrity, a failure of imagination? Is this failing apparent among the shoppers who stroll into your gallery/studio? Does the purchase of one of your pots prove the exception to the rule?

I will never know if Scarry and White surreptitiously got together to arrange their arguments prior to my exposure to their possible conspiracy. If not totally converted, I will offer a beautiful passage by White, suspend my critical intelligence, and fully accept:

"To socialize the imagination in the way we have socialized fear would be to take up not only creativity but also compassion. There is no such thing as a fascist, a repressive, or even a dominating imagination. That's a contradiction in terms. A fascist imagination could only be an imagination that seeks the death of imagination. Repression is the social imagination committing suicide. In our culture at present, as the Middle Mind illustrates, we commit this form of social suicide on a daily basis. Denying the necessary angel is a chore as regular as taking out the garbage for us. "Darling, did you remember to repress your sense of your own creative capacity before you came to bed? And don't forget to stultify the kids." The imagination's only true concept is freedom - the freedom for humans to create their own world. The mutual recognition that this is what we should all be free to do requires compassion for what others need in their turn. A socialized imagination requires justice."

I will now add C. Wright Mills, quoted in the last letter, to the conspiracy. They are all in this together. If this mighty band of brilliant commentators can agree with each other, who I am to resist?

I will provide a final solace to compensate for earlier accounts of sordid torture and a world possibly unmoved by imagination or art. It arrived in the mail just a few days ago. I was surprised when I saw it, even though I was impatiently awaiting its arrival. It was from the National Council on Education for the Ceramic Arts (NCECA). The letter from Jeremy Jernegan, Programs Director for the 2005 conference in Baltimore, announced:

"I am happy to report that your proposal for a panel entitled 'Letters to a Young Potter' was selected to be included as part of the conference program. The Board was interested in the topic and felt that the members of your panel could bring informed and provocative viewpoints to the discussion."

As I told you later on the telephone when sharing this news, it was your trust and positive note on that postcard you sent me after receiving my first letter that allowed me to continue. If your initial response had been negative, I would not have continued writing these letters. Now, two years and twenty-nine letters later, these messages to a fine young potter are going to be considered by your peers at the most important convocation of potters in the country. I am grateful for the opportunity to join you and such outstanding individuals on the panel as Walter Ostrom and Mary Barringer in engaging the assembled potters in a dialogue dealing with the endemic issues that provide meaning and value to their lives and work. I have a prideful independence and do not seek to curry favor, but you must know by now that I am sincere when I say that it is truly an honor to be so associated with such fine, active creators of pottery.

I do not know if this is the final chapter in my improbable life, but I think I have succeeded in yet another reinvention of self that will serve as a fitting entry to an arena that can only bring me great satisfaction. To be affirmed in this way is a joyous validation of those things that I hold dear. I take hope - and look forward to our future appointment next year in Baltimore.

Your friend,

Richard

Thirty

July 11, 2004

Dear Christa,

Virtue hopefully becomes a habit, although our usual habits are rarely virtues. Reading is one habit I would claim as virtue, a lifelong habit now apparently imperiled as obsolete behavior. I am a reader. It is a natural and normal activity for me. It is an activity in which I remain as active as the author of the text. We share authority. It is always a partnership. This is not a modern habit. Most people are now connected with electronic apparatus. I admit they are convenient, as some of these appliances can be stored in the purse or pocket, or in contrast, occupy as screen an entire wall. I cannot see the romance of this type of engagement. They can be a diversion as entertainment, or a functional necessity of doing business, but do not ask me to establish a relationship with these things. I might use them, but I do not love them. I do love the printed page. My love of reading is so intense that my memories of childhood and youth are largely memories of the times when I engaged the book and entered strange and wonderful worlds not otherwise available to me on that short dead-end street in west Los Angeles.

I remember my early rebellion, at a certain hour in the evening, when my father insisted that the lights go out in the bedroom, and I surreptitiously took my book from under the pillow and read by the distant glow of the hall light. My parents were not the sponsors of these childhood escapes, nor did I emulate their own habits in this regard. I do not know if I can even remember my parents reading at any moment in that remote past. I knew that, in almost all regards, they would remain strangers to my passion for reading, strangers to the worlds I discovered. Thus I had an early independence and separation from the normal authority of my parents. Early on, I knew that I knew many things they did not know or sadly, did not seem to even want to know.

Despite my early innocence and inexperience, I never transferred this authority over me from parent to author. I became master of my destiny through a careful selection of books in the local public library which stood on the corner of my childhood street. This premature liberation from family and neighborhood established a lifelong independence that has never been seriously threatened. Once you have read more than one author, you know and can never forget that diversity and disagreement about the most profound events in human history and culture are normal discontinuities. I never wanted a single truth. It would require giving up too many opportunities of further adventures with dissident authors that would unintentionally repudiate and rebuke, just by their differences, other authors previously read and experienced.

It is simply a foolish notion, although held by most reasonable people, that you have to abandon one notion if you embrace a different one. That differences in fact can be solved if information is available. The problem with that is that most information is insignificant and trivial. Differences in interpretation and value do not have to be finally resolved. This does not prevent action. I need to know why I prefer one story to another. I need to know why I shape my behavior by showing special affection for one idea over another. But I do not have to dispose of the neglected idea. In reserve, its influence can eventually become more influential than the idea in current favor. As I return to a book read long ago and reinterpret its meaning in the light of my present predicament, I reserve the right to return to my storehouse of possible ideas and overthrow and revise myself once more. If my taste in pottery is catholic and inclusive, it is because I accepted, long ago, the multiple possibilities and contradictions of the messages embedded on the printed page.

Christa, do I communicate with the potter when I gaze at the pot? After the point of purchase, the potter does not go home with the pot. Yet I do interact with the author of the text. I question the implied assertion, accept and slide inside the style, hoping to catch the rhythm and mannerisms of language and metaphor. I accompany the author's journey and consider her argument, seeking knowledge and wisdom for my own purposes. I never surrender my independence, but provide a leap of faith that must eventually be rewarded. To answer my earlier question, I do think I engage the potter as vigorously as the author of the written text. I seek to discover the creator's intention, to locate those imaginative deviations that mark originality, to place the object in context. The potter, fresh from the miraculous creation of the pot, might immediately claim a unique status for that object unmatched in previous ceramic history. As collector and perceiver, I must humble the pot by placement in a communal context that attaches that object to my world. The company of other pottery in my collection does not represent a hierarchy, but does teach that no individual pot or potter has a monopoly on creativity or aesthetic accomplishment.

What is the difference in my relationship to pot and potter? As a friend, you are always welcome in my home. I would even extend that invitation to all the potters represented in my collection. As host, I would try to provide my potter friends with food, drink and exposure to my beloved collection, home and garden. Your pot, in contrast, would join my family. I would take responsibility for the care and safety of that object. Accepted and housed, the pottery cannot cause me pain or disappointment. People are more volatile and uncertain in their possible behavior. This does not diminish the value and need of love and respect for family and friends. The risk is greater. As a teacher, my rewards were in the engagement with students. Whatever the differing degrees of anxiety, I still seek out and enjoy friends and family, the pot and potter. The creation and appreciation of pottery is a manifestation of the complexity and virtue of human beings and human culture. These gifts of the human hand encourage my contact and appreciation of people. I do not have to make a choice. Revealed insecurities do not embarrass me. I consider myself self-sufficient, social interaction does not come from concerns about individual isolation. Reading and art do not require the company of others. The sources of my life preferences and habits can be traced to the origins of my existence. A virtue becomes operational when it successfully compensates for the more obvious inadequacy. It is the inadequacies that give me humanity, it is the virtues that give me grace. Whatever virtuous habits I do possess, including the love of reading and pottery, they reflect both the joys and pain of a long life. I have no reason for complaint.

Do I dare to claim as collector and perceiver, as I did as reader with the author, that I become a partner of the potter? That this partnership is as necessary for the potter as for myself? Without modesty, I do so claim. I do restrict the validity of this claim to my own enrichment. I am not sure that it is necessary for the potter to know what I have gained from her pot. But if that is true, why am I writing these letters to you?

I do not expect you to change the next pot as a result of this communication. The partnership can be maintained if you continue to create the pottery according to your own intentions. The ambition to create a beautiful and original pot cannot be borrowed or imposed. There are reasons you do not destroy the pot after its completion. Aside from the necessary revenue derived from its sale, there are other more important reasons. I doubt if you could sustain your struggle if no one celebrated and embraced the creations of your potter's wheel. I demand of you only what I know you demand of yourself. The effort to achieve excellence on your part does not need my supervision. I would not spare you the stress and strain of that effort. It cannot be made easy. More importantly, I know from the aesthetic integrity of your previous efforts that you cannot spare yourself that terrible and wonderful crucible that forms the creative process. It is obvious we both have reciprocal responsibilities to the pot and each other.

John Ruskin, the 19th century art critic and social prophet, delivered two lectures, a week apart, in the British city of Manchester in 1864. These lectures, published together a year later as "Sesame and Lilies" contain a compelling defense of reading. In the first lecture, "Sesame: Of Kings' Treasuries" he makes his case:

"A book is essentially not a talked thing, but a written thing; and written, not with the view of mere communication, but of permanence. ... a book is written, not to multiply the voice merely, not to carry it merely, but to perpetuate it. The author has something to say which he perceives to be true and useful, or helpfully beautiful. So far as he knows, no one else can say it. He is bound to say it, clearly and melodiously if he may; clearly, at all events. In the sum of his life he finds this to be the thing, or group of things, manifest to him; - this, the piece of true knowledge, or sight, which his share of sunshine and earth has permitted him to seize. He would fain set it down forever; engrave it on rock, if he could; saying, 'This is the best of me; for the rest, I ate, and drank, and slept, loved, and hated, like another; my life was as the vapor and is not; but this I saw and knew: this, if anything of mine, is worth your memory.' That is his 'writing'; it is, in his small human way, and with whatever degree of true inspiration is in him, his inscription, or scripture. That is a 'Book'."

As with art, I am not a minimalist when it comes to the text. I do not mind the flourish and intensity of Ruskin's prose. It is dated in its specific style, and the contents must be forgiven for not transcending certain intellectual and social conventions that rightly rankle the sensibilities of contemporary progressive thought. But as Merle Rubin pointed out in his review of this new edition in the Los Angeles Times Book Review of January 19, 2003:

"Although his 'Tory' view of society was hierarchical, what now might be called 'elitist', he fiercely deplored the inequities brought about by extremes of wealth and poverty. His indignation on behalf of the poor kindled the imagination of countless reformers and philanthropists. But perhaps the best way to characterize him is as a Romantic visionary with radical leanings. Ruskin was one of the Victorian Age's great myth-makers, a prose poet whose erudite and imaginative metaphors offered a fresh way of seeing things. Too literal a reading can render him ridiculous."

Rubin finishes his review by concluding:

"But to read Ruskin in the open and imaginative spirit with which he himself urged readers to approach great books is to realize that his writings will survive any number of shifts in intellectual fashion."

The passage quoted earlier from Ruskin, edited by Charles W. Eliot in his Harvard Classics over a hundred years ago, has been recently joined by a new edition of "Sesame and Lilies" as part of a Yale University Press series called "Rethinking the Western Tradition", edited by Deborah Epstein Nord. Included in the volume is an essay by Elizabeth Helsinger entitled "Authority and the Pleasures of Reading". Here Helsinger points out that Ruskin required strenuous activity on the part of the reader:

"The reading Ruskin describes is markedly active, as his metaphors in Sesame suggest (mining - digging, crushing, smelting, chiseling, fusing - and hunting). The reader plays important roles in the interpretive process, participating silently in what could be described as the textual equivalent of the demanding spoken dialectics of early philosophical enquiry."

Two pages later Nord again addresses the idea of the 'free play of the associative imagination' in Ruskin's work.

"The aim of this kind of interpretive reading, where the controls of the logical mind are relaxed so that the reader may 'enter into the meaning' of an imaginative author more fully, is not to prove a set of relationships but to entertain them. Its potential rewards include both illuminating meaning in a particular context and expanding the mythical figure for future use, thus adding to the historical stores of culture."

Could it be that the observation and perception of reading and pottery require some of the same behavior? The pot is solid, has weight, and exists external to the perceiver. Although the book is a temporal object, the solitary auditing of the content is an internal process. Still, both require an 'open and imaginative spirit' on the part of the perceiver and reader. Surely pottery can meet Ruskin's injunction for the author and book, that it be true and useful, unique in source and shape. Ruskin demands active participation, Nord supports Ruskin in urging the co-construction of meaning by creator and participant. How do we prepare for this kind of work? What kind of work has the potter and author left for the participant/colleague? I fear that most people do not have the energy and time to construct their own meaning. They were not given permission or assignments in school to develop that capacity. They do not know that the significance and authority of the book and pot are not dependent upon your submission to them.

They do not know that, co-equal with the pot and book, your life is a primary source, as unique and complex as book and pot. All my books and pots comprise the raw resources for the construction of self. That attitude breeds respect, even love, surely not contempt, for I need them and they make all the difference in my life.

What a strange world we live in. An old man writing letters, harmless in their petition, therapy for his retired status and unlimited time. A young woman potter, creating in an ancient art obsolete in its technology and function, yet determined and persistent. We both exist on the margins. We attend to something called culture, largely undistinguished now from the entertainment which has become a weekend diversion from the demands of employment. You may claim to create culture, and I do seek to appreciate it. But it is the politicians and generals who make the decisions that become our daily history as recorded in the newspapers and on CNN. I will continue to write my letters, collect pottery, and read yet another book. You will make ceramics and become celebrated in the small circle of pottery devotees. The powerful in our society will leave us alone. We are harmless and cannot interrupt the powerful and awful stream of their tragic history.

Christa, I do not really want you to believe or accept that last paragraph. I hope that you, as reader, fully empowered and active, will argue with the thoughts, change my mind, reassure me and correct my pessimistic assumptions. It appears true to me only in the immediate despair I experience with the world beyond me. Show me some cosmic landscape where brutal power is tamed by the civilizing agents of both book and pot. ENTER INTO THE MEANING of these letters, Christa, as I enter daily into the meaning of your wonderful pottery on the shelves of my house. I promise I will prefer and choose your thoughts on this matter over mine if only you can convince me.

Judy and I have marked and tracked on the calendar our travel adventures for the summer and remainder of the year. The locations and possible acquisitions of pottery are as vital to this planning as the logistics of maps, travel guides and discount tickets. I know summer is a busy time for you.

Take care.

Richard

Thirty-one

July 28, 2004

Dear Christa,

The prospect of heat encourages me to get up early on summer mornings. Old patterns change with age. I do not sleep as long or as late now. This is an unplanned change. Up around 5:00 am, 4 or 5 cups of coffee while reading the morning newspaper, exercising on my stationary bicycle, and out of the house and in the garden by 8:00 am. I cannot eradicate poverty and war from the world but I do derive great satisfaction from removing garden weeds. Lately I have walked around the block to tend to the garden at my younger son's house. This particular garden, both sides of a corner house, was originally planted with ground cover. First I removed the ground cover, then designed with my daughter-in-law the possible organization of trees, shrubs, and perennial plants. The next step, after much arduous effort in preparation, the actual joy of planting. As with pottery, I cannot claim credit for the creation of the plant. But I do stake my claim as the designer and creator of the garden. I lose some control after planting as I reactively trim the often unanticipated directions of growth and expansion. I am content to allow the plant a measure of independence, pleased when rewarded with green growth and bursts of flowers. There must be similar satisfaction in surveying your pottery after removal from the kiln and the gardener's experience of viewing the results of their efforts.

Three authors, Charles W. Moore, William J. Mitchell, and William Turnbill, Jr., wrote a book with a wonderful title, "The Poetics of Gardens", in which they describe this great satisfaction:

"Making our own gardens is a pastime, a civility, a game, an obsession. But we cannot rely on a single comprehensive, authoritative set of rules to guide our actions. In an era like our own, with its dizzying intricacy of connections and its fast-forward pace, though our gardens may be simple and focused, any rules for them won't be, can't be, probably shouldn't be. The images we know about

are legion, our memories seethe with overlapping complexities. We admire mobility and embrace the notion of the movable feast, even as we yearn for roots and cherish a garden for the opportunity it gives us to put some down... (a few paragraphs later) ... Speculation about the forms that our own gardens might take is not, then, an orderly, linear process of deriving specific consequences from established general rules. It is a colloquium of the clamorous voices of memory - urging and intimating, sometimes reaching satisfying agreements and sometimes taking out contradictions, catching allusions and sharing jokes, making asides and getting back to the point, sporting with irony and flirting with whimsy, and finally concluding, somehow, that some particular ideas are right for a particular site at a particular moment."

I am impressed with the suitability of the description above as a generic description of the creative process. People like to receive full credit for the finished masterwork as a planned product. I am suspicious of any claim that you might have regarding the full image of the pot completed in your head before you turn the wheel. If you really did, I would think the process would become tedious and the pot obvious. The surprise of the wheel, and your inability to fully predict and control your own behavior at the wheel, allows that the rules of the game are made up as you experience the moment. I concede that the operating strategies emerge from the vast resources of previous experience. When you work on commission, I will further relent that creativity cannot become capricious. But I like certain words like whimsy and irony, because I really like what they mean to me in regard to the creative process. Maybe that's why I never trusted the assumption of complete mastery. If you only do what you know you can do, however brilliant and masterful, you are still playing it safe, controlled and rehearsed, the results preordained in every detail.

The artist is not a machine. The machine can manufacture a perfect product. In my view, the genius of the human hand resides in the possibilities of marvelous imperfections. The mechanical succeeds in the exact and endless replication of a previously approved perfection. The hand does not need to triumph over the machine. The machine never achieves the status of a worthy rival. The hand deviates in unexpected speculations. The victory over the machine is never a true competition because the machine is not qualified to compete. Disciplined deviation emerges from the human capacity to implement prior intent and yet to surrender to the creative chaos of infinite choices. The machine cannot be equipped with these virtues. If that should ever become possible, I do not wish to witness nor purchase it. The electronic machines of today do not carry any greater credit or currency with me than its iron or steel ancestors. Modern inventors might wire it with a surface personality but they can never give it internal character.

Christa, what aesthetic tradition do you claim? What tribe do you belong to? Do you need some single membership to feel secure? What category of humanity do you instinctively trust? I suspect you might embrace multiple identities. Some parts of you were given to you at birth, some imposed on you during childhood. Your so-called ethnic or racial identity, perhaps some religious affiliation of your family, maybe the immigrant status and national origins of your ancestors, some chosen mentor or hero, we all have interior shrines and light candles in our souls to those sources of support and inspiration that get us through the day. How about the importance of your gender? What does it mean to be a woman potter? Are you now so liberated that it does not carry any negative weight or disadvantage? Is there a sisterhood of women potters? Would it be a sign of weakness to join such a group? Do men potters play fair? Do they run the ceramics world, decide matters on the golf course and in the locker room? Are these questions and speculations just the ideological debris of an old activist?

As a man, as a collector, how do I escape that history of male domination? How can I be a patron of women potters without patronizing them? How do I support the women potters represented on my shelves? I do not buy the pots of women to display an affirmative action generosity. I did not buy these pots because of a guilty conscience and liberal sensitivities. I bought the pots because they contained qualities that give me pleasure. I bought the pots because they represented significant statements of the ceramic arts. If I should take an inventory, I would guess that over half of my collection is represented by pots from women makers. How did that happen? You are coming from a history where genteel women of the middle and upper classes decorated china ware imported for that purpose, from working class women who toiled in the factories of the ceramic corporations in the emerging industrial revolution. Do you claim that history and consciously defy it? Why are so many contemporary potters women? Men once threw the pots for previous generations of women, for most women. What makes you dare throw the pots now?

There is another important tradition. Moira Vincentelli explores the traditional pottery of indigenous cultures throughout the world. In many such cultures, women were the active potters who passed on knowledge about pottery from one generation to the next, from mother to daughter. In her book, "Women Potters: Transforming Traditions", Vincentelli describes the gender distinctions that existed:

"It is important to stress that there is nothing 'natural' about gender roles in ceramics: they are socially produced. But this area of the world (Asia) demonstrates again the characteristic model that women potters predominate where handbuilding methods have prevailed. Men become more involved in general when there is a strong economic incentive, and where new technology and workshop practices rather than home industry are beginning to develop. The association of men with high status, sculptural or ritual forms is also very notable."

Vincentelli roams the world in her book, looking at geographical areas divided in book chapters. As with the forests and jungles, as with the endangered species, so are the pottery traditions of women imperiled in much of the world.

She provides this mixed assessment of the present and the future:

"On every continent there are women potters who find a ready market for their handbuilt low-technology wares. There are still many places where such pottery plays a vital part in people's everyday lives whether for cooking, water and food storage, brewing and fermenting liquids, or dyeing cloth. But in a process that has been ongoing since at the very least the 19th century, these functions are increasingly being met by alternative means: from plastic containers and mass-produced tableware to running water, electric light and bottled gas. As one function disappears, however, women have had to be inventive in finding new outlets for their skills."

On the next page she discusses the difficulty of preserving traditional technologies in hi-tech societies and the lives of poverty for most of this population. Yet she ends this paragraph optimistically, noting that many women potters in various cultures are better off than those women who are not potters, and love and take pride in their work.

One manifestation of renewed interest and scholarship in the lives of women are their journals and diaries. Woman artists have often left us both art and text. One woman I greatly admire, Emily Carr, Canadian artist and writer, lived in Victoria, British Columbia. Independent, somewhat eccentric, she spent time in a caravan with her animals (monkey, dogs, etc.) in the forest, painting and sketching. Never married, forced to take boarders in her home and cook and clean house for them, all the time being one of the most gifted artists Canada has ever produced. She is of course celebrated now. One of my favorite places in the world, Granville Island in Vancouver, has the Emily Carr College of Art, an outstanding art school named in her honor. The Vancouver Art Museum has rooms full of her remarkable paintings. I remember from your vita that you visited and taught a workshop at this institution. It's a shame that you were not able to meet her and talk to her. You both have a toughness and determination that cannot be defeated.

Emily Carr kept a journal, where on April 6th, 1934, she reveals her grumpy unease at social gatherings and her articulate thoughts about art:

"Just came from the last lecture on art. This afternoon there was a tea for the lecturer - old women like me, very dull - refreshments drab and uninteresting. After the lecture tonight there was a reception at the Business and Professional Women's Club - mixed ages, vivacious old and stodgy young - peppy sand-wiches and snappy cakes - lots of chatter. What's it all about, this art? We've had the reason for the way each man worked. We've had the viewpoint of each man. We've had the thoughts of each man. We've had the man turned inside out and the work turned outside in, and how much of it is true? Who of us knows just why we do what we do, much less another's whys, or what we're after. Art is not like that: cut and dried and hit-at like a bull's eye and done for a reason and explained away by this or that motive. It's a climbing and striving for some-thing always beyond, not a bundle of 'rules' or a bundle of feels nor a taking of this man's ideas and tacking them on that man's ideas and making a mongrel idea and calling it 'my own'. It's a seeing dimly beyond and with eyes straight ahead in a beeline, marching right up to the dim thing. You'll never quite catch up. There will always be a beyond. It would be terrible to catch up - the end of everything."

Scholarship demands a clear and complete explanation. How could an expert on Emily Carr conclude at the end of a lifetime of research that 'there will always be a beyond' not accessible, not conclusive? A beyond that cannot be reached, a beyond that will always contain mysteries? Along with my chronic suspicion of experts is my chronic suspicion of artists when they assert complete self-consciousness in the creative process. I do not think that you, Christa, can provide the definitive explanation of why you do what you do any more than those scholars and critics that might some day seek to sum you up. I would maintain that this inability for you to fully expose your creative intentions is not a weakness, not a handicap of inarticulation. I agree with Emily Carr, art (and pottery) will never be 'cut and dried and hit-at like a bull's eye'. I would have more respect for scholarship in the humanities and the arts if they ended their narratives with confessions of an enriched ambiguity.

We are reminded of the world that existed during Emily Carr's life. Anne Newlands, in her book, "Emily Carr: An Introduction to Her Life and Art":

"… Carr had at last been recognized as one of Canada's most important artists. But it had sometimes been an arduous struggle for a woman born in

1871 in the staid provincial capital of British Columbia, where the role of most women was limited either to raising children or to teaching them. Women did not even have the right to vote until 1917, when Carr herself was middle-aged."

Are you truly liberated when you can declare that you are unaware of external discrimination of your own kind - of race or gender? Is this a sign of brave self-confidence or blind stupidity? Christa, are you a leading potter or a leading woman potter? I am not sure that the triumph of toleration is in the absence of these differences. I think it is imperative that we recognize and respect profound differences, not graciously subtract them from others in order to prove your own liberal lack of discrimination. Nor can I pretend to know the other. I cannot fully know myself - much less the hidden complexities of others that emanate from multiple identities I do not share or have ever experienced. I do not know how to make a pot, yet I fully enjoy them. I do not really know you, Christa, but I do fully respect you. The unknown need not be considered unfriendly. I would push further and say that intellectual activity is not in the knowing, but in improving the understanding. The mysteries that remain inspire the creative urge and imaginative spirit of human exploration and aesthetic adventure. I do not need to find impersonal taxonomies or organize knowledge and experience it within dependable categories. I am aware that the contrived patterns of meaning I create are for my own convenience and stability. I want my statements and attitude to represent an exception and defiance to the general application of traditional male stereotypes.

Sharyn Rohlfsen Udall, in her book, "Carr, O'Keeffe, Kahlo: Places of Their Own" explores three important women, three important artists of the last century. In a key chapter entitled, "Sexuality, Androgyny, and Personal Appearance", Udall states:

"Frida Kahlo, Georgia O'Keeffe, and Emily Carr were born into a world of strong gender dichotomies. In societies wedded to conventional definitions of 'masculine' and 'feminine' (whose roots lay deep in the Judeo-Christian past), the free interplay of such traits was viewed as dangerous. Commonly accepted was the view that, as linguistic theorist Deborah Cameron has written, 'sex differentiation must be rigidly upheld by whatever means are available, for men can be men only if women are unambiguously women'. In the arts, the rare designation of genius was still reserved almost exclusively for men. … In other words, if a woman's work was too accomplished, her output must be defined as abnormal. To critics who could not otherwise account for it, Emily Carr's power as an artist was sometimes construed as a gender aberration. Women's art, once distinguished from the 'lesser' artistic output of most women, could thus be ignored; despite occasional anomalies, the whole body of women's artistic production was rarely reexamined or reevaluated. With a few exceptions, this attitude defined the artistic world into the early twentieth century. Creativity and mastery of materials were inherently male; a concern with surfaces and the nuanced use of materials was gendered as female."

I must think about what I have just read. How does the culture celebrate the death of a stereotype? Is it premature in this case? I simply do not know. Freedom from discrimination does not ensure excellence. Given true liberation, there will be at least as many second-rate potters among women as men. Are the standards of excellence consistent for both men and women? When does a difference in result indicate gender? I resent traditional notions of masculinity, I reject their implications for my own personality and interests. Still, I must admit, these obnoxious notions never denied me life opportunities. Would anyone place a bet that given a hundred pots, they could successfully identify the majority as made by man or woman? Are pots inherently gendered, beyond deliberate and graphic evidence to make them so?

Frida Kahlo, in my art major days in college, was simply the wife of that towering Mexican artist, Diego Rivera. She did paint, I saw reproductions of her work, mostly self-portraits. But there was no doubt then about who was the important artist in that family. Her marital difficulties with and affection for her husband defined and fused her image with him. Her art was personal, his was political. His work now seems dated to past protests of settled or forgotten issues of his time. Her work pulls ancient Mexican cultural traditions and blends it with the pain and turmoil of the individual psyche.

Frida Kahlo is now a celebrated cultural icon, popular movies portray her life and posters are made of her paintings. The only modern complaint against her might be that she loved Diego too much and sacrificed energy and time on him when it should have been spent on her own art. Udall points out that with all three women, Carr, Kahlo, and O'Keeffe, their ultimate reputations exceeded that of their male mentors.

I remember a great exhibition I saw at the Autry Museum of Western Heritage in Los Angeles about ten years ago. The book that documented the exhibition, "Independent Spirits: Women Painters of the American West, 1890-1945", was edited by Patricia Trenton. In the Introduction, Virginia Scharff provides background to the theme and title of the exhibition:

"What must women have in order to create art? They have to have a source of inspiration, something worth making art about. And, not insignificantly, their right to express themselves must be recognized by somebody who matters.

Women have never been able to count on any of these things and have only achieved them through immense conscious, sometime collective effort. They must also be able to turn disruptive life changes into chances. The first half of the twentieth century witnessed a remarkable outburst of such effort, bringing American women the right to vote and hold office, the access to education that would open new economic and creative opportunities, and the social latitude to claim the right to pleasure and dignity on their own behalf. Women's access to artistic training, to the time and means to make art, and to the possibility of artistic recognition was assuredly part of this greater enlargement of women's possibilities. Most women remained committed to wifehood and mothering. Still, the possible combinations of what women should do, and what they might do, proliferated."

Well, Christa, what must you have to create art? Do you have any complaints? How did you acquire your 'independent spirit'? Do women potters know and appreciate their women pioneers in the arts? What woman artist do you identify with? Are all your heroes and sources of inspiration men? Where does your strength come from? Some people would say that your art work is simply compensation or sublimation for 'wifehood and mothering'. They would say that once you meet the 'right man' maybe you won't have to throw pots anymore? I have a feeling that you might say something rude to people who would say things like that. What combination are you searching for? What would suit you best?

I do remember Georgia O'Keeffe as a young naked woman. I have Stieglitz to thank for that. But that is not the last impression or thought I have about her. Male critics tried at first to attach her art to her well photographed body as the very essence of male notions of womanhood. Jack Cowart and Juan Hamilton were responsible for the publication of "Georgia O'Keeffe: Art and Letters". Sarah Greenough, who selected and annotated the letters of O'Keeffe for this volume, had this to say about O'Keeffe's thoughts regarding the identification of her art with her gender:

"Criticism made her 'shiver', she wrote, and gave her 'a queer feeling of being invaded'. Since 1915 O'Keeffe had been ambivalent about showing her work, fearing that it would be misunderstood and misinterpreted. When that fear was realized in the early 1920s she purposefully changed her style, making it less abstract, more representational. Her choice of apples, pears, plums, and especially flowers, however, only encouraged comment on the sexual qualities of her work. O'Keeffe's letters confirm that she believed that men and women saw and responded to the world in fundamentally different ways, but she did not think that women's art was any more or less sexual than men's. Because she was so distressed by much of the critical writing on her, which was primarily by men, and because she hoped that another woman might see her art more clearly, she solicited reviews from several women. These reviews were not always satisfactory, however."

At one time professional sports did not allow black athletes to play. Now, in numbers and quality, if you look at, say, baseball and particularly basketball, they dominate these sports. Will the same thing happen to pottery? Are men on their way out? How is ceramic talent distributed? Would any generalization or conclusion be mistaken? As a collector I want an inclusive representation of all regions, all humanity. But I am limited, the collection reflects where I have most traveled in my life. The art work reflects what attracts me but also what I can afford. My opinion of excellent pottery does not include an opinion about gender or culture or geographical region. Even for me, the ability to create memorable pottery is only one small segment of a total life of a culture. As with people that are physically disabled in one of their senses, culture compensates for lack of distinguished talent in one area with brilliance in others. I do try to stretch my understanding, but I cannot claim identities foreign to me. I am one gender, one origin, one language. Others will have to decide how these characteristics have limited my thinking and observations. I do not know how the artist works through this problem. To represent a particular culture or time or gender through your pottery might bring distinction, but to transcend them might bring universal affection.

In the O'Keeffe book I came across a letter written to Eleanor Roosevelt in 1944. It is not about art but about the political rights of women. In this rather brief letter she expresses regret that Eleanor Roosevelt does not support an Equal Rights Amendment for women. I was surprised at that information: Eleanor Roosevelt is one of my heroes, with deep convictions that exceeded the more expedient manipulations of her husband. I like the idea that people fight for the rights of groups of people that have suffered oppression and discrimination, even if they were the fortunate, privileged ones within that group. Here is O'Keeffe gently admonishing Roosevelt:

"The Equal Rights Amendment would write into the highest law of our country legal equality for all. At present women do not have it and I believe we are considered - half the people. Equal Rights and Responsibilities is a basic idea that would have very important psychological effects on women and men from the time they are born. It could very much change the girl child's idea of her place in the world. I would like each child to feel responsible for the country and that no door for any activity they may choose is closed on account of sex. It seems to me very important to the idea of true democracy - to my country - and to the world eventually - that all men and women stand equal under the sky."

I scanned all her letters in the book and did not see any other reference to the political rights of women. But in this one instance, she did state plainly her advocacy of the rights of women. As you know, despite the organized efforts over the years, we still do not have an Equal Rights Amendment that would enshrine the rights of women in the very Constitution of our land. Do we also need an equal rights amendment for women in ceramics? What would it say? You obviously did not need such documents or laws to make your mark. Are you one of those successful people who would insist that if you can make it, all other women can make it too?

Another account of the struggle of women to make art, this time fiction, was authored by one of the most important novelists of the last century, Virginia Woolf. It is a remarkable book, taking place over just a few days, with the interior monologues of intimate friends and members of a family, staying on the English coast at their holiday home. In this book, "To the Lighthouse", the very last words reveal the artistic struggle and eventual triumph of Lily Briscoe, painter, houseguest and friend of the Ramsay family:

"Quickly, as if she were recalled by something over there, she turned to her canvas. There it was - her picture. Yes, with all the green and blues, its lines running up and across, its attempts at something. It would be hung in the attics, she thought; it would be destroyed. But what did that matter? she asked herself, taking up the brush again. She looked at the steps; they were empty; she looked at her canvas; it was blurred. With a sudden intensity, as if she saw it clear for a second, she drew a line there, in the centre. It was done; it was finished. Yes, she thought, laying down her brush in extreme fatigue, I have had my vision."

I guess that's what I want for you. That you work very hard and that you finally have your vision. When you put down the clay each day, and until the end of your days, that as a woman and potter, you can emulate Lily and conclude with the same last words as she did, "I have had my vision". Virginia Woolf had the last word in her accomplishment, no future revisionist critic can erase her contribution. What does it take for that kind of achievement? I have mentioned a whole pantheon of significant artists in this letter. They have changed me in many ways. The sum total of their art represents a magnificent statement of achievement that the culture cannot ignore or fail to respect. Indeed, they have rightly become the culture. Great craftspeople and potters are fully qualified to be members of this band of treasured artists. Acceptance and recognition should not become dependent on some special and rare genius. The struggle to achieve excellence in itself provides a sufficient challenge for all of us. No one should have to endure a culturally systemic barrier of bias.

Like the Ramsays in another time and place, the Jacobs family has gathered on holiday on the central coast of California in the little town of Cayucos. We gather a block from the pier and ocean, in an old 1880s ship captain's house. I have written most of this letter here. My grandchildren display the constant drama of instant laughter and tears moments apart. There is a special delight for Judy and me in enjoying the presence of our beloved grandchildren. Our two sons and daughters-in-law are good company. Surely making friends of relatives is a major achievement, surprisingly easy in this case. We all made it to the lighthouse, we all survived intact and now, in this time, at this moment, we share food and close quarters in wholesome ways. I enjoy the company of Virginia Woolf, Emily Carr, Frida Kahlo, Georgia O'Keeffe, and the other towering women of supreme achievement. They too are all here with me in this old house on the central California coast. I am in very good company indeed. Take care.

Your friend,

Richard

Thirty-two

August 24, 2004

Dear Christa,

I am sitting, early in the morning, in a hotel room in Phoenix, aware of the three digit summer heat here, further warned by the TV news report that both heat and rain are quite possible today. We spent six hours on the highway yesterday, traveling with Judy, my daughter-in-law Joan and three remarkable and beautiful grandchildren. Why this particular journey? At this particular time of the year to Phoenix? To see pottery of course! At least that was my motivation. Joan lived in Scottsdale a few years ago, working on her Ph.D. in clinical psychology. She was coming back to see old friends, to show her daughter, Rainey, the places where she had lived as an infant before the big move to California. Are there limits to my pottery obsession? Just how far and how adverse would the conditions have to be to discourage my quest? I dare not answer those questions. Our trips are not planned around seeing beautiful natural scenery or staying at fancy resorts. I shun recreation and holiday release from my daily existence, or any other diversion. Oh, I am willing to visit cultural and historical sites, take in a good film or play, certainly a fine concert, an interesting bookstore. But when I received that brochure in the mail, the one about the exhibition of "British Ceramic Masterworks: Highlights from the Anne and Sam Davis Collection" at the Ceramics Research Center at Arizona State University in Phoenix, I rushed to the calendar on the side of the refrigerator in the kitchen, and after a brief discussion with Judy, confirmed the dates with a scribbled notation on the agreed days, and our fate was sealed. On to Phoenix in the middle of summer - such a reckless and dangerous gamble - proof of my chronic ceramic instability. Perhaps I should ask Joan, given her professional expertise, just how far I need to go before I fall within some category of pathological disturbance. Surely my serious condition can be partly blamed on the seductive lure created by potters determined to bait and agitate my fragile state.

Our preferences in life, those things we bless with uncritical favoritism, display much about ourselves. I love pottery, I particularly love British pottery. Why? One obvious good reason - I associate British pottery with Britain - a second home that harbors treasured memories for me. The possible danger of confessing positive bias is that it might be more revealing of my weaknesses rather than my strengths. I have lived there, visited often, have very positive recollections that only increase with time and age. One reason for an easy comfort is of course the language. The English accent sounds to my ear like a rather posh refinement of American English - anyone that has that proper BBC accent represents an indisputable authority that cannot be challenged. I do have trouble with foreign languages - can only speak and write my native tongue. It is simply not fair that any English idiot with that impressive accent seems to possess an awesome intelligence and innate superiority over the flat and dull pronouncements of the American mouth and mind. Maybe I award the same uncritical advantage to British pottery.

Britain did not rely entirely on its native genius to establish a modern reputation in pottery. Hitler did inadvertently sponsor two of its greatest potters, Lucie Rie and Hans Coper. World War II gave American literature W.H. Auden and Christopher Isherwood; American pottery was enriched with Gertrud and Otto Natzler; American music with Schoenberg and Stravinsky. The exile of war and the possibility of extermination provided rich imports of artistic and intellectual resources for both Britain and America. Rie and Coper became national treasures for Britain. They represented a deviation from the dominant influence of Bernard Leach. As Peter Held, curator of the Ceramics Research Center at Arizona State University Art Museum states:

"… Rie found it more difficult to gain acceptance for her pots in England, as her modernist aesthetic differed from the tradition established by Bernard Leach and his followers. Rie always favored wheel-thrown objects that emphasized refined forms and textures with a minimum of decoration. She experimented constantly with different glaze effects for her electric kiln, achieving a signature style through layering slips and glazes and using oxides or stains, either mixed into the clay or used on the surface of the clay or glaze. Her glazes ranged from smooth and satiny to thick and pitted, enhancing the elegance of her forms."

Now, on the very same day, after viewing and experiencing these wonderful exhibits, reporting on the impact and influence of this exhibition and the resources of the Ceramics Research Center, I must celebrate my elation at the pleasures of this experience. It was well worth it. The firecely hot climate, crossing vast expanses of desert, nothing can discourage me. I will return to this place. How ironic, that this near inferno can stage a display of cold, wet

British pottery and get away with it. In the past, I have risked dampness and possible pneumonia in England to savor its immense pleasures. I can now risk the burning heat of the summer to celebrate British pottery in Arizona. As this remark might indicate, I am severely limited in the range of natural climate I can tolerate without complaint. A collector by nature is an interior personality.

Christa, you came from some place back east, I think it was Pennsylvania, to the west coast, to California. At what point does your identity transfer? At what point can we give California, not Pennsylvania, credit for your contribution? At what point did Rie and Coper become English, and their pottery samples of English pottery? How liberal and generous can we be in the integration of immigrant potters in their new land? Are you a California potter now? Would you object if so identified? Does the association with a geographical region limit your possible universal status as a serious ceramic artist? In the very serious world of professional art criticism it seems OK for a particular art movement or style to originate in a specific site or region, and somehow represent indigenous aesthetic impulses in that place, but inherently limiting for an artist within that group to be too closely associated as representative of that area. The mysteries and conventions of writing about culture are as embedded with unconscious cultural presuppositions and hidden assumptions as the work and life of the artist under their review.

It is the next morning, early in the morning, about 4am. I have just read a few of the documents that Peter Held generously provided that describe previous exhibitions at the research center. They are most informative but do represent a moment of self-doubt and sudden humility. I am not a competitive person. I do not need potential rivals to goad my efforts in any endeavor. I am realistic about the modest dimensions of my collection and my limited financial capacity to further supplement it. Yet I am still very proud of the excellent potters and craftpersons that it represents. In the document that shares the same title as the exhibition last year at the center, entitled "Shared Passion: Sara and David Lieberman Collection of Contemporary Ceramics and Craft", Susan Peterson opens the essay with this splendid comment:

"Shared passion is what Sara terms the great love she and David have for ceramics, for ceramic artists, for the joy they find in the art, and for searching out and acquiring beautiful pieces."

A few paragraphs later we learn that David is an inventive and successful businessman who supported the initial interests of his wife. In fact they, at one time or another, have collected many kinds of things I have collected over the years, including functional pottery, prints and other craft objects. Peterson points out that their collecting is a joint activity, each with their own particular taste, yet sharing the experience and the beautiful objects that result from their mutual discoveries. I particularly respect the sensitive closing statement of Sara Lieberman:

"We want to live with these things, buying has nothing to do with it ... There is joy in living with extraordinary objects. It is a privilege to live with these, to stroll through the rooms, to drink from a ceremonial tea bowl. We have had fun, we have love for each other, we have wonderful children and grandchildren, friends that tie us together, but we count our collections as a wonderful extra."

We also share many of the same kinds of treasures with the Liebermans - children, grandchildren, friends, and our wonderful home enriched with beautiful things. I could not improve on her loving and generous words. I am further pleased when I find out that the Liebermans are involved in improving their community, supporting education and rehabilitation programs for children and adults with disabilities. That reinforces my own convictions about a love of art. It should not be an isolated appetite. The aristocracy were once the grand patrons, later the robber barons of the industrial revolution. Armies once looted defeated countries for the prizes of art for the victorious ruling classes. I do not seek placement in that tradition. The preservation and collection of art should be inspired and motivated by a generous and greater impulse than lust for the objects themselves. To love the aesthetic gifts of human civilization, you must first respect the dignity and humanity of all its members. It does not matter to me if this has not always been the case, I will not relinquish the principle. To conserve art by personal possession without also trying to conserve the culture of the greater community is an act of intrinsic self-centeredness and selfishness.

Another exhibition brochure from ASU and Peter Held, this time explores a movement that does not resonate with my own private preferences, "Humor, Irony And Wit: Ceramic Funk From The Sixties and Beyond." Here again there is a sensitive portrayal of collectors, Joyce and Jay Cooper. According to Held:

"The Coopers have spent the better part of the last twenty-five years enriched by personal relationships with many of the artists represented in their collection. The exhibition is made possible by their vision and commitment to the field. Like many collectors, they share a passion that has shaped their lives through art."

Further on in the exhibition guide, there is a question and answer interview with Dr. Jay Cooper by Held. Asked a question about forming his collection,

Cooper answers with great enthusiasm:

"I was fortunate in choosing an area to collect that was not too large, not too vast. Because it was focused, I was able to get my hands around it and really understand it. I also enjoyed the relationships that I've built with the artists. I felt empowered to learn more about what was going on and who was doing what … I thoroughly enjoyed getting to know the artists and being in their studios. It was an important part of the collecting process for me."

There is a brief italicized statement at the end of the interview: "This interview was conducted on December 2, 2003. Dr. Cooper passed away on February 4, 2004."

I re-read it, reviewing one of the last statements Cooper made at the end, "You never know what life's going to bring you." I thought about this generous man and of course I transferred my thoughts to my own situation. I have not resolved this essential question, should my own inevitable demise be calculated into my decisions about my collection? I am always receiving mail as a university alumnus, or from other non-profit organizations I support in modest ways, urging me to make immediate provision for a contribution of some element of my 'estate'. I never liked the term 'estate sale'. The term did not seem to convey a fitting tribute and memorial to the person whose demise was the occasion for the redistribution and recycling of treasured possessions. This is not a garage sale. It is a terminal closing of the documented artifacts that give meaning to the life that had just expired. It must be slightly ghoulish to attend such an event. I have not done so. How does one paw over these things, haggle over price, when I know that the monetary value assigned represents nothing of the joy that object provided to that deceased individual, this stranger whose funeral I did not even bother to attend. Should we not attempt in some fashion to mourn this collector at the estate sale? The rational and logical approach, which I do not support in this case, would state the obvious, that objects pass through time and sites, transported through collections and collectors. This history is called 'provenance' in antiques circles. At the moment, I resist the thought of being another sequential citation in the 'provenance' of any of my objects.

Like family, intimate objects have a long history in the home and an intimate relationship with people devoted to them. They cannot be efficiently depersonalized and abstracted from their former siting. I could be philosophically detached - after all, 'life goes on'. But it bothers me. It particularly reminds me of the potential absurdity of remaining an active collector into my seventies. I do not think I can bear to voluntarily let go of my precious objects. This might appear to make me selfish or weak but I cannot either defend my feelings or further explore them at this time. If I could only plan and determine the timing of my demise, I might be willing to consider the possible arrangements for and fate of my collection. In leaving this for Judy to work out, I will avoid responsibility and evade decision making.

Christa, you are too young now to even begin to think about this issue. I wonder how most potters deal with this? It is one thing to have a career strategy. How does one include mortality in the planning of a creative life? Death never appears as the final citation on a potter's resumé. What comprises a happy ending for the potter? Does the pottery just get better and better with age? At the end, does the culmination of ceramic greatness coincide with the termination of a potter's life? Does the pinnacle of life's work ripen into a final stage in which everything is reconciled in a final aesthetic triumph? How many times has that happened? In my own perverse way, I sort of prefer the George Ohr ending. An eccentric who stopped creating pottery, became the village idiot, died in obscurity, and became the legendary genius of American pottery decades after his death. Should potters be spoiled with earthly rewards or become the romantic heroines of tragedy as rejected failures redeemed only after their demise? Success has its own rewards, but just think of the great film or play that could be made if you suffer great tragedy and awful rejection during your lifetime and achieve fame only long after you could actually enjoy it.

What is the final triumph of the collector's life? The artist retains permanent credit, while collectors most often fade into historical obscurity. Perhaps that is why I highly valued the documents and the explicit tribute to the Liebermans and Coopers.

The Liebermans and the Coopers gave generously of their collections to the Ceramics Research Center at Arizona State University. They were not passive proprietors of inanimate objects, they were the active protectors and patrons of human genius and creativity. In my own humble and modest way, I am complemented by such worthy models and mentors. I dare not compare the scope and scale of my own life as collector with their results.

One reminder of this deserved modesty, I asked Peter Held for the names of local galleries where I could find pottery and he graciously obliged, identifying two galleries in Scottsdale. Judy and I went to the downtown area of old Scottsdale where galleries dominate the street. I had been there before and should have known better. We found the galleries but were disappointed. I do not usually find what I am looking for in galleries in places like Laguna Beach in California or in Scottsdale, Arizona. Why does expensive 'art' have to be so big and brazen to justify its high price? They usually advertise clay pieces as 'art' and celebrate exhibition openings with wine and cheese receptions. I must confess the ultimate embarrassment. I cannot remember ever attending or enjoying free wine and cheese at any reception. I just don't travel in those kind of elevated circles. I much prefer to go to a potter's studio, sometimes combined with a modest space for display, meet the potter and see the work. I much prefer to go to a gallery that proudly proclaims itself a haven for crafts rather than a salesroom for 'art'. The perfect example of these particular virtues is Seagrove, North Carolina. For the most part, home, studio and gallery occupy the same space and site. They are potters; some are graduates of art institutes and higher education; some are the living practitioners of generations of ancestors that were potters; but they are all potters. Some of them achieve great artistry, but they do not call themselves artists and do not project the arrogance of that claim with inflated prices. No one offered me wine or cheese during my tour of the potteries of the Seagrove area. Yes, I really feel at home in a place like Seagrove. And that said, I really like wine and cheese. I sense that I have just gone too far in my radical commentary. Please do not take offense. If you do occasionally offer wine and cheese at your gallery, please invite me next time. I have generally retained, during a long life, my virtues and values only because I have never been given the invitation or opportunities to corrupt them.

Another fine example is a small gallery in the little town of Cambria, California. Here Gayle Sewell provides a showcase for local and regional potters and other craftspeople. She supports and encourages their efforts and promotes the sale of their work. Here numerous galleries are not only a part of the commercial sector of the main street, they are the agencies that promote creative and cultural activities as an integral part of community and civic life. It must be the old public school art teacher in me, but I find that most commendable. Christa, I think you do much the same thing at your Verdigris Gallery in San Francisco. I know that you display the work of many potters, giving them the opportunity to present their wares and develop their craft and career.

Similar to my populist stance toward fancy galleries, I would never go to a franchise book store in a mall to buy a book. First of all, these places don't sell real books. They might have cook books, self-help books, travel books, but most of these homogenized fast food book stores lack the elegance of something once considered necessary at bookstores, something called literature. One great book store is in Ojai, a small town in the hills of Ventura in central California. Bart's Books occupies open air stalls and shelves, old houses and structures, books piled everywhere. When the store is closed, you can walk by on the sidewalk, browse through stacked boxes of books, make your selection and leave the money. I do not buy used clothing but I do love to browse used book stores.

One great book I discovered at Bart's was "In Praise of Hands: Contemporary Crafts of the World". This book was published in association with the World Crafts Council to commemorate an international exhibition of contemporary crafts at the Ontario Science Centre in 1974. It contains one of the most profound statements I have ever encountered regarding the handcrafted object. This essay by Octavio Paz, the Mexican poet/philosopher, in a used book most probably out of print and circulation, constituted a wonderful discovery for me. I took it home and keep it close, on the side arm of my big chair in the living room, where I sit and read, listen to music, gaze at my pottery and spend some of the best hours of the day. Christa, I wish I could reproduce the entire essay here for you but I will give you one small sample of this insightful and inspiring message - Paz is talking about the differences between the object manufactured by modern design and the objects crafted by hand:

"Modern design has taken other paths - its own characteristic ones - in its search for a compromise between usefulness and aesthetics. At times it has achieved a successful compromise, but the result has been paradoxical. The aesthetic ideal of functional art is to increase the usefulness of the object in direct proportion to the amount by which its materiality can be decreased. The simplification of forms and the way in which they function becomes the formula: the maximum efficiency is to be achieved by the minimum of presence. An aesthetic mindful of the realm of mathematics, where the elegance of an equation is a function of the simplicity of its formulation and the inevitability of its solution. The ideal of modern design is invisibility: the less visible functional objects are, the more beautiful they are. A curious transposition of fairy tales and Arabic legends to a world governed by science and the notions of usefulness and efficiency: the designer dreams of objects which, like djinn, are mute and intangible servants. The precise opposite of craftwork: a physical presence which enters us by way of the senses and in which the principle of maximum utility is continually violated in favor of tradition, imagination, and even sheer caprice. The beauty of industrial design is conceptual in nature: if it expresses anything at all, it is the precise accuracy of a formula. It is the sign of a function. Its rationality confines it to one and only one alternative: either an object will work or it won't. In the second case it must be thrown into the trash barrel. It is not simply its usefulness that makes the handcrafted object so captivating. It lives in intimate connivance with our senses and that is why it is difficult to part company with it. It is like throwing an old friend out into the street."

I think that the point that Paz is making is an important one. For someone like you, Christa, who is determined to make that successful compromise between aesthetics and function, he points out an inherent danger. The urge to subtract and to achieve perfect design and perfect function is to eventually produce that odd, bastard product - a hand-crafted object that would have been better designed and manufactured by machinery. It also implies an unconscious tribute to modern design and industrial production - an acknowledgement of conformity or defeat, or as Paz would say, "… the negation of meaning for the sake of the object". The rebellious response to industrial design in ceramics has taken another tack since World War II. The funk and pop movements derived, from post-war abstract expressionism, going further back to Dada and the effects of World War I, deliberate 'bad art' that combined satire and comedy, humor and obscenity. I don't know about you, but I am caught in the middle of all that. I reject the homogenized conformity and sterility of corporate manufactured products, but I am not ready to embrace the desperation and despair of the cynical response. In my opinion, funk and pop art are not funny, they are rather the sad messages of political and cultural losers. They may be right as an accurate historical judgment, yet I will stand with Paz - I will embrace 'tradition, imagination, and even sheer caprice'.

How do you make that pot project your humanity and imagination, and still be modern and contemporary in ways that go beyond expected tradition and simple cultural continuity? That is indeed a real challenge. Vulgarity and obscenity have become the calculated strategies of ceramic careers dependent on urban galleries, designed and packaged to attract sensational attention and to sell at inflated prices. This is truly as sordid and opportunistic a commercial enterprise as any critique inspired by middle-class consumerism and corporate greed.

Cynical 'bad art' does not protect the weak and oppressed, it congratulates the enemy as winner by the pathetic imitation of the vulgarity and obscenity necessary to exercise that oppression and exploitation. It becomes an inadvertent tribute to those they despise. Like Arneson's rejected memorial statue of George Moscone, it should be obvious that obscenity and/or vulgarity does not have the capacity to offer respect and homage, even to those people and principles they seek to defend. Moral outrage, embedded in those who have suffered loss, and others who historically suffer the loss of dignity and respect in this society, cannot be healed by ceramic protests that offend the victims in more severe ways than the intended targets of their 'art'. Vulgarity cannot protest moral outrage. When vulgarity becomes the prop of the artist's ego and individualism, it cannot be expected to carry the message to others. Art cannot be deliberately hostile to perceivers and then seek to convert them. Art becomes both morally and politically viable only when the contrast between the morality it is defending and the immorality of the offending party are clear by the contrast demonstrated in the character and representation imbued in that aesthetic work. In asserting that, I must then become very timid and liberal in seeking a definition of vulgarity that would support my argument and not display an intolerant and unthinking conformity with respectable conventions.

The most successful satires in art have demonstrated the capacity to gain access to the enemy by aesthetic devices that often adhere to acceptable forms of artistic media. Be it the savage satire of drawings by Hogarth or the current documentary films of Michael Moore, it is the critical content that rends apart the compliant and corrupt habits of the powerful. If Michael Moore had chosen to also include frontal nudity in his films, as is the naughty habit of some ceramists I know, it would have sharply reduced the circulation and display of the real obscenities of the powerful. The act of giving offense as purpose and end of the aesthetic act is as childish and meaningless as restroom graffiti. Sometimes I have to stand or sit in such a situation. I would never purchase such an object voluntarily nor keep company with it in my home. I am not offended by vulgarity. It does not violate my morals or my politics. It is simply not welcome in my own aesthetic search for the beautiful and the noble. I sense that this might make me old-fashioned or obsolete.

Paz further explores the qualities of craft-making:

"Because of its physical size and the number of people constituting it, a community of craftsmen favor democratic ways of living together; its organization is hierarchical but not authoritarian, being a hierarchy based not on power but on degrees of skill: masters, journeymen, apprentices; and finally, craftwork is labor that leaves room both for carefree diversion and for creativity. After having taught us a lesson in sensibility and the free play of the imagination, craftwork also teaches us a lesson in social organization."

Christa, I do not know what you call yourself or your work - artist, potter or craftsperson - art or craft. Frankly, I don't care. The issues will not go away if you avoid the discussion of terms and language. What best describes your aesthetic intentions and what best describes the result as represented in your work? I highly value the combination of supreme skill and creative imagination that results in great pottery.

I think the last few sentences of this essay by Paz brings us back to the earlier discussion and ideas in this letter. He offers me advice pertinent to my life placement:

"Between the timeless time of the museum and the speeded-up time of technology, craftsmanship is the heartbeat of human time. A thing that is handmade is a useful object but also one that is beautiful; an object that lasts a long time but also one that slowly ages away and is resigned to so doing; an object that is not unique like the work of art and can be replaced by another object that is similar but not identical. The craftsman's handiwork teaches us to die and hence teaches us to live."

Human life has sacred and noble dimensions. Art and crafts are visible evidence of those qualities. The shaped forms that emerge from the hands of potters and craftspeople form the very content and evidence of the cyclical rhythms of the human lifestyle. Make no mistake about it, Christa, this letter has been about death - and its ability to make life worthwhile. It is an event I admittedly prefer discussing rather than experiencing. Again I stand with Paz. I learn the lessons of life from the lessons of art and crafts and move forward in slow ageing into death.

Take care. Your friend.

Richard

Thirty-three

September 14, 2004

Dear Christa,

Impatience best describes my present condition. Impatience is bad practice for someone my age who naturally wishes to slow down the clock and calendar. This month wages a fierce defense of the summer season, often surprising for those who expect September to be a preview of fall. I wish to wait no further, summer surely must end soon. I can define seasons only in the immediate geography of my own existence, so others in other places must have different passions and prejudices about their state of climate and the time of year. I am impatient with the interminable political campaigns and the gnawing sensation of probable defeat for those causes I hold dear. I must gather energy to find devious ways of defending and rationalizing my minority views. I must convince myself that the tortured romance of self-exile can be achieved without the inconvenience of moving. I must convince myself that my perennial alienation is not the result of personal temperament but the external pressures of unfriendly forces. I will increase the time I spend with my pottery, that usually helps.

In the last few years I have given much time and thought to the aesthetics that govern my acquisitions. The benefits of such investigations not only provide clarity on those transactions, but further reveal my own nature and needs. I hesitate to share these ideas and the pattern of their meaning with others. I have been controversial all my adult life, in every sphere of professional activity. I wish I had had the accompanying ability to find pleasure in such hostile responses. I still expect and want the perverse pleasure of complete disagreement in aesthetic things and warm and accepting relations with the mistaken parties. I must find ways to assuage them without making too many concessions. The final disclaimer is the assertion that these stated standards are restricted, only for myself. I have no universal pretense of their truth for others.

Along with questions of God and country, questions concerning the core beliefs of aesthetic preferences are among the most sensitive matters to share with others. One cannot externalize and objectify these feelings. They leak out of your very soul. They are you - and when others do not share these feelings - are even offended and repulsed by the very contrast with their own aesthetic thoughts - conflict and confrontation loom. I cannot play it safe. I am going to declare an aesthetic devotion to notions of beauty and nature as the purest and finest sources of aesthetic inspiration, best enshrined at the domestic site of family life. More than my politics and my difficult and peculiar personality, this will solidify my isolation and gravely test my ability to keep up with the latest trends.

Let us take this idea of beauty first. Christa, when you finish a pot, do you step back and proclaim the beauty of your pot? Is the achievement of something you could call 'beautiful' even a goal of your efforts? The very word has an old-fashioned ring, obsolete and burdened with connotations of effeminate longings for the pretty decorations of a past world. I have had a lot of help lately in thinking over this notion of beauty. Wendy Steiner has written a wonderful book, "Venus in Exile: The Rejection of Beauty in 20th-Century Art", that leads me through a rich exploration of ideas on that subject. I am grateful for her leadership and good company as I try to integrate my aesthetic preferences for the beautiful with an understanding for the disreputable notoriety of this idea of beauty in the 20th century.

The very essence of modernism required the overthrow of beauty as an aesthetic standard. This was indeed a profound revolution. As Steiner explains:

"In modernism, the perennial rewards of aesthetic experience - pleasure, insight, empathy - were largely withheld, and its generous aim, beauty, was abandoned. Modern artworks may often have been profoundly beautiful, but theirs was a tough beauty, hedged with deprivation, denial, revolt."

This renunciation of beauty has progressive political attributes. Women had been trapped into conventional definitions of beauty that motivated them to become tempting objects of sexual desire and their lives a perennial 'beauty contest'. Can one encourage beauty as a worthy goal in aesthetics without supporting its invidious past as an oppressor of women? Steiner leads us through this discussion:

"Beauty is certainly a magnet for the cultural anxieties of our day: the readjustment of gender roles that has been in the works since the Enlightenment, the commodification of the body in consumer culture, the genetic and evolutionary discoveries changing our understanding of human nature. In the eyes of the geneticist, for example, female beauty is a competitive packaging that increases a woman's chances of perpetuating her genes; for the beauty industry, this packaging perpetuates multinational profits. One way or the other, female freedom and self-realization would seem to require resistance to such an aesthetic. But eschewing beauty comes at a high price if it closes off passion and procreation and self-understanding. For many women, beauty appears to set freedom and pleasure at odds."

As I read this book and process Steiner's argument, I keep three balls in the air. I must juggle the relationship of this discussion of beauty with my own rationale for the character of my collection, and my efforts to convince myself and others that my emerging aesthetic preferences will hold up to their scrutiny. If I hold out for the idea and ideal of beauty, will this book help me have a happy ending, helping to sponsor a renaissance of support for beauty as a worthy aesthetic standard?

Another idea treated in the book is the detested middle class, long a favorite target of Marxists, feminists, and modernists. My dad was a pharmacist. I grew up in a middle class neighborhood. As a young art student, I rebelled against my upbringing, aided by the reality of an insensitive father whose attitudes too often reflected the limitations of middle-class insularity and conformity. What about your origins, Christa? In Europe, there is a vast difference between working class and middle class. In the United States, there is persistent mythology that all working class people are really middle class. I do not know too many Americans that proudly proclaim that they were descended from peasants or factory laborers. The American middle class does not look back, they are eyeing the possibilities of further elevation into the upper classes. Unlike any other industrialized country, they are the most fervent supporters of the upper class, because they hope someday to join them. The definition of ascent involves income and acquisition of material goods, not aesthetic taste or any other manifestation of civilized refinement.

I try to balance these things. I do pay my bills, own a house and have an inventory of appliances. I am by definition and income middle-class. I am not conventional or conforming in my intellectual or political orientation, yet I would fail to meet the credentials of a true rebel according to some cultural standards. In the 1960s I did not drop out or turn to drugs or communal life. I left the country and went into exile, but I cannot claim the success of self-destruction or violent rebellion to establish my credentials. I did challenge the institutional racism of educational agencies and fought to save the minority victims of this professional treatment. I did not wear a Che Guevara t-shirt at the time. I bathe daily out of habit and regard disciplined adherence to duty and obligations paramount to an ethical life. How embarrassing an assessment, how tepid and timid the range of my political daring and compromised nonconformity. Is the range of conformity among potters the same as any other occupational group? Is there any relationship between the degree of artistic experimentation and personal appearance and behavior? Do the traditional potters who make viable containers carry over that conservative stance into their private lives? Do avant-garde clay artists have more fun than the staid craftspeople of the traditional pot?

Steiner explains this aversion of the avant-garde to the middle class:

"The avant-garde portrayed their resistance to philistines - women, the middle classes - as a heroic martyrdom, and they were so convincing in this role that it's hard even today not to believe in and respect their self-sacrifice. Like Socratic gadflies or Shakespearean fools, avant-garde artists told a truth that undermined the pious hypocrisies of conventional existence. They suffered (or embraced) ostracism for their pains, but that isolation from everyday life was, after all, what aesthetic experience was in fact all about. The artist lived art in his countercultural alienation. What could be nobler?"

Implicit in the modernist indictment of the middle-class was the antagonism toward that citadel of bourgeois life, the home. How ironic - the home was the target of both the feminist and modernist critic - yet the home is central to the development and use of craft, including pottery. Potters, in innocence, can claim that they did not order the women to set the table with their fine dinnerware, or fill the vases with cut flowers. Potters did not direct the distribution of duties and the washing and drying of their ceramic creations. In Steiner's book, Mary Wollstonecraft is quoted as comparing the home to a gilded cage for women, a prison where they are 'gentle, domestic brutes'. Christa, if you really believed this, would you want to provide domestic ware for imprisoned females to serve their male masters? Is domestic pottery today designed to attract women in order to make their domestic duties a bit more bearable?

Another voice condemns the American middle class and their dreams and aspirations: the urban planners and environmentalists take aim and fire. The middle class has fled the central city and created that disaster called suburbia, source of all kinds of dysfunctional problems in American society. James Howard Kunstler, in "Home From Nowhere", shows no mercy:

"The idea of a modest dwelling all our own, isolated from the problems of other people, has been our reigning metaphor of the good life for a long time. It must now be seen for what it really is: an antisocial view of human existence. I don't believe we can afford to keep pretending that life is a never-ending episode of Little House on the Prairie. We are going to have to develop a different notion of the good life and create a physical form that accommodates it."

Kunstler prepares us for this indictment of the American suburb by listing the crimes of the suburban middle class:

"Along with the suburb itself as a physical artifact, this notion of freedom from the consequences of one's social behavior has also persisted in the mental life of Americans. If anything, it has only become more gross and elaborate over time, so that today millions of Americans are employed in all sorts of destructive enterprises - killing other people's local economies, wrecking towns and cities with inappropriate 'development', paving over rural landscapes, ruining ecosystems - without the dimmest sense of remorse or responsibility, returning at night to their homesteads in an artificial wilderness, and the blue light of an electronic hearth with its diverting and reassuring imagery."

All right, I can agree with the underlying issues that suburbia represents, but the indictment leaves out the very human aspirations of those who made that trek to suburbia, who spend precious hours on clogged freeways each morning and late afternoon, in order to provide a reasonable and decent life for their families. In southern California, it was true that the first wave of refugees from the central city was often the white middle class, seeking escape from the crime and violence endemic to the urban world. But why did the emerging middle class minority families follow them? It was to secure that very same dream of the earlier migration. The historical origin of suburbia was once a dream of progressive planning in England after the industrial revolution, to flee the squalor, pollution, and poverty of the inner city to find the garden suburbs that would give them dignity and the good life. Progressive planners need to think twice about that savage indictment of suburbia. No wonder that the political forces that do not represent the economic welfare of the middle class now have their votes. You cannot reject human aspirations, however detrimental or mistaken they might be in long range consequences, and expect their loyalty and support at election time. I took up my lawn and replaced it with perennials, drive my Prius, and display conscientious concerns about my lifestyle. But I do not want to return to the density and intensity of life in the inner city, and I will not accept harsh judgments of guilt that do not recognize the compelling attraction of good schools, flourishing gardens and the family home.

One could develop a rigorous aesthetic and ethic of suburbia that would include profound elements of the integration of nature, art, and the human dwelling space. This suburban aesthetic and ethic would include exploring the balance between privacy and community participation, the design of the home interior and the utilization and preservation of the aesthetic artifact, architecture in the context of the garden and open space, the dynamics of family life as the agency of fully developing the human potential of its members. I totally reject those elements of the 'New Urbanism' that seek to make the suburb pay for its sins by so increasing the population density that it becomes assimilated into the inner city. I find it strange that this inadequate solution to the growing population of my area is never informed by any strategy of population control.

Steiner points out that the rejection of the middle class was basic to the modern aesthetic.

"... the twentieth-century avant-garde pursued its mission of public enlightenment by purifying the art of pleasure - the vulgar desire for comfort, charm, warmth, attraction, empathy. Since these despised virtues were identified with woman, the female subject in art underwent a violent transformation in meaning from the early nineteenth to the early twentieth century: from a supreme symbol of beauty to an object lesson in the need for aesthetic discipline. Ornament suffered a similar fate. Art was to be an experience of psychic freedom rather than seduction, a freedom guaranteed by the purity of form."

The middle class might represent the aesthetic essence of the sentimental and the most obvious representational conventions, but modernism was demanding that they forsake the ideal of beauty for 'vulgarity, primitivism, disorientation'. Steiner states the problem clearly:

"Disdaining a world of bourgeois limits, the avant-garde blamed the bourgeoisie for the unconstrained commodification that destroyed value, standing above this consumerism, above the masses, above exchange. But the way it saw fit to do so was, paradoxically, to fill art with waste, transgression, and obscenity."

This insistence on vulgarity has led to a curious appetite for the commercial 'art' object that can either entertain or shock with equal force. I recently went to a newly opened commercial gallery specializing in British ceramics, a favorite source of pleasure for me. It was a rather small space, with two-thirds of the front occupied with large ceramic cartoon figures, clever and cute. In the back were a few shelves with pottery. The proprietor, a most accommodating, charming man with an irresistible British accent, at one point in our conversation, expressed surprise and dismay that he was attracting a lot of interior decorators rather than pottery collectors. I did not reply, not wanting to criticise, but privately surveyed his merchandise. The cartoon figures were doing amusing things and were quite elaborate and very expensive, the ideal props for interior decorators with wealthy clients. In the same sense that I do not watch sitcoms with laughter tracks on TV, I do not want or value three dimensional ceramic jokes that replace the ceramic craft of pottery.

Steiner describes this attack on the sensibilities of the besieged middle class:

"Artists feel they must shock; audiences in the know feel they must applaud shock. The thrill of repulsion has become a positive and sought-after experience in itself, a nihilistic sublime in which horror, disgust, and lack of sympathy are accepted ends. To assimilate the latest challenge as art does not involve a victory of fellow feeling across the community but a proud gesture of superiority on the part of experts toward laypeople supposedly incapable of such feats of stamina and discernment. Moreover, insofar as those in society who are officially labeled as Other - women, minorities, immigrants, the insane, the disadvantaged, the poor - learn their situation by analogy to art, the lesson has been chilling. In the model art has recently presented, an Other can only be colonized or expelled, denatured or killed."

Can Steiner be right? Is modernism ultimately reactionary in the implicit disdain for the vast humanity that does not share its rarefied amusements? How does one locate some middle ground, avoiding the sentimentality of our Victorian past and the false humanity of a totalitarian social realism, yet feel grounded in the finely honed mastery of craft and the search for a subtle beauty that ennobles the human spirit? I am still pursuing this, still trying to put the pieces together, still uneasy that I might be backing myself into an aesthetic corner, pining for the old days, ruing a brave new world I do not understand or appreciate.

There are other more optimistic points of view about the middle class and the importance of the home, such as "The Ideal Home: The History of Twentieth-Century American Craft 1900-1920", edited by Janet Kardon, published on the occasion of the exhibition of the same name at the American Craft Museum in 1994. In one essay by Eileen Boris entitled, "Crossing Boundaries: The Gendered Meaning of the Arts and Crafts", she points out hopeful aspects of middle class suburban life:

"Women and men of the prosperous classes crossed boundaries - women into the world of work, men into the world of the home. Despite such behavior, they brought with them their concepts of manhood and womanhood. The Arts and Crafts movement incorporated dominant understandings of womanhood and manhood even as some of its major figures challenged them. Although this movement reflected a class response to social change, it facilitated the crossings of boundaries. Women's busywork became elevated to art, providing educated women an opportunity to become professionals. Manly furniture entered the home, no longer a feminized space. The crafts movement provided a material culture counterpart to the 'masculine domesticity' that historian Margaret Marsh found resulted from the joining of the suburban ideal with the cult of domesticity. Men returned to the home, aided in its maintenance, and supervised children, but on their own terms of recognized superiority. Although craft practice was divided along sexual lines, the home itself became a place of suburban togetherness."

It is a far cry from Kunstler's condemning rhetoric of the middle class home in the suburb as 'an antisocial view of human existence' to Boris's portrayal of the same phenomenon as 'a place of suburban togetherness'. It appears in general that the craft literature, although derived from the socialist dreams of William Morris, offers a far more positive and inherently conservative image of home and family life than the modernist avant-garde.

George E. Thomas, in his essay in the same book, points out that reform and utopian dreams shifted by the end of the nineteenth century from the city where 'no activism by socialites or political novices could redeem the fundamental inequities of the industrial city'. It was the country and suburbs that became sites for communal experiments and new innovations in architecture and design:

"Thus around 1900, when American architects and designers rediscovered the devices of simplification of form, expression of material, and representation of the manufacturing process, they gave the new movement a distinct national identity that could be seen in bungalows and cottages, in suburbs and villages, and in Mission furniture and interiors from the Atlantic to the Pacific."

It is simply historically inaccurate to blame the automobile for the suburb or to blame the suburb for the automobile. Although the automobile facilitated later migrations, the fundamental dreams of life in the suburbs was derived from the ideas and visions of important intellectual and cultural leaders in the nineteenth and early twentieth centuries who strove to provide the opportunity for the masses of workers to achieve recovery from the worst brutalities of the industrial revolution and applied this altruistic desire to aid the exploited working class to achieve a quality of life and simple dignity. The suburb seeks to balance family stability with the legendary lure of Eden. In many suburbs, these goals were obtained. The suburbs were made of the common dreams of ordinary people.

D.J. Waldie is the poet laureate and bard of the suburbs. He grew up in Lakewood, one of the earliest planned suburbs in the nation. He still lives in the house where his parents raised him and works as a municipal official at the local city hall. In a remarkable book that goes against the grain of the hostile literature about suburbs, "Holy Land: A Suburban Memoir" he contributes an account that is both romantic and honest.

"Daily life here has an inertia that people believe in. In the city's most recent survey, 92 percent of the residents believe this suburb is a desirable place in which to live. Such is the attraction of the suburbs. You look out your kitchen window to the bedroom window of your neighbor precisely fifteen feet away."

Waldie reminds us of the modest and hard origins of many of these people who purchased a slice of land in the tract and the standardized and mass produced house that allowed people with meager means to buy it:

"Some of the men and women in my neighborhood had lived part of their childhood on the outskirts of cotton towns in tents provided by the federal Farm Security Administration. Some had lived in tarpaper shacks among the oil fields outside of Bakersfield. The shacks didn't have indoor plumbing. Some had been the first of their family to graduate from high school."

Christa, it's time to touch base. Are you still with me? I want to establish the viability and virtues of the middle class, beauty, and the suburbs because they have been characterized and ridiculed by the same sophisticated, elite urban critics who have sponsored art that denigrates the very spirit of a democratic and inclusive involvement in the arts and crafts. Craft doesn't insult common folk. Pottery invites intimacy and welcomes new friends. It offers practical help yet provides an appearance that goes beyond function. One can, in the same moment, use a pot or cup and experience and interpret it.

This assessment does not remove the critique of popular culture. I do not visit or value popular, or more accurately, commercial corporate culture. But I have found much of the critical response and contributions of the counterculture of modernism to be as offensive and superficial as their target. Modernism has often settled for the same formula of mindless entertainment or shocking vulgarity as the most corrupt forms of commercial culture. Where does one go when the politics of both right and left leave out the most essential qualities that you value? I don't want an uncritical and soft center, I want a new politics in this country that recognizes those things that are important to me. Public policy is directly relevant and responsible for the possibilities and opportunities for the support of excellence in contemporary culture. A well planned community is based on the modesty of environmental impact and the generosity of the aesthetic qualities that make life worth living.

Nature is the most important source for a universal aesthetic for craft and art. I recently attended a wonderful exhibition in Los Angeles at the Craft & Folk Art Museum. Entitled "Celebrating Nature: Craft Traditions / Contemporary Expressions", it presented contemporary craft formed from the very stuff of the earth - wood, clay, metal, stones and natural fibers. The stated aim in the accompanying book clarifies the intention:

"The works in this exhibition are a marriage of tradition and contemporary expression, folk art and modern sculpture, the world we construct and the earth itself. The belief systems of ancient and indigenous people present the natural world as the domain of spirits. In the wake of Western civilization there is little appreciation for such a mystical, magical place and its ability to feed the soul. Contemporary artists who work in craft mediums embrace myriad world traditions while reflecting contemporary life, calling us back to nature and all that it has to offer. In so doing, they awaken the spirits, show us the magic and inspire our appreciation of natural beauty."

You will note that the last word in this statement is 'beauty'. That would truly describe the stunningly crafted artifacts on display in this show. Kevin V. Wallace, guest curator, wrote an introduction to the book that emphasized the integration of a rich variety of cultural traditions in joint efforts to connect or reconnect our lives to nature. None of the artists presented seek to merely duplicate the surface appearance of nature. These objects represent subtle and imaginative interpretations. Wallace values the harmony that comes from this interaction:

"The human sense of beauty and order has always been informed by nature, yet these artists have transformed the way I view the world. While all artists must have respect for their materials, artists who work with nature look to their materials for color, pattern and texture. When I look at the finest works in craft mediums, I see forms and textures that are in harmony with the natural world and celebrate it."

I seek to weave the threads of a compatible aesthetic that would explain after the fact my impulses and preferences in approaching and acquiring these things surrounding me on the shelves and walls of my home. I wonder if most potters feel the need to become so complicated in theorizing about their creative activities. One could assert with equal passion the need to explain why you create and, on the other hand, to remain adamant that the statement is in the work, no further communication is necessary. I remember visiting the Swedenborgian Church in San Francisco, an important example of Arts and Crafts architecture. I was with a group, sitting in the church with several notable experts explaining the building and its significance. One prominent expert was called upon to speak and he refused. I knew that he felt that it was important for us to experience the building, to allow that interior space to project its own message. We are discouraged in the cinema, and informed prior to the feature presentation, not to talk during the film and reminded that others in the audience would find it distracting. When experiencing pottery, do the same rules apply?

Christa, I am writing the last paragraph of this letter the same day I am going to pick you up in Riverside and take you to my home for the first time. Admittedly, I am somewhat anxious about your initial exposure to my pottery collection. You are the first 'pro' to see it. Except for Judy, who is my partner in our collecting adventures, I do not generally expect family and friends to show great enthusiasm or interest. For the most part, the collection for them is evidence of my eccentric nature. When invited to someone's house, I usually assess the host by scanning the books on their shelves. I have all this incriminating evidence around me, this declaration of self and celebration of choice. I cannot hide or evade the responsibility for it. I cannot separate the collection from me. We are indivisible. I do not expect others to have an uncritical agreement with all my choices or their arrangement. I do hope that you will at least affirm in your observations my dedicated embrace of pottery and my devotion to the work of artisans and potters. I look forward to spending a day with you and further exploring the issues and ideas that give meaning to what we do and how we choose to live.

Your Friend,

Richard

Thirty-four

October 12, 2004

Dear Christa,

According to Jack Putnam, staff member of the South Street Seaport Museum of New York and informed guide of our group of Elderhostel seniors, 'seafaring is an unnatural act'. On this second day of our odyssey across the Atlantic, I can testify to the accuracy of his statement. The sea is angry this first morning into our voyage. People walk down the long corridors parallel to the cabins with an unsteady sway that mirrors the roll of the ship. Jack, in our daily morning seminars aboard ship, in his fluid and articulate manner, explains the relationship of bodies of water and the maritime past of the human species. One of the great human inventions was the very first seizure of a floating log, sliding on top of it, and crossing the river to the other side. Jack also insists we are not cruising but we are involved in a crossing - a profoundly different experience. There are no ports of call on this vast and lonely sea. We are not true explorers - hardly discoverers - just a group of old people on a floating hotel - pampered and fed and cared for in a soft luxury that would shame our hardy seafaring ancestors. But all the same, I seize the romance and claim my connection to the legendary Celts, Vikings, and Phoenicians, the plundering pirates, explorers, and other courageous souls; some looking for gold or spices, some set upon the sea and sent into exile and the unknown as punishment; some endowed with courage and curiosity. I appreciate all that history. I must represent them in my current adventure on highly compromised terms, so Judy and I set sail on the Queen Mary 2 from New York, the largest passenger ship in the world and the only one left on the North Atlantic, due to arrive at Southampton, England, with a few days in London before flying back to Los Angeles.

Jack is still talking, a few individuals of the group are getting up and quietly leaving, not out of boredom but because of distress. The rolls are even more pronounced and stomachs recently filled with a generous breakfast are now rumbling in rhythm with the ship. Surely we have earned our membership in that heroic history of past maritime adventurers in keeping the contents of our excessive breakfasts in our bellies, refusing to surrender to the foreign movements of that cold and unfriendly sea. Like my ancestors, my courage is based on ignorance, not knowing the scientific principles of why this great ship is still floating above the white crested waves, trusting our survival to the unknown engineers responsible for this behemoth. They are not now with us as we surf on top of these gray waves that plunge and rise in continuous upheaval.

What constitutes a voyage of discovery for a potter? Why would you venture out from the secure and known boundaries of previous patterns and habits to try something new? I am not sure about the differences between tourist and traveler but one distinction must be that the tourist can only stare at foreign sights as a detached entertainment, while the traveler has something else in mind. The journey at the potter's wheel might appear static and stationary - but the signs of creative evolution provide artifacts that demonstrate the distance traveled and the dynamic changes of continuing exploration. Yet the irony of exploration - at the potter's wheel or across the North Atlantic - comprises the revelation that awaits our return to the familiar site of departure. I think T.S. Eliot said it best in the last stanza of "Little Gidding":

> We shall not cease from exploration
> And the end of all our exploring
> Will be to arrive where we started
> And know the place for the first time.
> Through the unknown, remembered gate
> When the last of earth left to discover
> Is that which was the beginning;
> At the source of the longest river
> The voice of the hidden waterfall
> And the children in the apple-tree
> Not known, because not looked for
> But heard, half-heard, in the stillness
> Between two waves of the sea.
> Quick now, here, now, always-
> A condition of complete simplicity
> (Costing not less than everything)
> And all shall be well and
> All manner of thing shall be well
> When the tongues of flame are in-folded
> Into the crowned knot of fire
> And the fire and the rose are one.

Thirty-five years ago, during the Vietnam war, I traveled the same route, accelerated by the flight of the airplane, determined to find permanent exile. The fires of war and racism sponsored that departure long ago. This morning, on board the ship, I choose to attend the meeting with Jack, instead of a competing seminar on the Iraq war. I do not think these two events, separated by half a lifetime, provide much evidence for the idea of human progress.

Christa, what do you find out about yourself when you arrive at the place you started and know that place for the first time? Do you keep a diary or rely on memory to record the history of your life at the potter's wheel? How do you realize the moment of discovery? Does the difference between the very first pot you threw years ago and the last pot you have just thrown provide comforting evidence of your devotion and work at the wheel? I cannot answer the questions I have just asked, because I am at sea and disconnected, waiting to understand what I already know; hoping that this understanding validates my past life and justifies the expenditure of funds on this crossing. I do not know if I will reach the promised land, but I do expect to reach the far shore.

If the fish does not know water, because that is the only thing the fish has experienced, and thus has no basis for comparison, how do potters know clay, if that is the only thing they have experienced? When does this very common experience, this daily habit at the wheel, become that voyage of discovery, that moment of revelation? Apparently, only a few passengers and group members are interested in abstracting this voyage as reflective metaphor. It has always puzzled me that so few people in life are self-conscious about the essential issues of their own biography. For most of us, unlike potters, the intimate artifact of our own personhood will be the only place in our lives where we will have any power and opportunity to craft some deliberate evidence of our nature. What I know about pottery is ultimately dependent on what I know about myself.

Christa, are you willing to take a voyage into the unknown? I want potters to risk everything, I want their work at the wheel to be dangerous. I want the finished products of their efforts to represent their voyage of discovery their tentative exploration of new possibilities, yet somehow connected with the mastery of their highly developed technical and aesthetic skills. Perhaps my demands are excessive. I do not want, of course, for you to travel so far that your new and strange shapes curl my aesthetic sensibilities. It is apparent that you must not be preoccupied with what I want, you must first satisfy yourself.

One of my first discoveries on board the Queen Mary 2 was an extensive and fine library. I found a book on ceramics! It is appropriate that it is entitled "Postmodern Ceramics". I will discipline my normal disposition and travel through the pages beyond my present ceramic preferences. Garth Clark wrote the introduction. Although severe in his treatment of Bernard Leach, he then proceeds to give an even-handed critique of postmodern ceramics:

"Postmodernism has produced the most heinous explosion of trite and often misinformed historical quotations, it has encouraged all the 'isms', from feminism to conceptualism, to play havoc with aesthetics in the name of postmodern content-based art, most of which has a lack of profundity and has subjected us to tedious artworld lectures on morality, political correctness, and even the meaning of life. It has resulted in an often incompetent and manipulative assimilation of the crafts. It has blighted the skylines of many a city with its pink, blue, and gray miasma of crudely proportioned buildings, seemingly made from giant children's toys. Postmodernism at its worst is admittedly much more of a visual catastrophe than modernism, which, at its lowest ebb, resulted in a boring, featureless sterility which can more easily be ignored; although it should be noted that some feel that modernism's post-1950s blight has been enormously corrosive. ... Postmodernism, being easy to mimic, is, at its worst, horrifyingly ugly and gruesomely vulgar."

I go this far, feeling some agreement, not knowing if I want to consider the next paragraph where a more favorable assessment is provided by Garth. There are plentiful photographs of a number of ceramic objects that illustrate postmodern ceramics in the book. As with all these convenient labels, rarely contrived by the potters themselves, a thousand varying styles and results are crammed into that single category. Your pottery, Christa, does not seem to fit here. From what I know of you and your pottery, you would not want your pottery to belong under that rubric. Could you move in style and outcome across these categories with ease and speed? How do I know when changes in your work are genuine gains earned by hard work and deep reflection, rather than expedient strategies motivated by the market place and the desire for quick membership in some trendy ceramic fashion? Do you have to have a postmodern personality to create postmodern work? Are all schools of art reactions to previous schools of art? Can a potter only claim significance after they have been labeled and placed in some box that provides their aesthetic pedigree? Is the conversion to a new ceramic school that rejects your previous ceramic school or style somewhat like the conversion of communist to Catholic or socialist to arch-conservative? The propensity to convert from one absolute system to another absolute system, despite surface differences, brings the same kind of closed comfort and security.

Clark, in rigorous fairness, provides the positive side to Postmodernism:

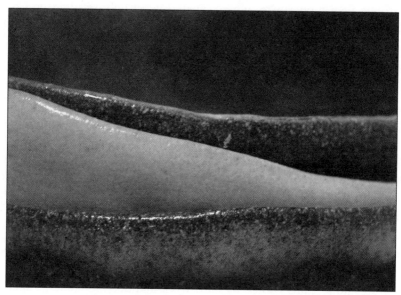

"...the stillness between two waves..."

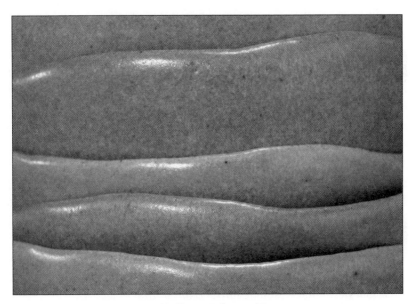

"Call me Ishmael"

"Postmodernism has been a tonic. Color has flooded back into our lives. Memory has been restored, often with remarkable insight and freshness. Society's love of decoration - seemingly an innate sensibility of the human being - has been revived. Architecture is free to be individualistic again. The concept of beauty is making a cautious reentry. But finally what makes postmodernism great is that one really cannot generalize about it because it has no singularity or hard boundaries and as a result it can never become the formidable, intolerant, and restrictive academy that grew out of modernism. Its practitioners are too diverse, its theory too broad, its freedoms too boundless to be able to install a regime and police the arts."

I suspect that most of us are not any one kind of thing. A single point of view does reinforce the purity of your theories about yourself and what you do, and provides a clear and direct logic that documents the structure and rhetoric of that theory. But what a price to pay. The need to strain and purge yourself of divergent impulses achieves the monolithic manifesto but does not permit the potentially illicit and surreptitious play of imagination to disturb the implementation of previously determined aesthetic dogma. A fellow member of our Elderhostel group told me this morning about a collector she knew who only collected pottery that contained the mistakes of the kiln. This collector was amused and fascinated by that unexpected dribble of glaze, the unplanned fissures and cracks, the drama of damaged goods. If the potter did not have the courage to plan these misfortunes, at least the kiln intervened and provided some delightful surprises. Surely both potter and critic must realize that this proclaimed membership in competing schools of thought and action fade with time and become largely meaningless to future generations. Context is invaluable but becomes quickly obsolete if you are not a direct participant in the struggle that produced that particular aesthetic attitude in the first place.

I hear the sea and know it is responsible for the constant motion but I do not feel connected to it. I am insulated behind glass and metal. I want to think I am involved in some basic and primal human activity. I am at sea, not in some Disneyland ride or theme park. But I know I am not really taking much of a chance. For the first time in our insulated cocoon of a ship, we decided to go outside, to feel the wind and cold, to see the waves directly without the filter of glass. We bravely walked for a bit, but then retreated to the lush interior. It is a small comfort to know that many of the upper class occupants of the Titanic suffered the same fate as those in steerage. I do not want the privileged to so enjoy their exalted position that they cannot question or challenge their right and responsibility for such easy and decadent pleasures. I have the interior deposition of the ascetic personality but not the temperament to self-impose excessive discomfort.

Maybe, Christa, this standard applies to you. If you become too successful, and you are close to that possibility, I might abandon you and find another potter in more dire straights. It is so damn difficult for me to tolerate success; knowing it must be a blatant symptom of a corrupt Faustian bargain totally unacceptable to me. I have a postmodern approach to a certain degree. I am eclectic and unaffiliated, pleased with appropriated bits and pieces from differing sources, preferring absurdity over certainty, comic and tragic episodes over planned pleasures. Yet I demand and expect rigorous protest, disciplined dissonance, all honed with the same devotion and dedication as possessed by those you wish to overthrow. The brutality of revolution can only be mitigated by the affirmative virtues of the imposed correction. This healing possibility has been rarely applied in history. Methodologies of violence, for whatever noble purpose, become bad habits that are continued after victory has been won.

Some people take vacations because they must escape the hell of their normal situations. Not so for me. Next week I will return home, to my garden, to my pottery, to my family. I am grateful but honestly feel at this time, considering the ordeals of my past history, that I fully deserve this good fortune. When I get home, I will open my posted mail, scan my e-mail, survey my garden, and dust my neglected pottery. What a full and satisfying life! I must first offer the indictment of my pleasant satisfactions, all the while fully enjoying them. This flexibility allows me to survive, critical intelligence and integrity intact, joined in an uneasy alliance with the animal pleasures of basic appetites realized and the joys of my credit card purchases. I do wish I could be a better model for you, Christa. Please forgive me.

I read the commentary of Mark Del Vecchio, who wrote this book, "Postmodern Ceramics", surveying each manifestation of this broad approach, including such oddities as 'post-minimalism', 'pattern and decoration', 'the multiple vessel', 'organic abstraction', 'the real/super-real', etc., etc. I realize that all, or almost all of these artists/potters are masters of their desired preferences, with refined examples that must be taken seriously. I am forced to admit that my flimsy aesthetic disposition, which regulates my personal decisions regarding purchase and placement within my collection, is arbitrary and isolated. I would not defend my own taste, but I can explain its attractions and will not abandon it. I do not think this attitude is unreasonable because it does provide me an organizing principle and direction. I can favor some pots and people with my love, this does not imply that other pots and people are unworthy of someone's love. This makes me a bit nervous. If I applied this same principle to politics, would I not truly be a dilettante? Does stated conviction in any matter require the moral strength to condemn all other matter outside the boundaries I have drawn? I do not have the heart for this type of combat, regrettably I cannot take myself that seriously. If this idea of critical intelligence, which I do indeed cherish, requires a passionate rebuke of those who differ, I am obviously not fit to participate in the cultural wars of the ceramic world. I know who are my adversaries in the political world and will continue my opposition to them, I do not know who are my adversaries in the ceramic world. Do I have to have them?

I reread the last few paragraphs, Christa, and wonder if you agree with me. Do you have nasty commentary for your fellow potters that differ in approach and style? Do you need to justify your own approach by denying the excellence and qualities of other approaches? Perhaps this whole idea of aesthetic disposition reveals its superficial character. After all, my politics, or yours for that matter, if ill-intentioned and implemented, could result in poverty, hunger, or war for others. My foreign policy, for example, if implemented by government edict, while benevolent and generous, could jeopardize major corporations and their profit margins. I could explain and provide reasons for my own ceramic preferences. But I cannot explain or otherwise insist why others should have the same view. What are the consequences for others of my aesthetic preferences? I do no harm. Let me be.

I am awake at two in the morning. The sound of the wind and waves became too loud and unexpected. I don't know how many times T. S. Eliot crossed the North Atlantic but I have yet to experience 'the stillness between two waves of the sea'. Tomorrow is the last day of the voyage. I will be back in England, a few days in London before our return home. We will make a dash to Marshall Street and the British potters represented there. We will take back t-shirts for our grandchildren and pottery for ourselves. I do not know if I can go back to bed now. I miss my home, family and pottery. The arc of separation from them reminds me of the inherent time limitations on my ability to enjoy the temporary distractions of travel. In the meantime, I allow myself an occasional room service for breakfast, the cleaning of my personal space by staff, and the wonders of creature comforts showered on me by others hired for that purpose. If only I could develop a politics and philosophy that approved of this treatment, my present joy would be complete. I try to prove to myself that my courtesy and appreciation for the efforts of the staff that attend to us is totally sincere, while knowing that their never-ending smiles and 'good mornings' represent merely a quality of professional service. I am not sure I am cut out for this fine life.

There have been several 'formal' nights where dinner in the grand dining room requires at least a dark suit and tie. I do not own a tie. On those evenings we dine at alternative sittings, away from the gloriously shimmering surfaces of evening gowns and black tuxedos worn by our fellow passengers, who live out for a few brief days the fantasy of membership in the aristocracy of our ship board society. As a result of our deficient wardrobe we could not get into that long line and shake the Captain's hand. Democracy is not entirely compatible with the customs and history of life on board these passenger liners. I attend seminars, concerts, movies, even donate small amounts of cash in the casino, but eventually tire of my easy ability to satisfy all my immediate desires. This does not imply regret for the entire journey. I am relaxed. I do enjoy the company of many of the group members. The sea is not yet a friend, but we do co-exist. I recognize its size and strength and appreciate more the dauntless courage of people who have ventured out in past history without all the assurances and protection of my present situation. Maybe T.S. Eliot was right. I might benefit from this experience and come to know what I already know for the first time.

I am struck by the sheer austerity of the sea. There is no diversion for my gaze. The horizon line is very simple and uncomplicated. The constant movement remains unfamiliar despite dependable patterns of crest and wave. That first night I was not sure it would tolerate our intrusion. At dockside, the ship was huge and imposing. Now, launched on our voyage, I wished I could fly far above and see that puny and rolling ship on that vast ocean. I do not necessarily identify with or understand the ocean's essence but I recognize and respect its power and permanence. I am not one of my species that insists on the domination of nature, I will soon humbly retreat to the more familiar and solid environs of human habitat. I simply hope that I can enjoy and learn more about the folklore, mythology, and culture of the sea with added insight, without an extended study and understanding of its complete complexity. I sense, with humility, that the sea does not depend on my attendance, it would represent the same impersonal and irresistible force without my presence. I cannot summarize that tremendous Atlantic Ocean, I cannot enclose and calm its potential power. It will remain a stranger to me, respected but distant. Long after I am gone, my pottery shattered into shards, the sea will remain. However severe the injury from our polluting habits, the sea will endure and outlast us. Eager to negotiate a truce, I can only conclude that the sea is primary to the geography of human existence and pottery is primary to human culture.

Toward the end of the voyage, in one of the last daily morning meetings of our Elderhostel group, Jack Putnam provided a remarkable performance. He recited, without notes or hesitation and with convincing mastery, the first few pages of "Moby Dick". I must pay respect to Jack and my experience with the unruly sea of the North Atlantic by quoting some of the same sentences that Jack quoted from Herman Melville and that immortal classic:

"Call me Ishmael. Some years ago - never mind how long precisely - having little or no money in my purse, and nothing particular to interest me on shore, I thought I would sail about a little and see the watery part of the world. It is a way I have of driving off the spleen, and regulating the circulation. Whenever I find myself growing grim about the mouth; whenever it is a damp, drizzly November in my soul; whenever I find myself involuntarily pausing before coffin warehouses, and bringing up the rear of every funeral I meet; and especially whenever my hypos get such an upper hand of me, that it requires a strong moral principle to prevent me from deliberately stepping into the street, and methodically knocking people's hats off - then, I account it high time to get to sea as soon as I can. This is my substitute for pistol and ball. With a philosophical flourish Cato throws himself upon his sword, I quietly take to the ship. There is nothing surprising in this. If they but knew it, almost all men in their degree, some time or other, cherish very nearly the same feeling toward the ocean with me."

I want to agree with Melville and join his company. But I do not think I will qualify. I do not know how the sea gets its energy. I observe its changing patterns of movement but cannot predict them. Nor do I understand why one would devote a life to experience it and live on its shore.

My own devotion to pottery remains a mystery. If solved, according to some theorists, it could provide some embarrassment. This fascination with a fixated subject can result in the acquisition of considerable information or the lean essence of some metaphysical meaning. Not so with pottery. I find pleasure in the pottery, in the actual experience of the material object and the interior resonance of aesthetic response. In most other things I want only convenient summaries of meaning.

I prefer artifice to reality, the painted seascape to the actual sea. I have visual memories of Winslow Homer's portrayal of the sea, John Marin a more modern treatment, a brilliant painting of a lighthouse and the surrounding sea by Edward Hopper. I have not retained the visual memories of the trips to the nearby seashore in my youth. I need even now to look outside the windowed balcony of my room and remind myself of the ocean's appearance. I have always preferred interpretation to explanation, subjective versions to objective conclusion. Unlike others, I have intuitively thought the world naturally subjective and only personally available, and am surprised and disappointed by the reminder of scientific narratives that indisputable information exists. I resist their authority to define what I see and experience. I have sufficient evidence of my adhoc investigations into multiple realities on the shelves and on the walls of my home.

At the end of our forward journey, in London, we traveled to the Victoria and Albert Museum and the sixth floor collection of ceramics. It must be one of the largest assemblies of ancient and modern ceramics anywhere in the world. I was pleased that several potters displayed there are also represented in my collection. Placement in a museum collection must be a final benediction of lasting significance. Or maybe not. I am sure that the storage rooms of museums are full of dusty relics that once occupied places of public honour. Even the informed judgment of museum curators remain within the ripe importance of one moment of history and a brief time and place.

I will be home soon. In the meantime, I hope things are going well for you. Take care.

Your friend,

Richard

Thirty-five

November 4, 2004

Dear Christa,

Why am I both grounded in the temporal reality of sordid politics and yet also capable of delight in the soaring pleasures of art and craft? Why do I care so much about the results of politics when the cheap manipulation of the message lacks even honest theater? There is no plot to politics, because policy and program are so secondary to the deceit of capturing voters by appealing to their basest instincts and fears. The verdict of the election does not just repudiate my candidate, it repudiates me. My thoughts and feelings must be extended beyond their present status as current event and short term reaction. Some comfort is provided by attempts at long term projections that dilute immediate despair. Readjustment is in order. Do I modify my present world view and opinions to join the greater part of American humanity who apparently do not agree with me? Or do I hold out - stay the course - and be prepared for a marginality that does not promise victory any time soon? I do not mind being in the minority, one can develop the necessary arrogance to assume a righteous pretension of superiority. But it is hard to see the values and concerns that you embrace and deeply believe diminish and wither as unrealized possibilities. There are indeed two Americas. We do not read the same books, attend the same films, or live in the same world. Place Mel Gibson's film 'The Passion of the Christ' next to Michael Moore's film 'Fahrenheit 911' and try to find some reconciliation and common vision. Both were big box office in 2004, yet I doubt that many people attended or accepted both films. I do not want to be a good sport and petition for unity as the weak peace of the defeated.

I cannot chastise or blame Protestant fundamentalists for voting for their values instead of their economic interests. I would ordinarily regard the decision to vote according to your moral conscience over economic advantage as an act of integrity. The issues that they care about are deeply held and perceived as integral to their religious beliefs. Why do the value positions of opposition to abortion, gay marriage, and gun control trump and triumph over the value positions of opposing poverty, war and lack of health care? Why do those that favor the first three issues rarely oppose the other three issues? Why are liberals, mostly urban and secular, completely unable to articulate, with passion and conviction, the ethical and moral basis of those things they care about?

Is it possible that both divided groups are suffering from the same malaise, but responding with very different reactions and assessments? Martin Jacques, in the September 24, 2004 issue of the Guardian Weekly, has an analysis that might enlighten us, entitled "The Death of Intimacy: A selfish, market-driven society is eroding our very humanity". Here Jacques points out three conditions that are making all of us unhappy:

"First, the rise of individualism, initially evident in the 1960s, has made the self the dominant interest, the universal reference point and one's own needs as the ultimate justification of everything. We live in the age of selfishness. Second, there has been the relentless spread of the market into every part of society. The marketisation of everything has made society, and each of us, more competitive. The logic of the market has now become universal, the ideology not just of neoliberals, but of us all, the criterion we use not just about our job or when shopping, but about our innermost selves and our most intimate relationships... Third, there is the rise of communication technologies, notably mobile phones and the internet, which are contracting our private space, erasing our personal time and accelerating the pace of life... Meanwhile the family has become an ever weaker institution: extended families are increasingly marginal, nuclear families are getting smaller and more short-lived, almost half of all marriages end in divorce, and most parents spend less time with their pre-school children."

I have never regarded pottery as a diversion or a pleasurable distraction. Yet at this time, I will seek in my pottery some healing of the heart, some mending of the mind. Pottery is primal, not trivial to human concerns. It is certainly central to my stability and balance. I pick up a book too long concealed in a stack of books on my desk, with the wonderful title, "The Soul of a Bowl". Kim Stafford, in an introductory essay, 'Personal Magnitude', provides me with a sensitive and moving essay that uplifts and restores my hope and reinforces my essential beliefs about the power and glory of those things that move and motivate my life:

"The fact is, the most important things in life are about the size of a tea bowl. The first is the mother's breast, held between the child's tiny hands. The breast doesn't have a handle because it is all handle, offering everything. Your little hands take all of it and it holds all you need - warm, full, private, bounteous. Some time later, growing, you close your own fingers into a bowl, and hold water in your hand. The first cup you make is your hand. … The knotted hands, the golden skein of human love. The human heart, faithful. About the size of your fist. The most important things are smaller than a house, a car, or a computer, but larger than a coin, a pen, or a spoonful of soup. The most important things are less symmetrical than a water glass, more intriguing than a perfect circle, older than the paper cup you throw away as you leave the coffeeshop. The most important things have the personal magnitude of a handshake, the tang of a handful of huckleberries all your own. These most precious things are a certain size, and they connect a person to another person, or they connect a person to the world as it is. They are what we ask for as we leave home forever: "Let me hold your hand one time." So your mouth meets the mouth of the tea bowl, your lips meet the rim, and a thread of tea, wine, or whiskey travels from one realm to another."

Well, at long last, a person who writes about ceramics with the voice of the poet rather than the stilted prose of the academic. Christa, get the book and be proud of your glorious craft. This book joins an inspirational literature that explores the profound and memorable experiences that pottery and other crafts bring to our lives. Five outstanding ceramic artists are explored in the book, Don Reitz, Frank Boyden, Jenny Lind, and Tom and Elaine Coleman. I have precious examples of three of these potters, Jenny Lind, and Tom and Elaine Coleman, in my collection. Christa, they are your colleagues. Potters can be the inspiration for a quality of life, pottery can facilitate the personal interactions that mark our humanity and make us a family of loved ones, friends, neighbors and community.

In a miraculous way Stafford joins in a dialogue with Jacques, providing a remedy that offers the personal rather than the commercial, the hand built object over market commodities, intimacy over impersonal communication technologies. Pottery sponsors the nourishment of the soul and body in equal proportions. I can think of nothing more practical and functional at the present moment. I do not know Kim Stafford. How do I thank her?

John Nance, author of the "Mud Pie Dilemma", an earlier book about the Colemans, and "A master potter's struggle to make art and ends meet", finishes the book with a closing essay, "Bowl Talk". Once again, Nance contributes, along with Stafford, a poetics of pottery that proves the metaphorical and cultural richness embedded in these clay containers. Their lyrical passages are not grounded in descriptions of technique, glaze, or shape. Nance says it better:

"A great bowl is somehow alive. The maker can divulge what clay, which glaze, oxide, and other ingredients are in use; and in what kiln, at what temperature a bowl was fired - but there is no way the maker can formulate the marriage of heart, head, hands and good fortune that infuse a particular earthy mixture with magic - with presence, with movement, with a voice. Yes, such bowls speak. They whisper invitations to be picked up, to have their curves fondled; for one to gaze at their gleaming inward parts; to have you touch your lips just so on their circling rims."

The intimacy of human contact, as depicted in the popular culture, has been too often reduced and limited to the sexual embrace. As Jacques pointed out, the intimacy of the family has been constricted by the excessive demands and interruptions of a consumer society that must be maintained by the continuous and strenuous efforts of the workplace. Aesthetic dimensions have been reduced to matters of interior decoration and largely satisfied by the standardized products of mass production. Yet Nance, in describing the elementary and fundamental role of the bowl to human beings, is really describing the nature of love, the possibilities that open when we are fully alive and fully conscious at each moment of engagement with others - with art - with life. His last sentences, the last paragraph of the book, urges us to listen, to feel, to awaken.

"Now it is clear - look, listen, and feel - that bowl is alive. It does speak. Its voice is almost always an invitation. So choose wisely, because what it invites you to is unique. And it is inviting you, provoking you to awaken to its message, to the moment. Be with it."

I have often thought of the protocols of pot and person. How close should we be to the pot or bowl? What is the proper space and distance? Is it necessary to hold, to feel the shape and texture? Nance and Stafford are urging me to grasp the bowl, to place it to the lips and receive the liquid gifts it contains. I know, Christa, that you have often urged me to actually use your pitcher or cup. Why is that so important to the potter? Many years ago I remember reading the books of Edward T. Hall, a cultural anthropologist who wrote books called, "The Silent Language" and "The Hidden Dimension". He explained that different cultures have a different sense of personal or private space. How close you stand to another person, the gestures and expression that define the relationship, all these have diverse cultural norms that profoundly differ. One can offend without intention. I cannot pick up a bowl in the museum, it is forbidden. In my own home I have many ceramic cups and containers that are used, that carry and contain food and and drink. But the vast majority are rarely touched. First of all, it is not practical. They are anchored to the shelf with a wax that hopefully will save them from the next California earthquake. Sometimes I just can't help myself. I softly twist the bowl or vase, lifting it up, enjoying the contact. It is very difficult to actively explore and experience the artifact with your hands behind your back.

Intimacy cannot be mass produced. It cannot be purchased. An act of kindness, even an act of kindness offered out of some personal need, even an act that could be described in psychological terms as driven by some deficient emotion, becomes generous and effective because we all are in such great need of that kindness. We respond, intimacy is reciprocal, of equal advantage, of equal benefit. Now we must move that intimacy to other possibilities. I know of two others, intimacy with nature and intimacy with art. John Armstrong, director of the Aesthetics Programme of the School for Advanced Study at the University of London, and author of "Move Closer: An Intimate Philosophy of Art" explores this phenomenon of intimacy with art:

"Reverie and imagination are not idle play - they provide a route by which our intimate concerns come to engage with what we see. And while they do not require that we bring prior learning to bear, they rely upon our willingness to pass time in a special way with the objects we encounter."

I continue my do-it-yourself therapy, walking through the rooms of my house. To paraphrase John Nance, to just 'be with it', with my pottery, not moving too fast, not seeking a total inventory but seeking compatible company. I pick up another book, with pictures of hundreds of bowls. In fact the number is precise, "500 Bowls: Contemporary Explorations of a Timeless Design". I slowly turn each page, marveling at the infinite variety of shapes, textures and patterns. The ability of the potter, fully informed of the ceramic traditions of the past, to continue that tradition with unique interpretations and reinventions of something as simple, common, and obvious as the bowl demonstrates the incredible possibilities of the human imagination. In a book that relies on the generous illustrations of bowls and little text, John Britt provides a short but insightful introduction that I must add to the homages of Stafford and Nance that pay poetic attention to the profound meaning of the humble bowl when it contacts and engages a human being.

"What makes the bowl so enduring? Obviously, it is the functional object par excellence. It can be both useful and decorative. It has everything: form, volume, surface, texture, and color. The bowl is both simple and complex. It can be, at once, deeply personal and yet it can also convey deep metaphysical insights. It is simultaneously mysterious and transparent. While the exterior is obvious, the interior conceals its form and content. Only when the viewer draws closer is that space revealed. That is when we are often surprised by a magical interior that was hidden inside a calm exterior, or vice versa."

Nature was the other possible source of intimacy mentioned above. I can think of no better representative of intimate communion with nature than Henry David Thoreau. This reminds me of one of my eccentric learning adventures when young. I wrote out by hand passages of the books I was reading, sitting at the dinner table in the evening. Dozens of notebooks filled with those passages that stimulated and thrilled me in my youthful passion for knowledge. I guess in a way I am still doing this with these letters. Decades ago, like some medieval monk determined to perpetuate human civilization, I hand-crafted and reproduced compelling thoughts from various texts, attempting to memorialize them by the repetition of manual copy. I recently discovered a small notebook from that time, page after page of handwriting in pencil. Passages from "Walden" filled this small notebook. It was written over fifty years ago, in yellowed pages, with a left-handed awkwardness that has not changed over the years. Thoreau is a very old friend.

Thoreau was the prototypical American individualist - as Emerson, his dear friend described him:

"He was bred to no profession; he never married; he lived alone; he never went to church; he never voted; he refused to pay a tax to the State; he ate no flesh, he drank no wine, he never knew the use of tobacco; and, though a naturalist, he used neither trap nor gun."

Another of his essays, one of his last before he died at a young age, was "Walking". The first words describe his deep love of nature:

"I wish to speak a word for Nature, for absolute freedom and wildness, as contrasted with a freedom and culture merely civil, to regard man as an inhabitant, or a part and parcel of Nature, rather than a member of society. I wish to make an extreme statement, if so I may make an emphatic one, for there are enough champions of civilization: the minister and the school committee and every one of you will take care of that."

Thoreau goes on to discuss the joys of walking in the nearby woods several hours a day. One passage is particularly helpful to me. I need to put politics in perspective just now. I do not agree with Thoreau about his disdain for civic obligations. But that doesn't matter just now. I will borrow his thoughts. In the following passage he puts puny politics next to the grand scale of nature:

"There are square miles in my vicinity which have no inhabitant. From many a hill I can see civilisation and the abodes of man afar. The farmers and their works are scarcely more obvious than woodchucks and their burrows. Man and his affairs, church and state and school, trade and commerce, and manufacture and agriculture, even politics, the most alarming of them all, I am pleased to see how little space they occupy in the landscape. Politics is but a narrow field, and that still narrower highway yonder leads to it. I sometimes direct the traveller thither. If you go to the political world, follow the great road - follow that market-man, keep his dust in your eyes, and it will lead you straight to it; for it, too, has its place merely, and does not occupy all space. I pass from it as from a bean-field into the forest, and it is forgotten. In one half-hour I can walk off to some portion of the earth's surface where a man does not stand from one year's end to another, and there, consequently, politics are not, for they are but as the cigar-smoke of a man."

I write this letter as collector. As I work down the computer screen, filling that downward sliding space in front of me, I am establishing a sequence of collected thoughts and images. It is a collage, an immediate experience that places ideas next to each other, on top of each other, in quick succession but soon integrated within my head before it becomes evident on the monitor. I join the bowl and become the container. I carry all these thoughts and visions of objects. Hopefully I become more complicated, my thinking more complex. The sheer grandeur of the noble thought or created artifact becomes my protection, my shield. I must attempt an inclusive analysis of my accumulated resources, it is the only way I know to find some transcendent wisdom. I become virtuous only if I become the active agent of the contents placed within my mind, heart and soul. Whatever the burden of accumulated years, I sense that growth is still possible. I am not through yet. I might regret the individual and collective judgment of others and their consequences but I can still find room for maneuver and hope. I have achieved a perfect union. I am now collector and container.

Every person who has ever transformed their thoughts to the printed page, every artist whose artifact has survived to this day, they are all now my potential advisors, my kitchen cabinet of unofficial guides. I use them for my own purposes, take them seriously but translate and place them according to my own needs. In this act of self-construction, person as container, I do not use the same materials as the potter, nor do I whirl on the wheel. I do feel the multiplicity and depth of those forces still working on me. For most people that view me, the erosion of age seems to be the active agent changing my appearance. But I know that this impression is mistaken. I am listening and considering all the voices recorded in human history, as many as I can, as many as I can fit in the day and my waking hours. They have joined me. They reside within. I am a strong and durable container. My thoughts pour out of me. I cannot trace them back to their interior location but they never fail to respond.

I have just been provided a clue for that amazing ability for interpretation and reinvention. Elaine Levin has been writing articles for Ceramics Monthly for a period of over 25 years, now collected in a book, "Movers & Shakers in American Ceramics: Defining Twentieth Century Ceramics". In one article considering Herbert Sanders, Levin quotes this former professor and founder of the ceramics department at San Jose State in which he offers this advice:

"The production of a work of art is the result of all experiences - emotional, spiritual, economical, social, and political, which the individual has during his existence. These frequently are beyond the range of ordinary consciousness but are so profound that they leave a lasting impression upon the unconscious and years later make their appearance in the work produced by the individual. The creative process 'is a spontaneous expression of inner urges or drives, through a chosen medium', the artist creating by standards uniquely his own with success depending on a 'depth of feeling'. The art object can be without life if an 'individual has great skill but nothing to say'."

Despite the homogenized conformity of a franchised economy and standardized commodities, this intrinsic diversity within the human species that Sanders is talking about provides great hope for the creative arts. We do have different experiences, different ways of processing and making sense of things, different ways of making and creating. I am the sum total of all my experiences, no one else has exactly duplicated those experiences. Each of us constitutes a variation on a general theme. Each of us has something to say, if only given the opportunity and encouragement. Who else would dare to write 35 letters over two or more years to a young potter at first unknown to me without benefit of the right academic major or other certified qualifications?

Should I have taken creative writing courses at the university or adult school before I started this venture? Do you need to be schooled in the proper techniques, practiced in apprenticeship, before your 'spontaneous expression of inner urges or drives' can have a disciplined success? Christa, you were schooled in ceramics long before you became a professional potter. Just in reading the book, "Movers & Shakers in American Ceramics", I find out that many of the most outstanding American potters were self-taught. What did you get out of your schooling experience? Was it a waste of time? Could you have gotten the same things by just doing it, working at the wheel and paying attention to the masters of your craft? Should I submit these letters to the English Department at my former university where colleagues could critique and grade my efforts before I mail them to you?

The savage rhetoric of the political campaign still rings in my ears. There is nothing sacred in either a person's personal or public domain that cannot be exposed in attacks calculated to leave severe wounds that result in the loss of respect and support among the citizenry. There is the same vengeance in cultural wars. We do need the sharp tongue and unforgiving voice of the critic to hold up charlatans and hacks in the creative arts. But sometimes the venom of such attacks causes me to want to protect the victim, however mediocre, however much I agree with the critique. One example of such savagery, all the more terrifying because it is done with great style and skill, is an essay by Walter Bagehot, 19th century English economist and critic, published in the Harvard Classics series under the title, "Essays: English and American". The subject of his essay was the same as the title, the poet, Milton. He started the essay with commentary about a previous book on the same subject:

"The 'Life of Milton', by Professor Masson, is a difficulty for the critics. It is very laborious, very learned, and in the main, we believe, very accurate; it is exceedingly long, - there are about 780 pages in this volume, and there are to be two volumes more; it touches on very many subjects, and each of these has been investigated to the very best of the author's ability. No one can wish to speak with censure of a book on which so much genuine labor has been expended; and yet we are bound, as true critics, to say that we think it has been composed upon a principle that is utterly erroneous."

The extreme cruelty exhibited by Bagehot, of course, was the long delay, after an apparently favorable buildup, to that final awful sentence, the exterminating angel of those last words. Isn't that prospect frightening to creative people? To work years on your art, and to be finally told that your entire work is built 'upon a principle that is utterly erroneous'. How do you recover? How do you determine the critic is wrong and you are right? Do mediocre potters deserve the same kindness and respect that excellent potters deserve? Do you have to point out the failures of other potters to prove the value of your pottery? Perhaps we should have some kind of ceramic rehabilitation or half-way house programs, some type of 12-step program to convert hopeless potters into other more appropriate fields of endeavor. Christa, I know you would never, never, tell me that my letters were based 'upon a principle that is utterly erroneous'. Needless to say, your pottery is safe from me.

There is a chronic issue discussed in education. Should you praise a child who is trying hard, making a sincere effort? Give her the same praise as the child doing excellent work? In doing so, perhaps increase motivation and self-confidence? Or should you set high standards that might constitute a severe verdict on present efforts but will drive the student on to eventually reach that higher expectation? I guess I have a double standard. I have seen failed films and plays, contrivances full of cliches calculated to reach a mass audience, but completely devoid of subtlety or substance. Here I remain unforgiving. But I have also seen failed films and plays where the effort to reach some sublime truth fell short, remained unconvincing but praiseworthy for the ambitious effort. Intention does mean something in most art forms. I do not know if this is true of pottery. Any great potter can make one or two failed pots - you would have to look at the range of work over time to make an informed judgement. One would hope that failed potters would cease activity voluntarily, certainly not achieve success with the public. I do not know if this is the case. I do think that was the case in the recent election. While incompetence in others can be toler-ated as an act of compassion, it cannot be rewarded if excellence and integrity in any field is to endure.

It is evident that my grandchildren will not inherit the kind of world I would have liked to leave them. Whatever happens to my pottery, I fear that my hopes and ideals for a just society will be dispersed after my demise. My son next door took down the campaign placards on his lawn - they did not help. The Jacobs family looks forward to further votes for condemned candidates and lost causes. I choose my comfort carefully, finding it in family, the pages of my books and with the pottery on the shelves of my home. We will wait it out.

Your friend,

Richard

Thirty-six

November 27, 2004

Dear Christa,

There are limits to tolerance. Liberals learned that during the last election. Mainstream male Americans were bullied and shamed during their lifetimes into accepting women, people of color, and the handicapped as eligible to full humanhood and citizenship. Their resilience and self-pride apparently cannot be further stretched or challenged. People with a different sexual orientation, people who attend a mosque instead of a church, immigrants without the proper papers, are among those groups being sent unfriendly messages in the attitudes and behavior of our dominant society. When does difference equate with threat? When does difference, just sheer difference, produce insecurity and fear? When does my voice and view become disloyal and subversive in a nation that proclaims itself at war? A war that by definition, since it is a war against terror-ism and not a nation state, cannot have an ending, cannot have a conclusion sealed with a peace treaty? Do we have a list of all the terrorists of the world, and when we finally kill them all, can we declare the war over? What happens when our very war against terrorists breeds more terrorists than we have already killed?

For those in power, these are logistical and tactical problems. For me they are moral and ethical quandaries. If some people are truly evil, whole groups of people truly evil, then I must hate them and approve of their extermination. I think I am nearing the point that, in order to be considered a good American, I must either agree with this proposition or become silent. There are limits to my tolerance. I cannot tolerate the wanton murder of innocent citizens in acts of terrorism. I cannot tolerate wars of preemption because they cannot distinguish between warriors and civilians as targets and victims. War has been made respectable, a viable policy choice, one option among many. War is a failure of human civilization. All who voluntarily engage are its common victims. For people like you, Christa, whose life is dedicated to creating rather than destroying, war must be the final atrocity of mind and hand. It is best that I not talk about these matters at social occasions. Only a few friends and family members can be trusted.

Yesterday, I saw a documentary, "The Fog of War", where the film maker interviewed Robert MacNamara, the Secretary of Defense during the Vietnam War. That eighty-five year old man peered into the camera and said he was wrong about the Vietnam war. How can he say that, over forty years after all those young Americans were killed as a result of his errors and orders? I went to the Vietnam memorial in Washington, D.C. a few years ago and looked up Isaac Romero Garcia, a student of mine at San Fernando Junior High, sent to his death at the age of 18 in Vietnam. What would surviving members of his family think if they saw and heard Robert MacNamara in that documentary? Guilt is not enough. The belated confessions of leaders whose full life span was of natural and normal length. That is not enough. The failed judgment, long after the fact, cannot resurrect those whose brief lives were expended as a consequence. I cannot tolerate the justification of wars as the necessary excuse and rationalization for the deaths of those who fought in them, even though this might bring some immediate comfort to the families of the deceased.

Should artists keep silent? Should they emulate Hollywood celebrities and pop star singers in partisan political activity? Creative people do not generally stay within the orthodox boundaries of conventional conservative thought. Christa, I remember your comments that most potters were progressive, and the ceramic community generally reflected a liberal consensus about these matters. I wonder if most wealthy pottery collectors would agree with their opinions? Perhaps it is best that potters refrain from political discussions with potential customers. Are so-called craftspeople more conservative than so-called artists? What is the working difference between being traditional and conservative? Can you be one without the other? How does one define these terms in ceramics? Can you arrange and organize conservative thought so it is inclusive and tolerant? The failure of progressive political forces to engage the traditional and conservative sectors of our society represents a complete disconnect. I remember that many 'folk singers' in the 1960s were in the forefront of that cultural revolution. In so doing, their songs sang of traditional communities, humble and hard-working people and the honest pleasures of a simple, rural life. Maybe today's liberals need to listen to those lyrics. Don't most potters, even those doing very experimental things, have respect for the traditions of pottery? If a potter chooses to create a non-functional clay object, could this be a tribute to those traditional forms rather than a repudiation? I ask these questions because I really believe that my opposition to current policies comes from traditional, even conservative beliefs rather than radical ones. An opposition based on ethical principles is inherently conservative.

I recently attended an exhibition at The Huntington Library of the papers of Christopher Isherwood, the English novelist who spent much of his later years in Southern California. Isherwood was a major twentieth-century writer of fiction. His work also constituted a significant contribution to the gay rights movement. Inspired by the exhibition, I read his novel, "A Single Man", about a gay man living in suburban Southern California, an outsider who had experienced recent tragedy and loss. This book, when published, shocked many by its sympathetic depiction of a gay man and his everyday world. Isherwood uses the voice of George, the main character, a professor at a state university, to lecture his students on this matter of differences among people and the reaction of people to those differences. George delivers these comments in a class discussion:

"All right. Now along come the liberals - including everybody in this room, I trust - and they say, 'Minorities are just people, like us.' Sure, minorities are people - people, not angels. Sure, they're like us - but not exactly like us; that's the all-too-familiar state of the liberal hysteria in which you begin to kid yourself you honestly cannot see any difference between a Negro and a Swede... So, let's face it, minorities are people who probably look and act and think differently from us and have faults we don't have. We may dislike the way they look and act, and we may hate their faults. And it's better if we admit to disliking and hating them than if we try to smear our feelings over with pseudo-liberal sentimentality. If we're frank about our feelings, we have a safety valve; and if we have a safety valve, we're actually less likely to start persecuting. I know that theory is unfashionable nowadays. We all keep trying to believe that if we ignore something long enough it'll just vanish... Well, now, suppose this minority does get persecuted, never mind why - political, economic, psychological reasons. There is always a reason, no matter how wrong it is - that's my point. And, of course, persecution itself is always wrong; I'm sure we all agree there. But the worst of it is, we now run into another liberal heresy. Because the persecuting majority is vile, says the liberal, therefore the persecuted minority must be stainlessly pure. Can't you see what nonsense that is? What's to prevent the bad from being persecuted by the worse? Did all the Christian victims in the arena have to be saints? And I'll tell you something else. A minority has its own kind of aggression. It absolutely dares the majority to attack it. It hates the majority - not without a cause, I grant you. It even hates the other minorities, because all minorities are in competition: each one proclaims that its sufferings are the worst and its wrongs are the blackest. And the more they all hate, and the more they're all persecuted, the nastier they become! Do you think it makes people nasty to be loved? You know it doesn't! Then why should it make them nice to be loathed? While you're being persecuted, you hate what's happening to you, you hate the people who are making it happen; you're in a world of hate. Why, you wouldn't recognize love if you met it! You'd suspect love! You'd think there was something behind - some motive - some trick..."

This is probably the longest monologue in the book, this diatribe directed to his students by George. The biographical similarities of George and Isherwood are evident. On the surface, his remarks are not very positive or hopeful; there is no inherent virtue in being a minority, no innate goodness in being a victim, the perception of tolerant liberals is as mistaken as those who persecute others. Both George and Isherwood have known the pain and prejudice of being different. I note that, understanding the historical placement of this early work before the public achievements of the gay rights movement, that George does not dare identify homosexuality as one of the minority groups under class discussion.

I do not know how this particular issue and difference plays out in the ceramics world. I do not know if the wounds incurred around differences in sexual orientation have been solved and healed or there are tensions and unresolved discrimination and bias. I would like to think that these things don't matter to people in the arts, that people in the arts know better. Yet, maybe George (and Isherwood) are right. Maybe I am expecting too much of the liberal pottery community. Maybe we just can't stop disliking, even hating, those people that are so different from us. Maybe like that poor old man, Robert MacNamera, we just confess our past sins and feel relieved about the whole matter, become harmless in our hate and mistaken ignorance.

Can you have a progressive politics without a belief in progress? John Gray does not believe in this thing called progress, according to John Banville, who reviewed Gray's book, "Heresies: Against Progress and Other Illusions" in the Guardian Weekly a few months ago. Secular heresies can be more difficult and persistent mythologies than religious ones. The latter is based on humble faith, but the former insists on the unlimited authority and arrogance of objective intelligence. Banville explains the position of Gray:

"Gray sees our faith in progress – 'the Prozac of the thinking classes' - as the illusion that underlies the most egregiously mistaken political and social policies of the present day. Certainly there is such a thing as progress, but it is a fact only in the realm of science, while 'in ethics and politics it is a superstition'. Throughout his work Gray hammers relentlessly against the notion that history moves inexorably in a straight line, and that human nature will necessarily improve as our knowledge accumulates. He grants that in some areas things do get better: we have abolished judicial torture, for example, and modern dentistry is a great boon. The mistake, he contends is to imagine that more dental implants and fewer thumbscrews will make us into better beings."

If we do not have a generous opinion of humankind, and a faith in its inevitable progress, how do we maintain the hopeful optimism that is the foundation for progressive thought? I do not know too many cynics that are liberal in their political persuasion. Can we be the agents of purposeful change if change and reform are not natural and normal phenomena? I do not wish to join the crabbed and grumpy old-men-of-destroyed-dreams club, victimized by the accumulation of years and disappointments. There is much of this sense of unfolding progress in writing about the arts. As commonly written, sequential movements and changes in style and attitude become reforms and improvements on the static and frozen conventions of the past. I think this notion of progress is more difficult with pottery. How can you demonstrate the superiority of the latest pot against the virtues of a Ming vase? To try to bring back the past is a reactionary impulse, but to respect the past and allow its wisdom and art to co-exist with what is known to us from our own experience is a form of progress that incorporates and employs historical references as contemporary resources. That might be the best revision and definition of progress that we can attain.

It is one thing to believe in progress, quite another to believe in the reverse. That is the other side of the coin, from the naivete and romance of progress to the condemning indictment of the decadence of the modern age. Perhaps both are mistaken, both are too simple. The best wisdom always carries and displays its equal contradictions, making a single summary difficult to prove. Estelle H. Ries, in her book, "Artists and Artisans" condemns our modern age and looks wistfully back to a more promising time:

"Today our chaotic times are reflected in a trend of decay in our arts. Music, art, literature, and drama feature debasing and pathological themes. Instead of ideal heroes we have criminals and freaks playing the leading roles. Debunking masks as realism. Discord in music, surrealism in art, vulgarism in the dance - these are the influences which surround us in our daily lives and accentuate the chaos and restlessness of our times. What a far cry from the works of growing eras like the Renaissance. Our decadent age is involved in a process of liking the lower instead of the higher, of choosing and emphasizing not the better part, but the worst - its stupidity, drinking, evil passions, and abnormalities in general. And these in turn, especially, in our literature, theater, movies, and painting, help to increase this decadence".

I do not know if Ries would include much of modern pottery in her indict-ment. Arneson and Voulkos should certainly worry about the application of her thoughts but I suspect they would only be amused. If one cannot go backward and one cannot go forward, for reasons I have been given from these resources, where else to go? If life is not linear, except for the life cycle and the calendar, is purpose lost when the apparent path becomes multiple detours to unknown possibilities? Most people simply do not have the constitution to contemplate this awful predicament. They hide out in dependable systems that provide a reliable compass. People in the arts essentially jeopardize that kind of stability for themselves. They potentially create new templates and systems each time they confront the wheel or face the canvas. Christa, you do not simply copy the ceramic past, yet you do not seek to create a completely new present. Do you occupy that middle ground in pottery that is no longer present in our politics? Could you be charged that your moderate stance in your work is due to timidity and conformity? Or could you reply that you are the active agent of a new synthesis, a new configuration that utilizes previous cultural references in the creation of an original pottery that also incorporates the realm of modern expe-rience? Few moderate people becomes public heroes - in politics or the arts. The media and the public require more dramatic fare. Genius by definition does not usually include moderate people. I do think a definition of excellence could well include moderation as a significant virtue and asset.

I did not know of Peter Dormer when I picked up the book he edited, "The Culture of Craft" a few months ago. I think I purchased the book in London on a recent trip. As is my custom before purchase, I read the table of contents, and since it was a paperback, I read the text on the back cover. There was a boxed segment of text that caught my attention:

"Peter Dormer has long been considered one of the most important thinkers on contemporary craft in the world. Over the last twenty years he has published a number of seminal books and articles, and curated several major exhibitions. This volume was planned while he was Fellow of Critical Appreciation of the Applied Arts at the University of East Anglia. He died on Christmas Eve 1996, as this book entered its final production phase. This volume is dedicated to him and his life's work in the crafts."

I really enjoyed the book, found many essays to be useful and insightful. I had not known of this person but I valued the book and his contributions to it. When I purchase a pot, I am also paying tribute to the life of the potter, to the integrity and courage of the potter to make that pot I find so attractive. When I purchase a book, I am also paying tribute and respect to the author or those individuals who fill its pages with ideas that challenge and inform me. Each pot and book purchased, by myself and all others who perform this act, pay this kind of tribute. The revenue derived is never just of monetary value, it is a revenue that subsidizes our common humanity and culture, that enriches the recipients in mysterious and wonderful ways. When we purchase a book or pot, we all become important patrons of the arts.

I found Dormer's introduction to one section of the book, "The Status of Craft" to be most helpful. He explains the present predicament of crafts:

"The separation of craft from art and design is one of the phenomena of the late-twentieth-century Western culture. The consequences of this split have been quite startling. It has led to the separation of 'having ideas' from 'making objects'. It has also led to the idea that there exists some sort of mental attribute known as 'creativity' that precedes or can be divorced from a knowledge of how to make things. This has led to art without craft. The fact that the practitioners of essay-writing, dance, theater and music, for example, have not accepted that creativity can be defined as 'art without craft' has been ignored in the visual arts. In the visual arts 'I don't want the craft to get in the way of my creativity' is a perfectly meaningful statement… Many of the practitioners of 'the crafts' have found themselves caught in a contradiction. For one thing, although the makers of pots, textiles and furniture have many understanding admirers, they have not found themselves admired as much as other 'artists'. Potters do not earn the same regard as sculptors, for example; and jewelry, for all its virtuosity, invention and ideas, remains a minor art. This is hurtful to the practitioners concerned but it is not a sudden development, it has been growing since the late nineteenth century. But as if this were not bad enough, they have also found that the 'ordinary consumer' does not admire them so much either, or rather, the ordinary consumer is puzzled by what the value of 'the crafts' is supposed to be (or, put yet another way, why are 'the crafts' so expensive?). The contradiction is that it appears to many intelligent craftspeople that they have actually reneged on craftsmanship to pursue their craft. The admirers of 'high art' are not interested in craft and the consumers of decorative objects and other trophies for the home do not see that high craft is really worth paying for. So what is a maker to do if he or she is to gain status or earn a living?"

Dormer has identified a central dilemma for the potter and other craftspeople. They often end up with the worst of both worlds. Not considered artists, not respected for their finely honed craft, not the makers of meaning but the makers of decorative objects for the home. I have seen pottery sold in furniture stores as accessories, along with book cases, lamps and other bric-a-brac. This problem is explored in a number of essays in the book. Dormer points out that this problem has been growing since the late nineteenth century. This is a case where time has not brought progress to pottery. Sometime in the emerging modern era, the skills of craft were no longer vital or universally appreciated in the fine arts. Their application in crafts suffered the same loss of value and respect as in the general culture. How do potters make the claim that their pottery is the nexus of craft and art, meaning and making? Maybe pottery has to find that middle ground between art and craft, a moderate bridge that embodies a contemporary application of both skill and art. How many potters are ready for that challenge? How many can articulate that aesthetic possibility?

After reading the book, I had added reasons for sharing the sentiments of that statement on the back of the book. I plan to locate other contributions by Dormer. It reminds me that we should provide gracious praise and recognition for valuable contributors to the culture when they are still with us. Their departure can be unexpected and the loss profound. Perhaps progress in human civilization is not as easy and evident as thought, but we can plan, experience and achieve the development of our own talents, and contribute to the general welfare of others. I will end this letter again in praise of moderation. I do not need to exclusively take one side or else remain neutral. I can vigorously strive for that balance and harmony that is sadly missing in our society right now. Christa, I think your pottery aspires to that same goal. We do not need to choose between conformity or chaos in our art, culture and politics. We do not need to choose between initiating violence or waiting to receive it. We do not need to chose between skill or expression, craft or art.

We need to further explore the aesthetics and principles of moderation for pottery and our very lives. Ironically, despite it's dull reputation, perhaps moderation is not composed of weak compromise, but rather requires the greatest concentration of moral courage and creative intelligence of all the possibilities. Perhaps moderation is that state of grace most difficult to attain and yet most despised by those on the extreme margins that seek to recruit and convert the center. Passion and creativity are not the natural or exclusive property of fanatic forces. Ego and ideology are not the only sources that could guide our individual and common behavior. We know their contribution to the twentieth century. We can be grounded in our time and place, devoted to our individual and common purposes, and find meaning in our behavior and in our culture. Stability is not the result of passive conformity. Stability can be the culmination and reward for a just society and a creative and intelligent citizenry. I do not need to believe in some sort of inevitable progress. The fact that this sort of hoped for achievement is not automatically ensured does not subtract from the possibilities of common effort to strive toward these goals.

We are going to have an opportunity to share our thoughts on these and other matters early next year at our exhibition of my letters and your pottery at The Collectors Gallery at the Oakland Museum of California Art and our panel presentation in Baltimore at the annual conference of NCECA (National Council on Education for the Ceramic Arts). Both these venues offer us the opportunity to articulate our thoughts on matters important to potters and the greater public. I want to end this letter with a very pertinent quotation from Peter Dormer, one of the last paragraphs in what turned out to be his last book. It poses the challenge of what we are trying to accomplish in our collaboration.

"The craftsperson cannot very easily explain the rightness of what she or he has achieved; other people have to recognize it. They have to see it. And because craftspeople cannot explain the reasons behind their work they are in an unhappy position in our society. Unless a person can explain the principles of his or her activity - unless there is a theory about it - then he or she may be credited with having skill but not understanding. This makes it easy for theorists to view the craftsperson as naive. And then, because we have made our minds up that craftspeople do not understand the real meaning of what they are doing, we look elsewhere for explanations and in so doing miss the integrity of a whole other world of knowledge - that of the craftsperson."

If we can make a small contribution to this problem, to help the potter reflect on the 'real meaning of what they are doing' and thus to articulate and demonstrate the integrity and significance of their knowledge as exemplified in their work and lives, then indeed our mutual effort and our joint hopes in this regard have a basis for fulfillment.

Take care. Your friend

Richard

Thirty-seven

December 9, 2004

Dear Christa,

It has been a wet November. Showers are continuing into December. Morning visits to my garden are restricted at this time of year, by rain, by wind coming down through the mountain canyons, by cold and damp weather that leaves the earth soft and soaked, by plants heavy with moisture. It is sunny and warmer today, and a visit to the garden fully warranted. Most plants are retreating into a dormant state that does not discourage me. They provide promises they have always kept in previous years. Fall is the time for gardens to make promises. The new year and spring is the time to keep them.

Beauty lacks precision. At best it is a generous word, lacking the edge of irony or the more favored force of aggressive criticism. It is a dangerous word to use. It signifies an uncritical and lavish exaggeration, a lapse in decorum that could prove embarrassing in sophisticated circles. Beauty has been restricted to the sentimental and saccharine expression of popular and easy taste. It is unsuitable for the modern age. It is old-fashioned, this word, this idea of beauty. It still doesn't qualify in this postmodern time. Bits of postmodern beauty are added like icing to architectural cakes as defiant commentary and belated homage to what they seek to reject or modify. The very term postmodern indicates that they have yet to find the right term for a transitional age that has not yet found its own permanent purpose and character.

There are those of us who believe in beauty and would make it the core of things, the very core of life itself. It is the one idea I do not want clarified or defined for me. Rigorous scholarship might exclude those things I favor and enjoy. I want to use the word promiscuously for anything and everything that pleases me and makes each day a bit easier. I embrace beauty, but I don't want to make it special. I want beauty to remain ordinary for me, as ordinary as the daily engagements with familiar sights that form my common habits. That is why my home and garden are the perfect places to find beauty. It is in the daily chores and rituals of my personal and interior existence in my modest cottage that I encounter treasured artifacts and memorable moments that I will arbitrarily bless as beautiful. The word serves me as a complement for my enhanced state. Others may use it or abandon it according to their own disposition. It will remain in my vocabulary.

It is more difficult to choreograph beautiful experiences. Beauty as experience is a bit more complicated than beauty as object. It often requires the cooperation of others. It is more predictable and dependable when observed on the stage as a result of yearly theatre subscription, or in the films on DVD ordered and received by mail order. In my forty years in the classroom, there were moments, times when there was a collective unity of insight and revelation that I knew would outlast that scheduled meeting and be taken home for a lifetime. I felt the rush of reverence and the collective beauty shared by all. Many of my beautiful experiences are solitary now, partly because I am fundamentally idiosyncratic in nature, partly because so few others have the vacant time necessary to experience beauty. Walks in public gardens with Judy almost always ensure a beautiful experience, and cost far less than the treasures on my shelves. We will often go to a pottery gallery or antique show, content to stroll and gaze, stopping to admire a beautiful object, not needing to own it, or not having the required money to purchase that particular one. I pick up the expensive object carefully, confirming the price on the sticker on the bottom, put it back on the shelf fully resigned, still feeling grateful for the encounter and experience.

We took our grandchildren yesterday to be professionally photographed. Judy made lovely dresses for the girls and a little outfit for the boy. When they were assembled on the raised stage, in front of the winter background screen and holiday props, smiling in perfect cooperation, a beauty was present that the finished photographs fully confirmed. I do not have space here to list all the things I consider beautiful; but surely a grandchild's smile, a ginkgo tree in the front garden dropping its golden fall leaves, the bursting smell of Jasmine tea when the hot water first makes contact, the peaty taste of any single malt Scotch from the island of Islay, the extravagant floral designs and deep colors of Belgian Art Nouveau tiles and the single color austerity of English Arts and Crafts tile (best enjoyed in near proximity in order to disprove a single standard of beauty), Royal Doulton and Mettlach vases from the late 19th century with intricate and brilliant glazed surfaces, the cello sounds of Yo Yo Ma, and pottery, so much pottery, old and new. They all deserve this honor, my personal benediction. They are all beautiful. A collector need not be a connoisseur of esoteric and obscure taste. A collector just needs to feel good, to feel fully human and awake when engaged by natural or created beauty. Collectors feel deeply indebted and grateful for the gifts of human civilization. That is why they are willing to take on the responsibility for taking care of a small portion of these cultural treasures for the brief measure of their lifetimes. Surely I am not the only one to experience beauty every day - all day?

There are things that are beautiful that I do not and cannot own. I claim a modern attitude when I declare that there are beautiful things that are not pretty or even attractive. I find beauty in the city. Huge sprawling cities where you sidestep dog excrement on sidewalks, violent noises of sirens and traffic, defeated strangers that inspire anxiety and apprehension as they walk by you on the sidewalk or sit opposite you across the narrow aisles on the subway, talking to themselves. I love cities. In order to enjoy the best of human culture, you must withstand or accept an array of human behavior. Peter Walsh understands me. He's in the remarkable novel "Mrs. Dalloway" by Virginia Woolf, a day in the life of a middle-aged woman in high society about to have a party that same evening; Walsh, an old flame of Clarissa Dalloway's, strolls the sidewalks of London and celebrates the sheer beauty in the chaos and jumble of the streets:

"Beauty anyhow. Not the crude beauty of the eye. It was not beauty pure and simple - Bedford Place leading into Russell Square. It was straightness and emptiness of course; the symmetry of a corridor; but it was also windows lit up, a piano, a gramophone sounding; a sense of pleasure-making hidden, but now and again emerging when, through the uncurtained window, the young people slowly circling, conversations between men and women, maids idly looking out (a strange comment theirs, when work was done), stockings drying on top ledges, a parrot, a few plants. Absorbing, mysterious, of infinite richness, this life. And in the large square where the cabs shot and swerved so quick, there were loitering couples, dallying, embracing, shrunk up under the shower of a tree; that was moving; so silent, so absorbed, that one passed, discreetly, timidly, as if in the presence of some sacred ceremony to interrupt which would have been impious. That was interesting. And so on into the flare and glare."

Beauty is not something you escape to. I do not seek some final salvation at some distant site where at last I will find peace and beauty. If I cannot find it now, in my immediate and everyday world, I will never find it. In that regard beauty is somewhat like the idea of love, also a notion out of fashion in our more enlightened and advanced circles. They may be the same thing. I can't divide them. Beauty and love bond me to life and connect me to those things that nurture and nourish me. A recent book review by Roberta Abrams in Guardian Weekly of "Why Love Matters: How Affection Shapes a Baby's Brain" by Sue Gerhardt brought home this idea. Gerhardt is a psychotherapist, drawing upon research on the impact of caring attention for babies.

"Gerhardt is not interested in cognitive skills - how quickly a child learns to read, write, count to 10. She's interested in the connection between the kind of loving we receive in infancy and the kind of people we turn into. Who we are is neither encoded at birth, she argues, nor gradually assembled over the years, but is inscribed into our brains during the first two years of life in direct response to how we are loved and cared for."

Could we find similar empirical proof of the importance of beauty in our formative years? Have such experiments been conducted? If beauty and love should prove to be essential for all of us, crucial in our infancy, why are these virtues so awkward for us to explore and so scarce for so many in their life experiences? Without quantifying these attributes, and reducing them to a single protocol and methodology, serious scholars prefer to leave such things to poets and other arty types. I can value such objective studies as that conducted by Gerhardt without surrendering the subjective richness and subtlety that I prize and experience.

Christa, could you ask the next potential customer that ventures into your gallery if that person truly values beautiful things? Ask them if there is beauty in their home and their lives? Follow up with the suggestion that one of your pots could be the loving gesture for that significant other that would make all the difference? Just think of it, for all those florist shops that hawk those dozen red roses for the very same purpose, instead we substitute pottery. We would both agree with Gerhardt that 'caring attention' is necessary to create loving people. The same virtue is necessary to maintain beauty. I venture that the benefits would be similar in the development of our humanity and personhood.

Christa, just how original are your various shapes and glaze results? Can I see the evident references to your mentors in the finished pot? Do you recognize and cede your debt to them? One reason I am asking right now is that the discussion in the last few paragraphs of this letter, exploring the relationship between beauty and love, were my ideas, spilled on the page out of my rushing and spontaneous thoughts. At least I think they were my ideas. Someone could point out that my novel and original idea, proud boast of authorship, could be traced to the forgotten references of books whose individual titles and content have long since faded into the general mass of my memory bank. Everything is derivative and in some slight variation, everything is original. I speak about this because, just after my mediation about beauty and love, just after writing the last few paragraphs, I came across an essay that verified and reinforced my thoughts. I was so pleased. I guess one could question why I needed that kind of assurance and verification but I am still pleased. I so respect the published, printed page. It makes their authors the official carriers of the culture. My printer does not have that kind of authority. By contrast, my pages look so home-made and tentative. My writing is such a modest craft.

Let me tell you about this fortunate reinforcement that led to my self-discovered brilliance. I was reading "Uncontrollable Beauty: Toward a New Aesthetics", edited by Bill Beckley and David Shapiro. In the essay, "The Practice of Beauty", by James Hillman, about two thirds into the book, I came across this passage:

"We want the world because it is beautiful, its sounds and smells and textures, the sensate presence of the world as body. In short, below the ecological crisis lies the deeper crisis of love, that our love has left the world. That the world is loveless results directly from the repression of beauty, its beauty and our sensitivity to beauty. For love to return to the world, beauty must first return, else we love the world only as a moral duty. Clean it up, preserve its nature, exploit it less. If love depends on beauty, then beauty comes first, a priority that accords with pagan philosophy rather than Christian. Beauty before love also accords with the all-too-human experience of being driven to love by the allure of beauty."

Well, you can see that Hillman fully agrees with me. It is a fine essay. Hillman is a psychotherapist, for ten years the director of the C.G. Jung Institute in Zurich and a Founding Fellow of the Dallas Institute of Humanities and Culture. I do not think, given my age and condition, that I should be embarrassed that the degree of appreciation of an author is directly calibrated with the author's agreement with me. It is a sign of my intellectual integrity that I even bring this matter up. His essay was apparently a talk he gave at some conference. Perhaps that is why it is so clear and incisive. I welcome his company and we fully agree - beauty comes first, then love, 'driven by the allure of beauty'.

Clarity in expressing your thoughts is more than a courtesy. It is directly correlated with the possibilities for comprehension by the reader. I trudge through the turgid prose of academic texts, suspicious that the convoluted density of words and thoughts is deliberately calculated to restrict potential readers to that small inner circle of narrow experts and colleagues of the author. Is it possible that the effort is deliberate, with the mistaken strategy of impressing and intimidating the puzzled and confused reader? Do you become a lax popularizer if the general reader understands what you are saying? I am willing to work hard, do my share as reader, to read and reread, eyes dropping to the bottom of the page for footnotes, hoping that the motivation for further effort will be rewarded and increased by the waiting revelation and insight. I do not think there is a natural relationship between the complexity of ideas and the struggle and difficulty of understanding them. Does the clarity of expression and exposition really endanger the idea? Does the process of clarification have to result in the consequence of simplification? I don't think so, but then, I don't write for a living.

Hillman seeks to guide us back to beauty, back from the repression, to invite beauty into our lives. He advocates the introduction of pleasure, provides a lovely quote from George Santayana, "Beauty is pleasure regarded as the quality of a thing." Christa, I felt that way when you presented that big beautiful pitcher you recently made for us, that imposing and striking dark object with the audacious red band around it. The pleasure that Hillman and Santayana are talking about is not restricted to the initial encounter. I lodge that object in my house, see it every day. Beauty does not desert your pitcher, my pleasure is also dependable and permanent. Such delight and joy are somehow made superficial by the culture. I don't know why.

Most people never make it to your studio/gallery. They find pleasure elsewhere. If you examine the most common sources of pleasure in our society, you begin to understand something about this idea of the repression of beauty. Most pleasure is now programmed into electronic entertainments or planned in advance by theme parks. The robot function of receiving the pleasure is a passive one, independent of your behavior or involvement, even your reaction is planned by them. The appreciation of an aesthetic experience that can reward one with pleasure cannot be that one-sided.

I just finished an essay by a great teacher of another time. Thomas Huxley was the British nineteenth century scientist who vigorously introduced and taught a hostile public the meaning and significance of the contributions of Charles Darwin. Huxley was concerned about the state of education in his time and the tradition of a humanities education that did not include the emerging discoveries of the natural world. In an address at the opening of a college to remedy this situation, on "Science and Culture", he wisely does not seek to discount or discredit this traditional emphasis on the humanities but to enrich them. What struck me was his stated conviction that we could direct the pleasure seeking drives of humans to a higher and more refined level. Huxley understood that science would bring technologies of prosperity and pleasure to the masses that had never known this opportunity. In a way, I think he anticipated that the direction of this opportunity was not going to uplift people but debase them. He felt that education could prevent this. Indeed, this was the purpose of education:

"If the wealth from prosperous industry is to be spent upon the gratification of unworthy desires, if the increasing perfection of manufacturing processes is to be accompanied by an increasing debasement of those who carry them on, I do not see the good of industry and prosperity. Now it is perfectly true that men's views of what is desirable depend upon their characters; and that the innate proclivities to which we give that name are not touched by any amount of instruction. But it does not follow that even mere intellectual education may not, to an indefinite extent, modify the practical manifestation of the characters of men in their actions, by supplying them with motives unknown to the ignorant. A pleasure-loving character will prefer pleasures which do not degrade him to those which do. And this choice is offered to every man who possesses in literary or artistic culture a never-failing source of pleasures, which are neither withered by age, nor staled by custom, nor embittered in the recollection by the pangs of self-reproach."

I look back over the previous paragraphs, trying to find the pattern of meaning in these three ideas, beauty, love and pleasure. If we can tie them to pottery, demonstrate how pottery will ensure all three possibilities, then surely you and all the other potters in the world will be besieged by demand and prosperity will result. I would, of course, have you follow the advice of Huxley in regard to how you spend that prosperity. Could it be that the creators of beauty would not seek beauty in their own lives? Tell me it isn't so, Christa! Would I catch a potter at Disneyland, playing video games, reading a comic book. Tell me it isn't so, Christa!

I realize the dangers of attempting to teach the virtues of beauty as moral duty. It could become like our current sex education programs where you teach sex by abstinence - by denying it and remaining ignorant of its nature. Given the religious fundamentalism so dominant today, one would teach beauty by denying the possible pleasure that might result. The seeking of pleasure is a dangerous activity - how can one instruct without being pious and righteous, yet demand standards of conduct that could restrict freedom. A democracy of pleasures is our birthright, who are we to deny them? Indeed, the current posture in the fine arts is to lead the debasement, to define art as debasement. As if the popular culture needed any help in this direction. I will side with Hillman and Huxley, yet hesitate to endorse some potential aesthetic catechism as curriculum even if it would bring the desired result.

How do I avoid becoming a hopeless and reactionary old man? Dusting my pottery and reading 19th century Victorian essays that provide classic preaching on the solid virtues of education and beauty? I will only look at contemporary texts that promise a return to the notions of beauty that have been debased by more modern contributions. I am withdrawing into a cultural cocoon of my own choosing. I vaguely remember my previous identity as educator and the liberation pedagogy I administered to free the oppressed masses. If at all successful in those efforts, I must now conclude I just made the waiting lines of people at Disneyland a bit longer.

The last remnant - the last fragment to fit in this conceptual collage - the ideas of a man totally unable to employ an aesthetic sense of harmony and beauty in his tragic and undisciplined life, but a man fully able to create beauty on the page - Edgar Allan Poe. Historically more appreciated in Europe than America, Poe wrote an essay on "The Poetic Principle". Poe shares my old-fashioned perspective, insisting that poetry should 'elevate the soul'. He does attempt to integrate his holy trinity of the human spirit and the human mind, attributes that lead to the promised land of beauty.

"Dividing the world of mind into its three most immediately obvious distinctions, we have the Pure Intellect, Taste, and the Moral Sense. I place Taste in the middle, because it is just this position which in the mind it occupies. It holds intimate relations with either extreme, but from the Moral Sense is separated by so faint a difference that Aristotle has not hesitated to place some of its operations among the virtues themselves. Nevertheless, we find the offices of the trio marked with a sufficient distinction. Just as the intellect concerns itself with Truth, so Taste informs us of the Beautiful, while the Moral Sense is regardful of Duty. Of this latter, while Conscience teaches the obligation, and Reason the expediency, Taste contents herself with displaying the charms; - waging war upon Vice solely on the ground of her deformity - her disproportion - her animosity to the fitting, to the appropriate, to the harmonious - in a word, to Beauty. An immortal instinct, deep within the spirit of man, is thus, plainly, a sense of the Beautiful."

Plainly the dialogue I am sponsoring in this letter about beauty, across centuries and generations, is a most reassuring one for me. The durability of this discussion must have something to do with its inherent importance. Despite a modern lull, even hostility, we must make room and take time for beauty. Like Poe, I have often thought about beauty, experienced beauty in art, but my life has not always been beautiful. That is a very difficult congruity to achieve - to appreciate or create art and document that commitment by living a beautiful life. If one can believe the gossip in the biographies of artists, few of them achieved the wisdom, beauty and virtue that Poe is talking about in his discussion of Pure Intellect, Taste, and the Moral Sense. It too often has seemed that the vulnerable sensitivity necessary to create and experience beauty removes the protection to endure and survive the harsh realities of our common existence. We do not question this, we contrive the romance of their suffering as central to their task.

I do not think it should be necessary. The need for self-destruction should not emanate from the same passion and energy that sponsors the creative impulse. That is a tragic and undeserved fate.

I wish you the best during this holiday season. We all must find time to balance the beauty we create and observe with the beauty we can experience in the quality of our lives. I hope this for you. It is a good last thought for this year and provides the basis for the great expectations we hold for the next.

Your Friend,

Richard

Thirty-eight

January 1, 2005

Dear Christa,

I have a bad attitude about New Year's Eve parties. I am not sure why people celebrate the new year, it is rash to predict a hopeful outcome so far in advance. I do not understand the celebration of the old year just passed; it might imply a blanket endorsement of every disaster and tragedy that occurred during its tenure. Certainly at this point in my life, anything that celebrates the continuing passage of time could lead to depression. We usually go out for an afternoon movie, then dinner. I sip Scotch, try to stay up until midnight, rarely succeed. It is not old age that governs this sullen behavior. I don't mind if people drink or seek company in small circles of friends or family on New Year's eve. I just prefer them to be morose and disappointed, preoccupied with the failure of the human species in yet another year of self-imposed catastrophe, humble and sincere in their petitions for collective and individual improvement for the next year. Admittedly the war in Iraq, election results, and the terrible destruction of the tsunami waves in Asia have influenced my current perspective.

Perhaps some summary or inventory must be made of the past twelve months in order to issue resolutions that might carry some modest reform into the new year. These resolutions are cheaply made and can be soon forgotten. On second thoughts, one should not be so cynical so early in the year. It is possible that such a review can lead to a change in personal habits or the rearrangement of household furniture.

Christa, I can envisage the perfect New Year's party. A party in complete harmony with my present frame of mind. A few friends and family in my living room, surrounded by prints and pottery. Trays of snack food, a variety of beverages, moderate drinking so as to maintain composure and self-control. I would prefer people to remain very quiet. It would be a multi-media event. Benjamin Britten's 'Requiem' would be played, composed for the new cathedral at Coventry, adjoining the ruins of the old cathedral bombed and destroyed in World War

II; images would be flashed on the wall, fragments of Picasso's Guernica, the bombing of a Spanish village that presaged what would soon happen to Warsaw and Dresden in World War II; Goya's series of prints of the French cruelties during their invasion of Spain, including that famous firing squad; images of suffering mother and dead child by Kathe Kollwitz, representing the poverty and tragedy of the vast masses of the lower classes everywhere; integrated with the more recent and modest attempts to revive the scale of the Holocaust - images of Srebrenica and Rwanda might do. I would show slides of all the bull-dozed and destroyed monuments of great architecture, the clay shards of pottery that civilization failed to preserve whole. Next would be pictures of the devastation of Iraq, still rich in promise for further contributions in the coming year. I would walk among the guests, if anyone fidgeted or started talking, I would freeze them with a stare. If some drunken fool cried out 'Happy New Year' or some soused idiot blurted out the refrain of 'Auld Lang Syne' they would be immediately evicted. Perhaps I will hold this party next New Year's day. I will put you down on the mailing list. It would be quite rude of you to decline.

Art can best articulate and celebrate human misery as well as joy. Above all, I do not want to be a superficial collector of pretty things. In my life, misery and joy deserve equal time, both have inspired great art, both co-exist in union within me. Misery and joy are not simple emotions, they deserve to be commemorated with subtlety and refinement. Profound misery becomes beautiful through the gift of earned insight and wisdom. One cannot attain a state of enlightened grace if the endemic tragedy of human life and experience are left out. The objects of desire, even pottery, cannot become a sedative or tranquilizer for me. Anyhow, aside from Walt Disney, who thought art should entertain? Marx was also wrong: entertainment, not religion, has become the opiate of the working class. Art should never simply entertain; it then becomes a distraction from life, not life itself. Now, I have made several declarative sentences in a row and I am fully prepared to suffer the consequences of a pretended authority solely dependent upon personal passion and prejudice. Reviewing the last two paragraphs, I must be in a bad mood or dangerously honest. Forgive me, I should not inflict either possibility on you so early in the year.

I saw a masterpiece the other day. The use of that term reveals too much about my quaint fondness for magnificent art. Like discussions of beauty, the term masterpiece represents a past age, now hopelessly obsolete. Nietzsche declared the death of God, modern artists have declared the death of the beautiful art object. Yet, damn it, I did see a masterpiece the other day. I stood before Renoir's 'Luncheon of the Boating Party', the great anchor of the Duncan Phillips Collection, subject of a current exhibition at the Los Angeles County Museum of Art, paying humble homage and feeling exhilaration and joy for those precious and intense moments of engagement. Perhaps my experience would be approved and accepted if I did not use that word - masterpiece. I could then be allowed my reverent engagement with that towering triumph of the painter's brush. Someone in authority could demand a definition from me, my defense of that word - masterpiece. What are the attributes associated with that term? Can I standardize some universal and unfailing formula? If I can't provide those standards (and I am sorry but indeed I cannot), then I have no choice. I must, according to the rules of the game, surrender the word and retreat to subversive rituals of hidden affection for that masterpiece, 'Luncheon of the Boating Party'.

I must compound my error. I have experienced not one, but two masterpieces recently. This confession should confirm the total decline of my critical faculties and my isolation from contemporary cultural commentary. I have just finished reading the novel, "Untouchable" by Mulk Raj Anand, the Indian writer who recently died aged 98.

This classic was written in 1935, the first major achievement by this son of a coppersmith and soldier who became a significant lifelong writer of cultural commentary and fiction. He embodied a progressive political philosophy, worked at the Workers' Educational Association in London, fought for the Republicans in the Spanish Civil War, later joining Gandhi in the fight for Indian Independence. Culturally he was that uneasy hybrid of two vastly different cultures; educated at Cambridge and graduate of London University with a PhD in philosophy, writing in the language of the occupying colonial power; yet after World War II, spending the remainder of his life in India, a university professor, writer of novels and art criticism, fine arts chairman at the Indian National Academy of Arts.

The "Untouchable" comprises one day in the life of Bakha, a young man trapped at the very bottom of the caste system. A latrine-cleaner, subject to constant abuse and humiliation, yet somehow proud and defiant. That one day encapsulates a panorama of Indian life at that time. Whatever the miseries imposed by the imperial racism of the British Empire, the indigenous culture contained its own divisions, its own injustices. Anand gives life and meaning to Bakha's plight with these words:

"Like a ray of light shooting through the darkness, the recognition of his position, the significance of his lot dawned upon him. It illuminated the inner chambers of his mind. Everything that had happened to him traced its course up to this light and got the answer. The contempt of those who came to the latrines daily and complained that there weren't any latrines clean, the sneers of the people in the outcastes' colony, the abuse of the crowd which had gathered round him this morning. It was all explicable now. A shock of which this was the name had passed through his perceptions, previously numb and torpid, and had sent a quiver into his being, stirred his nerves of sight, hearing, smell, touch and taste, all into a quickening. 'I am an Untouchable!' he said to himself, 'an Untouchable!' He repeated the words in his mind, for it was still a bit hazy and he felt afraid it might be immersed in the darkness again. Then, aware of his position, he began to shout aloud the warning word with which he used to announce his approach: 'Posh, posh, sweeper coming.' The undertone, 'Untouchable, Untouchable,' was in his mouth. His pace quickened and it formed itself into a regular army step into which his ammunition boots always fell so easily. He noticed that the thumping of his heavy feet on the ground excited too much attention. So he slowed down a little."

You will remember my last letter of December 9th, and my discussion of the novel by Virginia Woolf, "Mrs. Dalloway". This book represented one day in the life of an upper class English woman, Clarissa Dalloway, preparing for a party in her home that very night. How amazing, these two novels, read in succession, each taking place in one day, one in London in 1925, the other in India in 1935. I do not know if Woolf and Anand knew each other in England or even met. I do know that Bakha and Clarissa Dalloway could never have known each other, would never have met, worlds apart and separated by every conceivable barrier. Both are equally memorable, human and fallible. It must have been a literary convention of the early 20th century, novels taking place in one day. I like that device, I would like to think that a single day is long enough to experience the full range of a life, a sufficient sample of the nature of a life-time framed by particular placement and situation. I would like to think that one day could make a novel, containing the universe of all possibilities and behaviors. I need each day of my life to represent and last a lifetime, a normal desire of someone my age.

Two amazing novels, two amazing masterpieces. Moreover, I do not have to choose between them. I do not have to decide a preference or declare a partisan sympathy for one over the other. What a miracle of aesthetic generosity. I can claim both Clarissa and Bakha, knowing that shortly before they had been strangers existing in worlds unknown to me. I was provided entry by gifted writers to these foreign worlds, passports to lives that became carriers of meaning beyond the hours of that recorded single day, passing by me, passing through me, to a possible eternity of engagement with those who wish to invite them into their lives. Both books have dark shadows and human tragedy, moments of joy and humanity, conditions tentative and unstable, as are the conditions in all of our lives.

Back to another single day, another single moment caught on canvas, to Renoir and that boating party, on an island near Paris, in the open air. A social gathering composed of the friends of the artist; painters, wealthy businessmen, two or three actresses, a baron, a journalist, all portraits of individuals in inter-action, talking and drinking, standing and seated, enjoying each other's company over lunch. Johanna Halford-MacLeod, in the exhibition catalog, further describes the scene:

"… some of life's great pleasures: glorious weather, a day on the river, food and wine, and the company of friends. The painting commemorates no partic-ular event but reflects and celebrates modern life and the new social realities of the late nineteenth century."

The sensuous and ripe colors, the rich and complex composition that merged figures in close, overlapping proximity; a series of portraits of real people, some in profile, some partially concealed, all ignoring the viewer outside the painting. Why do I like this painting? I listen to another voice, that of Maurice Raynal, in "History of Modern Painting: From Baudelaire To Bonnard". Here Raynal offers tribute:

"Renoir may not be a modern painter in the current meaning of the word. He is, rather, one of the great masters of all time. If he joined in the Impressionists' cult of light, this was because he wished to place his expression of life in a setting as much 'alive' as life itself; for him light was to play a more vital part than that of an accessory of realism. In Renoir's art, colour is treated not as a lucky-bag of handy flummeries for milliners … but a solid substance like flesh or earth, fitted to serve the building of the dream of the master-builder that he was."

If Maurice Raynal, a distinguished art writer and critic, could use words like 'great masters' and 'master builder', then why can't this humble amateur use the same kind of language? Certainly a great master is qualified to paint a great masterpiece? Admittedly the quotation was extracted from one of the oldest art books in my library, one of three volumes on modern art published by Albert Skira in the late 1940's. I bought the books while still in high school or early in college - I just can't remember for sure - from wages earned in one of my very first part-time jobs. I was so proud of those books, proud of my purchase. Somehow I managed to retain them through many moves, transitions and upheavals over the years. At that tender age, I was so impressed that the repro-ductions of paintings were independent prints, adhered to but not printed on the page. It gave prestige to my library at a time when paperbacks dominated my book shelves.

I know by now that you have identified my big discrepancy, the glaring contradiction at the very heart of this letter. How could I approve and celebrate that joyous party on the island near Paris for the friends of Renoir and yet, early in the letter, initiate our discussion with a mean-spirited announcement of my future plans for a New Year's Eve party at my home, deliberately planned with a program to make people seriously miserable, albeit in a most refined manner? I know my explanation will not be convincing. I am not convinced. I am now willing to compromise. I will not eliminate any portion of the previous program but I am willing to enlarge it. Yes, I will permit spontaneous interaction, loud laughter, moments of appropriate gaiety. And I will add a Strauss waltz or two, the last movement of Beethoven's Ninth, the Ode to Joy (with images of the Berlin Wall tumbling down), perhaps Mozart's sunny 'Eine Kleine Nachtmusik', slides of the ripe interiors of Bonnard and the exterior landscapes of Pissarro. Paintings of mother and child by Mary Cassett would follow. All climaxed by a midnight walk through the ceramic collection. I will locate my single malt Scotch and share it (a considerable sacrifice in itself), and I will place several bottles of good wine, obtained through wine club membership, on the table. Now, I have restored balance to my life and the arts. I have fully restored joy, accompanied by tragedy, the two great gifts of art, to their rightful place as intimate companions in my life.

I used to tell my students that the only benefit a good education could provide was a more refined level of suffering. In the engagement with art, I cannot filter out the meaning extracted from human tragedy from the more pleasurable moments of human joy. I find the experience of pleasure and suffering derived from art necessary and memorable. I have no distinct preference between the two. I have always been aware that, in that regard at least, I do not have an American personality. Too often, for Americans, both spirituality and aesthetics exist as protections or distractions from their own mortality. Without the dread of death, I am not sure religion and art in America would otherwise have any popularity or function. I could never accept a religion dependent on the bribe of heaven as the chief rationale for belief; nor could I accept an art whose purpose was to conceal the sense of cosmic proportion and shared humanity that my morality provides me. This attitude comprises the only definition of courage where I might qualify.

Pottery is more benign. I have never experienced great suffering with pottery. Perhaps that is its chief limitation. I do know that pottery can offer a complex aesthetic message, that pottery contains masterworks that eventually qualify by the enduring embrace of generations as cultural masterpieces. Philip Rawson, in his book "Ceramics" made that case, pointing out the primal importance of pottery. I will repeat a short portion of a statement more fully quoted in an earlier letter:

"Inert clay, from the earth, is made into something which is directly and intimately related to active craft, to the processes of human survival, and to social and spiritual factors in the life of man, all at once."

I further reviewed Rawson, looking for a reference to the tragic potential of the pot. On the very next page, early in the book:

"A work of high ceramic art may even connect to itself whole chains or circuits of thought, feeling, and value, particularly those related to social status and identity (also valid ecological concepts), by means of the formal symbolism in its elaborated shapes and carefully treated surfaces. All these may be added, perhaps unconsciously on the potter's part, into the transformation image represented by the pot, and may raise it far above the category of primary utensil into a region of sophisticated expression. It may thus reflect into the mind of its owner an extremely complex image of his own identity, status, and personal value."

I find that last sentence interesting, Rawson is obviously referring to me as collector. Pottery does define me. Of the three attributes listed by Rawson, I am less interested in status, more so in identity and personal value. Can there be a merging of utility and expression? Do both contribute to the pot's significance? I can think of two meaningful functions historically carried by pottery - that of the urn and that of the bed chamber pot. I come close to humor here, as well as tragedy and ironic commentary. What credit can function make for its role in this case? Excrement is the spent fuel of human activity and ashes are the final waste product of a consumed life. The meaning, the symbolism of all that certainly must start with those containers and their content.

William Morris had thoughts on the healing power of craft, which he called the 'art of the people', to provide support through troubled times for both the maker and receiver. He stated that this art of the people:

"... has in many places and in many times solaced and sustained the people amid their griefs and troubles. And a great gift such an art seems to me; an art made intelligently by the whole body of those who live by their labour; instinct with their thoughts and aspirations, moving whither they are moving, changing as they change, the genuine expression of their sense of the beauty and mystery of life; an art born of their joy and outliving their sorrow, though tinged by it; an art leaving to future ages living witness of the existence of deft hands and eager minds not too proud to tell us of their imperfect thought and their glimpses of insight into wonders and terrors, as they passed amid the hurry of their daily work, through the sunshine and shadow of their lives."

Once again Morris helps me out. I can use his ideas of 'art born of their joy and outliving their sorrow' and the 'wonders and terrors' and 'the sunshine and shadow' of our lives. These qualities are usually present in some form in memorable art. In some ways, Morris and I exist within the same cultural envelope. He proposes these opposing dualities and I accept them as given or natural. As with all categories of thought, I assume I invent these things on the page but actually parrot or repeat the dualism of my culture and upbringing. Maybe I am not talking about two different things but one thing. I must struggle to go against my cultural grain, becoming aware of my limitations only when it is pointed out by someone outside my own reality. Soetsu Yanagi, in "The Unknown Craftsman: A Japanese Insight into Beauty" in a chapter on the 'Buddhist Idea of Beauty' helps me understand a very different way of looking and thinking about the 'sunshine and shadow' of our lives:

"The final objective of Zen Buddhists is, of course, liberation from all duality: good and evil, true and false, beautiful and ugly, one's self and others, life and death, consciousness and unconsciousness. All such dualistic forms must be discarded. Day in, day out, Zen Buddhists undergo rigorous training to that end, for so long as they are trapped in the polarized world, they are unable to achieve peace of mind, to attain Buddhahood. A true artist is not one who chooses beauty in order to eliminate ugliness, he is not one who dwells in a world that distinguishes between the beautiful and the ugly, but rather he is one who has entered the realm where strife between the two cannot exist. Only in the work of a man who has attained this state of mind is there no room for encroachment by the ugly or for the kind of relative beauty that is comprehensible only as an antithesis of the ugly."

The limitation of a utilitarian object occurs when the function is the source of social or cultural significance and the container is significant only because of its content and assigned ritual. This relationship can be reciprocal. I do not know how to assess the relative importance of the tea cup to the tea ceremony. As I am now beginning to understand, a Buddhist point of view would not recognize this distinction or my arbitrary methods of separation.

I can only try to understand, perhaps borrow these ideas. I will try to apply them to those two masterpieces I have been discussing. I thought them very different, that party on the island and poor Bakha in squalid poverty. I still do. Out of habit, I still sort out experiences and organize them in ad hoc but comfortable categories that might make sense to me. Each object of art has a special character, each cannot contain all qualities. But I can try to re-examine how I receive these things and thus recognize my constantly changing condition. I need to surface the hidden presuppositions that frame my reaction. For instance, I would like to think that the presence of a social conscience, an attribute I do claim, was important in receiving Bakha and that day in his life. Without the compassion that comes from the activation of a social conscience, why would anyone care about that distant untouchable? Christa, I am willing to permit you to stay at that party with Renoir's friends for a while, but request you leave a bit early in order to help Bakha clean the latrines. It is evident I must continue to work on the idea that the world and my life need not be polarized. I must still ask the question, why would one stay in the castle with Hamlet or go to the latrines with Bakha if one could go to Disneyland instead? I obviously need a Buddhist response to that question.

Perhaps my search and mission to defend the special delights of aesthetic misery simply reflect my own contrarian and irascible personality. But I am trying to be fair and balanced. I even picked up a book with the unpleasant title (given my current mood) of "Pleasure and the Arts: Enjoying Literature, Painting, and Music". Here, Christopher Butler does offer a direct response to my continuing inquiry.

"We have genuinely painful emotions and anguished thoughts in response to such works of art, and there are plenty of people who simply cannot take the fictional violence displayed in the cinema and on TV, who weep copiously when moved by the story of others' sad predicaments, and so on. When I choose between a Johann Strauss waltz and Richard Strauss's exquisitely mourning 'Metamorphosen' I know that the latter work is going to be tough for me in a way that the former certainly isn't (quite apart from thoughts of the destruction of Munich and Dresden through Allied bombing that a historically aware listener might associate with this music). Ella Fitzgerald or the Tritsch Tratsch Polka will generally do better in lifting my mood. Nor can I doubt that many of the cruelties described in books or enacted in films have their exact counterparts outside fiction, as in the case of Roddy Doyle's harrowing description of a battered wife in his novel 'The Woman Who Walked into Doors'. And yet, and so, there seems to be something which compensates us for the unpleasant emotions and sad or revolting thoughts that many works of art can make us have, so that pleasure is also involved. Doyle's book was extraordinarily painful to read, but one of the many compensations here was the extraordinary heroism, dignity, humour, and resource of the woman narrator ... There may be some kind of combination here that will resolve the tensions within the paradox of our enjoyment of the sad in artistic contexts. At least some of the pleasure we derive from such emotionally disturbing experiences seems to arise from their giving us the compensatory pleasure of an artistically ordered understanding."

Well, is that 'combination' that Butler talks about a dualism or an integration of a possible dualism? I choose an aesthetic experience, usually knowing in advance the promised or expected result. Whatever I have said above in this letter, I know I cannot choose for you, Christa. I do know that you have thought about these things. The first two pots I obtained from you had that 'gingerbread' glaze. I would characterize the effect as soft and peaceful, a most interesting combination of strong, simple shapes and subtle surface. But the last few ceramic pieces I have obtained from you reflect the drama of very dark glazes, with an audacious and rebellious square or ribbon of deep red. You are sending different messages in these two styles. You have displayed both sunshine and shadow. That spout on that big pitcher of yours is very aggressive. It cannot be ignored. The thin trickles of white that run down your gingerbread glaze would not belong on that pitcher. Your pottery can sponsor many moods. Continue to strive in your work and perhaps one day it will finally achieve the qualities to truly make me miserable.

Another setback in my quest for an informed misery - an article in the Guardian Weekly of December 24, 2004 on "The Pleasure Principle" where recent research at Laval University in Quebec finds the drive to seek pleasure is organic and central for humans. The author quotes Michel Cabanac, "Pleasure is the common currency that allows us to make any, and I mean any, decision in our lives". One brief ray of hope by the unnamed author of the article, who questions the correctness of the study, and offers an example of an incident in 1969, when Jan Palach, a Czech student, set himself on fire as a protest against the Soviet invasion of his country. This example supported my commitment, my conviction that I cannot separate aesthetic pleasure from issues of social justice and human dignity. The great heroes of my life, Martin Luther King, Gandhi, and Nelson Mandela did not live according to this pleasure principle. Art cannot provide the camouflage or distraction for the tragedy of poverty, war or discrimination. Art provides me with the opportunity to share the great pain and failures of humanity as well as those glorious achievements that encourage me that all the rest is not in vain.

Ah ha, good tidings at last! The Los Angeles Times newspaper this morning brought the welcome news. On the front page, an alarming article about the huge burgers now being served at fast-food restaurants. Burgers, loaded with two-thirds of a pound of beef, four bacon strips, three cheese slices and mayonnaise on a buttered bun, over 1,400 calories and lots of fat. Why this appetite for artery and heart clogging obesity? According to Amy Lanou, director of the nutrition department at the Physicians Committee for Responsible Medicine:

"Humans have an innate desire to harm themselves through indulgence, through pleasure and excess … I think it's unfortunate."

This discussion supports my own suspicion of pleasure. I somehow had sensed that pleasure could only make a person unhealthy and superficial. Could the same people who munch these monster burgers, seeking self-indulgent pleasure, be the same people who prefer the overripe joy of a Fragonard painting of French aristocrats playing and flirting, avoiding all the while the blue period of Picasso with his lonely absinthe drinkers leaning on a cafe table? Could these be the same people who would choose the gilded confection of Dresden china over the lean austerity of Arts and Crafts pottery? Would they really choose the vulgar piano tunes of Liberace over the demands and discipline of Horowitz when applied to Chopin or Scriabin? I do not need to choose tofu over beef to realize that there is a necessary nutrition for the soul that only memorable art can provide. Christa, I think I have convincingly made the argument for refined misery. My conscience is clear, if you do choose pleasure instead, you only have yourself to blame.

Are you as transparent and obvious in your moods as I am in this letter? Is it the role of the artist to suppress her dark emotions and the impact of harsh reality on her work or to use this emotional energy in her art? Does your pottery ever reflect the adversities of your immediate life? The program notes for Mahler's 6th symphony, written by Henry-Luis De La Grange, for the performance conducted by Boulez with the Vienna Philharmonic, offers a discussion of this work, his most tragic symphony. La Grange relates the attitude of the composer:

"As was so often the case, Mahler felt, while writing the Sixth Symphony, that he was the instrument of a power greater than himself. On this occasion, however, that power was mysterious, tragic and implacable, plunging him into a state of insurmountable anguish. What is this power that Mahler's symphonic heroes are forced to contend with, and to which they often succumb, as is the case at the end of the Sixth Symphony? It is a struggle that Mahler himself had to face, as he made clear in a striking remark when, following the final rehearsal, one of his friends asked him: 'But how can someone who is so good express so much cruelty and harshness in his work?' To which he replied: 'They are the cruelties I've suffered and the pains I've felt!' "

Laurie Rolland, a fine Canadian potter represented in my collection provided me with this commentary regarding the stern demands of her art:

"And how to justify a life spent in art is difficult - perhaps that it is a quality rather than a quantity. I juggled my work so I actually raised my child. With modest means there is a modest lifestyle. The result has been a solitary dedicated pursuit of excellence and a life lived with values and integrity. Does the handmade object make a difference in our lives? I have been told it does and the sincerity of these comments is often humbling."

Another outstanding potter also represented in my collection, the English potter Peter Wills, wrote these comments to me regarding his struggles:

"The ambiguities of making handpots in the 21st century, along with the idea of pots whose predominant function is aesthetic and not practical; added to the difficulties of making a living, make (as you seem to understand) one's function in life (as a potter? artist?) somewhat perplexing; if not at times frustrating and occasionally downright depressing! To an extent that there are times when it even seems such a pointless thing to be doing that I feel like walking away from my studio and pots forever. And then, on another day, one piece of work can keep me enraptured for hours and the whole process and its results are positively joyous."

I really have no basis to question you and all the other potters I know about the depth and seriousness of your efforts. You chose your destiny a long time ago. I appreciate the sacrifice that potters make every day in order to pursue their craft. The struggle to create the excellent pot, to hone the skills necessary for that pursuit, and to face an often indifferent world; all testify to an integrity that cannot be compromised or tempted by the ease of indifferent work or the pleasures of an affluent society. The satisfaction on completing your most recent pot must compensate for the prior history of struggle and devotion. You know more than I do that integration of misery and pleasure that every serious craftsperson and artist faces each day. We live in a world that offers us the same strange mixture of heartbreak and celebration. As a collector, I merely seek to join your company in acknowledging and sharing that burden and providing testimony to its glorious and untold benefits.

I will continue to use that word 'masterpiece' as a term of endearment for whatever aesthetic experiences that bring me exquisite misery and pleasurable delights. I can be equally inspired by aesthetic sunshine or shadow. To use a phrase of Butler's, it is 'the paradox of our enjoyment of the sad in artistic contexts' that allows the bittersweet opportunities for aesthetic engagement and lifetime enrichment.

I know this is a long letter. It has been the most difficult of all the letters to write. I thought I was finished, already embarrassed by its length, when I came across a passage from a remarkable person, M.C. Richards. I am going to participate, as you are, in an NCECA conference in Baltimore whose very focus and theme was inspired by this woman. I would like to think, in my own modest fashion, I am following in her tradition, trying to offer reflective commentary that sets pottery in an ethical and cultural context; to explore the profound human engagement that pottery represents; not only as a creative activity for the potter but also for the collectors or receivers of pottery such as myself. For custodians of such treasures, we experience pottery so rich with embedded meaning that it provides the creative life-giving forces that enrich our very existence. In a few sentences, she captures everything I have tried to do in ten or more pages.

"By accepting suffering, we may relate more to others, developing compassion. By grace we may come free. And best of all we may find our sense of humor enormously expanded through the warmth of our heart center, that deepset crossing point."

The best for the new year.

Your friend,

Richard

Thirty-nine

January 31, 2005

Dear Christa,

I don't think like they do. That has always been the case. I go to seminars and symposiums, at the Huntington Library, or the Los Angeles County Art Museum, or the Gamble Lectures Series in Pasadena, usually alone, sit there and at the end of the talk ask questions that appear baffling to the speakers. Most often they ignore the intent of the question, surprised I was not requesting some factual information inadvertently left out of the lecture. That is usually the only type of question they expect or receive. I remain alone, no one approaches me during the day or evening proceedings. I just don't think the way they do, I do not approach life or art the way they do. I cannot trust them with the power to sweeten or spoil my day. I will soon withdraw, protect myself and find comfort in the private world of my garden and the few rooms of my cottage.

Tell me, Christa, do you ever feel the same way? Are potters a special breed? Don't tell me that a conventional, conforming person can create an original and creative pot. Is it a good thing for a pot to be unique and original, but less acceptable in the person? It is not an affectation or attention seeking device, I simply do not think the way they do. I am ambivalent at this time of my life. The separation from others comes from different sources; the dissident pride of prolonged resistance as an outsider set against the potential ignominy of a perceived portrayal as an eccentric old fool. I don't care about the cost or consequences, I will never think the way they do.

My unappreciated task involves both pedagogical responsibility and personal temperament. I was an educator for over forty years. I must declare that, for the most part, my fellow teachers over the years didn't think like me either. Most teachers, on every level, including university professors, thought their job was to remove doubt, to confirm the single story proved by conclusive evidence. I always acted on the assumption that my role as teacher was exactly the opposite, to unravel the previous certainty of the unexamined presuppositions of students and to make them self-conscious about the inherited orientation of their world view and mentality. I wanted them to suspend their 'truths' so that they could consider other possibilities. I did not want to provide a new truth, the curricular catechism in current circulation. I just wanted to leave them in a crisis of doubt - without easy comfort but with the sympathetic support necessary to somehow carry on. The development of a critical intelligence depends on the integrity and humility of an unstable existence, willing to be dislodged by new discoveries, willing to jettison or abandon sacred and precious truths for the unknown possibilities that might bring some wisdom or insight.

Christa, if you thought you had finally accomplished the complete truth in a pot - a definitive breakthrough that could only leave you with the downhill aftermath of pale replications of that one true pot - why would you continue to work at the wheel? Any embraced truth is a superior fiction, necessary to stabilize life and provide some semblance of contrived security. Why does it have to be more than that? I am obviously not talking here about the essential scientific discoveries of physical phenomena, but rather the qualitative matters of assigning significance, establishing relationship and context, and placing value in the life-long construction of self and reality.

Why can't people be creative when they explore creative issues? It leads me to the disturbing idea that people devoted to the study of creative activities of others are not themselves creative. Those experts don't want my questions asked because they don't want to be caught in public having to make sense of something. The prepared presentation does not have room for comments not previously rehearsed. The museum talk is a replica of the academic lecture. I cannot believe that the audience, composed of interested and educated laypersons, really enjoy reliving their college days in the quiet stupor that forms the expected etiquette of the occasion.

I am not alone. I can claim a rich heritage of cultural ancestors who would understand my efforts. From the Socratic questions of that noble Athenian to the experiential learning activities inspired by John Dewey and progressive education, I have a proud heritage. With delight, I reach back and embrace Montaigne, the 16th century French founder of the modern essay. He wrote an essay, "Of The Institution And Education of Children" in which he described the goal of education:

"To a gentleman borne of noble parentage, and heire of a house that aymeth at true learning, and in it would be disciplined, not so much for gane or commoditie to himselfe (because so abject an end is far unworthie the grace and favour of the Muses, and besides, hath a regard or dependencie of others) nor for externall shew and ornament, but to adorne and enrich his inward minde, desiring rather to shape and institute an able and sufficient man, than a bare learned man; my desire is therefore, that the parents or overseers of such a gentleman be very circumspect, and careful in chusing his director, whom I would rather commend for having a well composed and temperate braine, than a full stuft head, yet both will doe will. And I would rather prefer wisdome, judgement, civill customes, and modest behaviour, than bare and meere literall learning; and that in his charge he hold a new course. Some never cease bawling in their schollers eares (as if they were still pouring in a tonell) to follow their booke, yet is their charge nothing else but to repeat what hath beene told them before. I would have a tutor to correct this part, and at first entrance, according to the capacities of the wit he hath in hand, he should begin to make shew of it, making him to have a smacke of all things, and how to choose and distinguish them, without helpe of others, sometimes opening him the way, other times leaving him to open it by himselfe."

Montaigne is talking about the empowerment of this 'able and sufficient man' capable of autonomous acts beyond 'meere literal learning'. He would prefer the developed capacity for 'wisdome, judgement, civill customes, and modest behaviour' over 'a bare learned man' with 'a full stuft head'. In a wonderful endorsement of the generalist profile and virtues, Montaigne would have a tutor educate a student to 'have a smacke of all things, and how to choose and distinguish them, without helpe of others, sometimes opening him the way, other times leaving him to open it by himselfe.' How do we 'open the way' for 'able and sufficient' lovers and protectors of the arts? Would a teacher hold up a series of finished pots to be duplicated by students as a basis for ceramic instruction? Why would an intellectual assignment or aesthetic experience require only the feat of memorization as the basis of the self construction of meaning? What is left for the participant to do after the expert has provided the official account of some historical movement in art or ceramics?

Montaigne warns us against this conformity of passive assent to authority:

"Our minde doth move at others' pleasure, and typed and forced to serve the fantasies of others, being brought under by authoritie, and forced to stoope to the lure of their bare lesson; wee have beene so subjected to harpe upon one string, that we have one way left us to descant upon voluntaries; our vigor and libertie is clean extinct."

Several years ago I developed an interdisciplinary general education program in the humanities, arts and social sciences at a nearby university where team teaching might bring together in the same classroom a poet and an historian, or a philosopher and a sociologist. If effective, they became sufficiently comfortable with each other and the students to offer different ways of thinking and living in the world as holders of methodologies and epistemologies that provided vastly divergent narratives of the same subject. They modeled civilized respect for the other viewpoint through their discourse, and their irreconcilable differences formed the perfect homework assignment for the students. Why not a panel, with people from different backgrounds, offering different points of view? A panel can respond to some central issue, provocative and stimulating in nature. Respondents are another device, even a good-natured debate is a possibility. Conference materials might offer attendees possible questions and issues to confront, challenge and consider. Laypersons who collect arts and crafts, people who live in homes designed in some specific aesthetic style, persons whose lives are devoted to the pursuit of an aesthetic existence are also possible recruits for active panel presentation. Why aren't poets and daydreamers put on panels too?

Why is the topic never transformed into a question, or a theme rich in contradictions or problematic elements? I have never observed an artist or craftsperson on one of these institutional panels. Why not? Do artists and curators speak the same language? Why are the passionate differences of art experts as revealed in their journals and periodicals so completely absent from the decorous monologues of the lecture halls of museums and other art institutions?

Christa, would you ever disagree with other potters in some public forum? Does a different perspective indicate conflict or disregard? When you look at other potters and their pots, profoundly different in approach and technique, do you have to nullify or dismiss their results in order to validate your own work? I do not want you to agree with my thoughts expressed in these letters. I would hope you could appreciate my fumbling efforts to arrive at some tentative meaning that stabilizes my daily life and directs my curiosity. When applicable, one can appropriate some insight and graft it onto our own lives, integrated in personal context. We can learn so much from people without sacrificing our individual right of interpretation.

The protocol of the art lecture, whatever the topic, is as predictable as the attitude of the lecturer. A darkened room, a screen, a series of images, the speaker in shadows except for the glare of the lectern light; all made easy and obvious by contemporary electronics and very old habits. A topic stated without the possibility of ambiguity or potential conflict, presented as a survey outline of facts. They are strung in a scholarly row, undisputed only because they are without explicit analysis or interpretation; unchallenged by any dialectical manifestation of irony or personal context. Third person experts expressing third person narratives, without stated doubt or unfinished explorations. Experts of one isolated subject, one particular frozen time, attached to a single geography settled in a definite location; a safe congruity of image and facts; all packaged and complete for the passive consumption of the audience. The Protestant Reformation was based on the premise that one does not need the mediating broker of the priesthood to know and speak to God. Surely I do not need the intervention of the curator or specialist to know and experience art. If their job is not to define that experience for me, what should they really be doing?

I have been critical in the past about one-way didactic lectures by expert scholars whose focused specialization makes it difficult to provide a contextual frame of reference that includes the interests of a lay audience. Sometimes the assumption or arrogance of mastery does not allow the expert to confess incompleteness. This is regrettable. The discrepancies, ambiguities, and contradictions of human knowledge are the most fruitful initiations of any search for meaning. Would it really be unprofessional for some expert to declare and express their love for something beautiful? Is the mark of a mature expert really the full and complete suppression of the youthful delight and joy that once heralded their experience of a sublime aesthetic moment? Could I really expect that they publicly demonstrate the joy and agony of their engagement and devotion to art? Is it really perverse of me to want them to tell me about what they don't know or understand in preference to what they already know and understand? I would truly respect a more refined bewilderment, a more mysterious and subtle bafflement, a full confession of the infinite mysteries that awaits one after a prolonged time of attempting to understand and make sense of things.

Why would experts on subjects of an aesthetic nature not know that their public performance also has an aesthetic dimension, as complicated as the subject of their lecture? Simply put, why can't people that talk to others about art demonstrate the same creative and imaginative elements that are so much a part of what they are talking about? Talking about art is an extension of the art itself, of the experience of that art. It should somehow embody the character and spirit of that artifact. Why does that sound so strange and why is it so foreign to current practice?

To my mind, the sponsorship of this type of event implies specific educational goals regarding the nature of the experience itself as well as the nature of conference content. I believe that the conscious effort to organize an authentic learning experience for others involves serious and substantial elements, fully as complex as the formal content of the conference. This requires the transforming of the habit of specialists to summarize and explain factual information into an interactive and dialectical process of the problematic character of divergent perspectives. The pedagogical principles embedded in this assertion include the active participation of learners in the on-going and dynamic struggle to make meaning of the offered subject matter; to assess significance, place normative value, stabilize and integrate configurations of knowledge within the biographical context of previous experience and knowledge. These are strenuous activities, seldom identified by conventional conference observers and organizers who assume that the speakers are doing all the work, received by a passive and docile audience. This is of course the dominant model too often in the university classroom, carried onto the conference platform.

Christa, are we going to play it safe when we give our talk at the reception for our exhibition at the Oakland Museum in a few months? Are we going to play it safe at our panel presentation at NCECA in a few weeks? I could not forgive myself if boredom is the only result for those who attend these events. Is controversy the natural result of a creative and original mind? Do the politics of career planning discourage remarks that might disturb others? Do curators and artists have the same worry in that regard? Why do they think that an intellectually critical question is inherently critical of their authority?

Density is often mistaken for complexity in higher education. Academic knowledge is rarely intellectual knowledge. They are not the same thing. The operational complexity is not in the inert information, but in the behavior of the learners as they perform the intellectual function of analyzing that content. The conference should provide the support system to facilitate this difficult activity for the learner/participant. These efforts are pragmatic as well as philosophical; we know from research that retention is much greater, as well as eventual application, when the process of appropriation is an active one.

The integrity of a question presupposes you do not know the answer. Thus it is an honest question. Something as precious as a question should never be wasted in asking for superficial information. This involves the shift from the trivial pursuit of low level information, based on successful school strategies learned as a student for exam purposes, to the honing of the question as an investigative research tool. The great question does not encourage a premature answer that nullifies further intellectual activity in the region of the question, but inspires new questions, more finely focused and profound that serve as the basis for further discovery. I have spent my lifetime seeking to create and improve the subtlety and sophistication of my questions. The search for wisdom is based on the nobility of a self-conscious ignorance. This should never be a source of shame. The stepping stones of that pilgrimage are the quality of the questions you ask, and the nature of the inherent petition within that question. The very best learning experiences require the remainder of our lives to find some approximate response. Memorable learning is always a series of reasonable failures.

I must return to Montaigne. In his essay "Bookes", he initiates the discussion with characteristic modesty, describing his efforts to make meaning of things, warning the reader that he will not find a single truth, complete knowledge or the promise of certainty:

"I make no doubt but it shall often befall me to speake of things which are better, and with more truth, handled by such as are their craft-masters. Here is simply an essay of my natural faculties, and no whit of those I have acquired. And he that shall tax me with ignorance shall no great victory at my hands; for hardly could I give others reasons for my discourses that give none unto my selfe, and am not well satisfied with them. He that shall make search after knowledge, let him seek it where it is: there is nothing I professe lesse. There are but my fantasies by which I endevour not to make things known, but my selfe. They may haply one day be knowne unto me, or have bin at other times, according as fortune hath brought me where they were declared or manifested. But I remember them no more. And if I be a man of some reading, yet I am a man of no remembering, I conceive no certainty, except it bee to give notice how farre the knowledge I have of it doth now reach. Let no man busie himselfe about the matters, but on the fashion I give them. Let that which I borrow be survaied, and then tell me whether I have made good choice of ornaments to beautife and set foorth the invention which ever comes from mee. For I make others to relate (not after mine owne fastasie but as it best falleth out) what I cannot so well expresse, either through unskill of language or want of judgement. I number not my borrowing, but I weigh them."

That's what I want from those expert speakers, not the accumulation of piled information, not descriptions of what I can plainly see in the galleries, not the sheer bulk of acquired knowledge about the subject, but to follow Montaigne's advice, 'I number not my borrowing, but I weigh them'. This weighing involves the active speculations of critical judgement combined with the personal soliloquy that intimacy and devotion to art inspires in our souls and fervid discourse.

I once invited the maker of my household furniture to one of my university classes. John had not graduated from high school, spoke a simple language. He designed his own furniture, inspired by medieval Spanish designs. He made the drawings, then he and his workers in his shop constructed the furniture. He brought pieces of wood to my class, spoke of the character of the wood. John caressed the wood, explaining softly and with love of the beauty and varieties of grain, hardness and other attributes. He respected the material, and tried to craft it in ways that did not insult or abuse its integrity. That was many years ago and he no longer has the shop, but I still have and treasure his furniture. Christa, I must never forget, as someone who writes to you about pottery, that you are the potter, you make the pots, as with John and his furniture. My own speculations are after-the-fact, are ruminations of 'my natural faculties'.

Why don't those experts ever talk about their first childhood encounters with art and craft? The elation and exhilaration of that first contact? Christa, I know you would not hide out in the objectification of the aesthetic mysteries of your lifetime. What were those early incidents in your childhood that now form the memories of your first attachment to a creative life? I value the example of Gabriel Garcia Marquez, the Colombian novelist, in his autobiography, "Living to Tell the Tale". Early in the book, Marquez relates a tale of early childhood:

"There, out of the blue, my mother gave me the most unexpected surprise with a triumphant emphasis: 'Here's where you were born!' I had not known that before, or I had forgotten it, but in the next room we found the crib where I slept until I was four years old and that my grandmother kept forever. I had forgotten it, but as soon as I saw it I remembered myself in the overalls with little blue flowers that I was wearing for the first time, screaming for somebody to come and take off my diapers that were filled with shit. I could barely stand as I clutched at the bars of the crib that was as small and fragile as Moses' basket. This has been a frequent cause of discussion and joking among relatives and friends, for whom my anguish that day seems too rational for one so young. Above all when I have insisted that the reason for my suffering was not disgust at my own filth but fear that I would soil my new overalls. That is, it was not a question of hygienic prejudice but aesthetic concern, and because of the manner in which it persists in my memory, I believe it was my first experience as a writer."

Ah, if only academics and curators could provide similar testimony of their early romance with art. Why are the lives and works of artists so filled with such rich and outrageous inconsistencies while the summaries of their art by experts appear so neat and tidy? It must be the intellectual equivalent of 'hygienic prejudice' as Marquez would say. I have never used the 'shit' word before. Lacking courage this first time I safely attribute it to another. It is only a matter of time before I shall try out the F-word. They are necessary additions to my letters if I aspire to meet the standards of contemporary literature.

I have two confessions to make before I complete this letter. It will further weaken any claim I can make as a serious collector and patron of the arts. The old spa in the patio was leaking, rarely used, high electric bills to keep the water heated, and taking up half the space of the room. For once, the yellow pages delivered the solution. They came, cut the spa in half and one of the central birthrights of a native Southern Californian was quickly removed. Then I discovered IKEA.

They say Ingvar Kamprad is the world's richest man, even richer that Bill Gates. He is the founder of IKEA, raised in Sweden, maker of furniture you buy in a box and put the parts together when you reach home. I went to a very big store with two storeys of stuff, simple and inexpensive, but you could tell it was designed. We went to get furniture for the half of the patio liberated from the spa. More room and shelves for pottery! I found the website in my usual clumsy and inefficient way and found out that Kamprad's vision includes a concern for ethical issues, according to Ms. Laurence Marocq, IKEA Canada's Director of Public Relations, 'Home furnishings that combine good design, good function and good quality with prices so low that as many people as possible can afford them'. I was very impressed with the examples given, understanding that the company was the source of the favorable publicity. For instance, on October 9, 1999, IKEA conducted an event in which the entire day's gross sales were divided among its employees; made an agreement with its worldwide solid wood suppliers, whereby all suppliers will guarantee that the wood does not originate in ancient forests; signed alliances with Greenpeace on environmental matters and with UNICEF, Save The Children, and other groups to prevent child labor in any factory that supplies material; conducts inspections of its supplier operations. I wanted to find out more. Kamprad had written a book in 1999. For some strange reason Amazon and Alibris did not have it. Another book, co-authored by him, on the design of his furniture, was over one hundred dollars. Too much for me. I was amused that the book was not available at IKEA, and cost more than much of his furniture. We bought book cases, chairs, corner hutch, and table; all in flat boxes. Following instructions without words, screwing and attaching parts together was made remarkably easy.

I wanted to find out if William Morris was an influence. What would Morris think of him? Kamprad succeeded in an area where Morris did not; he has made furniture affordable for the masses; furniture in simple Scandinavian designs, clean and economical. One was a pioneer socialist, the other had a brief flirtation with fascism. Why doesn't a curator organize an exhibition and lecture based on a comparison of the thoughts and objects of both men, helping us to understand the compatibilities and differences of the two approaches? Christa, they even had some pottery in that big store. Just think, if you could be a supplier for IKEA, you would have to hire a thousand assistants just to help you achieve your quota! Do I dare put your pottery on an IKEA shelf? Would you be upset - your wonderful pottery on such modest shelves? Hey, Christa, I just got an idea. Why can't you employ IKEA's marketing strategy and make your pottery in flat pieces, ready for assembly when taken home? Give it a little thought.

My final tale will leave you seriously incredulous about my intentions to shake the art world with the impressive scope and value of my ceramic collection. My daughter-in-law, Jennifer, wife of my younger son, Sean, took me to the Azusa Salvation Army Thrift Store. They had two or three tables with ceramic 'collectables'. I noticed a man without shoes, with very dirty feet examining some of the items. No doubt he was a serious collector, just like me. I found two objects; one a plate with abstract designs in ribbons of different colors, obviously hand painted, with a sticker on the bottom, 'Made in Macau', and a Chinese stamp; the other vase with a rich and detailed handpainted picture of two peacocks and flowers, on the bottom a "Made in Japan" sticker and a Japanese stamp. I purchased them without shame. Dare I put one of your vases next to them, given their unknown provenance? I hesitate to assure you that I did not find any of your work there. Perhaps it is too early for that. Along with various galleries and antique shops, I will now place the Azusa Salvation Army Thrift Store on my itinerary in the search for ceramic treasures. Please don't tell anyone. Only Jennifer and that other fellow without shoes and with the very dirty feet has so far discovered these precious objects.

Well, I do feel better. I can hold out. I am still a bit puzzled. A complete stranger and outsider, I have recently been published by "The Studio Potter" and welcomed as a major presenter at NCECA, the largest annual arts conference in the world. I have corresponded with potters in Britain, Canada and the U.S. who have expressed their positive response to my letters. But around my own immediate world, I am ignored by those members of little cliques at symposiums and lectures that do not welcome unknown strangers who ask unexpected questions. Well, in my splendid isolation, I will continue this quest, continue to write letters to you. See Christa, what I want you to understand, what you must know by now - I just don't think the way they do.

Take care.

Richard

Forty

April 10, 2005

Dear Christa,

There is a surge of Spring energy in the garden. I match the natural exuberance of new growth with my own renewed activity. I have been away from my garden, traveling to distant places for ceramics conferences and exhibitions. Spring is the worst time to ignore your garden. My guilt and pleasure combine to sponsor daily efforts. I manually prune and trim the vines on the house and shrubbery nearby into desired shapes. I could borrow garden appliances with long plugged-in cords from my son next-door but I want the exercise. It is hard but satisfying labor. I have never understood the idea or value of 'labor saving' devices. The notion might make sense in business but not in art, or gardening, for that matter. It is the labor that earns the result. The life lesson is in the experience of the effort. The virtues of the result comprise the profit of the labor. Time cannot be saved, only wasted. When given unlimited time, this bloody thing called 'retirement', too many Americans soon die of boredom and disappointment, having found no purpose or pleasure in finally obtaining that awful void of empty time. How sad that they really thought they were saving up all those years for some grand payoff only to find that their own human resources could not activate or fill the time suddenly available.

The roses around the edges of my corner house are bursting into bloom, almost a solid wall of pink flowers. I can still climb the high ladder, up to the second highest rung, trimming the tops of vegetation level with the line of the roof. I even shaped and trimmed the area in front of the house where, in a few weeks, they are going to remove all the plants and extend a room to provide a gallery for my growing pottery collection. I wanted the construction workers to see my garden at its best. It must be a matter of personal pride. A bit foolish. A continuation of the behavior when I used to sort and arrange things in the house before the house-cleaning crew showed up. I couldn't bear to think that they would find the house messy, as it would diminish the aesthetic experience for them. We have not used their services for some time - too many potential chips inflicted on my pottery.

It has been over two months since my last letter. I think this represents the longest lapse of time between letters since I started writing them. We have both been busy. Our joint appearance at the panel presentation 'Letters to a Young Potter' at the NCECA (National Council on Education for the Ceramic Arts) Conference in Baltimore was a smashing success. I was so pleased with the number of people that came up to me after the program and expressed their positive response. Judy and I enjoyed the shuttle bus tours of pottery exhibitions in the Baltimore area. We arrived in Baltimore a few days early, took the train to Philadelphia to visit Kathryn Narrow at The Clay Studio. What a great facility. We toured the studio, met many potters, and took away two of Kathryn's pots, along with a few items from their wonderful pottery shop. The night of our NCECA triumph, we had dinner with Kathryn, and some of her friends associated with The Clay Studio, including Gail Brown, who is on the Board of Directors and a curator. A most enjoyable evening.

Gail Brown curated one exhibition, 'Schools Out!' at a community college on the NCECA tour in a suburb of Baltimore County. I particularly liked her statement in the exhibition catalogue. I think we need to state our relationship with ceramic artists and their work with passion and energy. Some of her thoughts:

"History and culture inspire and sustain ongoing exploration of the visual arts. The quest for an expressive language of communication is as old as civilization. How does one identify a pursuit of meaningful inquiry? Individuality, imagination, time and place, all combine to offer untold, unique possibilities. School and apprenticeship are valid introductions. A wise university provost remarked that a liberal arts degree is simply the beginning of a lifetime of learning. Looking long and hard at accomplished contemporary works, delving into the masterful history of the decorative arts, and focusing expectantly on fresh work of younger makers, one marvels that human imagination can potentially offer something to stimulate each generation of passionate artists. The rewards for the earnest viewer are similarly abundant. We watch and absorb: ideas which bud and proliferate, creative daring being nurtured, inspiration flourishing and tentativeness becoming confidence, as skills are honed by the sense of purpose and enhanced life experience… Dialogue with many of the makers stimulates me - with apparent urgency, authenticity and focus. Goals are identified and explored. These young artists join the continuum of all those who find clay vital and extraordinarily accommodating to their own creativity. They celebrate aspirations and hard-won skills, quests to accomplish the next, self-defined challenges, each in their own inspired, personal language."

Curators and collectors have much in common. We both take responsibility for the welfare of pottery and potters. I fully agree with Gail that '… the rewards for the earnest viewer are similarly abundant'. I support her concern for the young potter, dedicated and committed to the making of ceramic art, emerging with evolving purpose and skill, associated with the rich promise of further accomplishments. Perhaps our mutual attempts at grateful testimony can help the young ceramic artist make self-evident the importance and meaning of their own intentions and goals.

I know, Christa, that we agree that our exhibition at The Collectors Gallery at the Oakland Museum of California Art was considerably less successful. They simply did not follow the plans we had discussed with them at the planning meeting. Still the panel discussion on this occasion went well, although poorly attended. How do you control all the variables associated with the display of your work? You surrender your precious creations to people who might or might not understand the aesthetic possibilities. They control the site, and their arrangement of your work in the physical context of that site can enhance or diminish the experience of engaging what you have provided them. Gail would agree with me about the importance of the curator as the sensitive organizer of an aesthetic event for all who enter and engage the contents of their arranged space.

I looked over the notes I made for the Oakland planning meeting. I have included them here to make the official record. They continue to speak to the essential aesthetic principles that comprise the possibilities of our collaboration.

The exhibition would attempt to integrate the two-dimensional texts of Jacobs' letters with the three-dimensional pottery of Christa Assad; this integration of language and the material artifact of the pottery enhances both. They are not only compatible and complementary, but they can enhance and empower each other; the perceiver - that is the collector - and the artist/craftsperson - the maker - are natural allies and collaborators. The collector sponsors and supports the arts and the maker gains the improved morale that comes from that attention and the material rewards of the purchased pottery. The collector obtains the privilege to live in his domestic environment with the objects that grace his daily life. The collector becomes temporary docent and protector of these examples of human civilization. This reciprocal relationship must be evident in the visual arrangement of the gallery; the improbability of the relationship - a young woman potter, distant and different from the collector in age, gender, and origin - finding a mutual and overlapping interest in their joint devotion and dedication to the making and preservation of craft and art. This exhibition would attempt to integrate the biographies of the two individuals with the making and collecting of the pottery. Making pottery and collecting it are the human activities of actual personalities; all objects of art and craft are functional. They operationally provide a quality of life that directly makes a difference. Some artifacts might have some specific function in addition to that central function but the contrived hierarchy of craft and art does not find support in this exhibition; it is still possible to make things by hand - to be a maker of original art - whatever the triumph of technology and mass production. These handcrafted objects still have the power to signify and celebrate the essential rituals and events of the life cycle and provide a daily margin of beauty and enhancement that compensates for whatever ordeals life brings to all of us.

My present review of these principles confirmed my previous favor and approval. If there are future opportunities for us to exhibit our pottery and letters together, I will try to be more assertive and demanding in the quality of their integration and the faithful implementation of these aesthetic principles.

Occasionally I am confronted with the use of pottery as agent and metaphor in other artistic arenas. Judy and I recently saw the play, "The Goat or Who is Sylvia?" by Edward Albee. This play, by an elderly male playwright of even greater age than myself, has shocked the respectable sensitivities of people since it opened. I observed people walking out in the middle of the play, striding defiantly toward the exit, faces frozen in great distaste and disapproval. In the play, a middle aged man declares to his disbelieving wife that he is having an affair with a goat. He is not only having a sexual relationship with the goat, he truly feels romantic love for the animal. Albee is pushing every button he can, and people in the audience laughed nervously and twittered in uncomfortable response. Now to my own confession. I was not shocked or even taken aback by the vivid descriptions of this man-goat affair. I myself have never contemplated such an unlikely combination. It was the wife that upset me. The stage set was quite sophisticated, an upper-class condo or apartment, furnished with a subtle and affluent interior of furniture and pottery. Well, I don't mind if the wife got upset, competing with that goat for her husband's passion and love. But at some point, after the incredulous shock wore off, she reacted with rage. She went around the living room, shouting at her husband, approaching piece after piece of pottery on shelves and tables, throwing them on the floor in a choreography of insane anger, smashing the pottery and sending their broken shards flying across the stage. I found myself sending silent and frantic messages to this wife, this actress, this person, preferring and urging her to assault her husband, strike him down, even murder the dumb bastard, but please, please, don't break any more pottery. I realize, in the telling of this tale, that my passion for pottery has now compromised my moral and ethical principles, but somehow I must go on. I now know, with great certitude, I will never allow a goat to get between my love of pottery and whatever other needs I might have.

Yet another unfortunate metaphor shook my soul with its possible results. We attended a performance of the 'Messiah' by Handel during December of last year at the Los Angeles Philharmonic. This fine performance celebrated that particular piece in its appropriate season. Yet I found a disturbing passage in the program notes, containing words from the Bible, in a passage for the tenor, 'Thou shalt break them with a rod of iron; thou shalt dash them in pieces like a potter's vessel'. (Psalm 2:9). I realized the widespread ancient and historical use of shattered pottery as religious and cultural metaphor. I would not want one of the more extreme of today's Christian fundamentalist militants to visit my pottery collection if they felt they needed to repeat and act out this injunction of the Lord. There must be a less radical way to subdue the heathen and yet spare the pottery. After a brief excursion in the King James version of the Bible to research this citation, I feel a need to further explore various theologies that would not only spare my pottery but allow me to take it with me to the promised land.

I simply want to declare a cultural armistice, no more metaphors that use the breaking of pottery, I cannot bear it. I must continue my search for citations in the world's literature that prefer the destruction of objects other than ceramics. I can understand the need for human catharsis and even righteous retribution, but surely the aesthetics of failed human civilization can provide other targets. I demand a moratorium on such talk. If it continues, I am sure it will eventually raise the insurance premium on my collection.

I do not dwell on my age. I ask no edge in any voluntary forgiveness that might reduce standards for my performance. I expect no golfer's handicap or early start. While I enjoy the generosity of others, I do not seek allowances or compensation for my long life. I do not think I require any affirmative action to comply with those standards of excellence and principle that have always guided my behavior. I do not need generous excuses or special dispensation. I hope to remain as stimulating and provocative as in earlier years, the sting of my critique and independent views not dulled over time. I wish only that the kindness of others corresponded with the effort made, given my natural limitations, and recognizing that the ageing process is an active agent that does not seek my prior approval. I might look fragile but I do not feel fragile. I am not sure what I will do when appearance and condition are in agreement and confirmed. In the meantime, to be taken seriously is a most satisfying pleasure. Old people need to feel dangerous.

This reminds me of an ad recently read in the 'personal column' of the New York Review of Books, which stated in bold print, "Destitute Retired Male Teacher", and proceeded to explain, '... 72, without television, e-mail, and cell phone, struggling to survive on harsh diet of reading, writing, exercise, attention to good causes, and a bit more: wants shallow, unscrupulous, grim, dull, vain woman or, perhaps, her opposite.' Well, this poor chap is only a year older, and I do feel fortunate that I do not have to place a similar ad at this time of life. We share many attributes, this destitute retired male teacher seeking a shallow and dull woman or whatever. I accept his rhetoric about the demanding and severe regimen of reading, writing, exercise and attention to good causes. I do hope he finds some desirable woman who more than lives up to his modest requirements.

The very next ad in the same column was not so clever but quite different in character. 'Optimistic Outlook is everything. Retired professional, widower, in excellent health, with great joy in life and endless curiosity, seeks fashionable woman in her sixties with similar positive temperament - mutual cultural interests are assumed - for compassion and LTR.' Christa, I do not know what LTR means. Perhaps you could tell me? My old-fashioned romantic soul leans toward the authenticity of unplanned and accidental meetings as the natural introduction to real love. Yet I know many people are now using the internet and commercial firms to screen potential candidates. I will not be answering similar ads, although I hope that someone does respond to these two deserving contemporaries. I have Judy. Well, potters have the annual NCECA Conference to sponsor such events. Perhaps they should schedule workshops for such a purpose. I have no idea what the demonstrations would look like.

In reading about older potters and other elderly creative people, I realize that the ageing process and our ultimate demise are factors that hover over all of us. As with those two ads, the language and attitude can be quite different. Do we ripen and mature like an old wine, more subtle with substance over time, or do we slowly surrender our fading powers in an uneven match with our mortality? Is it too early for you, Christa, to think about these things? One good example I recently came across was in the Los Angeles Times in the column, "The Big Picture" by Patrick Goldstein. Clint Eastwood is 74, full of energy and ideas, making very good films. A lover of films, I did not ordinarily go to see his work, never having found violence a satisfying cinematic art form. Yet his films are well made, the characters are most convincing, and worlds far apart are created with honesty and insight. It is not easy entertainment and he does not want to make it easy for the audience. From spaghetti westerns in his youth to a legendary actor and director in his old age. Quite a journey. Goldstein writes:

"... Eastwood has somehow defied time. A few months short of his 75th birthday, sitting in a hotel eatery, he looks as good as ever, lean, craggy and imperturbable - if a grease fire suddenly erupted in the restaurant, you'd expect him to show the firemen how to put it out."

Goldstein goes on to describe other people, in their 6th or 7th decade of existence who are contributing in various capacities to the excellence of film:

"What's especially fascinating, for anyone who grew up in our youth-obsessed culture, is that Eastwood is not alone anymore. Just weeks away from his 80th birthday, Robert Altman still works regularly, earned an Oscar nomination in 2001 for "Gosford Park" and is now directing an opera in Chicago. Roman Polanski and Mike Nichols are in their 70s, as vital as ever, Polanski having made "The Pianist" while Nichols is coming off "Angels in America" and "Closer". At 74, Jean-Luc Godard is as much of a provocateur as ever, earning glowing reviews for his recent film, "Norte Musique.""

In the concluding statement in the piece, ending the presumed interview, Eastwood points out the benefits of his age; he doesn't have to prove anything to anybody, doesn't worry about failure because his long career exists unchallenged. Old age allows an economy of statement, 'savoring economy over indulgence'. What does that say about older potters and their pottery? Christa, do you have any examples of potters that you could point to that you hope to emulate as models of productivity and creativity in old age? For every Eastwood, there are many more examples of those who have spectacular beginnings, fade quickly and disappear. How do potters combine excellence and durability? What would be the perfect pot of old age?

I attended a memorable panel discussion at NCECA, a panel of veteran writers and potters. Louana Lackey, Susan Peterson, Jack Troy and Robin Hopper together represent more than twenty books between them, contributing to the ceramics community for more than half a century. I have never personally met any of them, in some cases have not seen their pottery or read their work, but that did not matter. They were grand old contributors to ceramics, still feisty and insightful, acerbic and strong in their commentary. I felt a pride that ceramics can attract that caliber of intellectual and aesthetic depth in the people who investigate its complicated character. I do not know their exact ages. I suspect, as with Eastwood, that I might be the junior of more than one by a year or two. Yet, there was no farewell song here. No surrender to an easier standard. Mastery can be accumulated through time, in a dense and dynamic lifetime, in a long ripening lifetime. This mastery can be generic and complete, not any one thing alone, but in all things. Things like the use of language, humor that does not forgive mediocrity; critique that does not bestow on current fads the same approval as on the time-tested attainment of excellence; commentary that uses words to create thoughts with the same careful and creative effort as they would use clay to create pottery. Their evident traits of commitment and self-discipline were displayed without effort, because it is now ingrained in their very being. I felt a real pride, these individuals of my generation still displaying the talent and leadership that launched them so long ago. Aside from the richness and significance of their specific talents and contributions, their very presence supports the rest of us. Their long devotion to ceramics encourages us to follow their example. I would be proud to join these elders of the tribe around any campfire or at any conference.

I must now recognize someone who did not make it into her eighth decade. Mortality is an accidental and haphazard business. Virtue and prudent lifestyles have far less to do with it than genes and good luck. Marilyn Levine spent much of her life in California, studying with Peter Voulkos, with degrees from Berkeley, and teaching there later. She stayed with her vision, that hyper-realism that made clay into leather, never wavered, never strayed. Her stubborn uniqueness became an aesthetic virtue. She had a history, a record, and attention must be paid. It is not the sheer length of existence that counts, but the durability of sheer integrity. An integrity that does not blink or waver to pander to trends or fads, but stays the course. Integrity is rarely rational or in your self-interest. It ignores success but often perversely finds it as a result of ignoring it. Her work was one of a kind. I suspect Marilyn Levine was one of a kind. She received a half-page, with a wonderful picture of her smiling at the camera, a cat in front of her, additional pictures of her work on the page. I was surprised that the L.A. Times would devote that much space to a ceramic artist. I don't remember them ever devoting that much space in the past to the discussion of ceramic arts or living potters.

Mature judgment demands more subtraction than addition in its recognition of excellence. Like the first burst of Spring in my garden, youthful displays of an easy talent can fade and quickly lose their bloom. It is the long haul that determines both character and quality. It may appear self-serving to say this, a promotion for an ageing process that I cannot control. Still - I do believe it. Christa, you are not even half-way in your journey. I believe you have the aesthetic stamina to see it through - to stay the course. What was impressive about the Oakland exhibition was to see a considerable body of your work at one site. There was much inventive variety, yet a constant stamp of your personal vision. Your work was substantial and serious, and would certainly hold the attention of observers. I do not see how museum visitors could walk by that window without stopping, and after looking over your work, responding to the obvious need to go into the gallery and further explore your pottery.

This idea of consistency verses dynamic change or even overthrow of previous style works differently for various ceramic artists. I see evolving experiments and changes in your work over the time I have observed it; more dramatic glazes, darker and more intense, more angular edges with sharp geometric clarity. Do you know your future directions in ceramics? Can you predict the next creative deviation in your work? According to the obituary of Marilyn Levine in the Los Angeles Times, she did not shift in style during her long career. A Canadian reviewer said of her, 'In a lesser artist, this apparent lack of development would be interpreted as a severe limitation. However, in Levine's case, it confirms the unwavering power of her vision.'

Christa, I am still trying to make sense of the enthusiastic response to my remarks at NCECA. The number of people that rushed to the front of the room at the end of the panel discussion, the people who approached and thanked me the next day, and the generous comments of many others since then. They did not know me and could not have been impressed with my remarks by prior reputation. I have arrived very late in the day to this particular ceramics arena. I must use the remaining time carefully. Whatever the opportunities that might present themselves, I want to do whatever I can to support potters and pottery. My pottery collection exists as my homage to the significance of ceramic art. I wait to see how my words and thoughts can make their contribution. Our recent collaboration at Baltimore and Oakland reinforces the value of our mutual efforts together. The word and the pot are natural friends. The letters will continue.

Your friend,

Richard

Index

(Titles in italics)

Thanks and Acknowledgements

The author and publisher wish to show their gratitude to the following for permission to publish extracts from or show images of their work:

To Sam Hamill to quote from his poem 'To Bill and Chris' from his collection 'Dumb Luck' (published by permission of the poet and Boa Editions).

Thanks for the use of their images to the potters Christa Assad, Joanna Howells, Micki Schloessingk and Kaori Tatebayashi.

The author and publisher have made every effort to contact copyright holders.